GREEN BUILDING MATERIALS

THE WILEY SERIES IN SUSTAINABLE DESIGN

The Wiley Series in Sustainable Design has been created for professionals responsible for, and individuals interested in, the design and construction of the built environment. The series is dedicated to the advancement of knowledge in design and construction that serves to sustain the natural environment. Consistent with their content, books in the series are produced with care taken in selection of recycled and nonpolluting materials.

Design with Nature
Ian I. McHarg

Wind Energy Comes of Age
Paul Gipe

Audubon House: Building the Environmentally Responsible,
Energy-Efficient Office
National Audubon Society
Croxton Collaborative, Architects

Green Development: Integrating Ecology and Real Estate
Rocky Mountain Institute

Constructed Wetlands in the Sustainable Landscape
Craig Campbell and Michael Ogden

Green Building Materials: A Guide to Product Selection and Specification
Ross Spiegel and Dru Meadows

GREEN
BUILDING
MATERIALS

A GUIDE
TO PRODUCT
SELECTION
AND
SPECIFICATION

ROSS SPIEGEL • DRU MEADOWS

John Wiley & Sons, Inc.
New York • Chichester • Weinheim • Brisbane • Singapore • Toronto

The numbers and titles referenced in this product are from *MasterFormat*™ and is published by the Construction Specifications Institute (CSI) and Construction Specifications Canada (CSC), and used with permission from CSI, 1999.
For those interested in a more in-depth explanation of *MasterFormat*™ and its use in the construction industry contact:

The Construction Specifications Institute (CSI)
601 Madison Street
Alexandria, VA 22314
800-689-2900; 703-684-0300
CSINet URL: http://www.csinet.org

The authors advocate the use of environmentally friendly (green) building products, systems and materials; and believe that green products and innovative technology can enhance the outdoor and indoor environment, improve the quality of life of the user, and in general perform as well and even outperform their baseline competition. This book is intended to be a guide for researching environmental issues relative to building products. No warranty is made as to completeness or accuracy of information contained herein. References to manufacturers do not represent a guaranty, warranty, or endorsement thereof.

80%
TOTAL RECYCLED PAPER
20% POST-CONSUMER PAPER

This book was printed on acid-free paper. ∞

This publication is designed to provide accurate and authoritative information in regard to the subject matter covered. It is sold with the understanding that the publisher is not engaged in rendering professional services. If professional advice or other expert assistance is required the services of a competent professional person should be sought.

Library of Congress Cataloging-in-Publication Data:

Spiegel, Ross, 1947–
    Green building materials : a guide to product selection and
  specification / Ross Spiegel and Dru Meadows.
      p.   cm. — (The Wiley series in sustainable design)
    Includes bibliographical references.
    ISBN 0-471-29133-1 (alk. paper)
    1. Building materials—United States—Catalogs.   2. Green
  products—United States—Catalogs.   I. Meadows, Dru.   II. Title.
  III. Series.
  TH455.S65   1999
    691'.029'473—dc21
                                                                                99-21059
Printed in the United States of America.
10 9 8 7 6 5

CONTENTS

PREFACE

Much has been written in the last 25 years about the philosophical and moral impetus to design and construct "green" or environmentally-friendly buildings. Although more and more building owners are demanding that their design professionals take environmental concerns into account for new buildings, knowledge about the process of selecting and specifying green building materials has remained sketchy.

In this book, the reader will find not only a discussion of why one should use green building materials and what green building materials are, but a guide to their selection and specification as well. The reader will also find information about the construction process and how to guard against the substitution of non-green building materials. The information contained in the appendices and glossary serve to round out the package, providing the reader with valuable reference material, sample specifications, and a "kit of tools" to use on green building projects.

This book was a labor of love for the authors and its creation and birth were made possible by the encouragement and understanding of their families, friends, professional colleagues, and members of the green building movement. Our thanks also go out to the editors and staff at John Wiley & Sons who made the "birthing" process as painless as possible.

Ross Spiegel
Fort Lauderdale, Florida

Dru Meadows
Tulsa, Oklahoma

ACKNOWLEDGMENTS

My training as an architect taught me that the design and construction of a new building on virgin land—or the demolition of an existing building to make room for a new one—was unquestionably the most acceptable course of action.

In 1992 I was asked to locate a speaker for a day-long seminar on recycling in construction for a local government agency. After a lengthy and ultimately unsuccessful search, I volunteered to do the presentation myself. Over the next several months, I took a crash course on the subject, and when the time came for the presentation, I was ready for the challenge.

The research I had done and the education I received encouraged me to learn more. The more I learned the more convinced I became that using recycled-content building materials and recycling materials from demolished buildings was the correct action to take as an architect.

Building upon this start, I gave a presentation on using recycled-content building materials in construction at the 1993 Construction Specifications Institute (CSI) Annual Convention in Houston, Texas. At the same time, I was appointed to chair a CSI ad hoc committee on environmental issues, which produced several recommendations. One of the recommendations was to have CSI become a member of the U.S. Green Building Council (USGBC).

When CSI joined the USGBC in 1994, I was appointed CSI's liaison to the Council (a position I am proud to continue serving in today). My involvement in the Council intensified in 1997 when I was elected to serve a two-year term on the USGBC board of directors.

This book is the outgrowth of my experience as a specification writer, construction contract administrator, and architect. The inspiration for this book came from the input and encouragement of many people who I would like to thank here.

Thomas Young, FCSI, CCS, Former President of The Construction Specifications Institute, for believing in the importance of environmental issues when he appointed me to chair the ad hoc committee. Tom was instrumental in helping crystallize my thoughts on the environment and offered continuing encouragement over the years.

David Gottfried, co-founder of the U.S. Green Building Council, who helped me understand the importance of "green" buildings and encouraged me to learn more about the environment. He also showed me that green made economic sense.

Dru Meadows, my co-author, who showed me that being an architect without degrading the environment was not only the right thing to do but also the most sensible thing to do.

All of the CSI and USGBC members whose passion about the environment convinced me that this book was not only needed but essential to facilitate the use of green building materials in construction.

Finally, my wife, Dorine Shirinian Spiegel, who never doubted that this book would get written and who put up with the many hours of work necessary to write it and my daughter, Erica Shirin Spiegel, whose future existence on this planet spurred me to keep writing when I thought I could do no more.

If this book encourages you to design and build "green" and provides the tools that you need to do so, then my main goal in writing this book will have been achieved.

Ross Spiegel
Fort Lauderdale, Florida
June 1999

* * * * *

This book is a result of my experience as a "green" architect and specification writer. It required many, many long hours and would not have been possible without the encouragement and support of several people whom I would like to thank here.

Charles E. Bell, my partner in *theGreenTeam, Inc.*, who carried more than his share of our company's workload while I wrote and who provided valuable insights and comments on many draft versions.

Ross Spiegel, my co-author, who brought this project to my attention and convinced me to commit some of my experience as a green architect and specifier to paper.

John Thoman, who encouraged me years ago to write environmental procedure specifications when no one else was even listening.

Kelly Ingalls, with the City of Los Angeles, who used them and who has tracked their self-propelled migration over the years from Los Angeles, to New York City, to Canada.

James Blackburn, whose environmental law course at Rice University included a canoe trip down the Houston bayous which confronted me directly with the opaque, multi-colored, obviously contaminated water, one of the disastrous results of the way building professionals design the built environment. I am grateful for his teachings, and for the fact that I did not fall in the water.

Devin Meadows, my husband, who not only tolerated the process but is now challenging me to write yet another tome; Damon Meadows, my son, whose beautiful, young life depends upon our responsible actions; Franklin G. Fleischmann, my father, and Druenette L. Fleischmann, my mother, who taught me to respect others, myself, and the planet.

And finally, the readers who care enough to act on their convictions. Thank you.

Dru Meadows
Tulsa, Oklahoma
June 1999

CHAPTER 1

Introduction

No man is an island, entire of itself; every man is a piece of the continent, a part of the main. If a clod be washed away by the sea, Europe is the less, as well as if a promontory were, as well as if a manor of thy friend's or of thine own were; any man's death diminishes me, because I am involved in mankind, and therefore never send to know for whom the bell tolls; it tolls for thee.

Devotions Upon Emergent Occasions, Meditation 17
John Donne

In *Devotions Upon Emergent Occasions,* the seventeenth-century English metaphysical poet John Donne said "No man is an island, entire of itself . . ." Through this statement, Donne asserted that we all share a common humanity. In today's increasingly complex and interrelated world, not only is no man an island, but, similarly, no building stands alone. Every building exists within an environmental context upon which it not only acts but which also has an impact upon the building. Due to today's increased complexity and interrelatedness, no building can be constructed as a microcosm. Every building must consider the impact it will have on the environment into which it will be placed, locally and globally.

Donne's assertion that no man is an island is also an affirmation of sustainability. Sustainability is commonly interpreted to mean living in such a way as to meet the needs of the present without compromising the ability of future generations to meet the needs of the future.[1] It is frequently compared to the Native American concept of consultation with the as yet unborn future generations for their input on significant decisions, decisions that might impact them. Sustainability is a social concept in that it considers the needs of unborn. It is an environmental concept in that it addresses the affect of pollution and resource management (or lack thereof) on Earth's ecological systems. It is also an economic concept in that it seeks to quantify the tolerable limits for consumption such that we can live on Earth's "interest" instead of depleting the "principal." It is a perspective that focuses on systems and relationships instead of objects.

The term *sustainability* is not likely to appear in your dictionary. Likewise, the spell check on your personal computer will probably stumble over the word. Yet, the use of the term is quickly becoming widespread. *Green* is another term that has entered our working vocabulary. It is now used to describe not only a particular color, but as an adjective meaning "environmentally friendly." It refers to the color of lush, healthy, unpolluted vegetation. Some local and regional programs use *blue* in a similar manner to instill the idea of cool, clean, unpolluted water or air. *Brown* is indicative of dirty, barren, polluted areas, and has entered the industry vocabulary as a term referring to contaminated sites, *brownfields*. However, *green,* like *sustainability,* has entered the vernacular. Thus, a *green* building is not a comment on the shade of paint, but on the impact the building has on the environment. Simply stated, a green building is a building that is located and constructed in a sustainable manner and that is designed to allow its occupants to live, work, and play in a sustainable manner.

Over the last several years, interest among those in the building industry in green issues has grown considerably. The proliferation of green articles, conferences, publications, and projects attest to an increasing awareness. We have been made aware, in no uncertain terms, that we are a dirty and wasteful species. Each of us has had to accept responsibility for our part.

The United States generates more waste than any other nation. Each day, we produce enough garbage to fill 63,000 garbage trucks, which "lined up . . . would stretch from San Francisco to Los Angeles (about 400 miles)."[2] For many American schools, trash disposal is at least equal to the amount of money spent on textbooks.[3] The building industry alone accounts for approximately 20 percent of the waste stream.[4] The majority of this waste is "clean" waste—that is, scrap materials that have not been used but have merely paused momentarily on their brief and fairly direct path from manufacturer to landfill.

We waste energy: The Department of Energy has estimated that improvements in energy efficiency of buildings, utilizing existing and readily available technologies, could save $20 billion annually in the United States, and create 100,000 new jobs.[5] A significant percentage—40 percent—of the world's energy usage is dedicated to the construction and operation of buildings.[6] Even more is indirectly mandated by the thoughtless siting of buildings relative to each other. Urban sprawl has been denigrated for its negative impact on the quality of life. People regularly complain about the time devoted to traveling across town or the unfortunate aesthetics of their surroundings. However, as environmentalists will quickly tell you, urban sprawl is equally guilty of damaging the environment both directly and indirectly. It directly damages the environment as inexpensive, fringe property is hastily and wastefully paved over, and indirectly as the hundreds of thousands of energy-burning vehicles drive past to conquer the next bit of fringe real estate.

We also waste our natural resources: Over 50 percent of the wetlands of the contiguous United States have been destroyed—filled, contaminated, or otherwise "reclaimed."[7] The destruction of our wetlands and other natural resources has become much more efficient with technological advances. In recent

decades, ". . . the average annual rate of deforestation worldwide was approximately equivalent to an area the size of the state of Georgia."[8] James Lovelock,
creator of the GAIA theory, has predicted that, at current rates of deforestation,
we will have lost 65 percent of all the forest of the tropics by the end of this
century. This is a critical threshold. "When more than 70 percent of an ecosystem is lost, the remainder may be unable to sustain the environment needed
for its own survival."[9]

The building industry commandeers 3 billion tons of raw materials annually—40 percent of total global use.[10] It uses almost half of all the mined,
harvested, and dredged raw materials each year! It also diverts 16 percent of
global fresh water annually.[11] Most of the earth's water is located in our oceans
and is too salty for residential, commercial, or industrial use. Only 3 percent
of the water on the planet is fresh, and most of that is located in polar ice. Of
all the water on the planet, only about 0.003 percent is readily available as
fresh water for human use.[12] The estimate of 16 percent annual usage of available fresh water accounts for the quantity of water that is required to manufacture building materials and to construct and operate buildings. It does not reflect
the impact of the building industry on the quality of water. It is entirely possible
that future estimates of the percentage of available fresh water will decrease as
we contaminate our limited supply.

At some point, with continued unlimited growth, demand will exceed our
resources. But, at what point? There is a great deal of debate over the exact
numbers. How much fossil fuel do we have left? 10 years? 100 years? Determining the exact limit causes genuine concern because we want to know how
much we can use. And, of course, how much is it going to cost.

According to the United Nations Population Fund reports, from the beginning of time until 1950, the world population grew to almost 3 billion people;
from 1950 to 1990, that population doubled; and it is expected to double again
by the middle of the next century. The same resources we are now using will
have to support nearly 12 billion people. Each additional person requires food,
clothing, shelter, and assorted amenities. Most of this growth is anticipated in
Asia and in developing countries. Currently, these areas do not have the same
standard of living that developed nations do; but they are actively attempting
to acquire it. Also, these areas produce the majority of the raw materials, the
renewable and nonrenewable resources, that developed nations use to achieve
our higher standard of living. As available resources per capita decrease, the
costs will increase; there is even a question as to whether the developing nations
as they industrialize, acquiring not only the need for but also the capacity to
process their raw materials, will continue to supply raw materials to the developed nations.

A simple, objective comparison of available resources to increasing human
demands indicates that the system, as currently functioning, cannot continue
indefinitely. It must stop either voluntarily or involuntarily. Proponents of sustainability opt for the voluntary method.

Sustainable approaches focus on two questions:

What are we using?

How well are we using it?

What we are using may be perpetual resources, resources that are "virtually inexhaustible on a human time scale"[13] such as solar, wind, or tidal energy; renewable resources, resources that can be replenished through natural processes in a relatively short time such as trees and water; or nonrenewable resources, resources that require millions or billions of years to be replenished through geological, physical, and chemical processes such as aluminum, coal, and oil.

The law of conservation of matter states that matter can neither be created nor destroyed. What we have inherited—perpetual (exclusive of the solar input), renewable, or nonrenewable—is, ultimately, all we've got. We can take some from here and move it there, reshape it, burn it, bury it . . . . That's all we are going to get. What existed at the beginning of time is what we have now.

A significant ecological aspect of the law of conservation of matter is that matter goes through cyclical transformations. Matter cycles from physical reservoirs into biological reservoirs and back again. Water, for example, regularly travels through rivers, lakes, oceans, and the atmosphere, making detours through plants and animals (e.g., humans). Through transpiration, plants transfer water from the soil to vapor in the air. The rising vapor condenses to form clouds; rain falls, trees grow. Water vapor also condenses over the ocean. Algae in sea water produce dimethyl sulphide, which provides cloud-condensing nuclei, the particles that water condenses around to form clouds. The cloud cover lowers the temperature, causing differentials in temperature and air movement. The cloud collides with a land mass—rain.

There are some interesting environmental corollaries to the law of conservation of matter. If matter cannot be created, we never really get anything "new" and we never really "throw away" anything. We just move it around and combine it with different materials. Therefore, we are drinking the same water that has traveled through the cycle over and over and over since day one. And, if we deposit chemicals into a stream, they are likely to travel with the water to the next location in the cycle, and the next. Ultimately, everything is in your own backyard. The time a water molecule stays at any one point in the cycle is as follows:[14]

Location	Residence Time
Atmosphere	9 days
Rivers	2 weeks
Soil moisture	2 weeks to 1 year
Large lakes	10 years
Underground water at slight depth	10s to 100s of years
Ocean mixed layer to a depth of 55 yards	120 years
Seas and oceans	3,000 years
Underground water at depth	up to 10,000 years
Antarctic ice cap	10,000 years

How well we use our perpetual, renewable, and nonrenewable resources must be answered in terms of our affect upon the quality of the resource and our impact on the cycle of the resource (rate of flow, diversion, etc). According to the EPA, "as of 1996 about 40 percent of the nation's surveyed rivers, lakes, and estuaries are too polluted for basic uses, such as fishing and swimming."[15] That survey included only 19 percent of the nation's 3.6 million miles of rivers and streams, and only 40 percent of the nation's 41.7 million acres of lakes, reservoirs, and ponds. According to the Index of Watershed Indicators for 1997, only 16 percent of the nation's watersheds had good water quality.[16] Hose down your driveway and you have diverted a portion of the daily one-third of flowing water in the country and added an assortment of petroleum products, pesticides, herbicides, and debris which will flow down the street into the stormwater system. Thermoelectric power generation is responsible for nearly half of the annual water withdrawals in the United States, amounting to approximately 195 billion gallons per day in 1990.[17] A significant pollutant that power plants add to the water is waste heat.

The options for greener use of a resource are often complicated by political and economic factors. Water quite visibly travels across borders and is subjected to a variety of social, economic, and political values along the way. Of the 200 largest river systems in the world, 120 flow through two or more countries. Access to shared resources has triggered numerous conflicts over the centuries. Witness the tension in the Middle East. The 1967 Arab-Israeli war was fought in part over water rights to the Jordan River. Conflicting demands between agricultural, industrial, and urban uses are felt not only between countries, but also between and within states. The Los Angeles aqueduct project infuriates Northern California. The mighty Colorado river has so many users that it is virtually dry at its end.

While sustainable approaches could benefit from political advances and new technologies, there are many simple and innovative options currently available. Many not only improve the manner in which we use our resources, but also have financial benefits. For example, a water-recirculation system reduced the amount of water the Gillette Company used to make razor blades from 730 million gallons to 156 gallons per year. Companywide, Gillette now saves approximately $1.5 million a year in water and sewage bills.[18] Harrah's Hotel and Casino in Las Vegas asked its customers whether they wanted their sheets changed every day. Most said no. Harrah's reduced "its energy and water costs for cleaning sheets by $70,000 per year."[19] By utilizing a landscaping technique called *xeriscaping*™ which relies on native plants instead of water-intensive imported plants, Valley Bank in Tucson, Arizona, realized a $20,000 per year savings.[20]

The Earth has evolved thousands of intricately, delicately balanced cycles, each of which is woven into increasingly more complex systems to create the overall single system that is our world. The prospect of living sustainably in the midst of such complexity can be overwhelming. Some respond with a deus ex machina confidence that technology will "solve" the problems whatever they are, or that nature will adjust as necessary. Others, overwhelmed by the enormity of the challenge, reassure themselves by asserting that the impact one individual can make is negligible.

Technology may solve some of the problems, but only if we focus our attention on those problems and seriously endeavor to understand them. Nature will undoubtedly adjust; the question is whether that adjustment will involve the eradication of our species. And individual impact adds up, regardless of whether you choose to see it. Furthermore, the history books are full of individuals who did have tremendous impact culturally, economically, politically, and environmentally. As the anthropologist Margaret Mead pointed out, "Never doubt that a small group of thoughtful, committed citizens can change the world. Indeed, it is the only thing that ever has."

Solving all the problems simultaneously is as unrealistic as avoiding them. A more constructive approach is to do what you can and continue improving. Maintain the deep dark green goal, but don't let the fact that you are a few shades lighter stop you from achieving even that much.

Can you as a designer or building owner envision a building that neither imports not exports material or energy during construction? During operation? If not, can you envision a trade for the imported or exported material that will balance in a larger picture? To determine how closely you come to this goal, ask the questions: What am I using? And, how well am I using it?

With a basic appreciation of the law of conservation of matter, the answer to the first question will have implications relative to the impact of your choice on our natural resources and on the relative healthfulness of our environment. These two topics—resource management and toxicity—are valuable tools for evaluating materials. The answer to the second question will have implications for the performance of the material. Performance issues include durability, energy efficiency, waste generated, and potential for reuse or recycling. Performance is also a valuable tool for evaluating the greenness of a material.

Life Cycle Assessment (LCA) is the formal methodology for answering these questions. LCA is a process that investigates the impact of a product at every stage in the life of that product, from preliminary development through obsolescence. At each stage, you look at the materials and energy consumed and the pollution and waste produced. Life stages include: extraction of raw materials, processing and fabrication, transportation, installation, use and maintenance, and reuse/recycling/disposal. To date, there is not a single accepted LCA methodology. Experts are still trying to define precisely what is meant by "life cycle assessment." The Environmental Protection Agency, the American Society for Testing and Materials, the American Institute of Architects, and the International Organization of Standardization (ISO) are each attempting to outline the details of the process. Nevertheless, there is general consensus regarding the concept of LCA and its usefulness in quantifying sustainability.

Selection of materials is only one part (albeit a very important one) of making a "green" building. The LCA methodology helps to visualize the link between the big picture and the details, while bringing us that much closer to the goal of living sustainably.

Every human endeavor has as its basis a condition or state of being that we wish to attain. Call it an ideal of perfection for which we strive. In order to make our struggle more manageable, we break our efforts down into smaller pieces called goals. Goals are those steps that we can take on the path toward our ideal. Within the context of the subject of this book, our ideal can be described as a world of buildings that are located, constructed, and designed in a sustainable manner and that allow their occupants to live, work, and play in a sustainable manner.

An inherent quality of an ideal, of perfection, is that it is unattainable. This should not discourage us from making changes in the status quo. With a limited investment of time, money, and research, it is relatively easy to make measurable improvements. That is the crucial point: If you shift your paradigm from simple black-and-white answers to shades of gray (or should we say green), then there are unlimited possibilities for environmental successes.

The subject of green buildings has been widely discussed and often written about. This book does not attempt to be an exhaustive text on the pros and cons of "going green." It also does not try to engage in a detailed discussion of green buildings. There are many fine books available on both subjects.

The goal of this book is to help designers and other members of the building construction team better understand the green building material selection and specifying process. By attaining this goal, we hope to take one more step toward reaching our ideal.

Chapter 1—Endnotes

1. In the words of the landmark World Commission on Environment and Development (the Brundtland Commission), we should "meet the needs of the present without compromising the ability of future generations to meet their own needs." Cited in Joel Darmstadter, *Global development and the environment: perspectives on sustainability,* Resources for the Future, Washington, DC, 1992.

2. Valerie Harms. *The National Audubon Society Almanac of the Environment: The Ecology of Everyday Life,* New York: G. P. Putnam's Sons, 1994, p. 93.

3. *The Denver Post 1991 Colorado Recycling Guide.*

4. EPA Municipal Solid Waste Programs Division.

5. North American Energy Measurement and Verification Protocol, Department of Energy; DOE/EE-0081; March 1996; p. 1.

6. David Malin Roodman and Nicholas Lenssen, Worldwatch paper 124, "A Building Revolution: How Ecology and Health Concerns are Transforming Construction." Worldwatch Institute, Washington, DC March 1995, p. 23.

7. The National Science and Technology Council. *Technology for a Sustainable Future: A Framework for Action.* U.S. Government Printing Office, Washington, DC, 1994, p. 32.

8. *Ibid.*

9. James Lovelock. *Healing Gaia: Practical Medicine for the Planet.* New York: Harmony Books, 1991, p. 157.

10. David Malin Roodman and Nicholas Lenssen, Worldwatch Paper 124, "A Building Revolution: How Ecology and Health Concerns are Transforming Construction." Worldwatch Institute, Washington, DC, March 1995, p. 22.

11. *Ibid.*

12. G. Tyler Miller. *Living in the Environment: An Introduction to Environmental Sciences,* 7th Edition. Belmont, CA, Wadsworth Publishing Company 1992, p. 334.

13. *Ibid.,* p. 10.

14. World Resources Institute. *1994 Information Please Environmental Almanac,* New York, Houghton Mifflin, 1994.

15. EPA Document No. EPA 841-F-97-003, National Water Quality Inventory; 1996 Report to Congress.

16. Ibid.

17. Stephen A. Thompson, *Water Use, Management and Planning in the United States,* Academic Press, San Diego, CA; 1999, pg. 125, 127.

18. Joel Makower. *the e factor: the bottom-line approach to environmentally responsible business,* New York, NY; The Tilden Press, 1993, p. 217.

19. Joseph J. Romm. *Lean and Clean Management: How to Boost Profits and Productivity by Reducing Pollution,* New York, NY; Kodansha International, 1994, p. 4.

20. Joel Makower. *the e factor: the bottom-line approach to environmentally responsible business,* New York, NY; The Tilden Press, 1993, p. 217.

Why Use Green Building Materials?

An ounce of prevention is worth a pound of cure.

—Anonymous

Using green building materials can help divert indoor air quality (IAQ) liability claims, respond to consumer demand, and provide for compliance with certain regulatory requirements. And, oh yes, it's the right thing to do.

Liability concerns regarding healthy buildings and healthy sites are rising in proportion to our growing understanding of the potential hazards associated with certain materials. Classic examples include asbestos and lead. Green building products, especially those fabricated from nontoxic, natural, and organic materials, can reduce IAQ contaminants and the accompanying complaints and claims.

Consumer demand for healthy buildings and for energy efficient structures also drive manufacturers and designers to explore options for green products. Meeting consumer demand is good business. Failure to meet consumer expectations is likely to remind you about the liability concerns.

These economic forces are reflected in the regulatory arena. Voluntary and mandatory environmental guidelines developed at the local, national, and international levels are increasingly applicable to building design and construction. Environmental regulations can present economic and administrative headaches when approached from a business-as-usual standpoint. Conversely, green building materials and methods can make compliance much, much easier.

Altruism, however, is the most frequently cited reason to use green building materials, and we would be remiss to exclude it. As custodians of the built environment, daily decisions we make with respect to product selection have a ripple affect on the natural environment that merits a significant level of professional care. Selection of products used in buildings impacts the Earth directly and indirectly. The building industry is a major consumer of raw materials. Obviously, the type and quantity of raw materials that are extracted and how they are processed impacts the Earth directly. Which materials are selected also affects how the building occupants (and, often the community in general) use the building. By obligating occupants, neighbors, and the community in general to use buildings in certain ways, the selection of building materials can indirectly impact the Earth. If, for example, a building uses a membrane roofing system, the installation is likely to involve the release of solvents in the air. If the membrane is black, it is likely to have a negative impact on the energy demands of the building and of the adjacent structures due to the *albedo* (the reflected heat that raises temperatures in the microclimate). If it is a single-ply membrane system, it is likely to be fabricated entirely from synthetic chemicals and virgin materials instead of recycled materials. Single-ply systems, especially adhered systems, make future disassembly and recycling virtually unfeasible.

Altruism is certainly the most laudable reason to use green building products. Self-interest, however, is generally the most compelling. Using green building materials can satisfy some very self-interested motives: deflection of liability, economic gain, and simple regulatory compliance. Self-interested motives beautifully illustrate the relative worth of an ounce of prevention and a pound of cure.

Liability Issues

The Americans with Disabilities Act (ADA) of 1990 ushered in, among other things, a new term—*biochemically handicapped*—which, although not specifically cited in Title III of the ADA (the title that impacts building design), has been recognized under the ADA. Biochemically handicapped references individuals diagnosed with multiple chemical sensitivity (MCS). Such individuals are acutely affected to varying degrees by chemicals commonly found in many building products. They suffer headaches, nausea, rashes, and asthmatic attacks, which can be life-threatening. Remember the boy in the bubble? He now has recourse under the ADA, as do all of us. But, that recourse is still relatively nebulous. ADA case law presents an interesting phenomenon. While hundreds of cases involving MCS have been filed, few if any have gone to trial. Apparently, no building owner or material manufacturer wants to test this far-reaching document relative to responsibilities for environmental hazards. No one wants to risk the potential public liability. No one wants to set the precedent on the books. Nevertheless, various agencies and jurisdictions have recognized multiple chemical sensitivity as a handicap under certain circumstances. The Department of Justice in its summary and overview of the ADA stated that MCS is not specifically defined in the ADA as a disability, nor is it excluded. The determination will be based upon whether " . . . impairment substantially limits one or more major life activities."[1]

The single greatest culprit in triggering multiple chemical sensitivity reactions—and subsequent ADA filings—is poor IAQ, often referred to as sick building syndrome. According to the World Health Organization (WHO), as many as 30 percent of buildings experience some kind of sick building syndrome problems. The Environmental Protection Agency (EPA) has stated that the health risks associated with breathing indoor air are two to five times the risks of breathing outdoor air. The EPA places poor IAQ fourth on list of high cancer risks, with 3,500 to 6,000 deaths per year attributable to indoor air pollution. According to the National Institute for Occupational Safety and Health (NIOSH), the relative causes of indoor air pollution are as follows:

53 percent inadequate ventilation

15 percent indoor contaminants

19 percent outdoor contaminants

13 percent unknown

Poor IAQ is expensive; estimates range from tens of thousands to billions of dollars annually in employee sick leave, earnings, and productivity losses. There may also be significant costs associated with IAQ issues for those who find themselves part of a growing body of IAQ legislative case history. Examples of emerging IAQ case law include:[2]

- *Bloomquist v. Wapello County, 500 N.W.2d 1 (Iowa 1993).* Plaintiffs sued employers and builders for providing an unsafe work environment due to an inadequate HVAC system. The jury awarded $1 million, finding chemical exposure associated with pesticide application and inadequate ventilation. The judge set aside the verdict due to inadequate scientific basis. However, the Iowa Supreme Court reversed the judge's decision and reinstated the original verdict.

- *Flores v. Winegrad, No. 87-283 4 5 B, Harris County, District Court, Texas.* The owners and manager of apartment complexes terminated the services of a licensed pest control operator in April 1985 and used their own maintenance staff to apply termiticides. When they sprayed chlordane negligently, without any notice to tenants, 311 plaintiffs brought a class action seeking compensatory and punitive damages, alleging negligence on the part of the owners and manager. As a test case, a number of the plaintiffs were awarded by the jury $10.5 million as a result of the exposure to the misapplied chlordane.

- *Uricam Corp. v. Partridge Investment Co., No. CJ882691, OK D.C. (Oklahoma 1988).* The owner of an asbestos-contaminated building, occupied by the Oklahoma Department of Commerce, sued the building's prior owner for $2.9 million, the cost of asbestos inspection, abatement, and damages. The suit was based upon a breach of seller's representations and warranties. The asbestos was discovered by Department of Commerce employees. In addition to damages, the complaint sought indemnification against any third-party liability. The suit was settled.

• *Bloomfield Co. v. State, 3AN-87-2082 (Alaska)*. The State of Alaska moved out of a building owned by Bloomfield Co. alleging sick building syndrome. When the landlord sued the state for vacating the premises for $1.8 million, the state counter-sued for $1 million in moving expenses. The case was settled.

One of the main reasons that manufacturers, designers, and building owners do not want to set precedents relative to multiple chemical sensitivity and the ADA is that while IAQ may be the main culprit, it is not the only trigger for MCS reactions. It is just the tip of the proverbial iceberg. As scientific evidence continues to accumulate, chemicals previously considered inert or relatively benign come under suspicion. As we learn more about the complex workings of our ecosystems, we begin to recognize how naive we were not to ask more questions about the scientific wonders that the chemical industry heralded. And, of course, we look for the responsible parties, those who made the materials and those who profited from them. The potential legal exposure under ADA is immense. Any building occupant (employee or guest), can file a suit alleging discrimination on the basis of a disability. However unintentional, the Americans with Disabilities Act is perhaps one of the most powerful pieces of environmental legislation on record.

Economic Benefits

Obviously, the potential for liability has a considerable economic corollary. The use of green materials, particularly materials that are considered green because they are natural, organic or nontoxic, can help reduce claims made by MCS individuals under the ADA. The costs associated with potential liability are directly proportional to the size, location, type, and function of the building, and can be pretty hefty. Anyone caught in the situation, with the clarity of hindsight, can appreciate the wisdom of the old adage, *an ounce of prevention is worth a pound of cure*.

Similarly, it is easier and more cost-effective to prevent waste than to try and clean it up afterward. Waste costs money. An "ounce" of waste prevention can be worth a "pound" of waste mitigation. While trash may be the most familiar manifestation of waste, it is not the only one. Waste exists at every stage of a product's transition from a raw material through manufacturing, transportation, and use. Waste refers to the unused byproducts, the excess energy or heat, and the pollution produced along the way. It encompasses everything from packaging to greenhouse gases. Waste is lost profits. It is something you have purchased, but cannot sell or use. Cut the waste and you have reclaimed lost profits.

By performing an eco-audit of your building design, building operations, and manufacturing process, you can identify waste and possibilities for trimming the waste. An eco-audit is an earth-friendly review of the materials in your building as well as the operations in the building in order to identify cost-effective opportunities for: improving indoor air quality, improving water quality and efficiency, improving energy efficiency, minimizing waste, and improving the environmental integrity of the local ecosystem. An eco-audit is not a review for compliance with environmental regulations. It is a perspective of the building as a living system. An eco-audit reviews the system to identify the input (the energy, materials, and labor required to create the product or service), the output (the product or service itself), and the byproducts (the "waste" products created in the process). The systems approach examines processes and relationships in addition to materials. An eco-audit is useful for planned new construction and for evaluating existing construction. Opportunities exist to improve efficiency and to "green" a building and its operations within all schedules and budgets.

Green products can help mitigate economic losses due to waste. There are hundreds of opportunities in nearly every arena. Water conservation and water quality management, for example, boast numerous products and systems that can pay for themselves very quickly.

Water use in the United States doubled from 1950 to 1990, increasing from 910 billion liters (200 billion gallons) per day to more than 1.8 trillion liters (400 billion gallons) per day.[3]

Simply replacing a leaky faucet can save 160 liters (36 gallons) per day. Sensor-operated faucets and flush valves are classic examples of automatic controls to reduce waste. Low flow fixtures are another way to conserve water. Homes with older fixtures use about 75 gallons of water per person per day; homes with water-saving fixtures that are now required by most plumbing codes use about 55 gallons of water per person per day.[4] The Department of Defense, in compliance with Executive Order 12902, "Energy Efficiency and Water Conservation at Federal Facilities—March 8, 1994," installed new multistage dishwashing equipment in a federal cafeteria. Multistage dishwashers reuse water from the rinse cycle to prewash dishes. The DOD installation cost $57,800.00 and resulted in an annual savings of 500,000 gallons of water, $2,000 in water costs, and $19,000 in labor costs. Payback was 2.7 years and is projected to save almost $500,000 over the 25-year life of the installation.[5]

Selecting indigenous plant material (xeriscaping) instead of the decorative hothouse species could reduce municipal water requirements more effectively than low flow fixtures or sensor operated faucets. Because native plants are appropriate to the climate, they are easy to maintain. They do not need extra water or care, except perhaps during the 12-month establishment period. Buffalo grass is replacing many lawns in the prairie states. Buffalo grass requires 25 inches of water per year compared to Bermuda grass, which requires 40, Zoysia which requires 45, and St. Augustine, which requires 50. Compare such water requirements with the average 35.45 inches annual rainfall in the Dallas/Ft.

Worth area[6] area or the average 35.30 inches in Canton, Illinois[7]. Furthermore, not only is less water required, but also less chemical fertilizers and pesticides.

Ozonation equipment also offers the dual savings of reduced water requirements and reduced chemical requirements. To this, it adds energy savings. Ozone oxidizes bacteria, viruses, and other contaminants up to 3,000 times faster than chlorine, thereby reducing chemical usage up to 95 percent. With the addition of ozone as an oxidant, laundry and dish-washing machines can run at lower wash temperatures for shorter cycles. Washing time can be reduced by nearly half since the rinse cycle can be eliminated. Ozone reduces total dissolved solids, which reduces calcium and scale buildup so swimming pools need to be drained less and equipment life is prolonged.

Where droughts are common, rainwater harvesting systems are exceptionally useful at minimizing waste. Rainwater harvesting keeps rainwater on site. It lessens the burden to municipal water facilities and decreases erosion and flooding caused by runoff from impervious surfaces. Rainwater harvesting systems gained some high profile recognition when, in January 1999, the United States Post Office opened its first "green" post office in Ft. Worth, which incorporated, among other items, a rainwater harvesting system. Droughts are common in Texas; they have occurred somewhere in the state once every decade of this century.[8] Therefore, it is especially important for Texans to use water wisely. The system being tested by the United States Post Office is helping to develop a viable technology and bring it to the mainstream.

Energy-efficient products and, in some cases, water-efficient products can generate economic gains that are clearly documented on your utility bills. Many utilities, recognizing that it would be cheaper for them to help finance the replacement of thousands of inefficient appliances and equipment with new, efficient units than it would be to build new plants to serve anticipated loads, offered rebates throughout the 1980s and early 1990s. The incredible success of the EPA's voluntary programs, Green Lights and Energy Star, is due in large part to the improvements seen by the participants in their bottom lines.

Before computer-controlled, self-regulating heating and air conditioning systems, people built climate-appropriate buildings—buildings that caught the cool breeze on a hot summer day and allowed the sun to shine deep into the interior during the cold days of winter. This approach is called *passive solar design* and it has a long history. In 360 B.C., Socrates wrote: ". . . in houses with a south aspect, the sun's rays penetrate into the porticoes in winter; but in summer, the path of the sun is right above the roof so that there is shade. If, then, this is the best arrangement, we should build the south side loftier to get the winter sun, and the north side lower to keep out the cold winds." Technological advances permit us to build without regard for climate. However, if we combine the efforts—build in a climate-appropriate way and use convenient modern technologies, we can maximize our energy efficiency. Simply locating deciduous plants on the south and west sides of a building can cool a building in summer with their shade and allow warm sunshine to penetrate the building in winter when their leaves are gone. Another simple climate appropriate consideration is albedo. Albedo can affect energy efficiency because it affects the microclimate—that is, it is a lot hotter walking across a black asphalt paving than it is walking across concrete paving; and, it is hotter walking across a concrete paving than it is walking across grass; and it is hotter walking across grass than it is walking across shaded grass. Reductions in surrounding microclimate temperatures mean that the building air conditioning does not need to work as hard. In some urban areas, utility rates are as much as 10 percent greater than adjacent rural areas. This is due to the albedo of the paved roads and tall buildings in urban areas.[9]

Consumer Demand and New Markets

Green products can help recapture lost profits by mitigating potential liabilities and by reducing waste. Manufacturers and building owners have already learned this and are implementing efficiency upgrades in various forms. This raises the benchmark and creates a demand for the identification of other possible lost profits, other opportunities for green products.

In addition to mitigating economic losses, using green building products responds to a growing market demand for organic, nontoxic, energy-efficient, earth-friendly products across the board. Consumer interest in environmental issues has been gaining ground steadily. Health food stores and environmental mail order catalogs abound. It is rare to open a newspaper or watch television without being exposed to information about environmental damage, followed by what people are doing to fix it. How many surveys have you seen estimating the environmental surcharge people are willing to pay on gasoline, cigarettes, or energy? *The Green Consumer Guide,* published in 1988, was a best-seller. Since then, entire publishing companies have been dedicated to environmental issues. The public is hungry for green products and gravitates to green markets wherever they become available.

Mirroring consumer demand, in 1993, President Clinton issued Executive Order 12873, "Federal Acquisition, Recycling, and Waste Prevention," which directed each executive agency to "incorporate waste prevention and recycling in the agency's daily operations and work to increase and expand markets for recovered materials through greater federal government preference and demand for such products." In particular, the order required that all paper purchased by the federal government contain 20 percent post-consumer recycled content by the end of 1994, increasing to 30 percent by 1998. In 1998, Executive Order 13101, "Greening the Government through Waste Prevention, Recycling, and Federal Acquisition," expanded the earlier directive to encompass biobased (alternative agricultural) products as well. Such presidential mandates for the federal government, perhaps the single largest contractor in the world, drive new markets. The U.S. General Services Administration (GSA), which provides the buildings and supplies for the federal government, annually negotiates $40 billion of goods and services bought from the private sector.[10] It purchases the paper, which must contain a minimum of 30 percent recycled materials, that the federal government uses. It is not surprising that paper with recycled content is now readily available and comparable in cost and quality to paper manufactured from virgin trees.

The environmental market, encouraged by the federal government, is shifting away from clean-up to pollution prevention, from superfund activities to research and design. For years, the EPA has emphasized *end-of-pipe* regulations, which only control pollution after its creation. The EPA is increasingly focusing its efforts on pollution prevention—enter the architect, the manufacturer, the landscaper, and the specifier.[11] This shift in emphasis opens up a whole new market for products and services. The global market for environmental technologies in 1992 was approximately 300 billion dollars, and an estimated 400 billion dollars in 1997.[12] "Environmental technologies" are defined as technologies that "advance sustainable development by reducing risk, enhancing cost effectiveness, improving process efficiency, and creating products and processes that are environmentally beneficial or benign. The word technology is intended to include hardware, software, systems, and services." [13] Both green building products and green design services are factors of the burgeoning environmental technology market.

Some of the most visible displays of this shift in federal approach are the voluntary programs for energy efficiency. For a while, the EPA and the DOE stumbled over each other trying to establish programs. Finally, they have combined their efforts. The result is impressive. Green Lights is a voluntary program to assist conversion to more energy-efficient technologies such as T-8 lamps, electronic ballasts, occupancy sensors, daylight controls, and compact fluorescent lamps. The Energy Star program expands upon the concepts illustrated in the EPA Green Lights program, applying the approach to other technologies, including computers, office equipment, residential appliances, and buildings. The Energy Star Homes Program requires energy consumption 30 percent less than that allowed by the model energy code. Homes that comply are eligible for energy-efficient mortgages. Through 1997, the Energy Star programs have saved more than $2.6 billion in energy costs and an estimated 25.5 million tons of carbon dioxide emissions.[14]

Regulatory Requirements

Still, there are regulatory requirements in place at local, state, and federal levels that are not voluntary and that do emphasize end-of-pipe solutions. Regulatory requirements can also have significant economic impacts. Ask a lobbyist—any lobbyist. For example, compliance with environmental legislation, such as the National Pollutant Discharge Elimination System (NPDES), requirements of the

Clean Water Act, or the abatement requirements of the Comprehensive Environmental Response, Compensation, and Liability Act (CERCLA or Superfund) can be expensive. Green products can mitigate the expense and help streamline compliance.

NPDES prohibits discharge of pollutants into waters of the United States unless a special permit is issued by EPA, a state, or, where delegated, a tribal government on a Native American reservation. NPDES requirements affect permit applications, regulatory guidance, and management and treatment requirements. The Phase I Stormwater program permit application requirements address certain categories of stormwater discharges associated with industrial activity, including: manufacturing facilities; construction operations disturbing five or more acres; hazardous waste treatment, storage, or disposal facilities; landfills; certain sewage treatment plants; recycling facilities; power plants; mining operations; some oil and gas operations; airports, and certain other transportation facilities. Government-owned facilities must also comply. The Phase II Stormwater program applies to smaller municipalities and is estimated to include as many as 1.1 million commercial, institutional, and retail sources, and 5,700 municipalities.[15]

In many circumstances, retention ponds are required to obtain NPDES permits. However, pervious paving can often reduce or eliminate the need for retention ponds. Pervious pavement is a green building product. It includes pervious concrete and interlocking pavers that allow water to percolate through the joints between the pavers and paving forms specifically designed to support soil and grass. Most of the paving forms that are designed to support soil and grass are fabricated from recycled plastic. Use of pervious concrete paving or pervious pavers will reduce stormwater runoff from solid surfacing. Pervious pavement can be up to 90 percent permeable; which means that 90 percent of the moisture that hits the paved surface will percolate through the paved surface and 10 percent will run off.

Abatement of contaminated soil is another example of the potential for a green approach to save on regulatory requirement expenses. Ordinarily, contaminated soil is removed and mechanically or chemically treated off-site and burned or landfilled. *Phytoremediation* is an alternative treatment that can be as much as 50 percent less expensive than standard treatment. Phytoremediation is an innovative technology that utilizes plants and trees to clean up contaminated soil and water. It is an aesthetically pleasing, solar-energy-driven, passive technique that can be used to clean up metals, pesticides, solvents, crude oil, polyaromatic hydrocarbons, and landfill leachates. Plants can break down organic pollutants, those that contain carbon and hydrogen. Plants can also extract (phytoaccumulate) certain metal contaminants. Nickel, zinc, and copper are the best candidates for removal by phytoextraction because they are the favorites of the approximately 400 known plants. The plants are harvested as necessary and either incinerated or composted to recycle the metals. Trees have long tap roots that act as organic pumps/filters. Poplar trees, for example, can pull out of the ground 30 gallons of water per day. The pulling action of the roots decreases the tendency of surface pollutants to move downward toward groundwater or aquifers.

At the local level, environmental regulations take on a much more regional flavor, responding to local environmental quality issues and economic concerns. Like international agreements, however, local developments can translate into national policy. Concerns about air quality originally localized in New England and in California have gained federal attention. Recycling procurement policies, prevalent at the state level, are replicated in Executive Order 13101, "Greening the Government through Waste Prevention, Recycling and Federal Acquisition," which directs federal agencies to use recycled content materials for their supplies, everything from paper to concrete paving.

The international level can also birth national regulatory requirements. Although international agreements do not obligate the signatory nations per se, they nevertheless carry a great deal of political weight. More than 150 international environmental treaties have been adopted, most since 1970. Ultimately, many are internalized by signatory nations through national legal processes in each country. And, as seen in Kyoto, even when international environmental treaties are not internalized via the legislative process, they can impact a country. Nations that do not embrace global political agreements are often in an extremely unpleasant spotlight. Thus, despite their relative lack of enforcement mechanisms, international treaties can be powerful tools, impacting the development of national regulations and economic strategies.

The Montreal Protocol, authored in 1987, was an international agreement to phase out substances destructive to the ozone layer. It was amended in 1990 and accepted by 93 nations agreeing to phase out five key chlorofluorocarbons (CFCs 11, 12, 113, 114, and 115), carbon tetrachloride, and nonessential uses of fire extinguishing halons by the year 2000. It also stipulated the phase-out of HCFC by the year 2020 and established a Multilateral Fund to help developing nations finance this effort. In 1990, President Bush signed the Clean Air Act Amendments, which internalized the Montreal Protocol for the United States. The Clean Air Act Amendments mandated an increase in controls for acid rain, urban smog, car emissions, toxic air pollutants, and ozone depletion. Under this law, EPA sets limits on how much of a pollutant can be in the air anywhere in the United States. Individual states may have stronger pollution controls, but no state is allowed to have weaker pollution controls than those set for the country as a whole.[16]

Agenda 21, developed in 1992 at the Earth Summit in Rio de Janeiro, had no less of a goal than to stop and reverse environmental damage to our planet and to promote sustainable development in all countries. Agenda 21 contains 40 separate areas of concern with 120 separate actions and corresponding financial requirements to address: quality of life on Earth, efficient use of earth's natural resources, protection of our global commons, management of human settlements, chemicals and the management of waste, and sustainable economic growth. The U.S. Climate Change Action Plan was a partial internalization of Agenda 21. It emphasizes voluntary programs to achieve a reduction in greenhouse gases to 1990 levels by year 2000. Greenhouse gases (carbon dioxide, ozone, methane, nitrous oxide, chlorofluorocarbon, and others) act like the glass panes of a greenhouse. They allow light, infrared radiation, and some ultraviolet radiation from the sun to penetrate the atmosphere to the Earth's surface, which absorbs much of the solar energy and reflects infrared radiation. Some of the reflected radiation escapes into space and some is trapped by the greenhouse gases and reflected back to the earth as heat. When greenhouse gases build up in the atmosphere, more heat is trapped and reflected back to Earth resulting in global warming. Greenhouse gases have increased significantly since the Industrial Revolution. The plan addresses both economic and environmental concerns. By improving efficiencies, the United States improves our national bottom line and prevents the pollution associated with the energy generation. The U.S. Climate Change Action Plan detailed 45 separate actions and $1.9 billion in redirected federal dollars, along with an estimated $60 billion savings by year 2000. Estimated savings include 25 percent energy savings in construction and 40 percent energy savings in building operations. The plan is implemented in part through EPA and DOE programs such as Energy Star and Rebuild America.

Of equal importance to international agreements are international standards. Just as there are numerous standards-making bodies at the national level, there are numerous standards-making bodies at the global level. International standards developed by the International Organization for Standardization (ISO), for example, are the global corollary to national standards developed by the American Society for Testing and Materials (ASTM).

International standards are emerging as extremely powerful tools when wielded by global corporate interests. The World Trade Organization's (WTO) *Agreement on Technical Barriers to Trade* requires that signatories adopt international standards as the basis for national standards. Ostensibly, this means that voluntary international standards can preempt national regulations. Consider the European Union (EU) versus the United States regarding the import of beef containing growth hormones. In 1997, the WTO ruled that member nations could not impose health standards restricting farmers' use of growth hormones in beef cattle more stringent than those recommended by CODEX Alimentarius, an international food standards agency. This ruling came about as a result of a U.S. government challenge of European Union health standards that blocked the import into Europe of beef that had been injected with hormones. Despite EU regulations prohibiting the sale of beef containing growth hormones, the EU is now obliged under the rules of the WTO to allow the import of beef containing growth hormones. As of this writing, the EU is appealing the decision. Design consultants and building product manufacturers should learn from this example and be aware of the development of international standards for green building and green building products.

Altruism and Professional Responsibility

The costs that may be tracked on a typical assets/liabilities summary may appear significant to the bottom line of a particular project or product. But they pale in comparison to the environmental costs. It may be hard to economically justify basic "it's the right thing to do logic," but it will be impossible to continue without it—economically or otherwise.

We have only this one planet. It has the same amount of resources—water, air, minerals—that it has had since the beginning of time, yet demand for them is continually increasing. More people and higher standards of living require more and more goods. Most goods are derived from the Earth's natural resources, to be used briefly and then buried in a landfill. By the middle of the next century, the same limited amount of resources is expected to support nearly 12 billion people. We need to be very careful of the resources we use and how much of them we use. We must vigilantly ask and answer the questions:

What are we using?

How well are we using it?

Furthermore, our limited resources are not spread out evenly. There are centers of *biodiversity.* Biodiversity, or biological diversity, refers to the variety of plant and animal species and the ecological communities in which they live. Scientists have discovered that each species on Earth originated in only one location. Pecans and sunflowers, for example, are believed to have originated in the Oklahoma area. From there, they spread across the earth. Because they originated in Oklahoma, however, the greatest variety of pecan and sunflower types are still found in this area. We rely on biodiversity, the different characteristics of different species, for medical, agricultural, and industrial advances. When we remove all existing vegetation during the construction process, even if we landscape with "native vegetation" afterward, we have destroyed a portion of the biodiversity of our area forever.

We also contribute to the destruction of the Earth's biodiversity when we rely on a single species. Most lumber products, for example, are derived from an extremely limited number of species. Codes, standards, and industry structural tables are limited to a handful of species, such as southern yellow pine. Reliance on a single species or a limited number of species promotes *monoculture,* the antithesis of biodiversity. It was, in part, monoculture that devastated Ireland in the Great Potato Famine. The Irish relied almost entirely on a single species of potato. When it failed, thousands died of starvation.

Some techno-enthusiasts have argued that a little DDT would have put an end to the trouble that Ireland experienced in the mid-1800s. In the short term, that may have been true. But the next generation of Irish would have been that much worse off. How much simpler to plant several species (preferably native) of potato to benefit from nature's resiliency in the vast gene pool. How much healthier for us and for the planet to eat potatoes that survive blight without poison. The DDT solution overlooks a basic law of nature, the *conservation of matter.* Everything cycles. Everything. Everything moves from physical reservoirs to biological reservoirs and back again. In the summer, the carbon dioxide that we exhale may be utilized by the leaf of the tree, which will fall to the ground in autumn, decompose under the winter snow, and nourish our vegetable garden next spring. *Everything cycles.*

By specifying green products—products that are nontoxic, have recycled contents, and are easily recyclable—we can make it safer and easier to cycle materials responsibly and eliminate waste. Waste costs money. It also pollutes the planet and consolidates the Earth's resources in singularly useless pits around the world. Most landfill pits are hygienically isolated and rigorously compressed such that the contents are not exposed to oxygen or water, and consequently, do not readily decompose. Assuming a site that promotes decomposition, however, decomposition time for plastic is 1 million years; for paper, one month; for glass, over 1 million years; for apples, three to four weeks; and for aluminum, 200 to 500 years.[17]

Societal costs can be significant. There is a tiny island about 2,000 miles from the nearest continent "discovered" on Easter day in 1722—Easter Island. It was barren, a biological wasteland except for grasses and insects, and the statues. You have probably seen the statues, approximately 200 mammoth stone sentries, some more than 30 feet tall and weighing over 80 tons. These statues were a scientific and historic mystery for years. Now, based on analysis of ancient pollen stratified on Easter Island, we know a little more about the statues and the people who made them. Around 400 A.D., Easter Island was a subtropical paradise, rich in biodiversity, with abundant plant life and animal life. The most common tree was the Easter Island palm which grew more than 80 feet tall and would have been ideal for carving into canoes and equipment for erecting statues. The island also produced the toromiro tree, similar to mesquite, and good for fuel; and the hauhau tree, from which could be obtained a strong fiber ideal for making rope.[18]

We now know that the inhabitants of Easter Island developed a highly organized social structure of approximately 2,000 people. We also know that they exploited their resources to the extreme—to their own extinction. These people are gone. They paid the highest price for their environmental mistakes.

Of course, we have made a few mistakes of our own. Each has had significant societal costs. Recent examples include:

• *Love Canal, New York (1978).* Attributing high rates of illness and birth defects to highly toxic chemicals dumped at the site from 1942 to 1953, New York State forced evacuation of 740 families from the area. In 1980, the site became the first federal environmental disaster area.

- *Bhopal, India (December 3, 1984).* A chemical accident at a Union Carbide pesticide plant resulted in approximately 10,000 deaths and 200,000 to 500,000 injuries.
- *Chernobyl, Russia (April 25–26, 1986).* By far the worst single disaster in the world's nuclear power industry, resulting in a minimum of 50,000 deaths and radiation levels that 10 years later are reported to be 40 to 800 rads in the affected area (average normal background radiation is 7 rads; 12 rads is considered dangerously high and requires protective gear to avoid exposure).
- *Prince William Sound, Alaska (March 24, 1989).* An Exxon supertanker grounded on Bligh Reef, and spilled more than 11 million gallons of oil into Prince William Sound. Environmental damage is still being quantified and, unfortunately, debated.

These mistakes did not happen on isolated islands. Radiation, pollution, and chemical spills do not recognize geographical or political boundaries. They are not contained by mountains or oceans. These mistakes impact the global commons, the resources that we all share. It should be no surprise then, that we also share their economic impact. It costs each of us when the environment and our health and welfare are jeopardized. A 1984 World Health Organization Committee report suggested that up to 30 percent of new and remodeled buildings have poor IAQ.[19] Poor IAQ, according to the EPA, costs Americans $1.5 billion in medical bills and tens of billions in lost productivity. Up to 10 percent of urban electric demand is spent cooling buildings to compensate for heat gain due to a concentration of buildings, traffic, and dark paved surfaces.[20]

A growing number of statistics quantify societal costs, which, historically, have not been quantified. Nor have they even been recognized. If you are susceptible to poor IAQ that can be 100 times worse than poor outdoor air quality, your head may ache, your energy level may diminish, and you may become physically ill—perhaps even suffering long-term health effects. Typically, you will not trace any of these symptoms to the cause; you will merely call in sick to work until your body can rid itself of the debilitating toxins. Then, you will return to your daily routine until such time as the build-up of toxins in your system is, once again, more than you can tolerate. This susceptibility now has a name; it is called multiple chemical sensitivity (MCS) and is considered a handicap under the Americans with Disabilities Act.

Other aspects of societal costs are also beginning to be recognized. The Department of Commerce, Bureau of Economic Statistics, is developing measures of economic value for environmental assets, including renewable resources, nonrenewable resources, air quality, and water quality;[21] and, the President's Council for Sustainability, in its 1996 publication, *Sustainable America: A New Consensus for Prosperity, Opportunity, and a Healthy Environment for the Future,* recommended that measurements of our Gross National Product (GNP) be revised to incorporate environmental assets and reflect their consumption/degradation.

The GNP is an extremely poor indicator of a nation's wealth and economic stability. It is deceptive. It not only fails to subtract environmental damage from a country's assets, it generally views them as contributing to prosperity. Global warming, for example, is readily acknowledged as costly and problematic. In 1995, the United Nation's Intergovernmental Panel on Climate Change (IPCC), a group of approximately 2,500 scientists, determined that the greenhouse affect was real, that human activity, particularly the production of greenhouse gases, was impacting the global climate patterns. Furthermore, the IPCC advised that global warming would not mean an even temperature increase across the Earth. Rather, it would mean an uneven increase resulting in significant alterations to global weather patterns. The poles would warm more quickly than the equator and continents more quickly than the deep oceans. Gulf stream and wind patterns relied upon season after season, year after year, will be affected. In turn, climate "regulators" such as wetlands, rain forests, and oceanic plankton, will be impacted. Severe phenomena such as floods, hurricanes, droughts, and fires are likely to typify the changing climate. Over the last decade, the world has experienced a significant number of weather-related disasters. Under current economic systems, the costs to repair and replace damaged property, to feed the newly homeless, and to aid the injured are calculated as increasing the GNP. Money changes hands. Services and goods are provided. These are credits to the GNP. They make it appear to rise. But, there is no balance to the equation, no deduction for the property and lives lost, no deduction for businesses delayed or destroyed, and, no recognition of the part that global warming played in the event.

Government and academia are not alone in recognizing societal costs of environmental degradation. Industry, particularly those segments most directly affected by global warming, is also beginning to acknowledge societal costs. Hardest hit by the climate change have been agriculture, fishery, tourism, and insurance industries. The insurance industry is extremely powerful and wields a great deal of influence. It has taken notice of the cause and effect. The first five years of this decade cost the insurance industry $57 billion in weather-related losses, compared to $17 billion for the entire previous decade.[22] Because, under the current economic valuation system, the insurance industry carries a disproportionately large share of the fiscal burden for societal damage to the global commons, it is particularly interested in revising the status quo. Change certainly means accepting the cause-and-effect relationship. And, it means a commitment to reducing the pollution contributing to greenhouse gases, which contributes to global warming, which increases extreme weather and related disasters, which costs the insurance industry billions of dollars. It is also likely to involve new criteria for measurement and distribution of societal costs.

More often, economic equivalents are being developed that help us to quantify the enormity of damage. Wetlands, for example, play an important role in the purification of water on the planet, and the function that they perform can be equated to water treatment facilities. Of course, they simultaneously perform other services such as incubating the majority of freshwater aquatic life. If a vandal were to enter a water treatment facility and dump toxins or fill the holding tanks for "development," he or she (or "it" in the case of corporations) would be arrested, jailed, and fined. By establishing comparable values for ecosystems relative to their usefulness to humans, we create the mechanisms whereby vandals destroying wetlands are similarly penalized.

Forests are critical for air purification and planetary cooling. James Lovelock, a fellow of the Royal Society, developed the GAIA theory, the theory that earth functions as a single organism. He also developed an interesting economic equivalent for this one function of the world's forests. He wrote:

> *One way to value the forests as air conditioners would be to assess the annual energy cost of achieving the same amount of cooling mechanically. If the clouds made by the forests are taken to reduce the heat flux of sunlight received within their canopies by only 1 percent, then their cooling effect would require a refrigerator with a cooling power of 6 kilowatts per hectare. The energy needed, assuming complete efficiency and no capital outlay, would cost annually, $1300 per hectare. . . . A hectare of cleared tropical forest is said to yield meat enough for about 1,850 beefburgers annually, meat worth at the site not more than about $40, and this only during the very few years that the land can support livestock. . . . the 5 square meters of land needed to produce enough meat for one burger has lost the world a refrigeration service worth about $65.*[23]

Even this does not begin to address the value of forests as medical resources, construction products, and habitat. Nor does it consider the intrinsic value of forests in themselves, the inherent worth of a living thing and its innate right to life. (Those interested in legal arguments for the inherent rights of living things should review Christopher Stone's thesis, "Should Trees Have Standing: Toward Legal Rights for Natural Objects.")[24]

More recently, an international effort reviewed and tabulated hundreds of studies to compute the value of many of the services that the world's major ecosystems provide. Robert Costanza of the University of Maryland and colleagues calculated that the current economic value of the world's ecosystem services (pollination, water purification, climate regulation) is $16 to $54 trillion per year—compared to the gross world product of $28 trillion per year.[25]

Green Building Materials: An Ounce of Prevention

Buildings impact the Earth directly through their use of resources. They directly impact the quantity and quality of the Earth's resources—how much they use and how much they contaminate what they use. Buildings impact the Earth indirectly through their performance and through their effect on the performance of adjacent structures. Buildings impact the Earth indirectly through design decisions that help to drive the market. If you select a green product, you are making a philosophical and an economic statement. Manufacturers are listening.

Architects, as custodians of the built environment, have an opportunity and an obligation to confront these issues. Architects can have a huge impact, not only in the design of the building (which can impact those people who use it), but also in the design process (which can impact the market, regulatory requirements, and accepted practices). For building industry members associated with commercial or institutional projects, the potential impact is multiplied.

Often, however, the question is not so much whether a greener, more efficient solution exists, but how to identify it and how to implement it. The expectations of the design and construction industry tend to limit design choices to current industry standards—standards that are not necessarily the most efficient. They also tend to focus attention on problem solving during the construction phase, rather than problem identification during the design phase—further limiting the range of possible solutions. Standard design and construction strategies often require a pound of cure. Green strategies offer an ounce of prevention.

Chapter 2—Endnotes

1. Federal Register Vol. 56, No. 144, July 26, 1991, p. 35549.

2. Joe Manko, Manko, Gold & Katcher, as cited at the National Indoor Environment Conference, Baltimore, MD, 1996.

3. Department of Energy. *Greening Federal Facilities: An Energy, Environmental, and Economic Resource Guide for Federal Facility Managers.* DOE/EE-0123, 1997, p. 89.

4. Texas Water Development Board, in cooperation with the Center for Maximum Potential Building Systems. *Texas Guide to Rainwater Harvesting,* 2nd edition. Austin, TX, 1997.

5. Department of Energy. *Greening Federal Facilities: An Energy, Environmental, and Economic Resource Guide for Federal Facility Managers.* DOE/EE-0123, 1997, p. 59.

6. Texas Water Development Board, in cooperation with the Center for Maximum Potential Building Systems. *Texas Guide to Rainwater Harvesting,* 2nd edition. Austin, TX, 1997.

7. Canton, Illinois, Chamber of Commerce, 1998

8. Activities of the Texas Groundwater Protection Committee. Report to the 75th Legislature, 1996.

9. Environmental Protection Agency. *Cooling Our Communities: A Guidebook on Tree Planting and Light-Colored Surfacing.* 22P–2001, 1992.

10. GSA mission statement; www.gsa.gov/aboutgsa.htm.

11. Environmental Protection Agency. *Green Lights: An Enlightened Approach to Energy Efficiency and Pollution Prevention.* 430-K-93-001, July 1993.

12. National Science and Technology Council. *Technology for a Sustainable Future: A Framework for Action.* U.S. Government Printing Office, Washington, 800/ENV-6676.

13. *Ibid.*

14. www.epa.gov/energystar

15. EPA, Summary of Laws and Regulations, www.epa.gov/epahome/rules.html.

16. EPA, Features of the 1990 Clean Air Act, www.epa.gov/epahome/rules.html.

17. Metro-Dade County Department of Environmental Resources Management, Miami, Florida.

18. Environmental Building News. *Easter Island: Learning from the Past,* Vol. 4, Num. 5, September/October 1995, Brattleboro, Vermont.

19. EPA, Indoor Air Facts No. 4 (revised 1991), Sick Building Syndrome (SBS).

20. Environmental Protection Agency, *Cooling Our Communities: A Guidebook on Tree Planting and Light-Colored Surfacing.* 22P-2001, 1992.

21. National Science and Technology Council. *Technology for a Sustainable Future: A Framework for Action,* U.S. Government Printing Office, Washington, DC, 1994, p. 106.

22. Christopher Flavin and Odil Tunali. Worldwatch paper 130 "Climate of Hope: New Strategies for Stabilizing the World's Atmosphere." Worldwatch Institute, Washington, DC June 1996.

23. James Lovelock. *Healing Gaia: Practical Medicine for the Planet,* New York, NY Harmony Books, 1991, p. 183.

24. Christopher D. Stone, *Should Trees Have Standing: Toward Legal Rights for Natural Objects,* Avon Books, New York, NY, 1975.

25. Lester R. Brown, Christopher Flavin, Hilary French, et al, "State of the World 1997: A Worldwatch Institute Report on Progress Toward A Sustainable Society", WW Norton, 1997, p. 37.

What are Green Building Materials?

Our entire society rests upon—and is dependent upon—our water, our land, our forests, and our minerals. How we use these resources influences our health, security, economy, and well-being.

John F. Kennedy

Green building materials are those that use the Earth's resources in an environmentally responsible way. Green building materials respect the limitations of nonrenewable resources such as coal and metal ores. They work within the pattern of nature's cycles and the interrelationships of ecosystems. Green building materials are nontoxic. They are made from recycled materials and are themselves recyclable. They are energy-efficient and water-efficient. They are "green" in the way they are manufactured, the way they are used, and the way they are reclaimed after use. Green building materials are those that earn high marks for resource management, impact on indoor environmental quality (IEQ), and performance (energy efficiency, water efficiency, etc.).

Ideally, we specify only those products that use a minimum amount of perpetual or renewable resources and that use them very, very well at all stages. Ideally, we understand the basic environmental principle of finite, cyclical matter, and temper our every action accordingly. There are those "radical" environmentalists who do, even in the building industry.

We support this ideal and endeavor to work toward it. Nevertheless, there is an awful lot of progress that may be made by working with those who are not yet convinced and by demonstrating that green building, especially in "shades" of green, is possible and painless and often profitable. Furthermore, by so doing, we can collectively raise the benchmark and make it easier to build greener and greener buildings. This book is for those who recognize the necessity of addressing environmental issues and who must cope with those who do not. It is for those who want to do the right thing, but must balance ideals with tight schedules, limited budgets, and entrenched anti-green perspectives.

While people may recognize the term "green" to mean environmentally friendly, most have several misperceptions about how environmentally friendly products perform relative to the standard, more familiar products. In the building industry, it is not uncommon for the owner's initial response to the topic to sound something like this:

"Yes! Of *course,* I'm interested in protecting our environment."

"Yes, I'd like to discuss green building options."

"Yeah, so, what kind of cost are we talking about here?"

"Well. . . does it work?"

"And, um, what would this thing look like, you know, if we did go green?"

It is politically correct to express concern for the environment. Paradoxically, it is equally acceptable to express apprehension at implementing green approaches rather than standard approaches.

Information detailing environmental degradation, global warming, and chemical contamination of our earth is readily available. It is disseminated across society, from kindergarten through graduate school, in National Public Radio programs and in CNN newsclips. Leading scientists, including about 2,500 scientists from the United Nation's Intergovernmental Panel on Climate Change, concur that human activity causes pollution, vanquishes species, and is linked to global warming.[1] We know that we have a problem.

However, the correlating education and support network that would enable us to respond actively and positively to the environmental warnings is only now beginning to emerge. Partial information, outdated information, and misinformation plague the successful development of green building. The majority of building owners, designers, engineers, contractors, manufacturers, and building officials are receptive to protecting the environment, but are *not* receptive to using green materials to accomplish the task. The unfortunate perception of green building materials is that they look bad, cost a lot, and do not perform well. Understanding this perspective is essential for effectively resolving such concerns. Therefore, in order to better understand what green building materials are, we need to clarify what they are not. We need to get rid of the pervasive misperceptions about green building materials.

What Does Green Look Like?

It is important to recognize that there is an overwhelming societal prejudice in this country against environmental aesthetics. Environmental enthusiasts often overlook this. The resistance is reflexive—a fear of being different. And more, of being odd, and perhaps a little low-class. The stereotypical image of environmentalists is that they live off the grid and build with aluminum cans, tires, and straw bales. They wear unwashed jeans and tie-dye shirts. They have long hair, shaggy beards and eat obscure vegetables.

There is an awful lot of imagery associated with the term "environmental." It's not all pretty. Many of us are inclined to think about blue skies, lush green foliage, and clear, sparkling water. But, the average businessperson and the building owner immediately think low-tech, disheveled, overgrown, uncontrolled, and unprofitable. Translation: dangerous and unwanted.

If we believe that a green material will look trashy, we tend to actually see it that way. Perception filters reality. It adjusts the objective world into subjective information, upon which we formulate decisions and behavior.

It is true that a green product can look very distinctive. A photovoltaic panel, for example, is hard to miss. It is also true that there are a lot of examples of aluminum cans and old tires used directly as building materials. Some people do live in old school buses and decorate with found items (trash). This is reuse, pure and simple. But, that is *not* what we are talking about here—at least, not only that. We are considering alternative agricultural products, recycled content products, nontoxic products, and energy-efficient products—items that may very obviously display an environmental ethic. On the other hand, they may look just like the much more environmentally damaging products they replace. Sustainably harvested wood may have a label on it, but otherwise it will look like, well, wood. In fact, for decades, many products have contained recycled materials. For example, several acoustical ceiling tile lines are fabricated from recycled cellulose. And, gypsum board routinely utilizes reclaimed gypsum and recycled paper. These were economic decisions made by the manufacturers. They determined that the quality of their products could be maintained and the costs lowered if they used recycled content materials instead of raw materials. Previous perceptions, however, viewed such content as "trash" so manufacturers did not advertise the ingredients of their products. Many are still reluctant to claim "recycled content" for fear that the pendulum will swing again and they will be in the unenviable position of marketing "trash" products.

The options available in style and palette for a particular green product are sometimes more limited than for its conventional counterpart. However, such limitations are not necessarily inherent to green, but are often simply the consequence of a new and growing market. There are definitely more options available today than there were yesterday, and there will be more tomorrow. It is difficult to characterize the market impact of a more limited selection because individual response varies so greatly. There are building owners who balk at restrictions of any sort. They may have no desire whatsoever to install a metallic-flecked, hot pink, flooring system, but they hate the idea of losing the ability to do so. In other circumstances, the limitation has been received with elitist fervor. Some building owners glow at the prospect of being the first in the neighborhood to live in a straw bale house or install a rainwater harvesting system.

Decisions as to aesthetic acceptability, ultimately, depend on personal perceptions. They require project-specific evaluation and owner-specific review. We have worked on projects where the building owner felt the proposed green options appeared much more elegant than conventional construction materials; conversely, we have worked on projects where the very same green options were aesthetically unacceptable to that client. While there may be fewer green options relative to the buffet of styles, patterns, and colors to which we have become accustomed, there are still plenty from which to choose for interior and exterior finishes and landscaping. In general, now, there is enough variety in the market to make it accurate to say that, aesthetically, green options are neither better nor worse than conventional design options.

Does Green Work?

Yes, of course. Prior to the Industrial Revolution, society met most of its needs with materials obtained directly from the earth and then returned those materials to the earth after their use. The concern expressed in the "does it work" question is that we will need to decrease our standard of living to preindustrial levels. For some strange reason, we tend to assume that human ingenuity is limited to the development of petroleum products and synthetic chemicals. Fortunately, there is a host of entrepreneurs proving us wrong. New designs for photovoltaic panels have improved efficiencies. New plastics are being derived from agricultural products. Light pipes and heat film (film that becomes opaque when exposed to heat) offer new possibilities in the way we bring natural light into a building.

Perhaps the strongest evidence that green works is that so many green products and systems are gaining ground in the mainstream. That would be impossible if they could not perform. It would be equally impossible if the products were not cost-competitive.

Isn't Green Expensive?

The owner's question, "What kind of cost are we talking about?" reveals the economic perception of green. It costs more. There is a concern for the initial cost of the different, and perhaps risky, green product, as well as for the impact it may have on the overall value of the building investment. Economics is closely related to aesthetics. As many designers have experienced, it often dictates aesthetics. There is, after all, a tangible economic impact involved in appearances. What is the resale value of your house? Of your car? Can you get a job or a table in a nice restaurant without "proper" attire?

When cost is discussed relative to environmental issues, it is necessary to consider both the broader societal costs, the costs each of us bears for destruction of the global commons, as well as the costs directly borne by the individual under the current economic system.

The unfortunate perception of societal costs, however, is that one person does not make much of a difference. It is not going to matter much if I change the oil in my car and pour it down the storm drain. There is so much water in the world and this little bit is nothing in comparison. Besides, it is cheaper for me to do it myself than to pay a mechanic, who must comply with the environmental regulations, to do it. The reality, however, is that over 30 times more motor oil is dumped by oil changes and road runoff annually than was spilled by the Exxon Valdez supertanker.[2]

Nevertheless, until such time as societal costs are captured, such as with a revised GNP, and distributed proportionally, people will continue to believe that individually they cannot hurt the Earth and they will continue to act accordingly. That is, if they think about it at all. Even with the abundant wealth in the United States, most people spend the majority of their time devoted to survival tasks: the acquisition of food, housing, and transportation. There is not a lot of time or money for dealing with such esoteric issues as the health of the planet or community issues such as pollution prevention. We do what is easy and familiar, and what costs us the least. Our personal costs are determined by comparing the initial costs and, perhaps, the operating costs (typically maintenance and energy costs) of the readily available options. We are often guilty of the same, petty, daily calculations. Building owners are no different. Hardcore environmentalists may object, but if green materials and systems are to compete in the market—as the rules of the game are currently structured—they must compete on the basis of out-of-pocket costs. Happily, many can.

Simple economic comparisons show that green products are often competitive for purchase and installation—especially those that are considered green because they contain recycled materials. Back when recycled content material was called trash, many mainstream construction products, including ceiling tile, gypsum board, and steel contained recycled content materials. The manufacturers made economic decisions—the recycled material performed just as well and was cheaper than processing virgin material. But, perhaps most important, they could depend on the source. Increasingly, legislation is making it easier and cost-effective for manufacturers to use recycled content material as feedstock. Legislation that encourages recycling, for example, means that manufacturers are able to depend on recycled materials as a source material; they can retool their plants and redesign their procedures to incorporate recycling without the fear that recycling is simply a fad. Similarly, the elimination of economic subsidies for mining and forestry, originally enacted to encourage settlement of western lands, would decrease the discrepancy between the cost of such materials and the cost of alternative materials. As the infrastructure, legislation, and recycling programs continue to evolve, more industries can take advantage of them.

Energy-efficient products such as light fixtures and appliances must be evaluated in terms of life cycle, because they generally are more expensive to purchase and sometimes to install, but less expensive to operate. Probably the single greatest reason (without getting into political discussions of subsidies to oil and mining) is that these are new products; they have to bear research and development costs and they do not have the economies of scale of the less efficient competitors. Happily, if the energy efficiency rating (EER) is good, there is a quantifiable payback.

New, alternative products and systems (or revival of old systems) may be more expensive to purchase. New products may also be more expensive to install. Composting toilets, for example, aren't common. Although the concept may not be that difficult, the contractor isn't familiar with it and it may cost you more until he is. As the new markets continue to grow, however, the disparity in initial costs should decrease. As with energy-efficient products, these products are new. The debt they carry is proportionately larger than the comparable mainstream product, and they do not have the economies of scale . . . yet.

Both manufacturers and designers are changing the way they assign cost to a building and to building products. Some manufacturers are experimenting with *green leases*. Green leasing is a new, but dramatic shift in the traditional perspective of leased equipment. Under a green lease, the product manufacturer is responsible for the disposition of the product at all times. Thus, when the customer no longer requires the use of the particular product or requires an updated model, the manufacturer would be obligated to reclaim it and refurbish it or disassemble it for recycling as appropriate.

Green designers and building owners are developing *performance contracts*. The classic example of a performance contract is an Energy Service Performance Contract (ESPC). Overall, initial costs for green projects often cost 5 to 15 percent more than conventional projects. The increase in cost can be minimized by redefining traditional relationships and by accurately factoring operating costs. Design fees, which may increase to reflect the additional research and design, can be contractually linked to the operational savings experienced by the building owner. Operational savings can accrue not only from energy efficiency and maintenance procedures, but also from substantial increases in worker productivity. Studies indicate that green design (improved lighting and ventilation) has a tremendously positive economic impact on worker productivity in both manufacturing and service businesses. Since labor is the greatest expense by far for most companies, even a slight increase in worker productivity can have a significant impact on the bottom line. The trick is to determine what performance will be assessed against which benchmark, and how. The federal government is strongly supportive of ESPCs. In a 1998 memorandum, "Memorandum for the Heads of Executive Departments and Agencies Subject: Cutting Greenhouse Gases through Energy Savings," President Clinton directed federal agencies to make more extensive use of ESPCs. Along similar lines, the Department of Energy and some financial institutions are developing energy-efficient mortgages. An energy-efficient mortgage recognizes that an energy-efficient building will have lower utility bills and can therefore afford a larger mortgage payment or better terms.

Internally, many companies are adopting the principles of Design for the Environment (DFE). DFE encompasses the product concept, need, and design. Considerations include material selection, energy efficiency, possible reuse, maintainability, and design for disassembly and recycling. DFE is a prerequisite to green leasing. Green leasing necessitates a revision of administrative services. It also requires a basic redesign of products in order to allow for future disassembly and upgrade. DFE and green leasing have the potential to be cost-effective for manufacturers and customers alike because they save much of the energy and materials needed to manufacture the product from virgin materials. They are also extremely resource-efficient. Some major corporations, including Apple and Xerox, are exploring the possibilities of the twin approaches, DFE and green lease.

Perceptions

Perceptions are difficult to change. After World War II, we were surprised that Japan was producing quality merchandise. We are equally surprised today to find that manufacturers are producing quality *green* merchandise.

Suffice it to say that green may perform the task differently, but it performs it well; green can look very different, but it doesn't have to; and, green can cost a whole lot more, but it can also be more cost-effective, especially long term.

Shades of Green

The response to the question, "What are green building materials?" is less a black-and-white answer than it is a shade of gray—or of green. That is an obstacle for the building industry. We are accustomed to specific requirements in order to establish compliance with applicable codes and with accepted standards for professional care. But standards and measurable, prescriptive requirements delineating the greenness of a product are more difficult to define. They are the topic of Chapter 4, How Does the Product Selection Process Work?

Let us return to the fundamental benchmarks of sustainability.

What are we using?

How well are we using it?

Obviously, the responses are not simple. They involve a multiattribute decision-making process. In computer terminology, they involve fuzzy logic. Fuzzy logic develops a response to a complex problem by breaking the problem down into a series of simpler questions. As the answers to each of these simpler questions is derived, the solution to the original problem begins to take shape. In other words, you approach the answer and develop a workable solution, but, you are unlikely to ever generate a simple yes or no response.

The challenge of assessing the relative greenness of a product is that seemingly simple questions may still produce complex answers. For example:

- *Is it hazardous?* What if one of the byproducts at one of the stages happens to be a synthetic chemical—one of more than 65,000 synthetic chemicals in commercial use that, according the EPA, National Research Council, have *not* been tested for their effect on humans?

- *Is it locally obtained?* What if one of the input materials in one of the stages happens to be obtained from a location within an endangered ecosystem, such as bauxite for aluminum, mined in the rain forest?

- *Is it recycled?* What if the input materials are obtained entirely from recycled materials? From recycled petroleum-based materials? What if the only facility equipped to recycle those petroleum-based materials is overseas? What if a product is fabricated entirely from recycled materials, but the adhesive resin binder is a known carcinogen?

- *Is it energy-intensive to make?* What if the fabricating equipment is high-efficiency, non-CFC-producing, state-of-the-art equipment? What if the energy used to power the high-efficiency fabricating equipment is produced in a coal-burning utility plant?

- *Is it reusable or recyclable?* What if the product in its final stage will probably go straight to a landfill? What if it could be recycled at some point in the future . . . if the facilities or technology could be created to recycle it?

A single product may contain several materials. There are a lot of green characteristics that any one material might possess. Each material may involve hundreds of perpetual, renewable and nonrenewable resources. It may use some of them well in certain stages of acquisition, manufacture, distribution, and use; and, it may not use them very well at all during other stages. The information is often difficult to obtain. The product representative is unlikely to know the answers to these types of questions. But good representatives will find out for you—if you ask. Many are genuinely interested. Most want to represent a quality product and are often in the best position to communicate the quality requirements and new possibilities for meeting and exceeding those requirements to their company.

Balancing the "good" against the "bad" is an unfortunate and, hopefully, temporary reality. Under the current scheme of standards and threat of litigation, it can become an endless pursuit. To best manage the volume of information to assess it and render an educated, professional opinion, it is helpful to categorize the aspects of green into three categories: (1) resource management, (2) toxicity/IEQ, and (3) performance. These categories are tools to help quickly assess and compare the greenness of one product relative to another. Green building is an evolving field, and these tools are not necessarily the ones we will be recommending ten years from now. They are currently useful because we have in place ways to quantify and compare information within each of these categories.

Resource Management, Toxicity/IEQ, and Performance

Resource Management

Resource management is a common term in the environmental community, but it is misleading for those more accustomed to the business world. In business, we manage many tasks in great detail. Management hierarchies and methodologies permeate every company no matter how small. The single, overriding goal of management is to improve profit. Tangentially, we may focus on maximizing efficiency, improving morale, marketing to new customers, or cutting waste. But, the bottom line is the bottom line. In contrast, resource management is not concerned with profits. It is concerned with stewardship. It is not concerned with what can be extracted. It is concerned with what remains. The distinction is important because the term can be used intentionally in some circumstances to confuse the issue. For example, forest management is not necessarily forest stewardship. It might be. But it more likely refers to the operation of the forest to generate the most timber (profits) possible. Similarly, if you were to hire a waste management firm, your waste is just as likely to go to a landfill as to a recycling center.

Resource management relative to products refers to the impact on the Earth's resources—perpetual resources (solar, wind, tidal energy), renewable resources (timber, soil, grasses), and nonrenewable resources (oil, coal, aluminum)—due to the acquisition of raw materials and the manufacturing process. It considers the impact on biodiversity and ecosystems. Common measurements include recycled content (pre- and postconsumer) and independent environmental certifications of sustainability in acquisition or manufacture. Preconsumer recycled material is material that never made it to the consumer market; it is manufacturing scrap, and most industries utilize their own scraps in some manner. Postconsumer recycled material is the challenge and the better measure for greenness. Utilization of preconsumer waste is green; but, it is standard practice. It is baseline. If the product with preconsumer recycled content merely pauses in the consumer's hands en route to the landfill, then it is not a sustainable use of resources. If, on the other hand, a means for collecting the postconsumer material is available that will channel the material back to industry (ideally, back to the original manufacturer), then it is truly recycling.

When resources are managed for the benefit of the Earth and for the benefit of future generations, instead of for the maximization of profit, they are considered to be "sustainably managed." Sustainable resource management requires a perspective that is Earth-centered instead of human-centered. What are we using—from the Earth? How well are we using it—in terms of the consequences for the Earth, for the water, air, soil, and wildlife?

Sustainable resource management favors the theories of reduce, reuse, recycle, and renew. Opportunities to reduce, reuse, and recycle abound in the construction industry.

One opportunity for reduction of waste is utilizing alternative agricultural products such as soy resins, cork, or straw. These products frequently depend on agricultural byproducts (waste) and they are generally biodegradable. In addition, they tend to generate fewer hazardous pollutants during production than their traditional counterparts. This sort of innovative approach is the foundation of the American entrepreneurial spirit. Henry Ford, one of America's most renown entrepreneurs, developed Model T coil cases made of wheat gluten in 1915. In 1933, he developed soybean paint and plastics. By 1935, two bushels of soybeans went into every Ford car. Ford also developed ways to power vehicles with ethanol.[3] This approach contributes doubly to the nation's economic prosperity; it not only redirects money spent on waste, but also supports the development of new American industries.

Reuse is common in thrift stores and families with small children. For some reason, it frequently escapes consideration on a construction project. Potential sites with existing buildings are often overlooked in favor of previously undeveloped sites that can be manipulated more easily and quickly. In many cases, this is a false economy. Salvage! Adapt an existing structure. Redirect existing building components from the waste stream to local community groups, vocational schools, or church groups to give them a new home and you a tax break.

Recycling encompasses not only throwing your empty soda can in the specially marked receptacle, but also consciously selecting products with recycled content over products with virgin materials. That simple choice, referred to as "closing the loop," can save the natural resources, the energy to process them, and the waste associated with their production. In 1995, the United States recovered 56 million tons of materials from the municipal solid waste stream for recycling (including composting).[4] These materials are no longer classified as waste, but are considered raw materials, feedstock for new products. Estimates for the 1997 value of recovered materials totaled approximately $3.6 billion.[5] Of this, aluminum cans represent one of the highest market values, about $1 billion. Yet, every three months, Americans discard enough aluminum to rebuild our entire airplane commercial fleet. Not only is the material valuable in itself, but recycling one aluminum can saves enough electricity to power a TV or a 100-watt lightbulb for three hours.[6]

Options for building products with recycled content abound. Fiberboard, millwork, and flooring may contain reclaimed wood. Toilet partitions, car stops, and decking may contain recycled plastic. Sheathing and insulation may contain recycled cellulose. Floor mats, dock bumpers, and roof walkway pads may contain recycled tires. Upholstery, carpet cushion, and insulation may contain recycled textiles. Concrete and masonry may contain fly ash or slag. And steel generally contains some percentage of recycled content.

We need to develop opportunities to renew. It is widely believed by environmentalists that we have already exceeded the carrying capacity of the Earth. If this is true, we urgently need to rebuild ecosystems, nurture endangered species, and actively confront global warming as quickly as possible—before the Earth does it for us. If this is not true, renewal efforts will merely improve the quality of life for all of us. Fixing a problem is always more difficult and costly than avoiding it in the first place. Nevertheless, there are cost-effective options in the building industry. For example, we can reclaim brownfields and other abandoned or underutilized property. We can help stabilize greenhouse gas levels by designing building programs that effectively utilize urban infrastructure and encourage alternative transportation. We can help stabilize greenhouse gas levels by the simple act of planting trees. We can promote urban agriculture and develop wildlife corridors through urban areas, reinventing the classic garden cities. We can support conversion to renewable energy.

Of course, one of the many positive actions that building industry can take is to develop and use green building products.

There is not a lot of readily available information regarding the impact on the Earth's resources attributable to a particular product. We have a lot of information about what has been extracted. It is High Quality. It is Virgin Material. It is Imported. It is 100% Pure. But, not about what remains. The Depletion. The Degradation. The Contamination. The Social Costs of the Global Commons. However, we do have quite a bit of information about general practices and their results. So while we may not know specifics about Brand X resilient flooring, we do know what the environmental impacts are for the acquisition and manufacture of vinyl-resilient flooring in general. An excellent source of information describing the general processes and impacts on an industry-by-industry basis is the American Institute of Architects Environmental Resources Guide (AIA ERG).

There are some commonalties among the processes and impacts. Most generate *pollution;* they contaminate ecosystems. Most are guilty of *depletion;* they utilize nonrenewable resources and they do so inefficiently. And, most cause *destruction;* they ravage ecosystems in order to get at the non-renewable resources and/or they wastefully consume renewable resources.

Pollution: Raw materials for ore and stone ingredients are removed from the earth through mining, dredging, and quarrying. Raw materials for gas and petroleum ingredients are removed from the earth through drilling, pumping, and piping. Raw materials for cellulose ingredients are obtained by harvesting. These acquisition processes are typically responsible for soil erosion, pollutant runoff, and subsequent contamination of groundwater, and air pollution. Transportation of the raw materials to the manufacturing facilities involves trains, truck, and boats, and the accompanying fuel, roads, rails, and ports. The greater the distance, the greater the amount of pollution associated with transportation. Fuel is also required in the processing of the raw materials. Emissions from fossil-fuel-burning power plants that generate the energy that runs the manufacturing facilities include greenhouse gases (carbon dioxide, nitrogen oxides, sulfur dioxides), which contribute to global warming and acid deposition. Historically, factories have been located adjacent to natural waterways. Water is used to cool processes, to generate power, and to flush wastes. The ongoing struggle over PCBs in the Hudson River or the contamination of the Great Lakes offer classic examples. Depending on the process and environmental regulations governing the location of the facility, other hazardous substances may also be released into the air, water, and ground. The worst offenders are those who flee strict U.S. federal regulations and establish factories in less regulated areas, especially developing countries. In Mexico, such environmental abuse is so common that there is a word for the perpetrators, *maquiladoras,* companies that have factories just across the border, exploit the local population, rape their water and soil, export finished products back to the United States, and collect the vast profits that our domestic and international governing structures allow them to acquire in such an ignoble manner.

Depletion: In the acquisition of most raw materials, renewable resources and nonrenewable resources are depleted. That we have less of a particular resource is more than just a nuisance or hardship; it is a threat. Survival of any species is dependent in part upon the size of the gene pool. Fewer genes, less adaptability. This is especially harmful at a time when we are altering the ecosystems at a faster pace than any point in known history, and species need to be as adaptable as possible to survive. Survival of the ecosystem itself is also often threatened. A rain forest, for example, evapotranspires the water into the atmosphere that deluges the adjacent vegetation. When a portion of rain forest is clearcut, the neighboring portion is likely to suffer. Depletion all too often leads to destruction.

Destruction: Direct destruction of ecosystems during acquisition of raw materials or site preparation for construction is readily apparent. However, pollution also destroys ecosystems and habitats and the species that depend on them. The World Wildlife Federation considers the preservation of habitat a primary goal. Without appropriate habitat, the plants, animals, fish, and insects dependent on that habitat die. Many of these species are vital to the functioning of the ecosystems and, consequently, to our own survival. Insects, bats, and birds are crucial players in the web of life. They are pollinators; 80 percent of global crops and 33 percent of U.S. crops are pollinated by wild and semi-wild pollinators.[7] In addition to local habitats, migratory species depend upon appropriate sources of nectar-providing plants along their annual routes. Without wildlife corridors, many of these pollinators are unable to survive the journey.

Mining and drilling drastically alter huge tracts of land. Heat and contaminates flushed into our natural waterways destroy the aquatic balance at point of injection and for long distances downstream. Even localized disturbances (e.g., roadways or utility lines) that segregate habitat sufficiently to impede the travel of species for hunting and mating or the pollination of one patch of wildflowers with the next can devastate biodiversity and collapse ecosystems. Conversion of natural areas to "productive uses" (e.g., the conversion of natural forests to monoculture tree farms) eliminates the complexity of life dependent on the myriad of life within a forest ecosystem. By the time the temporary disruptions (sometimes lasting decades) are "restored," the local ecosystems are lost to us. And, perhaps the larger regional ecosystems are impacted beyond repair.

Toxicity/IEQ

Concern for toxicity encompasses indoor and outdoor contaminants and their impact on our health and the health of the planet. Toxicity issues include contamination of the planet and the corresponding degradation of ecosystems and biodiversity as described under resource management. However, because our culture is still focused on a human-centered perspective instead of an Earth-centered perspective, the primary measurement of toxicity in the building industry is indoor environmental quality (IEQ), and within this, indoor air quality (IAQ).

IAQ may be quantified by building owners in terms of worker productivity and customer satisfaction. It is determined more technically by industrial hygienists, researchers, and governing agencies in terms of parts per million (ppm) of a substance relative to current medical opinion of the threshold levels. Threshold levels are the points at which risk to human health is considered to transform from negligible to unacceptable.

Logically, this category should be pretty straightforward. Avoid synthetic chemicals in all forms. If nature didn't create a compound, chances are that it can't break it down. The classic example is polystyrene, which is completely nonbiodegradable. It floats across the surf at beaches and rolls around on the side of highways. It appears isolated from nature. An enigma. We also are learning that some of the thousands of synthetic chemicals are not quite as isolated from nature as we thought. Rather, they are absorbed up the food chain. Not digested and converted. Bioaccumulated. When water is contaminated with, for example, DDT, zooplankton living in the contaminated water may become themselves contaminated. They do not process the DDT. They cannot. Minnows eat the zooplankton, and, similarly, store the contaminants in their bodies. Larger fish repeat the process. And, at the top of the food chain, we eat the larger fish. We digest the nutrients and bioaccumulate the contaminants. Our bodies, like those of the creatures below us on the food chain, have no way to process the chemicals. The chemicals are not natural. So, they remain in our bodies until enough of them are accumulated to shut down our reproductive capabilities, our mental capabilities, or all of our life-sustaining functions. We die.

Bioaccumulation is not restricted to ingesting toxins. What we breathe impacts us. What we touch may be absorbed through our skin into our bloodstream. A friend of ours taught us this lesson the hard way. He was working on an art project—breathing and touching lots of chemicals—in a structure with poor ventilation and inoperable windows. He fell asleep in these conditions, and never woke up. He was 25 years old. IEQ, IAQ, and bioaccumulation are not typical health, safety, welfare concerns among governmental agencies that license architects, but they should be. By selecting environmentally healthy products, we can help protect the welfare of the community.

Material selection can have a significant impact on IAQ. Even though a product itself may have low volatile organic compounds (VOC) emissions, accessory products such as adhesives may emit VOCs. Also, maintenance may require or encourage the use of products containing VOCs. Similarly, if the product can function as a sink and adsorb emissions from other sources, then the original product's benign characteristics will be overwhelmed when the product is in place. All surfaces adsorb molecules of chemical substances and compounds or particles that are in the air. Adsorption is a chemical-physical bonding that may be permanent or reversible. The degree that surfaces sorb is a function of the volatility and polarity of the chemical and of the surface area of the sink material. Generally, the rougher the surface, the more sorption is possible. Glass and stainless steel sorb relatively low quantities compared to textiles, wood, and paper. Sinks can get very loaded during periods of elevated concentrations, then release (reemit) the substances later when the air concentration is lower.

Following are three general guidelines for assessing the potential for a product to impact a building's IAQ:

- If it outgasses, it will outgas forever, though with decreasing intensity.
- If it is a dry, packaged product, it was packaged promptly after manufacture, trapping the "new" smells in the packaging; these will be released when the package is opened.
- If it is a wet product, it will probably emit VOCs as it cures.

Unfortunately, toxicity/IEQ assessment is not straightforward for two reasons: First, a lot of high-performance building materials contain synthetic chemicals; second, a lot of litigation seeks to obtain compensation from those responsible for contaminating the environment (indoor and outdoor).

Many high-performance building materials, derived from petroleum and synthetic chemicals, have some green characteristics. High-performance glazing, such as low-emmisivity glazing, minimizes the thermal transmission through the glass, thereby improving the energy efficiency of the structure and reducing the amount of pollution generated as byproducts of electricity generation. This high-performance glazing utilizes laminated PVC interlayers and pyrolytic coatings. In place, the glass is inert, and it is potentially recyclable. However, the manufacturing process is guilty of pollution, depletion, and destruction. If we use the product, we share responsibility with the manufacturer for that pollution, depletion, and destruction of the Earth's resources. Single-ply roofing membranes are equally problematic. They offer significant improvements in performance, thereby lengthening the lifetime of the structure below. They are available in light-colored, reflective finishes for improved albedo and corresponding reductions in energy costs. They can be mechanically fastened, improving the capability of the parts of the roofing systems to be disassembled for easier recyclability. And they allow the creation of roof gardens, which also help reduce the albedo and reduce stormwater runoff, improve carbon sinking, and contribute to wildlife corridors through urban areas. But they involve those petroleum products and synthetic chemicals that nature cannot break down.

Obviously, high-performance building materials are preferable from a performance standpoint—hence the name. But they are a mixed blessing. Consequently, a lot of time is spent trying to establish acceptable compromises, and in turn defending against litigation that argues that the compromises have been breached or that they were flawed in the first place.

A lot of time and money is spent on defining, in legal terms, "toxic" and "hazardous" and on demonstrating scientifically that each of the new, non-natural materials is harmless to humans and to nature.

The Toxic Substances Control Act (TSCA), 15 U.S.C. s/s 2601 et seq. (1976), was enacted by Congress to test, regulate, and screen all chemicals produced or imported into the United States. The act, as its name implies, declares that there may be some potential harm to human health and the environment. The purpose of the act appears to be far-reaching:

§2601. Findings, policy, and intent
(a) Findings:
The Congress finds that
    (1) human beings and the environment are being exposed each year to a large number of chemical substances and mixtures;
    (2) among the many chemical substances and mixtures which are constantly being developed and produced, there are some whose manufacture, processing, distribution in commerce, use, or disposal may present an unreasonable risk of injury to health or the environment; and
    (3) the effective regulation of interstate commerce in such chemical substances and mixtures also necessitates the regulation of intrastate commerce in such chemical substances and mixtures.
(b) Policy: It is the policy of the United States that
    (1) adequate data should be developed with respect to the effect of chemical substances and responsibility of those who manufacture and those who process such chemical substances and mixtures;

(2) adequate authority should exist to regulate chemical substances and mixtures which present an unreasonable risk of injury to health or the environment, and to take action with respect to chemical substances and mixtures which are imminent hazards; and

(3) authority over chemical substances and mixtures should be exercised in such a manner as not to impede unduly or create unnecessary economic barriers to technological innovation while fulfilling the primary purpose of this chapter to assure that such innovation and commerce in such chemical substances and mixtures do not present an unreasonable risk of injury to health or the environment.

However, in the subsequent Definitions Section, the act dramatically limits the scope outlined in the previous section by defining the term "chemical substance" to mean any organic or inorganic substance, excluding "any pesticide (as defined in the Federal Insecticide, Fungicide, and Rodenticide Act (7 U.S.C. 136 et seq.)) . . . tobacco or any tobacco product . . . [and] any source material, special nuclear material, or byproduct material (as such terms are defined in the Atomic Energy Act of 1954 (42 U.S.C. 2011 et seq.) and regulations issued under such Act) . . ."[8] The Toxic Substances Control Act does not define the term "toxic."

OSHA offers the following definitions.

Hazardous chemical means any chemical which is a physical hazard or a health hazard.

Physical hazard means a chemical for which there is *scientifically valid* evidence that it is a combustible liquid, a compressed gas, explosive, flammable, an organic peroxide, an oxidizer, pyrophoric, unstable (reactive) or water-reactive. (Emphasis added.)

Health hazard means a chemical for which there is *statistically significant* evidence based on at least one study conducted in accordance with established scientific principles that acute or chronic health effects may occur in exposed employees. The term "health hazard" includes chemicals which are carcinogens, toxic or highly toxic agents, reproductive toxins, irritants, corrosives, sensitizers, hepatotoxins, nephrotoxins, neurotoxins, agents which act on the hematopoietic system, and agents which damage the lungs, skin, eyes, or mucous membranes. (Emphasis added.)

Under OSHA, the chemicals considered to be hazardous or carcinogens are those listed in the National Toxicology Program (NTP), "Annual Report on Carcinogens"; the International Agency for Research on Cancer (IARC) "Monographs"; or 29 CFR part 1910, subpart Z, Toxic and Hazardous Substances, OSHA.

In an appendix, OSHA affirms that determining the specific hazards is difficult and complex, stating, "The goal of defining precisely, in measurable terms, every possible health effect that may occur in the workplace as a result of chemical exposures cannot realistically be accomplished." The truth is that we do not know enough about the complex working of our planet to be able to predict how our actions may affect life's intricately balanced systems. We do not know how the products we use will directly and indirectly impact our own health. Already our ignorance has resulted in some nasty surprises. A more responsible approach would be to use known nontoxic, organic, and natural products to the greatest extent possible. Potentially toxic materials, materials whose reaction in the Earth's ecosystems is not known, should not be used.

Performance

Performance considerations address the indirect environmental impacts associated with a particular product. They examine installation methods; maintenance materials, and processes; durability; energy efficiency; and ability of the product to be recycled or reused at the end of its useful life in the building. Performance issues also include broader considerations regarding the impact of a product on the global commons, such as the albedo of the exterior finishes and the permeability of the paving. Typical measurements include energy efficiency ratings (EER) and, increasingly, worker productivity and customer satisfaction.

Energy efficiency improvements mean less energy. Less energy means less pollution. Simple.

Longer-lasting, more durable products mean less replacement. Less replacement means less total strain on our resources. Also simple.

In addition to these issues are considerations regarding the installation. Where acceptable to code, mechanical fastening is preferable from an IAQ perspective as well as from the possibility of disassembly for future reuse. Related materials which are required for installation of a particular product can have environmental consequences of their own. Which finishes, adhesives, caulks, or solvents are recommended by the manufacturer? How does the product cure? What, if any "waste" materials are generated due to the incorporation of the product into the building?

How much packaging is associated with the product? Opportunities abound on a construction project to reduce and to reuse packaging. Negotiate with manufacturers to explore packaging options. If the design professional never asks, the manufacturer is never made award of the need. Some, however, already understand the environmental need and economic benefits. Reuse of packaging is cost-effective for manufacturers and, consequently, their customers. Spec Mix, for example, distributes mortar mix for masonry construction in bulk packaging that it will reclaim and reuse. Another example is Alcoa, which offers two packaging reuse programs: Pallets Plus and Pallets Only. Under the Pallets

Plus program, Alcoa accepts return of pallets and packaging from its aluminum panels; under Pallets Only, a program for customers who already have a recycling method for packaging, Alcoa accepts return of its pallets. The pallets are refurbished and reused, and the customer receives a rebate.[9]

What kind of packaging is associated with the product? Plastic? Cardboard? Building product manufacturers can better position themselves in the changing market by proactively responding to packaging issues. Reduction is fairly commonplace because it makes obvious economic sense. Less money spent on packaging easily translates into more money received in profits. Reuse is beginning to generate comparable results. The type of packaging and the labeling as to type of packaging remains to be explored. Certainly cardboard with recycled content and the ubiquitous circular arrows are a step in that direction. There are developments on the horizon for greater use of starch-based plastics, not only for packing "peanuts," but for vacuum wrapping. Imagine the possibility of dropping a package of instant soup into your hot water—package and all. Soy-based inks used in the printing of labels is preferable. Also, if the plastic is petroleum-based, what kind? Many recycling programs distinguish between HDPE and PET, for example, just as they distinguish between colored paper and white paper. Unfortunately, most end users cannot readily distinguish plastic type. Plastic needs to be labeled.

Overcoming Entropy

If we discredit negative perceptions of the cost, the performance, and the appearance of green products, and if we educate ourselves regarding green evaluation of products relative to resource management, toxicity/IEQ, and performance, there is still one final hurdle to be overcome. Entropy.

Unfortunately, we use what we know, what we used on the last project—even if it wasn't exactly perfect. Why? Well, presumed liability for one. If a material has been in use for an extended period of time, even with only moderate success, the liability is known. And, it is shared. If everyone is using it, then the standard of care a professional can reasonably be expected to take is established at that level. If a manufacturer, or designer, or contractor steps outside of the circle and tries something new, the liability is entirely theirs. But so is the success.

Many times we fall back on the familiar because we are not permitted the time required to examine all the other possibilities. The pace at which our culture approaches life is astounding. The building industry is no exception. Fast-track is the norm and we are constantly searching for ways to further improve production speed—from design through construction. Does the use of green building materials slow a job down? Maybe. Design time may be extended depending on the project requirements, client's schedule, and the designer's experience with green building. Construction time may also be impacted. The contractor may not be familiar with the product or special in-stallation requirements; but then that could be true on anything you specify. It is also conceivable that the use of a green product could facilitate permitting and approval processes for sites subject to sewer moratoriums, waste mandates, and so on.

We need to reinvent patterns and habits as drastically as we did during the Industrial Revolution—which upset the balance in the first place. Prophetically, John F. Kennedy observed our dependence on the Earth's natural resources and the necessity for stewardship. Would that we had heeded his environmental message as ardently as his challenge to conquer space.

Chapter 3—Endnotes

1. *Setting the Record Straight: GLOBAL CLIMATE CHANGE.* United Nations Depart-ment of Public Information. DPI/1939/Rev.1 October 1998.
2. EPA National Research Council cited in Sierra Magazine, March/April 1999, pg. 17.
3. www2.ford.com/environment/featr3.html.
4. U.S. Environmental Protection Agency. Characterization of municipal solid waste in the United States: 1996 update. EPA530-R-97-015. Washington, DC, 1997. www.epa.gov/epaoswer/non-hw/muncpl/msw96.htm.
5. Tellus Institute. "Estimated value of MSW materials recycled in 1995. Prepared for U.S. EPA, Washington, DC, 1997.
6. City of Houston; Department of Solid Waste Management, Recycling Division; www.houstonrecycles.com/Facts.htm.
7. Lester R. Brown, Christopher Flavin, Hilary French, et al. *State of the World 1997: A Worldwatch Institute Report on Progress Toward a Sustainable Society.* New York: WW Norton, 1997, p. 102.
8. OSHA. § 2602. Definitions, The Toxic Substances Control Act (TSCA); 15 U.S.C. s/s 2601 et seq., 1976.
9. AIA Committee on The Environment, Waste Management Task Group Implications for Designers, 1992.

How Does the Product Selection Process Work?

Hurt not the Earth, neither the Sea, nor the Trees. . . .

Revelations 7:3

The product selection process is the same for green products as for standard (nongreen) products. All of the typical considerations for the quality, performance, aesthetics, and cost of a product are explored as usual. Add to this list, green. What are the environmental impacts of the product? How will the earth, the sea, and the trees be hurt? How will they be helped?

The standard product selection process includes the following steps:

1. Identify material categories.
2. Identify building material options.
3. Gather technical information.
4. Review submitted information for completeness.
5. Evaluate materials.
6. Select and document choice.

Obviously, some basic understanding is required at each step. You must understand requirements for how a building is put together in order to identify the material categories necessary for a project. Also, you must have a working knowledge of current construction techniques in order to assess building material options and to know what technical information is necessary for proper evaluation. Concrete, for example, has different performance criteria than does waterproofing. Some considerations, such as durability and cost, are common to all material categories, but the expectations for different materials will be different. A building owner may expect the roof to last 10 to 20 years with relatively little maintenance, but may anticipate replacing the carpet every 5 to 7 years.

Most design professionals are unable to personally assess the available material options. There are simply too many and their properties are too complex. Consequently, the building industry relies heavily on reference standards and on the expertise of consultants and trade associations to establish current standards of care for the various material options.

Green is an additional aspect to be considered in the product selection process. Like other considerations, it is imperative to understand the general concept of green (refer to Chapter 3, What Is Green?) and to know where to obtain the most current standard of care information regarding green. That is the subject of this chapter. You must know what green is in order to know what questions to ask and what technical information to request. You must know where to obtain current standard of care information to be able to verify a manufacturer's claims. The task is sometimes intimidating, but is in essence no different from exploring and evaluating other aspects of a product. If you are determining the strength of concrete, you would need to know enough about the nature of concrete to be able to ask informed questions and obtain technical information appropriate for the requirements of the particular project. You would also need to know where to obtain that information and where to validate it. The *process* of inquiry is the same.

Step 1: Identify Material Categories

During the schematic design phase, general material categories are identified. The Construction Specifications Institute (CSI) MasterFormat™ lists 15 broad material categories, CSI Divisions 2–16:

Division 2	Site Construction
Division 3	Concrete
Division 4	Masonry
Division 5	Metals
Division 6	Wood and Plastics
Division 7	Thermal and Moisture Protection
Division 8	Doors and Windows
Division 9	Finishes
Division 10	Specialties
Division 11	Equipment
Division 12	Furnishings
Division 13	Special Construction
Division 14	Conveying Systems
Division 15	Mechanical
Division 16	Electrical

During the design development phase, many different subcategories, CSI sections, will be explored. Although you may want to use masonry for the exterior walls, you may still be exploring different types of masonry—clay, concrete, or stone.

Step 2: Identify (Green) Building Material Options

In addition to the standard array of material subcategories, identify green subcategories. Adobe masonry units, rammed earth, and straw bale might be viable options for exterior masonry walls. Also, identify green options within the material subcategories. If you want to use masonry, consider clay masonry fabricated from petroleum-contaminated soil, or concrete fabricated with fly ash and slag. Explore local options for natural stone and reclaimed masonry units.

Greener options are available for almost every standard conventional building material. Though very few of them are listed in mainstream product references such as Sweets, there are several green building product reference books available and a growing amount of product information available via the Internet. Following are some resources listing green product manufacturers.

Alternative Energy Sourcebook
Real Goods Trading Corporation
555 Leslie Street, Ukiah, CA 95482
(800) 762-7325; fax (707) 468-9486
Lists energy-efficient products and technologies for the home, power
    generation, off-the-grid living, electric vehicles, and more.

Construction and Demolition Waste Recycling Guide
Integrated Solid Waste Management Office
200 North Main Street, Room 580 CHE
Los Angeles, CA 90012
(213) 237-1444
Lists options for recycling construction and demolition waste in the Los
    Angeles area.

Directory of Recycled-Content Building and Construction Products
Clean Washington Center (CWC)
Dept. of Trade and Economic Development
2001 Sixth Avenue, Suite 2700
Seattle, WA 98121
(206) 464-7040
Lists construction and building products manufactured partially or totally
    from recycled materials. Entries are classified under CSI MasterFormat
    headings and indicate the amount of recycled content and post-consumer

content in the product. Also contains Washington State GSA recycled product content guidelines.

Energy Efficient Building Products
Shelter Supply, Inc.
1225 E. 79th Street
Bloomington, MN 55425-1124
(800) 762-8399

WWW. SHELTERSUPPLY.COM

Lists products and technologies for energy-efficient, healthy homes construction. Includes an introduction describing energy problems frequently encountered in houses.

WoodWise Guide—Co-op America
1612 K Street NW, Suite 600
Washington, DC 20006
(202) 872-5307; fax (202) 331-8166
Lists wood products fabricated from alternative species and from wood obtained via certified sustainably managed forests.

Good Wood Directory
Certified Forest Products Council (CFCP)
14780 SW Osprey Drive, Suite 285
Beaverton, OR 97007
(503) 590-6600; fax (503) 590-6655.
Lists supplies and suppliers of independently (FSC) certified wood.

Green Building Resource Guide (1997)
John, Hermannsson, AIA, Architect
The Turnton Press
63 South Main St., P.O. Box 5506, Newtown, CT 06470
Lists green building materials in CSI MasterFormat™ classifications. Includes comparative cost information.

Green Home Product Guide
theGreenTeam, Inc.
5822 South New Haven
Tulsa, OK 74135
(918) 742-7593, (918) 599-0011; fax (918) 712-7593; arcvet.earthlink.net
Lists green building products and rates their greenness in terms of (1) resource management, (2) toxicity/IEQ, and (3) performance, relative to comparable standard construction materials. Entries include alternative agricultural products, recycled content products and energy-efficient products. Includes comparative cost information and an overview of environmental issues, focusing on residential construction.

Guide to Recycled Products: Building and Construction
METRO
600 NE Grand Avenue
Portland, OR 97232
(503) 234-3000; fax (503) 797-1795
Lists recycled-content building products in CSI MasterFormat classifications.
  Available on computer disk.

Guide to Resource-Efficient Building Elements (GREBE)
Center for Resourceful Building Technology
P.O. Box 100, Missoula, MT 59806
(406) 549-7678; fax (406) 549-4100
Lists green building products manufacturers. Contains information on
  resource-efficient design, job-site recycling, and resource management.

Harris Directory—Recycled Content Building Materials
508 Jose St. #913
Santa Fe, NM 87501-1855
Lists manufacturers of recycled-content building materials. Information is
  presented as a database for retrieval in CSI MasterFormat.

Interior Concerns Resource Guide
Interior Concerns Publications
P.O. Box 2386, Mill Valley, CA 94942
(415) 389-8049; fax (415) 388-8322
Lists green products and manufacturers in CSI MasterFormat classifications.
  Includes case studies, consultants, and additional sources for further
  ecological research.

McRecycle U.S.A.
McDonald's Corporation
McDonald's Plaza, Oak Brook, IL 60521
Lists products with recycled content that could be used in the construction,
  remodeling, furnishing, and supplying of McDonald's restaurants. Available
  in CSI MasterFormat classification upon request.

Minnesota Recycled Products Directory
Minnesota Office of Environmental Assistance
520 Lafayette Road North, 2nd Floor
St. Paul, MN 55155-4100
(800) 657-3843, (651) 296-3417
Lists recycled-content products made by Minnesota companies. Includes
  agricultural, construction, janitorial, landscape, office, and packaging. Also
  includes buy-recycled tips, and other resources.

Natural Choice Catalog
ECO Design Company
1365 Rufina Circle, Santa Fe, NM 87501
(800) 621-2591, (505) 438-3448
Lists healthy home products, including finishes.

Official Recycled Products Guide (RPG)
Recycling Data Management Corp.
P.O. Box 577, Ogdensburg, NY 13669
(800) 267-0707
Lists certified recycled product listings spanning more than 700 product
classifications, from paper to rubber and plastics. Entries are currently self-
certified according to EPA guidelines. However, the company is beginning
to work with Green Cross and other certification agencies to identify
products that have passed independent verification.

REDI Guide—Resources for Environmental Design Index
Iris Communications Inc.
258 East 10th St., Suite E
Eugene, OR 97401-3284
(800) 346-0104, (503) 484-9353; fax (503) 484-1645
Lists environmentally benign building and construction products available
throughout the United States. The guide enables users to find products by
manufacturer, brand name, product category, region of distribution, and
keyword.

Resource Guide to Sustainable Landscapes and Gardens
Environmental Resources, Inc.
2041 East Hollywood Ave.
Salt Lake City, UT 84108-3148
Lists information sources, landscaping materials, and products that are reused,
recycled, energy-efficient, or made from sustainable resources. Uses CSI
MasterFormat classifications.

Sourcebook for Sustainable Design: A Guide to Environmentally Responsible
Building Materials and Processes
Architects for Social Responsibility
c/o The Boston Society of Architects
52 Broad Street, Boston, MA 02109-4301
(617) 951-1433; fax (617) 951-0845
Lists green products and materials in CSI MasterFormat classifications.
Includes an overview of the environmental issues applicable to each CSI
division.

Step 3: Gather Technical Information

Technical information regarding the greenness of building products is much easier to obtain today than it was a few years ago. Sources include: product representatives, governmental agencies, building codes, trade organizations, industry standards, material safety data sheets, green rating programs, and environmental nonprofit organizations.

Product Representatives

If you have a specific green product in mind, the primary source of information is probably the product representative. Green product representatives can be extremely helpful in explaining the greenness of their product and potential applications for it. When researching green products, recognize that you may be dealing with someone who, while very familiar with the product and with the environmental issues, may not be as conversant with building industry practices as you typically expect, with things that you tend to take for granted. While the product representative is teaching you about environmental issues, you may need to teach the product representative about standard performance requirements such as compression testing or fire ratings. This is an extremely beneficial exchange for both parties.

For product representatives of green materials and systems, refer to the source listing in green material options just given.

Governmental Sources

When verifying manufacturer information or when researching general possibilities, one of the first sources of information that comes to mind relative to environmental issues is the government. Not a comfortable source for most industries that too often find themselves forced to deal with paperwork of mythic proportions and tangles of red tape in department after department. And for good reason; there are countless agencies enforcing myriad different, and sometimes conflicting, environmental regulations.

Nevertheless, federal, state, and local governments can provide excellent sources of information about the issues and the current requirements. Generally, regulatory requirements affect manufacturing facilities and procedures more than the product itself. There are some important exceptions for the building industry. Field-applied coatings, for example, may have VOC content limitations according to their intended application.

More than specific regulations, political activity is an important indicator of environmental trends and of related economic issues. Consider the effect on the HVAC industry after the international ratification of the Montreal Protocol and the subsequent amendments to the Clean Air Act (1990), which banned the manufacture of CFCs in the United States; and consider the effect on the lighting industry from the National Energy Act (1992), which banned the manufacture of certain lamp types and mandated minimum energy standards for new construction.

For designers and manufacturers who wish to remain ahead of the pack, it is vital to monitor political activity relative to environmental issues on a wide range in order to anticipate future developments and position themselves to take advantage of the opportunities. It is also advisable to monitor funding opportunities from governmental agencies. The Department of Agriculture, for example, sponsors the Alternative Agricultural Research and Commercialization (AARC) Corporation, a wholly owned government corporation that makes equity investments in private companies to commercialize nonfood uses of agricultural materials and animal byproducts. Some of the building materials that AARC has subsidized include: Agriboard, Environ by Phenix Biocomposites, and Primeboard.[1]

If you have not yet ventured into the arenas of politics and economics, perhaps the least painful way is by contacting the EPA and requesting information on their voluntary partnership programs; Green Lights and Energy Star provide assistance to improve the efficiency of building lighting and energy requirements, respectively. The EPA Building Air Quality Alliance Program was specifically defunded by the 104th Congress. In January 1996, the University City Science Center, a private nonprofit institution established in 1963 by a consortium of 28 educational and scientific organizations, finalized plans to develop a new private sector Building Air Quality Alliance. The University City Science Center approach, like the EPA program, is to provide building owners and managers with a set of guiding principles from which to develop a building-specific plan to promote acceptable IAQ. The University City Science Center will not be a certifying body; however, it will provide recognition for buildings where a proactive IAQ plan is in place.

As you enter the fray, you will find that many environmental specialists will speak a language consisting almost entirely of abbreviations and acronyms. And, as you become greener, you will of necessity learn those that are most integral to your particular market(s). Many have to do with governmental agencies or policies. Following are examples; refer to the Glossary for additional terms.

CAA   The Clean Air Act (CAA); 42 U.S.C. s/s 7401 et seq. (1970): "The Clean Air Act is the comprehensive Federal law that regulates air emissions from area, stationary, and mobile sources. This law authorizes the U.S. Environmental Protection Agency to establish National Ambient Air Quality Standards (NAAQS) to protect public health and the environment. The goal of the Act was to set and achieve NAAQS in every state by 1975. The setting of maximum pollutant standards was coupled with directing the states to develop state implementation plans (SIP's) applicable to appropriate industrial sources in the state. The Act was amended in 1977 primarily to set new goals (dates) for achieving attainment of NAAQS since many areas of the country had failed to meet the deadlines. The 1990 amendments to the Clean Air Act in large part were intended to meet unaddressed or insufficiently addressed problems such as acid rain, ground-level ozone, stratospheric ozone depletion, and air toxics."[2]

CERCLA   Comprehensive Environmental Response, Compensation, and Liability Act (CERCLA or Superfund) 42, U.S.C. s/s 9601 et seq. (1980): "Congress enacted the Comprehensive Environmental Response, Compensation, and Liability Act (CERCLA), commonly known as Superfund, on December 11, 1980. This law created a tax on the chemical and petroleum industries and provided broad Federal authority to respond directly to releases or threatened releases of hazardous substances that may endanger public health or the environment. Over five years, $1.6 billion was collected and the tax went to a trust fund for cleaning up abandoned or uncontrolled hazardous waste sites. CERCLA established prohibitions and requirements concerning closed and abandoned hazardous waste sites; provided for liability of persons responsible for releases of hazardous waste at these sites; and established a trust fund to provide for cleanup when no responsible party could be identified. The law authorizes two kinds of response actions. Short-term removals where actions may be taken to address releases or threatened releases requiring prompt response. Long-term remedial response actions that permanently and significantly reduce the dangers associated with releases or threats of releases of hazardous substances that are serious, but not immediately life threatening. These actions can be conducted only at sites listed on EPA's National Priorities List (NPL). CERCLA also enabled the revision of the National Contingency Plan (NCP). The NCP provided the guidelines and procedures needed to respond to releases and threatened releases of hazardous substances, pollutants, or contaminants. The NCP also provided the NPL. CERCLA was amended by the Superfund Amendments and Reauthorization Act (SARA) on October 17, 1986."[3]

CWA   The Clean Water Act (CWA); 33 U.S.C. s/s 121 et seq. (1977): "The Clean Water Act is a 1977 amendment to the Federal Water Pollution Control Act of 1972, which set the basic structure for regulating discharges of pollutants to waters of the United States. The law gave EPA the authority to set effluent standards on an industry basis (technology-based) and continued the requirements to set water quality standards for all contaminants in surface waters. The CWA makes it unlawful for any person to discharge any pollutant from a point source into navigable waters unless a permit (NPDES) is obtained under the Act. The 1977 amendments focused on toxic pollutants. In 1987, the CWA was reauthorized and again focused on toxic substances, authorized citizen suit provisions, and funded sewage treatment plants (POTW's) under the Construction Grants Program. The CWA provisions for the delegation by EPA of many permitting, administrative, and enforcement aspects of the law to state governments. In states with the authority to implement CWA programs, EPA still retains oversight responsibilities."[4]

EPACT
The Energy Policy Act of 1992: Increases previous regulatory requirements for conservation and energy efficiency for both government and the public. For federal agencies, it requires a 20 percent reduction in per-square-foot energy consumption by the year 2000 as compared to 1985 baseline.

EPCRA
The Emergency Planning & Community Right-to-Know Act (EPCRA); 42 U.S.C. 11011 et seq. (1986): "Emergency Planning and Community Right-to-Know Act, also known as Title III of SARA, EPCRA was enacted by Congress as the national legislation on community safety. This law was designed to help local communities protect public health, safety, and the environment from chemical hazards. To implement EPCRA, Congress required each state to appoint a State Emergency Response Commission (SERC). The SERC's were required to divide their states into Emergency Planning Districts and to name a Local Emergency Planning Committee (LEPC) for each district. Broad representation by fire fighters, health officials, government and media representatives, community groups, industrial facilities, and emergency managers ensures that all necessary elements of the planning process are represented."[5]

ESA
The Endangered Species Act (ESA); 7 U.S.C. 136; 16 U.S.C. 460 et seq. (1973): "The Endangered Species Act provides a program for the conservation of threatened and endangered plants and animals and the habitats in which they are found. The U.S. Fish and Wildlife Service (FWS)

of the Department of the Interior maintains the list of 632 endangered species (326 are plants) and 190 threatened species (78 are plants). Species include birds, insects, fish, reptiles, mammals, crustaceans, flowers, grasses, and trees. Anyone can petition FWS to include a species on this list. The law prohibits any action, administrative or real, that results in a 'taking' of a listed species, or adversely affects habitat. Likewise, import, export, interstate, and foreign commerce of listed species are all prohibited. EPA's decision to register a pesticide is based in part on the risk of adverse effects on endangered species as well as environmental fate (how a pesticide will affect habitat).[6]

Ex. Or. 12843
Through Executive Order 12843, Procurement Requirements and Policies for Federal Agencies for Ozone-Depleting Substances, April 21, 1993, President Clinton officially recognized the impact of ozone-depleting substances on the stratospheric ozone layer, citing the Montreal Protocol on Substances that Deplete the Ozone Layer, to which the United States is a signatory. In order to reduce the federal government's procurement and use of substances that cause stratospheric ozone depletion, the order directed federal agencies to maximize the use of safe alternatives to ozone-depleting substances, evaluate the present and future uses of ozone-depleting substances, and revise procurement practices to substitute nonozone-depleting substances to the extent economically practicable.

Ex. Or. 12873
Through Executive Order 12873, Federal Acquisition, Recycling, and Waste Prevention, October 20, 1993, President Clinton directed each executive agency to "incorporate waste prevention and recycling in the agency's daily operations and work to increase and expand markets for recovered materials through greater Federal Government preference and demand for such products." Specifically, the order requires agencies to "consider the following factors: elimination of virgin material requirements; use of recovered materials; reuse of product; life cycle cost; recyclability; use of environmentally preferable products; waste prevention (including toxicity reduction or elimination); and ultimate disposal, as appropriate . . . for all procurements and . . . contracts." Replaced in 1998 by Executive Order 13101, which expanded the directive to encompass bio-based (alternative agricultural) products as well.

Ex. Or. 13101
Executive Order 13101, Greening the Government through Waste Prevention, Recycling and Federal Acquisition, Sep-

tember 14, 1998, builds upon and replaces the previous order (EO 12873), which gave EPA its original mandate on environmentally preferable procurement. EO 13101 requires EPA to issue new guidance to federal agencies, encourages federal agencies to conduct pilot projects based on this guidance, and incorporates biobased products into federal EPP efforts. The EO also has requirements related to the purchase or use of paper products that contain at least 30 percent "postconsumer" fiber by January 1, 1999.[7]

NEPA

National Environmental Policy Act of 1969 (NEPA); 42 U.S.C. 4321-4347: NEPA is the basic national charter for protection of the environment. It establishes policy, sets goals, and provides means for carrying out the policy. "The purposes of this Act are: To declare a national policy which will encourage productive and enjoyable harmony between man and his environment; to promote efforts which will prevent or eliminate damage to the environment and biosphere and stimulate the health and welfare of man; to enrich the understanding of ecological systems and natural resources important to the Nation; and to establish a Council on Environmental Quality."[8]

NPDES

National Pollutant Discharge Elimination System (NPDES), created by EPA in 1972, under the authority of Public Law 92-500, the Federal Water Pollution Control Act: ". . . intended to control discharges to the Nation's waters from industrial, commercial, and municipal point sources; these discharges presented a threat to water quality and health. Initial efforts focused on traditional pollutant discharges from industrial manufacturing processes and municipal waste water treatment plants. Later amended to become the CWA, this law provides broad authority for EPA or States (authorized by EPA) to issue NPDES permits. Specific reporting requirements are established in the permits to require monitoring and reporting of discharges. The CWA establishes two types of standards for conditions in NPDES permits: technology-based standards and water quality-based standards. These standards are used to develop effluent limitations and special conditions in NPDES permits. Numeric effluent limitations establish pollutant concentration limits for effluents at the point of discharge. Since the implementation of the CWA requirements, EPA has begun to address nontraditional sources of pollution, such as those that result from Wet Weather Flows (WWF). The NPDES program currently requires permits for point sources, but not for NPSs."[9]

Phase I	Typically refers to an Environmental Site Assessment: Financial interests in particular want to determine potential environmental concerns on a given site since environmental regulations place responsibility for abatement and liability for contamination upon ALL entities that have touched the material, including building owners, contractors, and architects. Insurance companies and lending institutions do not want to inherit environmental debts. The primary purpose of the Phase I environmental site assessment is to observe site conditions and identify any areas of potential environmental concern. ASTM E 1527, *Standard Practice for Environmental Site Assessments: Phase I Environmental Site Assessment Process* and ASTM E 1528, *Standard Practice for Environmental Site Assessments: Transaction Screen Process,* are alternative approaches to records review, site reconnaissance, interviews, and reports. One offers broad guidance for investigation, the other specific questionnaires. Both seek to define commercial standards for conducting environmental site assessments with respect to contaminants under CERCLA and to petroleum products; that is, to establish the practices that constitute all appropriate inquiry under CERCLA. The goal is to determine the requirements necessary for the user to claim an innocent landowner defense to CERCLA liability.
Phase II	Typically refers to an Environmental Site Assessment: The goal is the same as for Phase I, limiting liability. When suspicious conditions are identified in a Phase I Site Assessment, a Phase II Site Assessment is recommended to perform more detailed analysis. ASTM E1903, *Standard Guide for Environmental Site Assessments: Phase II Environmental Site Assessment* Process was developed specifically to identify a professional standard of care for conducting a Phase II Site Assessment. It outlines customary practices relative to a range of contaminants, which are within the scope of CERCLA, as well as petroleum products.
RCRA	The Resource Conservation and Recovery Act (RCRA); 42 U.S.C. s/s 321 et seq. (1976): ''RCRA (pronounced 'rick-rah') gave EPA the authority to control hazardous waste from the 'cradle-to-grave.' This includes the generation, transportation, treatment, storage, and disposal of hazardous waste. RCRA also set forth a framework for the management of nonhazardous wastes. The 1986 amendments to RCRA enabled EPA to address environmental problems that could result from underground tanks storing petroleum and

other hazardous substances. RCRA focuses only on active and future facilities and does not address abandoned or historical sites (see CERCLA). HSWA (pronounced 'hiss-wa'—the Federal Hazardous and Solid Waste Amendments are the 1984 amendments to RCRA that required phasing out land disposal of hazardous waste. Some of the other mandates of this strict law include increased enforcement authority for EPA, more stringent hazardous waste management standards, and a comprehensive underground storage tank program."[10]

TSCA   The Toxic Substances Control Act (TSCA); 15 U.S.C. s/s 2601 et seq. (1976): "The Toxic Substances Control Act of 1976 was enacted by Congress to test, regulate, and screen all chemicals produced or imported into the United States. Many thousands of chemicals and their compounds are developed each year with unknown toxic or dangerous characteristics. To prevent tragic consequences, TSCA requires that any chemical that reaches the consumer marketplace be tested for possible toxic effects prior to commercial manufacture. Any existing chemical that poses health and environmental hazards is tracked and reported under TSCA. Procedures also are authorized for corrective action under TSCA in cases of cleanup of toxic materials contamination. TSCA supplements other federal statutes, including the Clean Air Act and the Toxic Release Inventory under EPCRA."[11]

Building Codes

Building codes are intended to protect the health, safety, and welfare of the public. They are inherently flawed in that they must respond to changing conditions and empirical evidence after the fact. New technologies present new hazards as well as new benefits previously unimagined. We try to codify the new systems based on old understandings. Fire standards, which became the focus of attention after the great Chicago fire, were developed around our understanding of how wood burns. These test methods must be continually reviewed and revised to adapt to changing materials and expected combinations of materials. Smoke released in a wood fire is different from smoke generated in a treated wood fire, and still more different from that released from plastics. Seismic regulations changed drastically after the San Francisco bridge collapsed and, shortly thereafter, the Northridge quake toppled apartment buildings. We learned a lot about security construction, and lack thereof, after the Murrah Federal Building in Oklahoma City was bombed. Federal agencies quickly revised their security design requirements and remodeled many facilities accordingly.

The limitation of hindsight is magnified in a world moving as rapidly as ours does today. Unfortunately, if the environmental experts are correct, we have already exceeded the carrying capacity of the Earth. We are already using more of the Earth's natural resources than can be replenished annually. We are already polluting and destroying ecosystems faster than the Earth can renew itself. We have already damaged the ozone layer and altered the Earth's global climate patterns. We have already irreparably lost precious species and biodiversity. But no single disaster has focused our attention on the need for revising building codes. There has been no calamity that we recognize as on par with the Chicago fire, the San Francisco quake, or the Oklahoma City attack. When we do recognize the need and determine an appropriate response, it may be too late.

In the interim, we have the opportunity to obtain variances. Anyone who has attempted to build a structure just a little bit differently from the manner outlined by the applicable building code will appreciate the hurdles many green designers and builders face. It is not an easy proposition. Most of the traditional, time-tested building methods, such as adobe, rammed earth, and straw bale, are today classified as "alternative" methods. Perversely, native, indigenous materials are required to demonstrate their ability to meet structural, energy, and fire standards on a project-by-project basis. This is a costly proposition because it must be done on an individual basis. It may also be difficult, since most test method standards were designed to accommodate specific materials and systems, which generally do not include straw or mud. The challenge is further intensified because most indigenous building methods are not proprietary. Therefore, no manufacturer has a stake in paying for the testing necessary to demonstrate compliance, even when appropriate test methods exist.

Happily, many jurisdictions are beginning to respond to pubic demand. And several environmental interest groups are helping to create an information and support network. The Development Center for Alternative Technologies (DCAT) is a nonprofit organization dedicated to the research and development of green building codes. DCAT is working to impact the development of the International Building Code. DCAT's goal is to develop model code language for alternative indigenous, earth-friendly building materials and methods. (Refer to the appendices for contact information on DCAT and other environmental organizations.)

Straw bale construction has a well-defined network of designers, builders, and consultants. Assistance is readily available for details, mortgage financing, and code compliance. While there are many jurisdictions that allow straw bale building under the alternative materials and methods provisions of the existing codes, there are also some that have specific provisions for straw bale construction, including parts of Arizona (the City of Tucson, Pima County, Pinal County, the Town of Guadalupe); California (State Guidelines and several counties and municipalities); Boulder, Colorado; the state of New Mexico; and Austin, Texas.

The City of Boulder has added environmental requirements to its residential permitting process. Unlike other green building programs such as in Austin, Texas, and the statewide program in Colorado, the City of Boulder has developed a green building program that is mandatory. Its Green Points Program applies to new residential construction and additions larger than 500 square feet. The program requires building permit applicants to earn a minimum of 25 points from the city's green points list. By requiring an additional point for every 200 square feet of floor area over 2,500 square feet, it balances "excess" use of the Earth's resources with proactive environmental efforts. Items that are fairly straightforward may be self-certified; otherwise, inspection by the city is required. For example, recycled content roofing earns 3 points and may be self-certified by the building owner. Structural alternatives to wood earn 10 points and require city inspection.

Trade Organizations and Publications

Many independent sources of technical information exist for environmental issues. The challenge is that historically, these sources have been isolated from the channels of communication and information exchange in the building industry. Slowly, connections are being made. These first connections, however, have discovered that the language and methods of communication for environmentalists and for building industry are very, very different. They differ on specifics. "FS" to a specifier means "federal specifications," but to an environmentalist, it is likely to mean "forest service." More important, they differ on fundamentals. Environmentalists stress ideals, whereas the building industry (or any industry, for that matter) focuses on the practical. Where they come together in increasing numbers is on improving efficiencies—improving energy efficiency, reducing waste, improving water quality, and improving indoor air quality. Similarly, both the captains of environmentalism and the captains of industry are "big-picture" people and recognize the global impact of human activity.

Sources of green information are beginning to develop a very cohesive and reliable network that, at certain points, overlaps the mainstream building industry information network. Professional and trade organizations dedicated to green issues and green building can be very helpful. Examples include: U.S. Green Building Council, the Electric Power Research Institute, Environmental Business Association, Institute of Scrap Recycling Industries, Urban Land Institute, and Global Environmental Management. (Contact information for these organizations and others are available in the appendices.)

Sources of green information also include specialty publishers, such as:

• John Wiley & Sons/AIA Environmental Resource Guide: (800) CALL-WILEY
• Island Press: (707) 983-6432

- Lewis Publishers: (800) 272-7737
- World Resources Institute: (800) 822-0504

And they include specialty magazines and periodicals such as:

DESIGNER/builder
2405 Maclovia Lane
Santa Fe, NM 87505
(505) 471-4549
Features the latest ideas in architecture and design. Includes articles on
  environmentally conscious building, urban design, affordable housing,
  environmental psychology, alternative construction materials, and on people
  who are pushing the limits of design and community development.

Environmental Building News
122 Birge Street
Brattleboro, VT 05301
(802) 257-7300.
Focuses on environmentally sustainable design and construction, featuring
  checklists, latest news, reviews of building products, case studies, and
  information sources. Provides well researched, in-depth technical articles.

Indoor Air Bulletin
Indoor Air Information Service, Inc.
P.O. Box 8446
Santa Cruz, CA 95061-8446
(831) 426-6624; fax (831) 426-6522
Focuses on indoor air quality, but considers all aspects of indoor environment
  important to occupant health, comfort, and productivity.

Solar Today
The American Solar Energy Society
2400 Central Avenue, Suite G-1
Boulder, CO 80301
(303) 433-3130
Features articles on solar technologies for transportation and building
  applications. Includes thermal systems, photovoltaics, environmental
  concerns, legislation, and products and services.

Industry Standards

The contractual agreements that designate professional responsibilities and
corresponding liabilities depend upon measurable, assignable requirements.
Generally, they depend upon established industry standards. Similarly, manufacturers market their products by advertising compliance with established industry standards. Either the assembly is UL rated or it is not.

Standards-developing organizations exist on many levels. There are trade and professional organizations that set quality requirements for their own areas of expertise. Examples include the American Concrete Institute, the Ceramic Tile Institute, and Architectural Woodwork Institute, and (from a green perspective) the Forest Stewardship Council. There are federal specifications and military standards that are being slowly phased out as private sector standards are developed to replace them. And there are national and international standards development organizations. The American Society for Testing and Materials (ASTM) is the primary standards development organization in the United States.

The International Organization for Standardization (ISO) is the primary standards development organization internationally. ISO is a nonprofit, volunteer standards development organization. It has a 50-year history of standards development. The mission of ISO is "to promote the development of standardization and related activities in the world with a view to facilitating the international exchange of goods and services, and to developing cooperation in the spheres of intellectual, scientific, technological and economic activity."[12] The technical work of ISO is highly decentralized, carried out in a hierarchy of some 2,700 technical committees, subcommittees, and working groups. Each technical committee has subcommittees, and each subcommittee has working groups. Although the greater part of the ISO technical work is done by correspondence, there are, on average, a dozen ISO meetings taking place somewhere in the world every working day. Every country is allowed a single vote. To render the vote, each nation designates a voting member body. For the United States, the voting member body is the American National Standards Institute (ANSI). ANSI is essentially a figurehead that designates (for each ISO technical committee) an entity responsible for developing the American opinion and directing the ANSI vote. Most of the entities reside in ASTM.

ASTM is a voluntary organization created at the turn of the century that develops standards for everything from dishwashing liquid to concrete curing compounds. It has produced more than 10,000 standards. The 132 main committees are organized into subcommittees, and each subcommittee is further divided into task groups. ASTM is designed to be a balanced organization and voting membership on any given committee is limited to 50 percent manufacturing interests. The remainder is composed of users, government, academia, and general public. While most voting is conducted by mail, negative votes are resolved at the biannual meetings where the simple majority rules on interpretation (including dismissal) of negative votes.

Both ASTM and ISO have several committees dedicated to environmental issues, and to green building issues in particular. The ISO Technical Committee (TC) on Environmental Management (ISO/TC 207) covers "standardization in the field of environmental management tools and systems" with the exception of those specific topics covered under other ISO TCs. Excluded are: test methods for pollutants, which are the responsibility of ISO/TC 146 (Air Quality),

ISO/TC 147 (Water Quality), ISO/TC 190 (Soil Quality) and ISO/TC 43 (Acoustics); setting limit values regarding pollutants or effluents; setting environmental performance levels; standardization of products. TC 207 works closely with ISO/TC 176 in the field of environmental systems and audits. ISO has developed several environmental performance standards, including:

- ISO 14001 Environmental Management Systems
- ISO 14004 Environmental Management Systems—General Guidelines on Principles, Systems, and Supporting Techniques
- ISO 14010 Guidelines for Environmental Auditing—General Principles on Environmental Auditing
- ISO 14011 Guidelines for Environmental Auditing—Audit Procedures— Auditing of Environmental Management Systems
- ISO 14012 Guidelines for Environmental Auditing—Qualification Criteria for Environmental Auditors

In 1997, ISO designated an ad hoc committee to investigate the international viability and necessity of standards for sustainable building. It is also intended to review the many building rating systems that have been produced in the United Kingdom, Canada, Norway, Sweden, and the United States. By unanimous agreement, the Ad Hoc Group on Sustainable Building proposed that ISO/TC 59 develop a new Subcommittee for Sustainability, with a scope as follows: "To develop guidelines and standards for sustainable building and construction that are based on the principles of the ISO 14000 series." Furthermore, by unanimous agreement, the Ad Hoc Group on Sustainable Building proposed the following working groups for the new Subcommittee on Sustainability:

- General Principles
- Tools and Methods for the Assessment of the Environmental Sustainability of Buildings and Building Products
- Environmental Declaration and Labeling of Buildings and Building Products
- Tools and Methods for the Design of Sustainable Buildings
- Sustainability Indicators for the Built Environment and the Construction Industry
- Terminology

It is anticipated that ISO will follow the recommendations of the ad hoc committee.

Committees in ASTM that are addressing environmental issues include those that are responsible for concrete, plastic, and glass, each responding to environmental issues specific to its arena. Committees attempting to respond to more holistic concerns include: Committee E06 on the Performance of Buildings and E50 on Environmental Assessment. ASTM E06.71, Subcommittee on Sustainability, closely parallels the ISO Sustainable Building effort.

Trade organizations are also beginning to publish standards and opinions relative to environmental issues specific to their arena. The American Society of Heating, Refrigerating, and Air Conditioning Engineers (ASHRAE) is a prominent example. ASHRAE has developed standards relative to indoor air quality and energy efficiency, including: ASHRAE 62, Ventilation for Acceptable Indoor Air Quality; ASHRAE 90.1, Energy Efficient Design of New Buildings Except Low-Rise Residential Buildings, which presented code language to help states meet the October 1994 federal deadline to write codes that meet or exceed the standard as per National Energy Act; and ASHRAE 100, Energy Conservation standards for existing industrial, institutional, and commercial buildings.

Most standards and codes govern individual building products and individual buildings. They do not attempt to address the collective impact of buildings. For environmental issues, this oversight is unacceptable. The environmental impact of buildings in aggregate, as for example, in the classic case of urban sprawl has generated a new genre of standards, *sustainability indicators*. Indicators augment the typical array of measurement tools, particularly with respect to complex, shifting, and holistic areas such as economics and the environment. In many diverse efforts around the world, indicators are being developed to assess the environmental and economic impacts of buildings in aggregate. "Indicators are useful because they point to trends and relationships in a concise way. They provide meaning beyond the attributes directly associated with them. In this sense, they are different from primary data or statistics, providing a bridge between detailed data and interpreted information. Indicators have been used for many years and are common in planning and economics where indicators such as GDP [Gross Domestic Product], the unemployment rate, the literacy rate and the population growth rate are widely monitored."[13]

In 1987, the World Commission on Environment and Development (Brundtland Commission) called for the development of new ways to measure and assess progress toward sustainable development. Subsequently, at the Earth Summit in Rio de Janeiro in 1992, the United Nations Conference on Environment and Development, reiterated the importance of indicators. Chapter 40 of the UNCED Agenda 21 calls for the development of indicators for sustainable development. In particular, it requests countries at the national level, and international governmental and nongovernmental organizations at the international level to develop and identify such indicators.[14]

Many local, national, and international efforts have attempted to respond to this need. For example, the Commission on Sustainable Development (CSD), which grew out of the Earth Summit, is working with 21 countries to test indicators (developed through the UN and discussed with the Expert Group on

Indicators of Sustainable Development in September 1996 in Geneva) in relation to its own national priorities and interests. These countries include: Maldives, Pakistan, the Philippines, China, Ghana, South Africa, Kenya, Morocco, Austria, Belgium, United Kingdom, Germany, Finland, France, the Czech Republic, Barbados, Brazil, Bolivia, Costa Rica, Mexico, and Venezuela. The goal of the CSD is to document viable sustainability indicators for development by the year 2000.

Another important international development in sustainabilty indicators are the Bellagio Principles, developed in late 1996 by the International Institute for Sustainable Development with support from the Rockefeller Foundation, in Bellagio, Italy. The Bellagio Principles outline a holistic perspective with consideration for: equity and disparity within the current population and between present and future generations; for the ecological conditions on which life depends; and for economic development and other nonmarket activities that contribute to human/social well-being. The Bellagio Principles cite the need for adequate scope in terms of both human and ecosystem time scales and spatial needs. And it requires a practical focus with openness and the capacity to adjust goals, frameworks, and indicators as new insights are gained.

An ISO standard on this topic is under consideration, which would coordinate with the work of the Commission on Sustainable Development, the International Institute for Sustainable Development, intergovernmental organizations, and nongovernmental organizations.

Material Safety Data Sheets

Much information regarding the chemical composition of a product and the corresponding precautionary recommendations is available via Material Safety Data Sheets (MSDSs). MSDSs are required under the Occupational Safety and Health Administration (OSHA) Hazard Communication Standard (1910.1200) as one of the vehicles for employers to inform their employees about the hazards of the chemicals in their workplace. They are also extremely useful tools for greening a building.

MSDSs address chemicals. They do not address articles, such as door hardware. They do address coatings, adhesives, sealers, and cleaning agents. And, while they contain some very technical data, they include a lot of useful information for evaluating the toxicity of a product.

According to OSHA, an MSDS must include the following information (1910.1200(g)(2)):

- Product name
- Chemical and common name(s) of all ingredients that have been determined to be health hazards or physical hazards
- Physical and chemical characteristics of the hazardous chemical (such as vapor pressure, flash point)

- Physical hazards of the hazardous chemical, including the potential for fire, explosion, and reactivity
- Health hazards of the hazardous chemical
- Primary route(s) of entry
- OSHA-permissible exposure limit (threshold limit)
- Whether the chemical is listed in the National Toxicology Program (NTP) Annual Report on Carcinogens or the International Agency for Research on Cancer (IARC) Monographs, or by OSHA
- Precautions for safe handling and use
- Control measures, such as appropriate engineering controls, work practices, or personal protective equipment
- Emergency and first-aid procedures
- Date of preparation of the material safety data sheet or the last change to it
- Name, address, and telephone number of the chemical manufacturer, importer, employer, or other responsible party preparing or distributing the MSDS

There is no OSHA-specified format for an MSDS. However, the American National Standards Institute (ANSI) has developed recommendations for a standard format (ANSI Z400.1) that is commonly used. The ANSI standard is intended to promote consistency and to help convey information in a manner that is useful and understandable across education levels, from the janitor to the emergency room physician. It includes 16 sections. The first 10 address the specific requirements under OSHA; the last six identify information that OSHA does not require, but that may be necessary in order to better address requirements in other countries. Because the last six sections are not legal OSHA requirements, many MSDSs do not provide data for them. Nevertheless, these last six are of particular interest for specifiers of green building materials because they identify the impact of the chemical(s) on the Earth in addition to the impact on human health.

Following is a summary of the 16 sections of the ANSI standard MSDS format:

Section 1   *Chemical Product and Company Identification:* This section indicates the name, address, and phone number of the company, manufacturer, or distributor of the chemical. Emergency contact information should be included here.

Section 2   *Composition/Information on Ingredients:* This section is of limited use to most building industry professionals. It identifies chemicals and their percentage content. Note that only those chemicals referenced in 29 CFR part 1910, subpart Z, OSHA Toxic and Hazardous Substances, are likely to be listed. This section may also include OSHA Permissible Exposure Limits (PEL) and American Conference of Governmental Industrial Hygienists (ACGIH) Threshold Limit Values (TLV).

Section 3	*Hazards Identification.* This section will tell you whether the material is considered a carcinogen and what the known potential health effects are. Note that only those chemicals referenced in the National Toxicology Program (NTP), "Annual Report on Carcinogens"; the International Agency for Research on Cancer (IARC) "Monographs"; or 29 CFR part 1910, subpart Z, OSHA Toxic and Hazardous Substances, are likely to be listed. The "Registry of Toxic Effects of Chemical Substances," published by the National Institute for Occupational Safety and Health indicates whether a chemical has been found by NTP or IARC to be a potential carcinogen.
Section 4	*First-Aid Measures.* This section is fairly self-explanatory. It should be written for untrained individuals.
Section 5	*Fire-Fighting Measures.* This section indicates the flammability and explosivity of the product, with fire-fighting instructions. It also indicates potential hazardous byproducts due to combustion.
Section 6	*Accidental Release Measures:* This section describes responses to material spills, leaks, or accidental releases.
Section 7	*Handling and Storage:* This section is self-explanatory. It might include overexposure warnings and hygiene instructions.
Section 8	*Exposure Controls/Person Protection:* This section describes the engineering controls and protective gear that will reduce personal exposure. Obviously, the greater the danger, the more protective gear is required.
Section 9	*Physical and Chemical Properties:* This section may be of limited use to building industry professionals. It should include information regarding the appearance, odor, pH, physical state, vapor pressure, boiling point, vapor density, freezing/melting point, solubility in water, and specific gravity or density.
Section 10	*Stability and Reactivity Data.* This section will indicate known incompatibilities with other materials and potential hazardous decomposition. This information provides an indication of the potential interactions in the ecosystem.
Section 11	*Toxicological Information:* This section should include data used to determine the hazards cited in Section 3. This information provides an indication of the potential toxicity/IEQ impacts. It may discuss acute data, carcinogenicity, reproductive effects, and target organ effects. Do not be surprised to find "No data available."
Section 12	*Ecological Information.* This section should include data regarding environmental impact in the event of an accidental release. This information provides an indication of the potential interactions in the ecosystem. Do not be surprised to find "No data available."

Section 13   *Disposal Considerations.* This section should include data regarding the proper disposal of the chemical. It may include information regarding recycling and reuse. It may indicate whether or not the product is considered to be "hazardous waste" according the U.S. EPA Hazardous Waste Regulations 40 CFR 261. This information provides an indication of the potential interactions in the ecosystem.

Section 14   *Transportation Information.* This section should include basic shipping information such as the hazard class. As with Section 8 for exposure control, the greater the precautions, the greater the environmental and health risks.

Section 15   *Regulatory Information.* This section should include the regulations applicable to the material. References may include federal regulations such as TSCA or SARA, and state specific information such as California's Proposition 65, the Safe Drinking Water and Toxic Enforcement Act.

Section 16   *Other Information.* This section may include hazard ratings, preparation of the MSDS, and additional labeling information.

Last, although it is not part of the OSHA requirements nor the ANSI format, there will be a disclaimer. Following is a sample.

The information and recommendations set forth herein are believed to be accurate. Because some of the information is derived from information provided by our suppliers, and because we have no control over the conditions of handling and use, we make no warranty, express or implied, regarding the accuracy of the data or the results to be obtained from the use thereof. The information is supplied solely for your information and consideration, and we assume no responsibility from use or reliance thereon. It is the responsibility of the user of our products to comply with all applicable federal, state, and local laws and regulations.

Labeling

We are a litigious industry in a scientific society. We like to measure, monitor, assess, and label. Green buildings and green building materials are no exception. This decade has seen a veritable flood of green rating systems and assessment tools, each vying for public recognition and industry acceptance. Green building does, however, present a unique challenge to our desire to quantify and label. In order to create simple, apples-to-apples comparisons, each assessment tool inevitably must assign single numbers to complex interrelationships. Not surprisingly, each of the tools focuses on certain aspects of our web of life and neglects others. Nevertheless, each new generation of green building rating tools offers improvements on the predecessors.

There are many examples of rating systems for green building products. The most viable offer independent third-party verification. One of these, Green Seal, a nonprofit environmental organization, develops standards for a variety of consumer and building products. When in compliance with a Green Seal Standard, the Green Seal certification mark may appear on the packaging and on the product itself. However, when the certification mark appears on a package or product, the product or package must contain a description of the basis for certification. Another, Scientific Certification Systems, is a for-profit company that reviews specific manufacturer claims and offers endorsement for products that pass its review. In 1998, the National Institute of Standards and Technology (NIST) released Building for Environmental and Economic Sustainability (BEES), a tool for generating relative scores for building product alternatives. BEES explores environmental issues in accordance with ISO 14040 LCA methodology to weight the environmental impacts of raw materials acquisition, manufacture, transportation, installation, use, and waste management. It does not address impact on human health. It does not address regional environmental issues. It does incorporate economic information in accordance with ASTM E917 for initial costs, replacement costs, operations costs, maintenance and repair costs, and disposal costs.

There are even more green rating programs for buildings. With the notable exception of the City of Boulder's Green Point Program, the programs are voluntary. However, by establishing minimum requirements in various categories, voluntary programs can help establish professional standards of care for the greenness of both the building as a whole and the component green materials/products/systems. Examples of green building programs include the following:

- Austin Sustainable Building Program: The City of Austin's Green Builder Program received a United Nations Award for Local Government Initiatives at the Earth Summit in Rio de Janeiro. The goal of the voluntary program is to influence home builders to use "sustainable" building practices. The program bases its rating system on the premise that a house is a single system, with four major components to consider: energy, water, materials, and waste. It offers certification using a simple scale of one to four stars—the more stars, the more green features in the home. The Austin program is extremely regional. It emphasizes locally available materials and regional factors both for the particular building and for the community in general. The Austin Green Builder Program has since been expanded to commercial and institutional structures. A separate initiative, the Austin Sustainable Communities Initiative, has been launched.

- Building Environmental Performance Assessment Criteria (BEPAC): BEPAC was originally designed for new and existing office buildings in British Columbia, although regional variants have subsequently been developed for Ontario and Atlantic Canada. BEPAC evaluates two main categories, the base building and tenant buildout. Each category is assessed according to five criteria: ozone layer protection, environmental impact of energy use, indoor environmental quality, resource conservation, and site and transportation. Each of the criteria are assessed within a 10-point scale. BEPAC weights the points to reflect the relative importance of aspects within each criteria, but not between criteria. BEPAC is no longer used, but remains of academic interest.

- Building Research Establishment Environmental Assessment Method (BREEAM): BREEAM is a tool developed by the BRE in the United Kongdom in 1990 and is widely used in Europe, Hong King, Singapore, Australia, New Zealand, and Canada. A North American version for use in the United States is under development. BREEAM is based on energy and environmental principles. It evaluates a building in two stages, before and after, identifying opportunities for improvement that may be implemented prior to final assessment and certification.

- Colorado Green Building Rating Program: The Governor's Office of Energy Conservation and the Home Builders Association (HBA) of Metro Denver developed a voluntary, statewide Green Builder Program to recognize builders who construct homes that conserve natural resources and preserve the environment. Homes built under the program's guidelines receive the designation "Built Green." In addition, the Energy Rated Homes of Colorado's (ERHC) E-Star program rates a home's energy efficiency on a 100-point scale, which translates into scores of one to five-plus stars. ERHC's Energy Improvement Mortgage can allow prospective home buyers to add cost-effective energy upgrades into a mortgage loan for payback over the life of the loan. Home energy upgrades also can be financed through an Energy Improvement Mortgage. ERHC is operated by the Colorado Housing and Finance Authority.

- Energy Star: Unlike most building labels, this one does not examine the design of the building, but evaluates the performance. An Energy Star label is earned by comparing 12 months of utility data (including energy efficiency, IAQ, thermal comfort, and lighting levels information) against an industry-established baseline. The EPA/DOE Energy Star Building program is a voluntary, performance-based benchmarking and recognition initiative. It benchmarks against current market averages. President Clinton has directed federal agencies to pursue the Energy Star Building label. The Energy Star building label is available for private construction as well, and makes available a web-based tool capable of assessing performance of a particular building against comparable averages. With certification by a licensed engineer, any qualifying building can obtain an Energy Star label.

- Good Cents: Utility-sponsored programs to improve energy efficiency are the oldest green building programs in the United States. The Good Cents program was developed in 1976 to encourage the construction of energy-efficient homes. To date, more than 750,000 Good Cents homes have been built across the country with another 60,000 added annually.[15]

- Home Energy Rating Systems (HERS): HERS was developed by the U.S. Department of Energy, in accordance with the Energy Policy Act of 1992. DOE has also developed guidelines for Energy-Efficient Mortgage Programs (EEMS). DOE is encouraging utilities and the mortgage industry to adopt them. Homes are awarded an energy-efficiency rating between 0 and 100, with 100 being a home that is completely energy-self-sufficient. In 1995, the National Association of State Energy Office Officials and Energy Rated Homes of America founded the Residential Energy Services Network (RESNET) to develop a national market for HERS and EEMS.

- Leadership in Energy and Environmental Design (LEED), developed by the U.S. Green Building Council is a tool to designate the relative greenness of buildings. It contains certain prerequisites. The building must be asbestos-free, CFC-free, and smoking-free. It must comply with ASHRAE 90.1, ASHRAE 62, ASHRAE 55, EPACT requirements for low flow fixtures, and EPA standards for water quality. It must contain areas that allow occupants to recycle. And, it must be commissioned. Any building meeting these prerequisite requirements can earn credits in a variety of ways. Final scores place buildings in a category of "greenness" and entitle the building to be labeled as a Green Building under the LEED program.

A growing international movement, the Green Building Challenge (GBC), is culling the best of each of the national efforts. If it can avoid the dilution that tends to accompany international compromises, it is likely to dominate the green building rating arena. The GBC is developing the Green Building Assessment Tool (GBA tool), the second generation of which was unveiled in October 1998. The GBA tool uses a series of criteria with subcriteria weighted to accommodate both hard and soft data, a typical impasse for many green rating tools, and has defaults that can be modified to reflect regional priorities. This is also an asset. Most tools are averaged over a broad area and are ill equipped to adapt to local and regional environmental concerns.

At some level, most of these rating systems require a subjective, albeit educated and professional, opinion. This is especially true for the whole building rating programs. Pure objectivity is nearly impossible given our limited understanding of the functioning of ecosystems. We do not know the number and type of species living with us on this planet, let alone how they interact in the web of life. Except in limited applications such as energy efficiencies, informed, subjective opinion is almost unavoidable for green rating systems. Each label implies an endorsement of the rating systems and the rating entity. After arriving at reasonably acceptable rating systems, whom should we trust to assess building products and buildings themselves? The usual array of testing laboratories and governing agencies having jurisdiction does not generally possess adequate understanding of the environmental issues.

There is a new player in the construction industry that does understand environmental issues and is likely to become a critical partner in green building: nongovernmental organizations (NGOs). Long on the sidelines, accustomed to educating the public and exposing environmental abuses, environmental NGOs are now being sought after by mainstream organizations to consult on green approaches and, ultimately, to certify the greenness of the product, system, or building in question. With increasing numbers, mainstream corporations are seeking the counsel of environmental NGOs. Some do this quite publicly, such as the now famous assistance that the Environmental Defense Fund (EDF) provided to McDonald's in the wake of the public outcry against McDonald's use of styrene. Subsequently, McDonald's not only developed less environmentally damaging paper containers for its food products, but also began incorporating recycled content materials in its buildings. Furthermore, it developed and distributed free of charge a listing of the building and furnishing materials that it had identified. Many reputable, for-profit, green consulting firms are now established. Such firms are generally familiar with both the building industry and the environmental arena, and can readily assist building owners in design and material selection. They are also equipped to assist product manufacturers in improving efficiencies and in marketing green products. For certification of a product's greenness, however, independent nonprofits are the most desirable. For authenticating a product's greenness, the environmental NGO is likely to become the primary figure.

Certification

Certification, and, specifically, independent third-party certification, is necessary because our society long ago abandoned the "gentleman's agreement" as an acceptable contractual arrangement. Because in our increasingly complex and litigious world it is impossible for one person to have detailed knowledge on all topics, we rely heavily on the impartial expertise provided by independent experts. The design and construction industry, for example, no longer relies on the innate desire of a contractor to produce quality craftsmanship or the reliability of the owner to fairly compensate a contractor. Rather, the industry relies on form contracts, legislation, building codes, and trade standards. It is natural in this system for an owner to expect to verify the authenticity of the "sustainable" aspects of sustainably harvested wood through such independent methods. Questions subsequently arise as to what defines "sustainability," who verifies the parameters, what are their qualifications, and how much does it cost. Enter certification.

The certifying entity and method are critical. Independent environmental organizations, for so long considered to be on the radical fringe, are quickly stepping in to fill this void. Their environmental expertise and enthusiasm for educating industry and the public can be extremely valuable assets.

Environmental NGOs have credibility due to their long history of altruistic pursuits. They are exquisitely objective. In contrast to industry organizations whose primary goals are to facilitate commerce and promote the products of their membership, environmental organizations have one purpose: protect the environment. The goal involves complex, holistic considerations. Too often the standards organizations are demarcated into isolated specialties, unable to address holistic concerns adequately. In this arena, the NGOs are, without question, the experts. It is entirely likely that the environmental NGOs, not ASTM, ANSI, ISO, or other established groups, will lead the practical shift to new ways of thinking, new standards, and new measurements. For example, the Forest Stewardship Council (FSC), an international nonprofit organization that trains, accredits, and monitors independent, third-party certifiers for well-managed forests around the world, has gained an acceptance in the construction industry unheard of for NGOs in previous decades. Green designers who wish to specify wood from sustainably managed sources, specify that the lumber bear the Forest Stewardship Council (FSC) label. This is a harbinger of a new era and a new player in the construction industry. Certifications from environmental NGOs can offer the green equivalent of the UL endorsement.

Step 4: Review Submitted Information for Completeness

While some standards for green building products do exist, there are not enough. Not yet. Furthermore, where they do exist, they are often performance-based, not prescriptive-based. Consequently, the designer is left in the position of recommending products in the absence of industry-recognized acceptable minimums that we like to have to clearly designate responsibilities and liabilities. The designer is forced to render an educated, professional opinion. This is not a comfortable position for architects in a litigious society. But it is a necessary one. The codes and standards that guide our decisions today evolved via this same process of trial and error mixed with educated, professional opinion. Undeniably, environmental issues are health, safety, and welfare issues for the individual occupants of a given building and for the community as a whole. Eventually, we will evolve specific industry-recognized standards addressing all aspects of construction relative to environmental issues.

In some cases, such as products with recycled content, the comparison of green products to their conventional counterparts is apples to apples. It is possible to use existing standards to establish performance quality and use other certification or assessment processes to demonstrate green qualities (biodegradable, energy-efficient, nontoxic, recycled contents).

In other cases, the comparison is apples to oranges. For those products that are meeting a need in a new way, such as agriculturally based products and alternate energy systems, there may be no existing appropriate performance standards. The green products perform differently from their conventional counterparts, although they accomplish the purpose of the assembly. Many of these products are viable, but have difficulty competing in an industry that relies so heavily on independent third-party qualification. Recognizing this, new standards are being developed. Green building is a rapidly evolving industry segment. New products, systems, regulations, and standards appear with increasing frequency to meet growing consumer demand.

Although the performance of a green product may be comparable to the conventional counterpart, the difficulty is finding credible information to make the comparison in the first place; in this respect, green is not yet on equal footing with conventional design and specification methods. Architects and specifiers must spend additional effort to determine not only that a product exists, but also that the quality assurance information exists. It is not unusual that a new manufacturer needs some education as to what type of quality assurance information may be required.

As time goes on, the testing data that officially documents greenness will be developed. The empirical evidence may be more difficult to come by. While some of the green products are simply rediscovered products we used to use, others are new and cannot cite 10 to 20 years of satisfied customers. Keep in mind that manufacturers of green products want to make a profit just like the next guy. They can't do that if you don't buy their products. You won't buy their products if those products don't perform.

Step 5: Evaluate (Green) Materials

Perhaps the most important step in the product selection process is the evaluation. In a perfect world, all the information you need would be readily available and well organized so that you could simply add up the scores and pick the best. Realistically, at some point, even if you haven't obtained all the information you want, the bell rings and you must make a decision. As in all matters, there is the theory . . . and then there is practice.

First, let's review the theory. Practice is nearly always altered by reality. But it is founded in theory, so it's a good place to start. In theory, the greenness of materials is determined by answering as best you can the two questions:

What are you using?

How well are you using it?

Are you using perpetual resources, renewable resources, or nonrenewable resources? How are you affecting the quality of the resource (present and future) and the cycle of the resource (rate of flow, diversion, etc.)? Consider local, regional, and global implication of choices. This is especially important for people in the United States to understand. We have the money and the power. What we do matters a lot. But it is amazingly difficult for the average American to grasp that. Many—most—of the negative consequences of our actions (energy inefficiency, resource mismanagement, and waste) are felt in developing countries. Not only do Americans consume a vastly disproportionate share of the Earth's limited resources, we export waste (including hazardous waste) to developing countries for 'disposal' there at a nominal fee. Furthermore, corporate America may site its factories in developing countries to avoid the more stringent environmental regulations at home. The immediate damage is removed from our direct view, but it will drift back to us.

In practice, answers to the two questions will be both descriptive and quantitative. They will also have economic implications. In theory, there is a universally accepted formula—the holy grail of life cycle assessment methodologies—that will process all the variables and spit out the answer. The LCA concept sounds fairly straightforward: quantify the input, the output, and the byproducts and you will have your answer. But LCA is not simply a matter of adding and subtracting all the variables and comparing the total to some EPA approved matrix. It is a complex, intricate, holistic approach that defies the codes and standards with which the design and construction industry is familiar. The EPA estimates that a complete LCA of a product costs $100,000.00.[16] That is a bargain. But, how many of us have worked on a project where there was enough money and enough time to perform the kind of research necessary in a complete LCA? And even if given an open checkbook and an open schedule, much of the information is hotly debated within the scientific community, let alone the political and economic communities.

Even more distressing, the solution that you do manage to find often reveals an apples-to-oranges comparison between green products and standard construction products and between one green product and another. Many green products are charting new territory. The existing standards have been developed over decades by the industries they support, by the industries that have a vested interest in maintaining the status quo. Their power base is founded in current valuations of resources, tax structures, and subsidies, and in the current interpretations of regulatory requirements. The coating companies in California spent a great deal of money and effort lobbying against the development of VOC regulations by the South Coast Air Quality Management District (SCAQMD). Nevertheless, each of them developed coatings with low VOCs in compliance with the applicable SCAQMD regulations. Consumers were adamantly in favor of reducing the VOC content of coatings. Similarly, alternative wood treatment, such as borates, is handicapped by the monopoly the chromated copper arsenate (CCA) industry has on standards and the inclusion of those standards in model building codes. With increasing public awareness, this too is likely to shift.

In practice, green design solutions are not always simple and straightforward. For example, the knee-jerk reaction to tropical wood is to avoid it so as not to devastate the rain forest. But consider that if there is not some economical value to the tropical wood, and if there is tremendous financial encouragement to clearcut to raise cattle (which there is), there is no reason to respect and protect the wood. The tropical wood needs some economic value in order to be venerated and protected.

Through informative, responsible evaluation, building industry professionals can help improve the process. By making green information an integral part of the design process, building industry professionals can provide a higher quality of service to their customers and better protect the health, safety, and welfare of the community.

Step 6: Select and Document Choice

Whatever you do, including electing to avoid making a decision, will have an impact on the environment. What you do will shape the daily reality of the people who use the building. What you design will affect energy and water usage. The building will use a great many of our limited natural resources. The building will probably create pollution directly and indirectly.

Solving all of the problems simultaneously is as unrealistic as avoiding them. A more constructive approach is to do what you can and continue improving. Sustainbility is the goal. It is difficult to define, let alone achieve, in all areas today, but we can work toward it and raise the benchmark for everyone. Following are general rules of thumb for designing, specifying, and building green:

- Maximize the durability.
- Maximize the energy efficiency.
- Maximize the future recyclability: Mechanical fastening is preferable to adhesive/solvent welding.
- Maximize the maintainability.
- Maximize the recycled content: Close the loop. Collecting and recycling is not the goal. We must incorporate the recycled products into the building, and, when the product's current usefulness wanes, it should be recyclable into yet another useful product—not sent to a landfill.
- Maximize the use of local materials/regional materials.
- Minimize embodied energy: Promote the highest and best use of a material to avoid wasting the embodied energy. The highest and best use of a 500-year-old redwood tree is not paper pulp.
- Minimize the use of hazardous natural chemicals (asbestos, lead, etc.).
- Minimize the use of synthetic chemicals: Synthetic chemicals should be considered guilty until proven innocent.

That's not too difficult. Even in practice.

While the product selection process is essentially the same for both green and nongreen products, the lack of green certifications and standards places a greater burden on the specifier. Similarly, because green building product information is not typically available through mainstream building industry information resources, the burden on the specifier is also increased. However, once you have become familiar with environmental resources and with environmental issues, the selection process is no more difficult than for mainstream products—and it is much more satisfying.

The next step is to specify what you have selected.

Chapter 4—Endnotes

1. Alternative Agricultural Research and Commercialization (AARC) Corporation Sourcebook 1998; Department of Agriculture, Washington, DC.
2. EPA, summary of laws and regulations, Internet listing as of 9/98; www.epa.gov/epahome/rules.html.
3. *Ibid.*
4. *Ibid.*
5. *Ibid.*
6. *Ibid.*
7. *Ibid.*
8. The National Environmental Policy Act.
9. EPA, summary of laws and regulations, Internet listing as of 9/98; www.epa.gov/epahome/rules.html.
10. *Ibid.*
11. *Ibid.*
12. www.iso.ch/infoe/aboutiso.htm.
13. The United Nations Department of Economics and Social Affairs, *Indicators of Sustainable Development (ISD) Progress from Theory to Practice,* 1/14/98.
14. United Nations Committee on Environment & Development Agenda 21, paragraph 40.6.
15. Good Cents Home home page; www.goodcents.com/.
16. Annual USGBC Conference. (1994). EPA presentation on Life Cycle Assessment; NIST, Gaithersburg, MD.

How Does the Product Specification Process Work?

"Sometimes the specifications even work against sustainable design, as when virgin materials are specified for work that could have been done with used materials."

The Next Efficiency Revolution: Creating a Sustainable Materials Economy
John E. Young and Aaron Sachs

There are many people involved in a construction project. The primary participants in the average construction project include: the building owner, the contractor, the design professional, the product manufacturer, and the building official. Additional players include: the building cccupant, the fabricator, the subcontractors, and other consultants. Understanding their roles and perspectives is crucial to the successful integration of an unfamiliar building material, green or otherwise, into the project.

Design and Construction Relationships

The Building Owner

The building owner is the person or company, either public or private, whose idea the building was in the first place. The owner is also responsible for funding the construction of the project and for operating it once it is complete. The owner is the one party who enters into separate contracts with both the design professional and the contractor. This creates a third-party relationship between the design professional and the contractor. For example, certain responsibilities of the design professional during construction, acting on the owner's behalf, are included in the owner-design professional contract. They are also included in the owner-contractor contract.

The building owner rarely cites environmental concerns as a reason for building. The reason for building is to meet a specific need of the owner. The owner also rarely cites spending money as a reason for building. Spending money is viewed as an unfortunate consequence of meeting the identified need. Another necessary evil is the time required to transform the owner's need into a building.

The building owner may be a single person, several persons, or an organization. The organization, public or private, will probably be represented by several key contacts (e.g., director of construction, facilities manager, marketing/sales, vice president in charge of construction, etc.), who may or may not have a clear understanding of the hierarchical relationships among themselves. However, to successfully incorporate green building materials into a project, it is as important to understand the relationships between the various contacts within an organization as it is to understand the relationship of the owner to other parties on the project. Finding a champion of green materials within the organization is nice; finding the right champion is better.

With increasing frequency, building owners are including environmental concerns in their design requirements. The design professional must recognize that this does not imply that the owner's attitude about cost or time has changed. Nevertheless, more and more Fortune 500 companies are elevating environmental responsibility to higher levels within the corporate structure. It is not unusual for the director of environmental affairs to be a vice president or board member. According to a 1994 survey of Fortune 500 companies by Global Environmental Management Initiative (GEMI), approximately 50 percent tracked environmental costs and most expected environmental cost accounting issues to become more important in the future.

The Contractor

The contractor is the entity that enters into a contract with the building owner to build the project. The contractor in turn subcontracts with a multitude of subcontractors and suppliers to furnish and install specific portions of the work. The contractor, however, retains responsibility for completing the project in accordance with the contract documents. For this reason, it is important that contractors incorporate provisions of their contract into the contracts with their subcontractors and suppliers.

Typical provisions of the contract documents that should be incorporated include submittal procedures and substitution request procedures. The subcontract or purchase order should reference the relevant drawings and specifications that pertain to the portion of the work being performed or building material being supplied.

When green building materials are included in a project, the contractor must deal with the additional demands of purchasing and installing unfamiliar materials into the project. The contractor must ensure that the subcontractors and suppliers are aware of and follow the environmental requirements associated with these products. The contractor must also be familiar with substitution request procedures (which are discussed in greater detail in Chapter 6).

To avoid conflicts with both the owner and the design professional, the contractor should be aware of the owner's reasons for requiring the use of green building materials on a project and understand how flexible or not the contract documents are in regards to substituting nongreen materials for green ones.

The Design Professional

The design professional, who may be either an architect or engineer, is generally the primary consultant on a building project. Based on licensing laws and training the primary design professional on a project is usually the architect. The architect typically subcontracts portions of the work to other design professionals, such as structural engineers, landscape architects, electrical engineers, civil engineers, mechanical engineers, and others as necessary. As the primary consultant, the architect usually has the most direct contact (and, theoretically) influence upon the building owner. The architect will probably also be involved in construction contract administration.

Many architects are interested in environmental issues. Some are concerned. Some do not place any priority on green at all. Others are actively attempting to improve the world to the extent that they can. In short, architects are like everyone else.

When the actively committed design professional and the inspired green product manufacturer meet, the synergy can be tremendous. On average, though, the architect typically experiences more frustration than usual when searching for green building materials. Similarly, the manufacturer often feels equally frustrated trying to market a green product. This is true primarily for two reasons: Architects have extremely limited time to research new materials, and green building material manufacturers often lack a working knowledge of the building industry.

Many architects do not know where to go to get information on green building materials or know how to evaluate it once they have it. For a small firm, the time involved in researching these materials is prohibitive. Further, green building materials represent a rapidly changing segment of the industry that must be constantly monitored. Although a few small firms specialize in green architecture, many do not have the time or the expertise. Larger firms can support more overhead activities. The green building material manufacturer would do well to identify those firms, large or small that have indicated a commitment to green architecture, to which to market their products.

The Product Manufacturer

Green products are developed by two types of manufacturers: established manufacturers who produce a line or lines of green building materials, and the novice manufacturer who has a good idea and wonders why the rest of the world hasn't caught on yet. The most common difficulty facing the novice manufacturer is a lack of understanding of the target industry. A lack of basic understanding of the contractual relationships between the contractor, architect, and owner means that green product representatives may not know whom to contact, when, or how to get their product used on a project. They do not know what information needs to be conveyed or why. They are not familiar with the standard procedures of the typical construction contract and contract documents.

The architect is frequently in the position of both student and teacher, learning about a new product or method while instructing the product manufacturer on the prerequisite testing and applicable building codes that pertain to the materials they are providing.

It is important that the manufacturer or supplier understand the design and construction process in order to effectively operate within it. Most new manufacturers—especially those who are addressing environmental issues—do not understand the process. They do not know how to get into it or how to follow it and to stay in it. And even though they have a great idea and a great product, they go out of business almost as quickly as they got into business.

One of the primary actions that a green material manufacturer or supplier can take is to establish an efficient method for distribution of product information and product. For example, sustainably harvested wood, almost by definition, involves many small suppliers. It would be extremely useful for the small suppliers to organize through one or two "brokerage agents," such as the nonprofit certifiers with whom they are already working to bring their products to market.

An example of how this can work successfully is the use of Environ material manufactured by Phenix Biocomposites, Inc., in two Wal-Marts. "The Environ material might have been one of those missed opportunities, except that in this case the manufacturer—Phenix Biocomposites, Inc.—was responsive to . . . [the architect's needs]. As a result, over 1,000 feet of Environ is now in place in each of Wal-Mart's two new environmental demonstration stores, one of which recently received Oklahoma's Governor's Award for Environmental Achievement."[1]

The manufacturer realized that it did not know how to enter certain markets of the construction industry. It was willing to work with the design professionals to learn how to enter the market while continuing to develop its product.

"When Environ first came out, it had so many possible uses that our marketing wasn't very focused. Everyone loved the look, and liked the fact that it was recycled. We had people interested in using it for sushi bowls, rifle stocks, and our marketing staff was promoting every possible use. Technical support only got the calls when tough questions came up. For example, Environ isn't meant to be used for structural purposes, but some of our early sales staff weren't clear about that."[2]

What was unusual for a product manufacturer was that it had more people involved in research than in sales. This permitted the company to readily offer technical information as required by the design professionals involved in the project. The technical information included test results from its own testing based on a version of ASTM standards.

Manufacturers of new products often focus their marketing efforts on a contractor working on a specific project. That doesn't usually work well. Contractors generally base their bid on past experience, and they may be reluctant to substitute a new, unfamiliar product for a more familiar one. It is rare that this substitution will not increase the budget or impact the schedule and, therefore, rare that the contractor will use the green building material on the project.

This brings up another stumbling block. The manufacturer who has successfully marketed to the architect, has to be ready to deal with different parties who are responsible for making decisions at different stages of the project. The manufacturer has to be prepared to assist the contractor during construction and, perhaps, to convince the contractor and owner to stay with a product, even after it was specified.

The Building Official

The building official is the chief code officer for the location at which the project is being constructed. Since the building official's primary responsibility is to ensure the health, safety, and welfare of the building's occupants after its completion, he or she takes a very conservative approach to permitting new and unfamiliar building materials into projects.

Most building codes contain provisions governing the use of nontraditional and new materials in buildings. To avoid lengthy delays in the approval of these materials, providing the building official with extensive testing reports and, where available, engineering documentation, will speed up the process of getting them approved for use on a project. Providing a list of other projects where the material has already been used is also beneficial.

The building official is also burdened by an ever-increasing workload that limits the amount of time available to review nontraditional and new materials. An example of how difficult it is to get approval for nontraditional and new materials is the use of straw bale in construction projects. This material, which has been around for a long time, was not an approved material under the current building code. The code authorities required extensive testing and demonstration of its abilities to function as well as other more traditional building materials, even though it has been used to construct homes in various areas of this country for many years.

The Building Occupant

This may or may not be the building owner. Broadly, the occupants of public facilities, commercial buildings, and private residences are the public. They are the ones who are directly and indirectly affected by design choices made in the building. If the only area for collecting trash is the leftover space under the kitchen sink, it is doubtful that even the most well-intentioned building occupant will separate materials for recycling or composting.

All of us are affected by the Urban Heat Island effect—the rise in temperatures in urban landscapes of 2 to 8 degrees as a result of the reflection of heat and light from solid surfaces (asphalt, concrete, etc.). The Urban Heat Island effect obligates the typical urban building occupant to use an additional 1 to 2 percent more energy per degree rise in temperature than if the building were in a rural area or utilized alternative construction materials.[3]

The building occupant may or may not be in a position to directly influence the selection and implementation of a green building material. However, many building owners are taking note of the public's growing interest in the environment. *The Green Consumer Guide,* published in 1988 was a best-seller.[4] For three years in a row, the Times Mirror Magazine survey, conducted by the Roper Organization, found that most Americans (66 percent) believe that environmental protection and economic development go hand in hand. When obliged to choose between the two, 6 out of 10 Americans stated that the environment was more important; 9 out of 10 feel that they can personally help the environment; 48 percent are willing to pay an extra 25 cents for a gallon of gasoline if the money is used to help the environment.[5]

The Fabricator

The fabricator is a company that manufactures specific assemblies or products for incorporation into a project under a contract with the contractor. The assemblies or products may be fabricated from a combination of different materials. It is important that the fabricator understand not only the special requirements on green building materials but also the standards that may govern the materials used in the assembly.

The design professional should include references to the applicable standards in the contract documents. Where compliance with the standards is critical to the success of the project, the design professional should also require that a copy of the standard be maintained on the construction job site.

On a green building project, the design professional also considers the environmental impact of the manufacturing process when evaluating which products and assemblies to include. In selecting materials for the Audubon House in New York City, the Croxton Collaborative, Architects, and the National Audubon Society team "looked at criteria such as embodied energy, the overall environmental policies of manufacturers, health and safety conditions at their factories, and even social responsibility."[6]

As in their contracts with subcontractors, contractors will incorporate applicable provisions of their contract with the owner into their subcontracts or purchase orders. Fabricators not only manufacture but also install. This requires them to be familiar with requirements for working at the job site, such as: recycling, material and trash disposal, and air quality control. A fabricator's familiarity with the environmental issues involved in the fabrication of assemblies or products on a green building project will make their selection more likely.

The Subcontractor

The subcontractor is a company or individual that enters into an agreement with the contractor to perform a specific portion of the construction contract or to supply materials for a project.

As the use of subcontractors has grown, the need to ensure that provisions of the construction contract are included in subcontracts has increased correspondingly. Subcontractors are usually selected in much the same manner as contractors, through competitive bidding. In some instances, contractors may select subcontractors based on past experience rather than purely on price.

With subcontractors performing more and more of the work on a project, it is not only contractors who must be sensitized to special requirements of projects that include green building materials. Since subcontractors compete for work through variances in labor costs and by the use of competing materials and products, they, too, must clearly understand the limitations placed on them when green building materials are specified, because acceptable alternates for green materials may not always exist.

The Consultant

Much as a contractor has subcontractors, consultants are the design professional's "subcontractors." Design professionals "subcontract" for the services of specialists such as: civil engineers, acoustical consultants, and with growing frequency, green building consultants.

Design professionals are responsible for providing their consultants with information about the project, including: the owner's programmatic requirements, any special needs or requirements of the project, and conditions governing construction of the project. When the project is a green building, the design professional must relay special instructions regarding selection of green building materials, energy conservation, and waste management to the consultants so they can incorporate them into the contract documents.

The Design Team

Ideally, a green building material is designed into a building in such a manner so that it can function optimally. Good communication and a focused understanding of the environmental goals for the project will help the design team identify, specify, and utilize green building materials effectively.

Of all of the players, the relationship between the Architect and the Manufacturer is the most important in terms of successfully implementing green building materials. They must work together. Neither can fully implement "green" building materials without the other. The architect relies on the manufacturer for applicable performance data, installation expertise, and product service. The manufacturer relies on the architect for product consideration at the critical first moments of design when the green product can be implemented most efficiently, economically, and successfully. Together, they can support a growing market and have the satisfaction of knowing that they have "done the right thing."

Green Documents: Overview

The design and construction process for most projects can appear excessively complicated, but the basic intent is pretty simple. Someone, usually the owner, wants a building; someone, usually the architect, is going to design it; and someone, usually the contractor, is going to build it. Everything after the initial decision by the owner to build a building, is about communication—how does the owner communicate his or her needs to the architect and how does the architect communicate the design to the contractor.

Much as we may want to, we cannot issue commands from the heavens; instead, we use contracts, samples, drawings, specifications, building codes, standards, and lots of meetings. The product manufacturers or suppliers may never see any of these things, but they are there; and if the product manufacturers understand them, they will know what questions to ask, of whom, and when. They will know how best to communicate what they have to offer to the owner, architect, and contractor. The basic tools of communication in the construction process are the drawings and the specifications.

The drawings are fairly straightforward; they indicate the type, quantity, location, and dimension of materials.

The specifications are the written documents that accompany the drawings and describe what the materials are and how to install them; they also dictate the level of quality of construction expected on the project. For example, if the drawings indicate a plaster wall, the specifications will describe the plaster mix, lath and paper backing, and application requirements (e.g., three coats, finishing techniques, moist cure).

As explained in Chapter 4, the specifications are organized into 16 divisions. The purpose is to provide a standard framework for locating information. The framework does not vary from project to project or from architect to architect. It was developed after World War II by a group of government architects who sought to bring consistency to construction specifications. This led to the formation of The Construction Specifications Institute (CSI) in 1948. The building industry was becoming progressively more complex and more regulated; every architect was organizing information for building requirements in a different way, which made contractors' lives more and more difficult. In 1963, CSI introduced a standard organizational format, known as MasterFormat™, which today is used by manufacturers, architects, contractors, government agencies, and building officials across the United States and Canada.

According to CSI's MasterFormat, information is located in an outline form. The 16 divisions are divided into sections each of which contains three parts. There is also a standardized system of articles and paragraphs within each part. In the 16 divisions, Division 1 defines the general administrative requirements for the project, such as submittal procedures and requirements for progress meetings. Divisions 2 through 16 contain the technical specification sections, which specify the materials and installation requirements. The sections describe units of work under each division, and are identified by five-digit numbers. The section numbering system is described in MasterFormat. The first two digits of the section number represent the division number (01–16) and the last three indicate succeedingly precise units of work. The sections are organized into parts: General, Products, and Execution.

Green Specifications

Division 1

While the best response to environmental issues is more comprehensive, it may be the simplest thing to begin at the beginning, with Division 1. Division 1 addresses general administrative and procedural requirements for a project. It is important to recognize that some environmental controls are already common in most contract documents. For example:

- Section 01100, Special Project Procedures: This section is sometimes used to address project-specific concerns such as the existence of hazardous materials on a renovation project, noise restrictions for construction near a hospital, or special environmental procedures.
- Section 01500, Construction Facilities and Temporary Controls: This section commonly includes requirements for tree and plant protection, cleaning of the site during construction, dust control, and erosion control. It may also restrict access to the site, thereby limiting the impact of construction operations. Many architects and specifiers are currently trying to see how far they can expand these environmental controls. How large is the job? What will the client accept? What will the contractor do willingly? Almost willingly? Are the environmental concerns too different from standards currently employed by the industry? What is the risk if environmental concerns are implemented? If they are not implemented? One way to address these questions, is to expand the controls globally, in Division 1.

Divisions 2 through 16

For Divisions 2 through 16, communication of green requirements can be improved by identifying them in separate articles under each of the three main parts. A sample of applicable articles that should be used may be found in Section 00000, Environmental Specifications Format, given in Appendix C.

Consider the specifications format when investigating product options, and record the information gathered accordingly. Refer to the sample Environmental Impact Questionnaire and the sample Indoor Air Quality Test Report included in Appendix C. These research tools organize product data to coordinate with the major articles and paragraph format in the Environmental Specifications Format.

Develop new sections as necessary. Many of the green building materials do not correspond to an existing CSI section. CSI is beginning to address this growing need. In the meantime, it will be necessary for the design professional to create broadscope and mediumscope sections appropriate to the new categories of materials, such as: alternative agricultural products, plastic lumber, and constructed wetlands. It may also be necessary to create new narrowscope sections to more efficiently organize the proliferation of similar competing materials, such as: fiber insulation (cellulose, fiberglass, mineral wool, cotton), rock insulation (perlite, basalt), and foam insulation (polystyrene, polyisocyanurate, polyurethane, glass, and cementitious).

Public Works Projects

It is important to consider the specific requirements applicable to public works projects commissioned by public agencies. Public agencies are, by definition, organizations wholly created for the welfare and benefit of the public. Public agencies are responsible for and responsible to the public. In some ways, this means that their operations have certain restrictions. It also means that they have incredible opportunities. This is definitely true for green building material specifications produced by a public agency.

Public agencies have the ability to affect positive change, or compromise, on a large scale. When people joke that "you can't fight city hall," they mean that it is difficult for a private entity, a single person, to make much of a difference. But if city hall fights, what a difference it could make. City hall can fight for environmental improvement in several ways:

• Education: City Hall can issue public announcements and create promotional campaigns that educate the public and sensitize them to environmental issues. The water conservation effort during the height of the drought in California is an excellent example. It makes for a better, and more amicable, compromise in the long run if everyone is informed of the facts and the options.
• Legislation: Legislation establishes the framework for meaningful change. When California Assembly Bill 939 requiring a measurable reduction in the waste stream was passed, it established the necessity to redirect waste. It indirectly created an entire new realm of opportunities—businesses to collect

recyclable material, businesses to manufacture items from recyclable material, and businesses to monitor the process. Concerned citizens who would not separate glass from plastic in their garage and carry it to a plant 15 miles away, could now set out separate containers in their driveway for standard, convenient pick-up.

- Assistance: Price preference programs and information hotlines already help fledgling groups such as minorities, women, and veterans. A little extra assistance will help the novice who has a great new idea compete with big corporations and their established old ideas. This can extend to environmentally sensitive products, processes, and companies to help get them off the ground. Energy companies, for example, frequently utilize this route. They are large enough to manage it and business-oriented enough to see the cost savings.

- Leadership: Public agencies can take the lead and set the example for environmentally sensitive design and construction. By establishing environmental requirements for purchase orders and project specifications, public agencies can create the standard for green building material specifications. That is the primary logic behind Executive Order Number 13101 (refer to Chapter 4). An excellent example of leadership by a public agency is the green program operated by the United States Postal Service (USPS). USPS has one of the nation's largest construction programs and recognizes the role it can play in environmental leadership. The USPS has revised its standard master specifications for all building programs to incorporate green materials and methods. This impacts all of the 300–500 new USPS facilities constructed annually. Incorporated items include: aggregate from recycled concrete and asphalt, recycled plastic wheel stops, xeriscaping, biodegradable form release agents, concrete with fly ash, alternative agricultural sheathing, fiberglass with 25% recycled glass, improved albedo for roofing materials, adhesives and paint with low/zero VOCs, hook/loop carpeting, recycled plastic toilet partitions, dock bumpers made from recycled tires, increased efficiency requirements for mechanical insulation, instantaneous point-of-use water heaters, pre-occupancy ventilation, and increased efficiency requirements for lighting.

These innovations were carefully researched by a cross-functional team that included representation from USPS Facilities, employees who would work in the building, design professionals, and the contractor. They were tested and modified in response to user comments and have now been implemented in the USPS Design and Construction Program. It is anticipated that, pending the results of continued monitoring of the First Green Post Office in Fort Worth, Texas, and feedback from users and the public, additional green materials and methods will also be incorporated.

Green building material specifications are the cornerstone for leadership on this issue. Project-specific documents are really the only forum a private entity can access directly. A large private corporation might establish a special interest scholarship fund or research and development fund, but it will never have as much impact as the assistance a public agency can provide. So, apples for apples, the contract documents are the only common ground.

Public agencies have a unique opportunity here. The documents that they produce are frequently used as industry standards. Public agencies are custodians of our health and welfare; consequently, the level of care that they establish is often viewed as a standard for private work.

On the other hand, public agencies have unique concerns and unique methods for addressing the concerns that are not typically the province of the private entity. The investment of time and money can limit private entities. Often, they simply do not have the resources or they do not occupy new construction space for a long enough period of time to warrant the type of investigation and documentation that public agencies can support.

This is not meant to imply that there is unlimited funding in the public coffers. But as guardians of public heath and welfare, part of their job is to investigate issues that affect public health and welfare—such as environmental design, construction, and demolition.

A public agency is in a position to see the big picture. Further, while the impact of the findings may be limited to the private entity itself, were it to undertake such a program, the impact for a public agency is much broader. It can affect the long range building program of the agency, and it can also affect leadership, education, and legislation.

Methods unique to public agencies include:

- Monitoring processes that extend beyond the construction period: Monitor indoor air quality and energy consumption. Compare them to predicted values. Also, compare operating costs to similar "nonenvironmentally sensitive" facilities. How many sick days are used? How often are the high efficiency lightbulbs replaced? The monitoring program doesn't need to be any more extensive than one morning a month, to check the status and plot the information on a chart. Even such a rudimentary investigation will help to evaluate the effectiveness of environmental controls implemented on the particular project.

- Carrot Programs: Establish goals for recycled tonnage. Establish percentages for recycled content. Create a benefit or reward system for contractors when they reach the predetermined goals and percentages. Contractors are in the low-bid system. They certainly will take advantage of opportunities to make a little extra money on the job. This is an option if the agency cannot afford the time, money, or personnel to adequately research the recycling possibilities prior to issuing the contract documents. Set up a carrot program and let the contractor find the savings. Then document it and incorporate the contractor's research into your next project.

Requirements for recycled content (either pre- or postconsumer) may be stated generically for each material in the individual specifications sections or as an overall project goal. This allows for creativity and encourages new ideas; but be extremely cautious when setting an overall goal. In large, complex programs, this is destined to produce apples-to-oranges comparisons that do not allow for equal consideration. It may be more time-consuming initially to put the requirements in the individual sections, but it will probably save a lot of time and grief in the long run.

• Ratings systems: The intangibles that the private entity subjectively analyzes are often converted into measurable quantities by public agencies by means of rating systems. Add "environmental sensitivity" as one of the categories for evaluating products, architects, and contractors. Establish ratings systems that give preferential treatment to products with recycled content or to contractors/architects who have demonstrated commitment to environmentally sensitive construction.

Public agencies are not free agents, so while there are a lot of exciting possibilities, there are also some restrictions for public agencies creating contract documents:

• A private entity can negotiate with a single architect and a single contractor, determine exactly what they want and what is affordable. A private entity represents only their own interests. They can behave subjectively, willfully—as long as it is within legal boundaries—without repercussions. Public agencies represent a larger team than the standard architect-contractor-owner relationship. Public agencies represent the people, all of the people, and all of the different opinions and interests that those people have.

• A private entity can identify exactly which product by which manufacturer it wants in the building. Public agencies cannot show favoritism. Contract documents for public work cannot be proprietary. Different agencies interpret this rule in different ways. Some say that you may specify by a single brand name, but must review any and all proposed substitutions for equivalency. Some say you must list three and state "or equal." Some refuse to accept any naming of manufacturers. Further, you must be careful not to describe a particular product so specifically that, in fact, you have eliminated all but the single product around which you wrote the specifications.

That said, there is no reason that environmentally friendly documents should be any different from a performance specification. Environmental quality is simply one more control to be used to govern the overall quality of any given product or material.

Ultimately, every product should be defined not only in terms of fire resistance and durability, but also in terms of recycled content, toxicity, and outgassing.

Just as there is no caveat against public agencies specifying terrazzo in the lobbies of their buildings, there is no reason why they can't require that the aggregate in the terrazzo be recycled colored glass instead of aggregate from newly quarried stone.

Another restriction is that public agencies must take the "lowest, responsible bidder," which generally translates into the lowest bidder.

- A private entity can evaluate intangibles such as attitude, experience, personality, and professionalism when engaging a contractor. Public agencies are often destined to contract with the lowest bidder. The contractors know this. You know they know this. It becomes a game of low bid-change order.

Again, there is no reason that green building material specifications should be any different from specifying for any other project. If your documents are not complete, you will never be able to add to them.

The contractor will claim an additional cost, and if the money is not in the project's budget you won't get it. The sad thing is that, though a few years ago it was true that products containing green materials (especially recycled materials) generally cost more, they now generally cost the same or less. Include the requirements at the start, preferably in the individual specification sections and at least in the alternates specification section.

Project Examples

One company that has successfully implemented green design in its real estate program is Wal-Mart. Through development of an Environmental Demonstration Store program, Wal-Mart is testing the viability of green design solutions for application throughout its building program. In 1996 two environmental demonstration stores opened, one in the City of Industry, California and the other in Moore, Oklahoma. Although investment in new technology raised initial store development costs by approximately 10 percent, due to energy-efficient design, the anticipated savings per project are $70,000 to $125,000 *each year*. In addition, comparable store sales in skylit areas for the environmental stores are higher.[7] Wal-Mart has also received substantial public relations benefits for its efforts. All in all, this program has proven to be both an economic and an environmental success.

Another example of the successful integration of green design into the building design and construction process is the Audubon House, the home of the National Audubon Society, located in lower Manhattan. The Audubon House project is instructive for several reasons:

- The collaborative approach to design and construction taken by the owner and the design professionals
- The holistic concept of green being an integral part of the design and construction process
- The consideration given to the effect on the environment of existing building reuse versus constructing a new building.

The project team recognized early that in order to achieve the goals they had set for the project—that is, incorporating environmental criteria, controlling construction costs, and maintaining the aesthetics and functionality of the building—they would have to work in close collaboration with each other. "It necessitate[d] the cooperation of parties with a stake in the project, from the owner, architect, and designer on down to subcontractors."[8] It required team members to think in an entirely new way—working to complete individual tasks while not losing sight of the project's goals. Working together enabled the team to select nontraditional building materials more frequently.

This team spirit extended to the contractors and subcontractors. At a reception held at the contractor's offices, the team members explained the project's goals and "pointed out to the subcontractors the competitive advantage to be gained by acquiring skills with new materials and striving for environmental performance."[9]

Equally important to the success of the project was the holistic approach to the design. "Also known as 'integrated, high-performance design,' this system relies on the cumulative effects of no-cost or low-cost design solutions, in tandem with advanced technologies, to bring about the desired level of building performance."[10] The clearest outcome of this approach was the integrated lighting design used in the building, blending the use of natural and artificial lighting to obtain a substantial savings in energy costs.

The last lesson to be learned from the Audubon House project is that the best solution to an owner's need for a new building may be renovating/reusing an existing building. It sent out the message that instead of expending money to develop a "clean" site elsewhere, by using a holistic, team approach to the design, an existing building could be reused at the same cost, with the added benefits of using green building materials.

Beyond Selection and Specification

Once the job of selecting and specifying building materials has been completed, the formidable task of ensuring that green building materials make it through the bidding process and are incorporated into the constructed building begins.

Following sound procedures during this next phase of the project ensures a successful green building in the end.

Chapter 5—Endnotes

1. "Getting New Products into Buildings: An interview with architect and manufacturer." *Environmental Building News* Vol. 5, No. 4, pgs. 8–9, July/August 1996.

2. *Ibid.*

3. Environmental Protection Agency. *Cooling Our Communities: A Guidebook on Tree Planting and Light-Colored Surfacing.* 22P–2001, pp. 5–6, 1992.

4. Connie Koenenn, "Green: New Tide in the Affairs of the Nation's Consumers." *Los Angeles Times,* Thursday March 15, 1990.

5. "America and the Environment: The Sky Isn't Falling," *Skiing,* September 1994.

6. National Audubon Society, Croxton Collaborative, Architects. *Audubon House: Building the Environmentally Responsible, Energy-Efficient Offices,* New York: John Wiley & Sons, Inc., 1994, p. 118.

7. Joseph J. Romm. *Lean and Clean Management: How to Boost Profits and Productivity by Reducing Pollution,* New York, NY: Kodansha International, 1994, p. 100.

8. Audubon House, p. 58.

9. *Ibid.,* p. 60.

10. *Ibid.,* p. 53.

CHAPTER 6

How Does the Construction Process Work?

Worldwide, the building industry is beginning to recognize the shortcomings of its products, and to discover that there are readily available, cost-effective remedies.

A Building Revolution: How Ecology & Health
Concerns Are Transforming Construction
David Malin Roodman and Nicholas Lenssen

Every building construction project, green or not, goes through several phases. Beginning with the planning phase and concluding with the postconstruction phase, the bidding and construction phases are where "the rubber meets the road" for the building's design professionals. By examining the process of bidding and construction, we can understand the actions required to ensure the successful incorporation of green building materials into a project.

The Bidding Phase

Using the construction documents prepared by the design professionals during the preceding phase, the owner solicits construction bids either by advertisement in the case of public projects or by invitation in the case of private projects.

During the bidding phase, each bidder solicits bids from various subcontractors for those portions of the work that they are not going to perform with their own forces. The purpose of the competitive bidding process is to determine the lowest responsive and responsible bidder who will be able to construct the project with the funds the owner has available. In public projects, the owner generally must accept the lowest bid. In private projects, the owner usually preselects the bidders and has the freedom to choose any one of them.

Whether bids are solicited by competitive bid or negotiation, it is during the bidding phase that bidders review project specifications and drawings to determine which products and systems are included. When green building materials and systems are specified, the design professional will have two important responsibilities during bidding: 1) educating bidding general contractors, subcontractors, suppliers, manufacturers' representatives, and others about green building materials and systems that may be relatively unknown to them; and 2) processing substitution requests for green building materials and systems.

Since many green building materials are manufactured by small or new companies, most bidders may not be familiar with them or know how to contact them. In addition to the contact information that the design professional provides either in the specifications or on the drawings, the subject should be covered at the pre-bid conference. Another issue that must be dealt with at that time is the tendency on the part of contractors to use materials with which they are familiar. The fear of the new or untried is a powerful issue when the contractor is responsible for guaranteeing or warranting the entire building for a year.

The pre-bid conference, at which the design professionals, owner, and bidders are present, can be used to dispel some of these concerns. A full discussion by the design professionals of the importance and reasons for using green building materials and systems on the project should be conducted, along with a review of the materials and systems and how to contact the manufacturers. A discussion of alternates and substitution request procedures would also be helpful. Bidders should be encouraged to raise any questions or concerns they have about these products and systems at this time. Minutes of the pre-bid conference should be kept and distributed to all holders of bidding documents. Documenting information discussed during the conference is extremely important to prevent misunderstandings later on in the project. Of course, any clarifications, revisions, additions to or deletions from the bidding documents should be incorporated into an addendum.

Another useful practice is to notify the manufacturers of the green building materials and systems when a building project that incorporates their products and systems is released for bidding so they can contact the bidders directly. To further encourage the dialogue between bidders and green building material and system manufacturers, the design professional can provide a list of bidders to the manufacturers.

Alternates and Substitution Requests

Alternates are typically included in bidding documents to allow the bid price to be adjusted to fall within the limits of the funds available to construct the project. Another use for alternates is to identify the cost of specific materials and systems in comparison to alternate products and systems.

When green building materials and systems are specified, alternates can be used to compare the cost of green versus nongreen. When a project's budget is limited and there is a concern on the part of the owner that using green will be more costly, the use of alternates can establish the true cost, thereby allowing the owner to make a judgment based on weighing the cost of green over the life cycle of the building.

If alternates are used, reference to them should be included in several locations in the bidding documents, including:

- Invitation to Bid/Advertisement for Bids
- Instructions to Bidders
- Bid Form
- Agreement
- Specifications

The Invitation to Bid/Advertisement for Bids document should alert bidders to the inclusion of alternates on the project. A simple statement, similar to the sample in Figure 6.1, may be used.

The Instructions to Bidders should explain how bidders are to prepare alternates and how the alternates will be considered in evaluating bids. Figure 6.1 includes sample provisions that may be included in the Instructions to Bidders.

The Bid Form should include a list of alternates that matches the list in Section 01230-Alternates. To avoid confusion, the order of alternates on the Bid Form should be the same as they appear in Section 01230. Each alternate on the Bid Form should be followed by a blank space where the bidders fill in their price. A sample alternate is given in Figure 6.1.

If a standard form of agreement, such as AIA Document A101 or EJCDC Document 1910-9, is not used, those alternates that have been accepted by the owner must be acknowledged within the Agreement. A sample is illustrated in Figure 6.1. When one of the standard forms is used, the accepted alternates should be listed in the space provided on the Agreement form.

To complete the series of bidding documents containing information about alternates, Section 01230—Alternates, should be used to identify the alternates. Unlike the Bid Form, which contains only a title for each alternate, Section 01230 includes a detailed description of each alternate. This enables bidders to prepare accurate prices for the alternates. Each alternate should reference the applicable technical specification sections as well as the drawings. The affected technical specification sections in Divisions 2 through 16 should have an article in PART 1 GENERAL which refers to the provisions for alternates (see Figure 6.1). If design professionals wish to emphasize environmental considerations, they can use a special alternate section to do so. (A sample Section 01231-Environmental Alternates is included as part of Appendix C.)

Invitation to Bid/Advertisement for Bids
[The following text should be incorporated into the invitation to bid/advertisement for bids.]
Bids shall be on a stipulated-sum basis for the lump-sum base bid, and include prices for alternates.

Instructions to Bidders
[The following text should be incorporated into the instructions to bidders.]
Alternates are described in the specifications and are listed on the Bid Form.
The price bid for each alternate will be the amount added to or deducted from the Base Bid Price if the Owner selects the alternate.
The Owner may accept alternates in any order, regardless of the order in which they are listed, and determine the lowest responsive and responsible bidder based on the sum of the base bid plus any selected alternates.

Bid Form
[The following is a sample alternate format for listing on the bid form.]
Alternate No. 1-Erosion Control Blankets (Note: title of alternate should be derived from description in Section 01230)
(ADD)/(DEDUCT) _____ Dollars ($_____)
                          (In words)   (In numerals)

Agreement
[The following text should be incorporated into the agreement between the owner and the contractor.]
The Contractor shall perform all work required by the Contract Documents for the Environmental Resource Center at 2332 Green Street, Paradise City, USA, including Alternates No. 1, 3, and 5 as described in Section 01230-Alternates, of the Specifications.

Section 01230/01231
[The following is a sample alternate description which can be used in building a section of alternates in Division 1 of the Project Manual.]
1.05   ALTERNATE NO. 1-EROSION CONTROL BLANKETS
      A. Furnish and install degradable, natural-fiber erosion control blankets where indicated on the Drawings and as specified in Section 02370-Slope Protection and Erosion Control.

Section 02370 Slope Protection and Erosion Control
[The following is a sample article referencing the Division 1 section on alternates, which should be incorporated into the technical specification section.]
1.05   ALTERNATES
      A. Refer to Section [01230] [01231] - Alternates/Environmental Alternates for description of work of this section affected by alternates.

FIGURE 6.1   Examples of Alternates in Bidding Documents

Alternates are used primarily to adjust the bid price prior to the signing of the agreement, whereas substitution requests are generally used by contractors, subcontractors, manufacturers, and suppliers to propose a different manufacturer, product, material, or system than the one specified.

Depending on how the project requirements are written, substitutions may be requested only during the bidding phase, only during the construction phase, or during both phases.

It is important that the bidding/contract documents contain clearly defined procedures to control and manage substitution requests whenever they occur. This is especially true when green building materials and systems are specified on a project due to their special nature. It is fairly common to receive substitution requests to use nongreen materials instead of green building materials and systems. The inclusion of specific requirements regarding how substitution requests for green building materials and systems will be evaluated by the design professional will make the process clearer and perhaps prevent the submittal of frivolous substitution requests.

Substitution request provisions should appear in various bidding/contract documents in much the same manner as alternates. To supplement and expand the provisions that appear in AIA Document A201, General Conditions of the Contract for Construction, and EJCDC Document 1910-8, Standard General Conditions of the Construction Contract, Section 01630-Product Substitution Procedures, should be included in the Project Manual. This section should include a standard form for use by bidders/contractors to submit substitutions. (A sample section and form can be found in Appendix C.)

The Instructions to Bidders will state when substitutions are permitted before bids are received, on which form they are to be submitted, who may submit a substitution request, and how notification of approval will be given to bidders. Once a substitution request is approved by the design professional during bidding, all bidders have the opportunity to use the substitute product or system. The benefit to the project's owner is that any savings realized by using the substitute product or system will be incorporated into the bid price.

The Division 1-General Requirements section cited above, which applies during both bidding and construction, outlines procedures governing substitutions. Once the construction contract is signed, substitutions can only be submitted by the contractor. During construction, the substitution request also has to indicate any changes in the contract price and time. If the substitution request is approved, a change order will have to be issued to incorporate these changes into the contract.

The disadvantage to permitting substitution requests during bidding and construction is that there may not be enough time to properly research the proposed substitution. The design professional should not approve a substitution request if he or she is concerned about the substitution's level of quality or whether it will perform as well as the specified product. When substitution requests are proposed for green building materials and systems, the complexity and time required for review by the design professional is increased because of the additional properties that must be examined as compared to nongreen materials. Because of these concerns, it is preferable to consider substitutions during the design and construction document phases of the project. In this way, the design professional can minimize the approval and use of unacceptable materials on the project.

The Construction Phase

The construction phase of the project usually begins when the bid award is made by the appropriate authority on a publicly financed project or when the contract is signed on other projects. If the contract documents require it, the contractor will have to submit a list of proposed products and a schedule of submittals to the design professional, usually within 30 days after the contract is signed. In some cases, the owner may require that the list be submitted at the same time that the bids are submitted.

The list of proposed products, prepared by the contractor, is reviewed by the design professional and then forwarded to the owner for approval. The submittal of the list by the contractor to the design professional is a means of confirming that only specified products or approved substitutions are being used. The preparation of the list also allows contractors to confirm that their suppliers and subcontractors are following the contract document requirements. The design professional must specify which products the contractor must include on the list since the typical project includes a substantial number of products.

When green building materials are specified on a project, the submittal and review of the list takes on added significance. The design professional must clearly express in the contract documents that substitution requests cannot be proposed through the list of proposed products. If the list contains unapproved substitutions for specified green building materials, the design professional must quickly and clearly notify the contractor that the list is not in conformance with the contract documents. The contractor must revise and resubmit the list until it is acceptable to the design professional and the owner.

Once the list is found to be acceptable, the design professional distributes the approved list to the contractor, owner, and consultants. The contractor is responsible for distribution of the approved list to subcontractors and suppliers. The approved list serves as a checklist throughout the construction of the project to ensure that only specified green building materials and approved substitutions are incorporated into the completed building.

A schedule of submittals is another useful tool for the design professional to use to monitor the flow of information and tasks during construction early in the project. The schedule of submittals is usually submitted in conjunction with the construction progress schedule. The design professional should review the schedule to confirm that the contractor has included all of the submittals required by the technical specification sections. Since the contractor must take into consideration many factors when preparing the schedule, the design professional should verify that the submittals are not scheduled to be submitted all at the same time; that submittals for materials in an assembly are submitted together; and that the contractor has allowed adequate time prior to the need for materials on the project for preparation of submittals, review by the design professionals, and resubmittal in the event that the submittal is not acceptable the first time. The design professional should encourage the contractor to allow more time for submittals for green building materials due to the possibility that submittal information may be more difficult to obtain.

As mentioned earlier, many manufacturers of green building materials are either new or small or both and may require more time to assemble a submittal. With this understanding, the contractor and design professional can easily accommodate the green building material manufacturer's submittal time schedule.

The Submittal Process

Once the list of submittals has been reviewed and approved, the contractor will begin the submittal process. Submittals may include shop drawings, product data, samples, manufacturer's installation instructions, test reports, manufacturer's certificates, material safety data sheets, and other information as required by the individual technical specification sections.

The standard general conditions, either AIA Document A201 or EJCDC 1910-8, require that the contractor obtain the approval of the design professional for submittals required by the contract documents prior to ordering or incorporating those materials into the work.

The review and approval of submittals is a very important part of the design professional's contract administration phase services. During the submittal review process, the design professional must be alert for unauthorized substitutions for specified materials. The design professional must also carefully compare the submittal against the requirements of the corresponding technical specification section to ensure that it includes: 1) all of the submittal documentation required, and 2) sufficient technical information to compare the submittal to the specification.

Green building material specification sections often contain requirements for special submittals such as: toxicity test reports, material-content/recycled-content data, and installation environmental considerations. Since these submittals are not normally required for nongreen building materials, special attention must be given by the contractor and the design professional to these special requirements to ensure their timely submittal, review, and approval.

On projects that include the requirement for a preconstruction conference, a portion of the agenda should be set aside to review the substitution request process (if the contract documents permit them during construction) and the submittal process. Any special submittals required for green building materials should be reviewed and clarified so that there will be no confusion regarding the requirements. It would also be appropriate at this conference to review the design professional's responsibilities regarding verification that materials delivered to the job site and installed in the project are those specified and submitted.

The contractor should clearly understand his or her responsibility for reviewing the submittal prior to forwarding it to the design professional, and ensure that the subcontractors and suppliers are knowledgeable regarding their responsibilities as well. The contractor should not forward incomplete or incorrect submittals to the design professional. The design professional, in turn, should refuse to review any submittal that does not comply with the specifications.

All members of the construction team should familiarize themselves with the provisions of the Division 1 section that covers submittals prior to beginning the submittal process. This will shorten the time required for review and increase the likelihood that the design professional will approve the submittal the first time around.

Construction Administration Activities

The standard contract between the owner and the design professional requires that the design professional observe the work during construction. This is to be done periodically to keep the owner informed as to the progress and quality of the work and to prevent defects and deficiencies in the work. It is not meant to be exhaustive nor to make the design professional responsible for the means and methods of construction, which is contractually the responsibility of the contractor.

The design professional's periodic visits to the job site help improve coordination between design and construction, improve communications between the design professional and contractor, and ensure conformance of the work to the contract documents. The design professional's responsibilities are normally coordinated with the general conditions of the contract for construction. This is important to verify when non-standard documents are used, to avoid conflicts since the design professional and contractor are not in contract with each other. The design professional's contract with the owner typically defines not only his or her role during construction but how often he or she will visit the job site to make observations. In some instances, the owner may hire the design professional to make more frequent visits to the job site or to assign a part- or full-time individual on the job site when the project scope or complexity requires it.

Although the design professional is not required to make an exhaustive review of the work during the periodic visits to the job site, it is beneficial to the project to pay special attention to the incorporation of green building materials into the work, for two reasons. First, to verify that the specified materials are being used, and second, to verify that the manufacturer's installation instructions are being followed by the contractor. As mentioned earlier, this is important because of the relative unfamiliarity of contractors with these green building materials.

The design professional can also facilitate the participation of the green building material manufacturer in the construction process because of the relationship established during the design phase of the project. As a result, any questions or concerns that arise during construction can be dealt with quickly and with the least amount of disruption to the construction schedule.

The Construction Phase as the Successful End to the Project

Many design professionals, after investing a great deal of their energy and talent in the design and specification of a building project using green building materials, are disappointed when the materials are changed during the bidding and construction phases without their agreement. By putting an equal amount of effort and care into the bidding and construction phases of the project, the design professional can ensure that the green building materials they selected and worked so hard to include in their project will actually be incorporated into it. By working to make the contractor's job of using relatively unknown materials easier, the design professional can serve both the owner's needs and those of the environment at the same time.

Conclusion

The Congress, recognizing the profound impact of man's activity on the interrelations of all components of the natural environment, particularly the profound influences of population growth, high-density urbanization, industrial expansion, resource exploitation, and new and expanding technological advances, and recognizing further the critical importance of restoring and maintaining environmental quality to the overall welfare and development of man, declares that it is the continuing policy of the Federal Government, in cooperation with State and local governments, and other concerned public and private organizations, to use all practicable means and measures, including financial and technical assistance, in a manner calculated to foster and promote the general welfare, to create and maintain conditions under which man and nature can exist in productive harmony, and fulfill the social, economic, and other requirements of present and future generations of Americans.

The National Environmental Policy Act[1]

The first generation of green building projects were not particularly representative of the majority of the building industry. Some projects involved high-end facilities (private residences or high-end services) that had the accompanying high-end budget. Other projects were sponsored and subsidized by interested nonprofit groups or governmental agencies and had flexible schedules and even more flexible allowances. Then there were the projects developed by people who live "off the grid" and built their own residences rather cheaply, and without benefit of a building inspector, using old tires, bottles, straw bales, wind or solar power, and various unique collectibles.

More recent projects bring environmental issues—and possible solutions—within reach of mainstream design and construction. They introduce green building products that are affordable, functional, and beautiful. They clearly demarcate a new direction in architecture.

History of Green Building Materials

Out of necessity, building design by early civilizations was heavily influenced by natural elements. Structures were oriented toward available daylight and desirable breezes. Roofs were pitched to shed water. Walls were thickened to insulate against the cold. Consequently, buildings in hot, arid regions looked distinctly different from those in cold, wet climates.

Material selection was limited to the regionally available natural resources and the use of materials was molded by regional climate patterns. Depending on the prevalent ecosystem, building materials included: thatch, adobe, sod, straw, stone, timber, brick, wattle and daub (the precursor to lath and plaster), and fabric. Homes were constructed on raised platforms in warm, wet, flood-prone areas of the tropics. Homes were constructed from collapsible frames and lightweight breatheable fabric (that swelled when wet to shed water) by desert nomads. Northern regions consistently produced thicker, denser walls to defend against the cold. In every location, people built their own buildings with materials that they acquired locally.

Ironically, today, indigenous building materials, materials that evolved in harmony with the land and the people over hundreds of years, are deemed "alternative" materials. Where there are exceptions, such as stone and wood, it is largely because commercial interests privatized the acquisition of natural resources and have promoted the market value of that resource. Natural materials are largely unrecognized in building codes. Alternative materials are, by their very nature, nontoxic. Most comply with basic performance requirements for fire-resistance. Most can be detailed to meet seismic and lateral load requirements as well. Still, "original" building materials are considered to be "alternative". They have been replaced with modern building products, synthetic materials, and composites.

Modern civilization's mastery of an array of scientific principles has enabled us to create artificial environments unimaginable in previous eras. A flick of the thermostat provides almost instantaneous comfort. Point-of-use water heaters provide a seemingly endless supply of hot water. Appliances in the kitchen offer relentless conveniences. With a push of a button or turn of a dial, we adapt the parameters of our built environment to suit the whim of the moment. Our buildings reflect these new technology-driven expectations. As a result, an office building in New York is likely to resemble one in New Mexico. Worse, a company can design a prototype (a fast food restaurant or retail space) and build it almost anywhere with little modification. Twentieth century architecture is much more homogenous than any previous period. Differences in building design and choice of building material that were once due to the influence of nature's elements are now primarily a factor of aesthetics and budget.

The turning point was the dawn of the Industrial Revolution, marked architecturally by the Crystal Palace in the mid-nineteenth century. The Crystal Palace epitomized the Industrial Revolution, a grand vision constructed with new materials in repetitive, standardized sizes. Today, it is a staple in history of architecture courses, lauded and immortalized over the years. Very few histories relate the rest of the story, however. Unfortunately, the difference in thermal expansion between the glass and the metal frame was ill-considered, the glass sheets were prone to popping out, and the building leaked like a sieve. The analogy is plain. Society embraced the promises of the Industrial Revolution as it did the image of the Crystal Palace. And it tolerated similar oversights. Society failed to acknowledge the new problems that accompanied the new solutions. Nothing is free. There are always trade-offs, whether we recognize them or not.

The Industrial Revolution ushered in a fabulously exciting time of new and improved products for buildings—steel, sheet glass, reinforced concrete, elevators, and curtainwalls. It thrived on standardization and mass production, which helped make all these technological wonders affordable to an eager public. It permitted the construction of taller buildings. It allowed construction at a faster pace than ever before. More and bigger and "better" buildings changed the fabric of our cities. Many of the deplorably polluted conditions of older cities were improved. Indoor plumbing alone can be credited with mitigating many of the diseases pervasive in urban areas. But, it was a trade. This we failed to realize. The new technologies replaced older forms of pollution with new ones. While we no longer fear treading in the deposits left by horse-drawn carriages, we have no way of avoiding the air pollution caused by some 500 million vehicles on the road today. The sooty fog caused by coal combustion has been replaced by ozone (smog) and worse. Fires, always a hazard for dense urban areas, may be relatively less frequent due to improvements in building materials and systems, but they now present the added component of toxic smoke from the burning of myriad plastics and synthetic chemicals.

The Industrial Revolution was followed closed by a scientific revolution. Post-World War II society expects technological marvels in daily life that even the pioneers of the Industrial Revolution did not envision. The scientific revolution heralded a period of chemical discovery that paralleled the physical discovery of the Industrial Revolution. It fostered new attitudes towards materials, dissecting matter into atoms, neutrons, and quarks. The building industry witnessed mass production of new products from previously unknown substances. We now take for granted the benefits of stain-resistant carpet and fiber-optic communications. As did our forebears, we overlooked the new problems that accompanied the new solutions, the wonder materials. We are just beginning to acknowledge these new problems—the toxins, carcinogens, and mutagens. We are gaining a better, fuller perspective of the impact on our natural resources and on urban congestion and quality of life.

Both the Industrial Revolution and the scientific revolution altered the business of building as well. The process of building came to mirror the process of standardized manufacturing. We design to standard sizes with standard products, tested and qualified by industry recognized standards, and contracted on standard industry-recognized forms. The craftsman era is largely gone. Where it survives, it is extremely expensive. In many ways, this makes innovation more difficult than it was before the Industrial Revolution. Innovation requires a certain freedom from prescriptive standards in order to find better ways to meet basic performance requirements. Innovation is exactly what we need to solve the problems overlooked by the Industrial Revolution and scientific revolution. And that is exactly what green building is. It is a recognition of the benefits as well as the problems presented by these revolutions. It combines the affordability and convenience of standardization with the quality and thoughtfulness of craftsmanship.

Our society has developed many conveniences and made many improvements in the quality of life. However, wisdom from history should not be discarded. The benefits associated with designing buildings in response to nature have been largely forgotten over the years. Green building design and green building products are rediscovering these benefits. A building design that takes climatic conditions into consideration requires less energy to operate, while providing improved lighting, indoor air quality, and healthier places to live and work.

The Future of Green Building Materials

The architecture of the Industrial Revolution and the scientific revolution expresses the values and world views of society at that time. Future "revolutions" are likely to impact the building industry as much as those preceding. New fields of scientific investigation such as holographic philosophy, virtual reality, and chaos theory, may alter our perspective dramatically—and so our building. The information revolution of the computer age might alter our working relationships and daily interactions and the corresponding need for certain types of buildings. Space exploration may birth new technologies, new needs, and new world (or worlds) view. Collapsing economies and dwindling natural resources may salute an energy revolution, impacting building design and promoting new markets for renewable energy products.

The design of buildings individually and collectively (urban design) reflects our culture, our consistently shifting attitudes about issues beyond the simple need for shelter. It also reflects the very real and very significant economic and environmental factors. Traditionally, economic and environmental issues have been isolated from each other. More and more, we are coming to understand how closely linked they are. Any one of the possible future revolutions just cited will have economic and environmental components. The difference from previous eras, however, is that we are more likely to recognize them as they occur.

Over the last five years or so, a new field of accounting has developed. It is called *environmental accounting,* and it is supported by many economists and politicians, including Vice President Al Gore. Basically, environmental accounting revises the financial systems in this country, (taxes, prices, GNP evaluations, etc.) to reflect the value of forests, minerals, clean air and water, erosion of soils, and so forth. The theory requires a complete restructuring of global economic systems. Obviously, without a magic wand, such a wholesale restructuring is unlikely. Nevertheless, piecemeal applications of environmental accounting are becoming more numerous. Piecemeal applications are already directly impacting the building industry in the sun rights, sewer rights, and pollution rights instituted at the local levels in cities such as New York, Houston, and Los Angeles.

Broader examples will have indirect, but ultimately more significant, impacts in the building industry. Broader applications of environmental accounting include:

- *Elimination of federal subsidies to forestry, mining, and various agricultural industries:* Historically such subsidies were enacted to encourage the claiming and taming of Wild West lands. The federal government wanted to assist pioneers and support industry that attracted settlers into the wilderness, effectively bringing it under the national umbrella. However, long past the accomplishment of the goal, such subsidies remain entrenched. Consequently, taxpayers fund the roads that logging companies now use to burrow into our dwindling natural forests, and the federal government contracts to sell timber below market rate to the mainstream timber industry. Many taxpayers are outraged for purely economic reasons. Add to their voices, the voices of environmentalists, and politicians are taking notice. The topic of forest subsidies surfaces fairly regularly. Obviously, if such subsidies were reduced or removed, many sectors of the building industry would be impacted.

- *BTU tax:* The taxation of energy—and more particularly the pollution it spawns—is also a recurring subject politically. Many countries tax energy. Gasoline, for example, is consistently cheaper in the United States than anywhere else in the world due in part to the fact that other countries levy a considerable tax on gasoline. If in the United States gasoline were taxed commensurate with the cost for pollution clean-up, the ripple effect would permeate all industries, including the building industry.

- *Raw materials tax:* This is an ideal discussed by environmentalists and economists more than politicians. A raw materials tax is conceived as a deterrent to consuming the Earth's resources. Not only is forestry subsidized in the United States, but the value of the land is not seen to diminish once the forest has been harvested. A raw materials tax would invest the forest with a measurable value in and of itself.

- *Pollution tax:* Like a raw materials tax, a pollution tax works on the principle of taxing that which is undesirable, versus that which is desirable (such as earnings). Generally, pollution taxation is proposed as a combination of penalties and incentives. For example, in a given industry sector as determined by existing IRS designations, a median pollution level for each measurable pollutant would be established. Those who exceeded the median would pay a tax (a penalty) and those who emitted less than the median would receive a bonus. If the bonus were derived from the penalties, the taxation would essentially pay for itself, and continuous improvement would be encouraged as industry members vied among themselves to reduce pollution, thereby lowering the median.

- *Trading credits:* Various examples of trading credits are already emerging in both the private and pubic arenas. When items such as solar access, sewer rights, wetlands, and "trash" are assigned a limit, they immediately gain financial value. In the late 1980s, Houston was so overbuilt that it did not have sufficient wastewater treatment facilities to handle the new construction. The city implemented a system of sewer rights, where properties were assigned an allowable number of water closets based on the square footage of the property. By virtue of the limitation, the sewer rights became valuable, tradable commodities. The EPA has developed guidance for the establishment and use of wetland mitigation banks. "Land owners needing to 'mitigate' or compensate for authorized impacts to wetlands associated with development activities may have the option of purchasing credits from an approved mitigation bank rather than restoring or creating wetlands on or near the development site."[2] There are approximately 100 mitigation banks in 34 states, including the first private entrepreneurial banks.

- *Full disclosure of corporate environmental impact:* This is a significant issue for many corporations, and tends to be driven more by economic vectors than by political debate. In environmental arenas, it is referred to as "transparency." It is one thing to state that one is operating in an environmentally friendly manner, but it is quite another to document it. As ISO 14000 standards, which have the support of the World Trade Organization, become more prevalent, stakeholders are starting to ask for verification and documentation of environmental stewardship. A growing number of investment funds advertise themselves as "socially" and/or "environmentally" responsible, and purport to use social and environmental screens to build their portfolios. Stockholders are asking questions and demanding answers.

- *Green leases:* Green leasing of building products offers a potentially profitable new merchandising approach. It represents stronger, more lasting business relationships, and provides the groundwork for better environmental stewardship by all parties.

- *Revised GNP:* The Department of Commerce, Bureau of Economic Statistics; is developing measures of economic value of environmental assets, such as renewable resources, nonrenewable resources, air quality, and water quality.[3]

Green Building Material Response to Changing Conditions

Current and continuing market impacts of green considerations on products include considerations for packaging, labeling, sourcing, processing, and of course, development of new products. Reducing, reusing, and recycling packaging is one of the "low hanging fruit" options that most competitive manufacturers have already embraced.

- *Alternative packaging:* Alternative packaging, such as starch-based pellets and wraps, is likely to become more prevalent.
- *Labeling:* Labeling of both product and packaging is in the process of becoming more sophisticated and more common. At one time, the ubiquitous arrows-chasing-arrows symbol for recycling was the banal attempt of manufacturers to support recycling. Now, many are indicating the type of plastic used in order to facilitate the sorting of feedstock for the most efficient recycling. Furthermore, under the auspices of the Federal Trade Commission, environmental information given on labels is becoming more substantial. *Greenwashing,* the superficial and unreliable endorsement of green issues, is becoming less and less frequent. And, because so much good information is becoming available, where greenwashing does occur, it tends to be readily apparent and not likely to fool consumers. Green information presented in labels may include certification of nontoxic content, organic content, recycled content (pre/post), life cycle impact, and recycling classification of both product and packaging.
- *Alternative feedstock:* The sources of feedstock for manufacturing once heralded "virgin materials"; now they are equally proud about recycled content. The infrastructure that delivers recycled material to manufacturing facilities is growing. Similarly, the support of biobased, alternative agricultural products is growing.
- *Manufacturing processes:* New technologies for improved energy efficiency and cleaner process are gaining ground environmentally and economically. Low-emission microwave finishing, for example, can allow a fabricator to minimize the energy required in the coating process and reduce the waste heat generated. Cleaner operations lower regulatory and insurance costs. The Design for the Environment (DFE) approach, combined with green leasing is also likely to play a role in manufacturing processes of the future.
- *New products:* Perhaps the most noticeable change is the growing availability of new, greener products. Such products include a wide variety of alternate energy systems and a renaissance in agricultural products. Solar-powered roofing shingles, waterless urinals, soy-based adhesives and plastics, bamboo flooring, and strawboard sheathing panels offer an ideal response to the federal commitment ". . . to create and maintain conditions under which man

and nature can exist in productive harmony, and fulfill the social, economic, and other requirements of present and future generations of Americans."[4]

Recommendations

Hundreds of green building products are currently available. They offer a range of aesthetic options. They perform well. They are cost-competitive. It is not only possible to incorporate green building products into our design and construction practices. It is imperative.

It is our sincere and earnest hope that this book contributes to the redevelopment of our economic and political infrastructure in the support of sustainable approaches to green building. By promoting the use of green building products, we better serve our clients and the public. We provide a more efficient, less toxic building that respects the health, safety, and welfare of the building occupants and the community in general. And we help to change the business of building in a positive way, one that helps to safeguard the "the social, economic, and other requirements of present and future generations of Americans."[5]

Chapter 7—Endnotes

1. Section 101 [42 USC § 4331], Title 1, The National Environmental Policy Act.
2. www.epa.gov/OW/facts/fact11.html
3. *Technology for a Sustainable Future: A Framework for Action;* National Science and Technology Council. U.S. Government Printing Office, Washington, DC, 800/ENV-6676.
4. Section 101 [42USC . . .]
5. Ibid.

Sources of
Further Information

To assist readers in learning more about green building materials and green buildings, this appendix lists various resources of additional information.

Air Quality Management District (AQMD)
21865 E. Copley Drive
  Diamond Bar, CA 91765
(909) 396-2000; www.aqmd.gov
Public information, governing board
  agenda, minutes and committee
  agendas, rules and regulations,
  business assistance.

Alliance to Save Energy
1200 18th St. NW, Ste. 900
Washington, DC 20036
(202) 857-0666; fax (202) 331-
  9588; e-mail: info@ase.org;
  www.ase.org
The alliance focuses on improving
  energy efficiency in new and
  existing buildings. It promotes
  energy-efficient housing through
  energy rating systems, assesses
  impacts of federal and state fiscal
  policies, and identifies energy-
  efficient products and services
  nationwide.
Publications: *Energy Efficiency
  Resource Directory: A Guide to
  Utility Programs, Energy
  Innovations*

**American Council for an Energy-
  Efficient Economy (ACEEE)**
1001 Connecticut Avenue, NW,
  Ste. 801
Washington, DC 20036
(202) 429-8873; fax (202) 429-
  2248; e-mail: info@aceee.org;
  aceee.org/index.htm
ACEEE explores the links between
  energy efficiency, economic
  prosperity, a cleaner environment,
  and other aspects of national and
  global concern. It conducts

technical and policy assessments,
  advises governments and utilities,
  works collaboratively with
  businesses, and organizes
  conferences.
Publications: several

American Gas Cooling Center
400 N. Capitol Street, NW
Washington, DC 20001
(202) 824-7141; fax (202) 824-
  7093; www.agcc.org
Resource Provides information on
  natural gas air conditioning,
  dehumidification and refrigerant
  technologies and applications.

**American Institute of Architects
  (AIA)**
1735 New York Avenue, NW
Washington, DC 20006
(202) 626-7300; www.aiaonline.com
The AIA's Committee on the
  Environment (COTE) works to
  create sustainable buildings and
  communities by advancing,
  disseminating, and advocating
  environmental knowledge and
  values to the profession, industry,
  and the public. Members provide
  volunteer resources and expertise
  to fulfill its mission of guiding
  architects toward sound
  ecological and economic
  decisions.
Publications: *AIA Environmental
  Resource Guide*

American Local Power Project
1615 Broadway, #1005
Oakland, California 94612
(510) 451-1727 (Tel/Fax);
  www.local.org

A national clearinghouse for communities interested or already engaged in efforts to utilize local powers to gain a voice in the electric deregulation debate.

American Nature Study Society (ANSS)
5881 Cold Brook Rd.
Homer, NY 13077
hometown.aol.com/anssonline/ index.htm
ANSS is America's oldest environmental education organization, and continues to disseminate environmental information via its journal and newsletter.
Publications: *Nature Study* (journal), *The American Nature Study Society Newsletter*

American Rivers
1025 Vermont Ave, NW, Ste. 720
Washington, DC 20005
(202) 347-7500; fax (202) 347-9240; amrivers@amrivers; www.amrivers.org
American Rivers has helped preserve over 10,000 river miles for clean water, threatened fish and wildlife, recreation, and scenic beauty. Emphasis is on wild and scenic river systems, dams, diversions, channelizations, and adverse development.
Publications: *American Rivers* (quarterly newsletter)

American Solar Energy Society, Inc. (ASES)
2400 Central Avenue, Ste. G-1
Boulder, CO 80301

(303) 443-3130; fax (303) 443-3212; ASES@ASES.org; www.ases.org
ASES focuses on advancing the use of solar energy by promoting its near-term use, encouraging basic and applied research and development in solar energy, and providing information.
Publications: *Solar Today*

Architects, Designers and Planners for Social Responsibility (ADPSR)
P.O. Box 18375
Washington, DC 20036-8375
www.adpsr.org
ADPSR promotes protection of the natural and built environment and socially responsible development among architects, designers, planners, and related professionals.
Publications: *New Village; ADPSR News*

Associated Air Balance Council (AABC)
1518 K St., NW, Ste. 503
Washington, DC 20005
(202) 737-0202; fax (202) 638-4833; AABCHQ@AOL.com; www.aabchq.com
AABC is a professional organization for consultants and contractors in the HVAC and mechanical profession. Many provide commissioning services.
Publications: *TAB Journal*

Association for the Environmental Health of Soils (AEHS)
150 Fearing Street

Amherst, MA 01002
(413) 549-5170; fax (413) 549-
0579; AEHS.com; www.aehs.com
AEHS is a clearinghouse for
technical and regulatory
information on soil issues,
including chemistry, geology,
hydrogeology, engineering,
modeling, toxicology, regulatory
science, and the law.
Publications: *Journal of Soil
Containment, Soil &
Groundwater Clean-Up Magazine*

Alliance of Foam Packaging Recyclers

2128 Espey Ct, Ste 4
Crofton, MD 21114
(410) 451-8340; fax (410) 451-
8343; www.epspackaging.org
Formed in 1991 by over 80
companies, representing every
major manufacturer of EPS
protective foam packaging, their
raw material suppliers and
equipment manufacturers work to
facilitate EPS recycling between
EPS mfrs.
The alliance has more than 110
plant locations nationwide to
serve as central collection points
and help produce foam packaging
made with recycled content.
Emphasis is on encouraging the
reuse of loose-fill foam
packaging and the recycling and
reprocessing of molded foam
packaging.

Bioenergy Information Network

Bioenergy Feedstock Development
Program
Oak Ridge National Laboratory

P.O. Box 2008, MS-6422
Oak Ridge, TN 37837-6422
(423) 574-7818; www.esd.ornl.gov/
bfdp/
The network organizes renewable
energy outreach activities. The
DOE-funded projects focus on
the domestic production,
recovery, and conversion of
energy crops (fast-growing trees
and grasses) and residues to
economically priced,
environmentally beneficial fuels
and power generation.

Brobeck, Phleger & Harrison LLP

One Market Spear Street,
San Francisco, California 94105
(415) 442-0900; fax (415) 442-
1010; www.brobeck.com/docs/
envinscv.htm
Law firm highlights important court
decisions about coverage under
environmental insurance.

Business for Social Responsibility (BSR)

609 Mission Street, 2nd Floor
San Francisco, CA 94105-3506
(415) 537-0888; fax (415) 537-
0889; www.bsr.org
BSR is a professional organization
that provides leadership to
address economic, social, and
environmental problems that
confront business and society.
Among BSR's charter members
are: Reebok International, Ltd.,
Levi Strauss & Company, the
Body Shop USA, Ben & Jerry's
Homemade, and the Calvert
Group. Environmental programs

utilized by BSR members include green design, waste reduction, and energy-efficiency programs.

Canadian Institute of Chartered Accountants
277 Wellington Street West, Toronto ON M5V 3H2 Canada
www.cica.ca/new/fp/p18.htm
Presents Financial Post awards for corporate environmental reporting.

Center for Holistic Management
1010 Tijeras, NW
Albuquerque, NM 87102
(505) 842-5252; fax (505) 843-7900; center@holistic
management.org; wwwholistic
management.org
The center focuses on community development that encourages communities to become involved to restore their well-being and the natural resources on which they depend. Emphasis is on expanding the number of individuals capable of offering training in holistic resource management.
Publications: *Holistic Management Quarterly*

Center for Marine Conservation
1725 DeSales St. NW, Ste. 600
Washington, DC 20036
(202) 429-5609; fax (202) 872-0619; dccmc@ix.netcom.com;
cmc-ocean.org
The center is dedicated to the conservation of marine wildlife and habitats. Emphasis is on five major goals: conserving marine

habitats, preventing marine pollution, conserving fisheries, protecting endangered species, and promoting and educating about marine biodiversity.
Publications: *Marine Conservation News*

Center for Maximum Potential Building Systems, Inc.
8604 FM 969
Austin, TX 78724
(512) 928-4786; fax (512) 926-4418;
CMPBS@Greenbuilder.com;
www2.cmpbs.org
The center works with public entities, professional organizations, community groups, universities, and individuals to develop sustainable building policies and practices, ranging from individual buildings to entire regions.

Center for Our Common Future (CCF)
Palais Wilson, 52 rue des Paquis,
Geneva CH-1201, Switzerland
+41227327117; fax
+41227385046; www.gsf.de/
UNEP/swiccf.html
CCF was formed by Our Common Future, the report of the World Commission on Environment and Development (WCED), as a means to monitor its follow-up activities. Emphasis is on promoting the WCED report, disseminating objective information, and including public participation in sustainable development.

Publications: *The Brundtland Bulletin, Network 92*

Center for Plant Conservation
Missouri Botanical Garden
P.O. Box 299
St. Louis, MO 63166-0299
(314) 577-9450; fax (314) 577-9465; CPC@MOBOT.org; www.mobot.org/CPC/
The center focuses on conserving rare and endangered native plants through research, cultivation, and education at botanical gardens and arboreta in the United States. Emphasis is on five priority regions: Hawaii, Florida, California, Texas, and Puerto Rico.
Publications: *Plant Cogeneration Directory, Seed Storage Guidelines*

Center for Resourceful Building Technology (CRBT)
P.O. Box 100
Missoula, MT 59806
(406) 549-7678; fax (406) 549-4100; CRBT@Montana.com; www.montana.com/crbt/
CRBT focuses on educating the public on issues related to housing and the environment, particularly environmentally responsible building materials and technologies. CRBT also conducts research and demonstrates resource-efficient building materials and practices.
Publications: *The Guide to Resource Efficient Building Elements*

Center for Social and Environmental Accounting Research

University of Dundee
www.dundee.ac.uk/Accountancy/CSEAR.htm
Provides list of resources on environmental accounting.

Certified Forest Products Council (CFPC)
14780 SW Osprey Drive, Ste. 285
Beaverton, OR 97007
(503) 590-6600; fax (503) 590-6655; www.certifiedwood.org.
CFPC is a nonprofit, voluntary business initiative committed to promoting responsible forest product buying practices throughout North America in an effort to improve forest management practices worldwide. Emphasis is on the purchase, use, and sale of third-party, independently certified forest products.
Publications: *Understory* (quarterly newsletter), *Good Wood Directory*

Citizen's Clearinghouse for Hazardous Waste
P.O. Box 6806
Falls Church, VA 22040
(703) 237-2249; fax (703) 237-8389; cchw@essential.org; www.essential.org/cchw/
Also known as Center for Environmental Justice, the clearinghouse assists communities in combating environmental threats. Emphasis is on contaminated sites campaign, including convicting the EPA for child abuse for not cleaning up these sites.
Publications: *Everyone's Backyard* (quarterly), *Environmental Health* (Monthly)

City Bikes
2501 Champlain St. NW
Washington, DC 20009
(202) 265-1564; fax (202) 462-
7020; www.citybikes.com
City Bikes supports local, regional,
and national bicycle and other
nonmotorized transportation
advocacy groups and events,
maintains a comprehensive
recycling program, and provides
support for cycling awareness and
safety programs for the children
in the area.

Clean Sites, Inc.
1199 N. Fairfax St., Ste. 400
Alexandria, VA 22314
(703) 683-8522; fax (703) 548-
8773; http://clu-in.org/programs/
clnsites/cleaninc.htm
A coalition of businesses,
environmental groups, and senior
EPA officials organized to help
find ways of accelerating the
clean-up of hazardous wastes, it
emphasizes the use of dispute
resolution and facilitation
techniques, and offers technical
services in project design and
management, peer reviews,
environmental audits, and
technical mediation.

Clean Water Action
4455 Connecticut NW, Ste. A300
Washington, DC 20036
(202) 895-0420; fax (202) 895-0430
A citizen's organization that focuses
on obtaining clean and safe water
at an affordable cost; controlling
toxic chemicals; conserving
wetlands, groundwater, and
coastal waters; safe solid waste
management; public health; and

environmental safety of all
citizens. Emphasis is on citizen
organizing and education.

The Cohousing Network
www.cohousing.org
An extensive cohousing guide to
sources, general information, and
information about specific
communities.

**Consumer Product Safety
Commission (CPSC)**
4330 East-West Highway
Bethesda, Maryland
(800) 638-CPSC; www.cpsc.gov
Issues product safety alerts and
recalls.

Co-op America
1612 K St., NW, Ste. 600
Washington, DC 20006
(800) 58-GREEN; (202) 872-5307;
fax (202) 331-8166;
info@coopamerica.org;
www.coopamerica.org
Co-op America focuses on
developing a just and sustainable
economy by promoting socially
and environmentally responsible
businesses.
Publications: *National Green Pages,
Co-op America Quarterly,
Financial Planning Handbook*

Conservation International
2501 M St., NW, Ste. 200
Washington, DC 20037
(800) 429-5660; fax (202) 887-
0193; www.conservation.org
Conservation International focuses
on the conservation of
ecosystems and the preservation
of biological diversity. Emphasis
is on working with partner

organizations and locals in tropical and temperate countries to develop and implement ecosystem conservation projects. Publications: *CI News, In the Front*

Corporate Environmental Strategy: Elsevier's Journal of Environmental Leadership (CES)
www.elsevier.nl/inca/publications
International publication dedicated to describing the connection between environmental management and sound business strategy.

Council on Economic Priorities (CEP)
30 Irving Place
New York, NY 10003
(212) 420-1133; fax (212) 420-0988; cep@echonyc.com; www2.realaudio.com/cep/home.html
CEP evaluates and encourages corporate social and environmental responsibility. CEP has established the Corporate Environmental Data Clearinghouse, which profiles the environmental performance of hundreds of companies.
Publications: *Shopping for a Better World*

Development Center for Appropriate Technology (DCAT)
P.O. Box 41144
Tucson, AZ 85717
(520) 624-6628; fax (520) 798-3701; www. azstarnet.com/~dcat

DCAT is a nonprofit organization involved in research, testing, consulting, and development of green building codes. Emphasis is on appropriate sustainable building technologies.

Earth Architecture: An Overview WebPage
Rainforest Action Network
www.ran.org/ran/ran_campaigns /old_growth/earth_arc.html
Provides basic information on adobe, rammed earth, and plastered straw construction.

Earth Island Institute
300 Broadway, Ste. 28
San Francisco, CA 94133-3312
(415) 788-3666; fax (415) 788-7324; www.earthisland.org
The institute develops innovative projects for the conservation, preservation, and restoration of the global environment. Emphasis is on the International Marine Mammal Project, the Sea Turtle Restoration Project, Baikal Watch, Urban Habitat Program, and International Green Circle.
Publications: *Earth Island Journal*

Earthwatch Institute
P.O. Box 9104
Watertown, MA 02471
(800) 776-0188, (617) 926-8200; fax (617) 926-8532; www.earthwatch.org
Earthwatch focuses on archaeological finds, the study of pollution effects, and development of management plans to help alleviate crucial environmental problems.

Emphasis is on rain forests and endangered species.
Publications: *Earthwatch* (magazine)

Sustainable Architecture Building & Culture
P.O. Box 30085
Santa Barbara, California 93130
(805) 898-9660; fax (805) 898-9199; www.sustainableabc.com
Offers extensive links under a variety of topics.

Energy Crossroads
eetd.lbl.gov/CBS/eXroads/ EnergyXroads.html
This is Lawrence Berkeley National Laboratory's contribution to organizing a wide array of pointers to energy-efficient resources on the World Wide Web. It currently contains nearly 400 links to other Web sites.

Energy Efficient Building Association (EEBA)
P.O. Box 22307
Eagan, MN 55122-0307
(612) 994-1536; fax (612) 994-1914; info@eeba.org; www.eeba.org
EEBA is an international association focusing on the development and dissemination of information relevant to the design, construction, and operation of energy- and resource-efficient buildings. It also sponsors conferences and workshops.
Publications: *EEBA Excellence Journal* (quarterly); *Energy*

Efficient Building List; Builders Guide

Energy Ideas Clearinghouse
Operated by the Washington State University Cooperative Extension Energy Program
(800) 872-3568; www.energy.wsu.edu/eic
Established in 1990, the Energy Ideas Clearinghouse provides fast, centralized access to comprehensive and objective energy information, education, resources, and technical assistance.

Energy Outreach Center (EOC)
Olympic Renewable Resources Assoc.
610 E. 4th Ave.
Olympia, WA 98501
(360) 943-4595; fax (360) 943-4977; eoc@olywa.net; www.eoc.org/index.html
EOC provides information to the public about home energy conservation and renewable energy. Emphasis is on home energy analysis service, residential heat loss calculations, classes, and workshops, information center, newsletters, and research.
Publications: several

Environmental Access Research Network (EARN)
P.O. Box 426
Williston, ND 58802-0426
(701) 837-0161
A research and educational service that provides medical, legal, and governmental information

regarding the health effects of chemicals and related issues. Sponsored by the Chemical Injury Information Network (CIIN), a charitable support group.
Publications: *Our Toxic Times,* several other publications and databases

Environmental Building News (EBN)

122 Birge Street, Ste. 30
Brattleboro, VT 05301
(802) 257-7300; fax (802) 257-7304; info@ebuild.com
www.ebuild.com/
Provides articles, reviews, and news on energy-efficient, resource-efficient, and healthy building practices.
Publications: *Environmental Building News* magazine, *The Environmental Building News Product Catalog;* other: E Build Library CD-ROM; Green Building Advisor.™

Environmental Careers Organization (ECO)

179 South St.
Boston, MA 02111
(617) 426-4375; fax (617) 423-0998; www.eco.org
Resource for paid, professional-level positions of 3 to 24 months, with dozens of private, public, and nonprofit environmental employers. Emphasis is on college students and recent graduates. ECO has helped more than 5,500 people launch environmental careers since 1972.

Publications: The *New Complete Guide to Environmental Careers*

Environmental Defense Fund (EDF)

257 Park Ave. S.
New York, NY 10010
(212) 505-2100; fax (212) 505-2375; www.edf.org
EDF focuses on developing innovative, economically viable solutions to environmental problems by linking to science, economics, and law. Emphasis is on solid waste management, global climate change, tropical rain forest deforestation, and toxin control.

Environmental Health Foundation

1760 East River Road
Tucson, AZ 85718
(520) 577-7899, (602) 577-5225; fax (602) 577-5180
The foundation focuses on environmental health research and education. Emphasis is on long term effects of low-level toxic exposures, short- and long-term effects of various toxic exposures, "sick building syndrome," and environmentally related physical disorders experienced by many Vietnam and Persian Gulf War veterans.

Environmental Information Resources

The George Washington University Green University Initiative,
2121 Eye St. NW
Washington, DC 20052
www.gwu.edu/~greenu/index2.html

Provides environmental information, including pollution prevention and environmentally conscious manufacturing.

Environmental Law Institute (ELI)

1616 P St. NW, Ste. 200
Washington, DC 20036
(202) 939-3800; fax (202) 328-5002; www.eli.org
ELI provides information services, training courses and seminars, research programs, and policy recommendations to environmental professionals in government, industry, the private bar, public interest groups, and academia.
Publications: *Environmental Forum, The Environmental Law Reporter, National Wetlands Newsletter*

Earth's 911

(800) CLEANUP;
www.1800cleanup.org
The hotline is a public-private partnership with the EPA, Bank of America, Edison International, Sprint, and others. It provides recycling information and related small business information.

FacilitiesNet

www.facilitiesnet.com
This Web site is sponsored by Building Operating Management. It provides several energy-related links for products, organizations, state-specific lists of power organizations, legislative updates, and other energy information.

Public Citizen

1600 20th Street N.W.
Washington, DC 20009
(202) 588-1000;
www.publiccitizen.org
Produces the Renewable Energy Sourcebook.

Fish and Wildlife Reference Service

5430 Grosvenor Ln., Ste. 110
Bethesda, MD 20814
(301) 492-6403; fax (301) 564-4059; swrs@mail.sws.gov
The service maintains a clearinghouse of fish and wildlife management research reports. Emphasis is on fish and wildlife management and protection of endangered species.
Publications: *Fish and Wildlife Reference*

Friends of the Earth

1025 Vermont Ave., NW, 3rd Floor
Washington, DC 20005
(202) 783-7400; fax (202) 783-0444; foe@foe.org; www.foe.org
An advocacy group focusing on ozone depletion, agricultural biotechnology, toxic chemical safety, groundwater protection, nuclear weapons production wastes, tropical deforestation, and various international projects.
Publications: *Friends of the Earth Newsmagazine; Close to Home Newsletter*

Global Environment Options

www.geonetwork.org
A clearinghouse of information on sustainable buildings, development, and communities.

Global Environment Management Initiative (GEMI)
818 Connecticut Ave., NW, Second Floor
Washington, DC 20006
(202) 296-7449; fax (202) 296-7442; www.gemi.org
GEMI is a coalition of corporations that encourages and facilitates sharing information regarding processes and approaches to sound environmental management, including health and safety issues.

Global Network of Environment & Technology (GNET)
Global Environment & Technology Foundation,
7010 Little River Turnpike, Ste 300, Annandale, VA 22003.
(703) 750-6401; www.gnet.org
Conferencing system for technology issues.

Government Institutes, Inc.
4 Research Place
Rockville, MD 20850
(301) 921-2300; fax (301) 921-0373; www.govinst.com
Publishes a guide with Web site information about recycling and waste management.

GreenClips
(415) 928-7941; solstice.crest.org/sustainable/greenclips-info.html, www.greendesign.net/greenclips
GreenClips is a summary of of news on sustainable building design and related government and business issues.

Green Corps
1109 Walnut St.

Philadelphia, PA 19107
(215) 829-1760
The environmental movement's equivalent to the Peace Corps. The Green Corp training program teaches everything from how to organize effective mail campaigns to how to study a gas station's compliance with the Federal Clean Air Act.

Green Lights/Energy Star Buildings Programs
U.S. Environmental Protection Agency
401 M St. SW, 6202J
Washington, DC 20460
(202) 775-6650; fax (202) 775-6680; www.epa.gov/energystar.html and www.epa.gov/greenlights.html
Managed by the Atmospheric Pollution Prevention Division of the U.S. EPA, the Green Lights and Energy Star Buildings Programs seek to work cooperatively with companies, governments, and other institutions to encourage the use of energy-efficient lighting and other building technologies, including air conditioning and air distribution systems.
Publications: several

Greenpeace USA
1436 U St. NW
Washington, DC 20009
(202) 462-1177; fax (202) 462-4507; www.greenpeace.org
Greenpeace is an international organization dedicated to protecting the environment. Emphasis is on campaigns to eliminate nuclear and toxic

pollution, protect marine ecology, and end atmospheric destruction.
Publications: *Greenpeace*

Green Seal
1001 Connecticut Ave., NW, Suite 827
Washington, DC 20036-5525
(202) 872-6400; fax (202) 872-4324; www.greenseal.org
Green Seal is a nonprofit organization dedicated to protecting the environment by promoting the manufacture and sale of environmentally responsible consumer products (including doors, windows, and appliances). It develops environmental standards and awards a Green Seal of Approval to products that cause less harm to the environment than the conventional products that they replace
Publications: Several, including standards for environmental consumer products. The Web site defines standards for environmentally responsible products as well as providing general information on health concerns, energy efficiency, and so on. A list of products with Green Seal certification is also provided.

Greenware Environmental Systems Inc.
145 King Street East, Suite 200
Toronto, Ontario, M5C 2Y8
(416) 363-5577; fax (416) 367-2653; www.greenware.ca
Provides concise overview of environmental accounting from quarterly journal.

Greenwire
www.cloakroom.com
Subscription service gives daily briefing on environmental news.

Home Energy Rating Systems (HERS) Council
1331 H Street N.W., Suite 1000,
Washington, DC 20005
(202) 638-3700; fax (202) 393-5043; e-mail: HERSCDC@aol.com; www.hers-council.org

The Institute for Earth Education
Cedar Cove
Greenville, WV 24945
(304) 832-6404; fax (304) 832-6077; IEE1@aol.com; http://sInet.com/cipliee
The institute focuses on developing and disseminating educational programs to promote harmony with the Earth. Emphasis is on Earth education program development and support for teachers and leaders.
Publications: *Talking Leaves*

Institute for Local Self-Reliance (ILSR)
2425 Eighteenth St. NW
Washington, DC 20009-2096
(202) 232-4108; fax (202) 332-0463; ILSR@IGC.APC.org; www.ilsr.org
ILSR works with nonprofit organizations, businesses, and government toward self-reliance through resource management. It offers technical assistance, organizes conferences, conducts research, analyzes public policy issues, and disseminates information.

Publications: several

Institute of Scrap Recycling Industries, Inc. (ISRI)
1325 G St. NW, Ste. 1000
Washington, DC 20005-3104
(202) 737-1770; fax (202) 626-0900; www.isri.org
This trade association represents processors, brokers, and consumers of scrap commodities, including metals, paper, plastics, glass, and textiles, as well as suppliers of equipment and services to the industry.
Publications: *SCRAP* (bimonthly magazine)

International Alliance for Sustainable Agriculture
1701 University Ave. SE
Minneapolis, MN 55414
(612) 331-1099; fax (612) 379-1527; IASA@MTN.org; www.mtn.org/iasa
The alliance focuses on the development of sustainable agriculture. Emphasis is on publication of a national directory on humane sustainable agriculture.
Publications: *Planting a Future: A Resource Guide to Sustainable Agriculture in the Third World, Manna* (quarterly)

International Institute for Bau-biologie® and Ecology (IBE)
P.O. Box 387
Clearwater, FL 33757
(813) 461-4371; fax (813) 441-4377; baubiologie@earthlink.net; www.bau-biologieusa.com
The institute focuses on the education of the building industry and the public regarding healthy houses. Emphasis is on electromagnetic radiation and the offgassing of building materials.

International Institute for Sustainable Development (IISD)
161 Portage Ave. E., 6th Fl.
Winnipeg, Manitoba R3B OY4, Canada
(204) 958-7700; fax (204) 958-7710; www.iisd1.iisd.ca/
IISD promotes sustainable development in decision making within government, business, and the daily lives of individuals. Emphasis is on policy research, international trade, business strategy, and national budgets.

Investor Responsibility Research Center (IRRC)
1350 Connecticut Ave. NW, Ste. 700
Washington, DC 20036
(202) 833-0700; fax (202) 833-3555; irc@aol.com
The center maintains an Environmental Information Service with corporate profiles detailing the environmental activities of major U.S. companies.
Publications: *Investor's Environmental Report* (newsletter)

ISO 14000 Infocenter
www.iso14000.com/
Covers ISO environmental management standards.

Journal of Industrial Ecology
MIT Press Journals
Five Cambridge Center
Cambridge, MA 02142-1407

(617) 253-2889; fax (617) 577-
1545; mitpress.rait.edu/journal-
home.tcl?issn=10881980
International, multidisciplinary
quarterly designed to foster both
understanding and practice in the
emerging field of industrial
ecology.

Keep America Beautiful, Inc. (KAB)

1010 Washington Blvd.
Stamford, CT 06901
(203) 323-8987; fax (203) 325-
9199; keepamerbe@aol.com; http:
//204.127.239.150/index.html
KAB focuses on improving waste-
handling practices in American
communities. It is a national
organization with 500 local
affiliates in 41 states, including
21 official statewide affiliates.

The Land Institute

2440 E. Water Well Rd.
Salina, KS 67401
(785) 823-5376; fax (785) 823-
8728; theland@midkan.com;
www.midkan.com/theland/
The institute conducts sustainable
agriculture research. Emphasis is
on genetic diversity, land
stewardship, and alternative
agriculture.
Publications: *The Land Report*
(newsletter)

Land Trust Alliance (LTA)

1319 F St. NW, Ste. 501
Washington, DC 20004
(202) 638-4725; fax (202) 638-
4730; www.lta.org
The alliance provides technical
assistance for land trusts and
other land conservation

professionals, fosters public
policies supportive of land
conservation, and builds public
awareness of land trusts and their
goals.
Publications: *Exchange* (quarterly),
*National Directory of Conservation
Land Trusts*

League of Conservation Voters (LCV)

1707 L St. NW, Ste. 750
Washington, DC 20036
(202) 785-8683; fax (202) 835-
0491; www.lcv.org
The league is a national,
nonpartisan organization that
seeks to have proenvironmental
issues better represented in the
U.S. Congress. Emphasis is on
endorsing and supporting
candidates for election to the
U.S. House and Senate.

Management Institute for Environment and Business

10 G Street, NE, Suite 800
Washington, DC 20002
(202) 729-7600; fax (202) 737-
1510; www.wri.org/wri/meb/
Provides abstracts of cases.

Million Solar Roofs Initiative

www.eren.doe.gov/millionroofs
Supports U.S. goal for businesses
and communities to install solar
panels on 1 million rooftops
across America by 2010.
Coordinated through the
Department of Energy's Regional
Support Offices located
throughout the United States.

MIT Technology, Business and Environment Program

tbe.mit.edu
Offers product and industrial design
information.

The National Arbor Day Foundation
100 Arbor Avenue
Nebraska City, NE 68410
(402) 474-5655; fax (402) 474-
0820; www.arborday.org
The foundation is dedicated to tree
planting and environmental
stewardship. Emphasis is on
community programs such as
Trees for America and the
National Arbor Day Program.
Publications: *Arbor Day*

National Association of Conservation Districts (NACD)
509 Capitol Court, NE
Washington, DC 20002-4946
(202) 547-6223; fax (202) 547-
6450; www.nacdnet.org
The association promotes
conservation, management, and
orderly development of America's
natural resources.
Publications: *Forestry Notes; The
District Leader*

National Association of Regulatory Utility Commissioners
1100 Pennsylvania Avvenue
N.W., Suite 603
P.O. Box 684
Washington, DC 20044-0684
(202) 898-220; fax (202) 898-2213;
www.naruc.org
Provides links to state public utility
commissions and other industry
and association sites. It also
features news items on regulatory
issues.

National Audubon Society
700 Broadway
New York, NY 10003
(212) 979-3000; fax (212) 979-
3188; www.audubon.org
The society focuses on protecting
wildlife and its habitats through
research, lobbying, litigation, and
citizen action. Emphasis is on
ancient forests, wetlands,
endangered species, Arctic
National Wildlife Refuge, Platte
River, the Everglades and the
Adirondack Park.

The National Coalition Against the Misuse of Pesticides
701 E. St. SE, Ste. 200
Washington, DC 20003
(202) 543-5450; fax (202) 543-
4791; ncamp@ncamp.org;
www.ncamp.org
The coalition focuses on pesticide
safety and the adoption of
alternative pest management
strategies that reduce or eliminate
dependency on toxic chemicals.
Emphasis is on effecting a
change through local action and
providing assistance to
individuals and community
organizations.
Publications: several

National Energy Information Center
1F-048 Forrestal Building
1000 Independence Ave. SW
Washington, DC 20585
(202) 586-8800; fax (202) 586-
0727; www.eia.doe.gov
The center provides information on
Department of Energy (DOE)
programs, and distributes fact
sheets and publications on energy

resources, consumption, imports, exports, and related economic and statistical information.
Publications: several

National Environmental Balancing Bureau (NEBB)
8575 Grovemont Circle
Gaithersburg, MD 20877
(301) 977-3698; fax (301) 977-9589; www.nebb.org
NEBB is a professional organization of consultants and contractors in the HVAC and mechanical profession. Many provide commissioning services.
Publications: several

National Ground Water Association (NGWA)
601 Dempsey Road
Westerville, OH 43081
(800) 551-7379, (614) 898-7791; fax (614) 898-7786; www.ngwa.org
NGWA is a nonprofit, international, professional society for the groundwater industry. NGWA provides leadership and guidance for sound, scientific, and economic management of our underground resources.
Publications: several

National Materials Exchange Network (NMEN)
4708 E. Jaremko Street
Mead, WA 99201
(509) 466-1532; fax (509) 466-1041; www.earthcycle.com/nmen
NMEN publicizes unwanted materials to potential users for reuse and recycling. It lists more than 11,000 entries in material categories on the Internet,

including construction materials, paint and coatings, and construction equipment.

National Pesticides Telecommunications Network (NPTN)
Oregon State University
333 Weniger
Corvallis, OR 97331-6502
(800) 858-PEST; fax (541) 737-0761; nptn@ace.orst.edu; ace.orst.edu/info/nptn/index.html
The network provides information about pesticides and how to recognize/respond to poisonings.
Publications: Fact sheets, available on Web site.

National Lead Information Center and Clearinghouse (NLIC)
8601 Georgia Ave, Suite 503
Silver Spring, MD 20910
(800) 424-LEAD; fax (301) 585-7976; www.epa.gov//lead/nlic.htm; www.nsc.org/ehc/lead.htm
The center provides lead information and state contacts for local information. It also operates a clearinghouse that provides a list of laboratories that can analyze paint and dust samples for lead.
Publications: several

The National Safety Council's Environmental Health Center (EHC) National Radon Hotline
1025 Connecticut Ave., N.W. Suite 1200
Washington, DC 20036
(800) 505-radon; fax (202) 293-0032

Provides information about radon to callers

National Solid Wastes Management Association (NSWMA)
4301 Connecticut Ave. NW, Ste. 300
Washington, DC 20008
(202) 244-4700; fax (202) 966-4841; www.envasns.org/nswma
The National Solid Wastes Management Association represents the interests of those with responsibilities for the management of solid wastes in public agencies.
Publications: *Waste Age* (monthly magazine), *Recycling Times* (biweekly newspaper)

National Trust for Historic Preservation
1785 Massachusetts Ave. NW
Washington, DC 20036
(202) 673-4000; fax (202) 673-4038; www.nthp.org
The mission of the National Trust is to foster an appreciation of the diverse character and meaning of our American cultural heritage, and to preserve and revitalize the livability of our communities by leading the nation in saving America's historic environments. It has seven regional offices, owns 18 historic house museums, and works with thousands of local community groups in all 50 states. It also provides technical advice and financial assistance; sponsors educational programs, technical workshops, and an

annual preservation conference; advocates for protection of the country's heritage in the courts and with legislative and regulatory agencies; sponsors programs to demonstrate how preservation can stimulate community revitalization and economic development; owns and operates historic house museums.
Publications: *Historic Preservation* (bimonthly magazine), *Historic Preservation News* (monthly newspaper), *Preservation Law Reporter* (legal quarterly), *Historic Preservation Forum* (bimonthly journal), books and brochures on a variety of related topics

Lady Bird Johnson Wildflower Center
4801 Lacrosse Avenue
Austin, TX 78739
(512) 292-4100; fax (512) 292-4627; www.wildflower.org
Promotes the preservation and reestablishment of native wildflowers, grasses, shrubs and trees in North America. Emphasis is on public education on native plants and incorporating native plants in the repair of ecosystems.

National Wildlife Federation (NWF)
8925 Leesburg Pike
Vienna, VA 22184
(800) 822-9919; fax (703) 790-4040; www.nwf.org
Promotes conservation, responsible use of natural resources, and

protection of the global
environment. The federation
distributes education materials,
sponsors nature programs, lobbies
Congress, and litigates
environmental disputes. Emphasis
is on endangered species, forests,
wetlands and water resources,
grazing and mining reform,
biotechnology, toxic pollution
sunsetting, and backyard habitat
program.
Publications: *National Wildlife*
(bimonthly magazine), *The
Conservation Directory*

Native Seeds/SEARCH
526 N. 4th Avenue
Tucson, AZ 85705-8450
(520) 622-5561; fax (520) 622-
5591; desert.net/seeds/home.htm
A conservation organization that
preserves seeds of crops grown
by Native Americans in the
Southwest United States,
including more than 200 varieties
of vegetables, such as corn and
squash. Promotes the use of
traditional desert foods to prevent
and control diabetes.
Publications: *Native Seed/SEARCH
Seed Listing*

**Natural Resources Defense
Council (NRDC)**
40 W. 20th St.
New York, NY 10011
(212) 727-2700; fax (212) 727-
1773; www.nrdc.org
Protects America's natural resources
through legal action, scientific
research, and citizen education.
Emphasis is on energy policy and

nuclear safety, air and water
pollution, urban transportation
issues, pesticides and toxic
substances, forest protection,
global warming, and the
international environment.
Publications: *Amicus Journal*

The Natural Step (TNS)
P.O. Box 29372
San Francisco, CA 94129-0372
(415) 561-3344; fax (415) 561-
3345; tns@naturalstep.org;
www.naturalstep.org
TNS is an educational organization
that uses consensus building to
help guide businesses,
communities, governmental
agencies, and individuals toward
sustainability.

The Nature Conservancy
4245 North Fairfax Drive, Suite 100
Arlington, VA 22203-1606
(703) 841-5300; fax (703) 841-
1283; www.tnc.org
Conserves plants, animals, and
natural communities that
represent the diversity of life on
Earth by protecting the habitats
they need to survive. Manages a
system of more than 1,300 nature
sanctuaries in all 50 states.
Emphasis is on demonstrating
that biodiversity protection can
also accommodate human
economic and cultural needs.
Publications: *Nature Conservancy
Magazine*

**Northeast Recycling Council
(NERC)**
139 Main Street, Suite 401

Brattleboro, VT 05301
(802) 254-3636; fax (802) 254-5870; www.nerc.org/
NERC provides information on regional recycling issues and state programs
Publications: *NERC News*

Northeast Sustainable Energy Association (NESEA)
50 Miles St.
Greenfield, MA 01301
(413) 774-6051; fax (413) 774-6053; www.nesea.org
NESEA promotes energy efficiency, sustainable energy design, and the use of renewable energy. Sponsors annual conferences on green building. NESEA offices are in the Northeast Sustainability Center, an evolving project that will serve as a renewable energy design model.
Publications: *Northeast Sun* (quarterly magazine); *NESEA News*

Nuclear Information and Resource Service (NIRS)
1424 16th St. NW, Ste. 404
Washington, DC 20036
(202) 328-0002; fax (202) 462-2183; nirsnet@nirs.org;
www.nirs.org
Serves as a networking information clearinghouse for environmental activists concerned with nuclear power and waste issues. Emphasis is on challenging radioactive waste policy; publication of energy audit manual for towns and universities; and preventing new nuclear reactors.

Publications: *The Nuclear Monitor* (monthly newsletter)

Oikos Green Building Source Published by Iris Communications, Inc.,
P.O. Box 5920
Eugene, OR 97405-0911
(541) 767-0355; fax (541) 767-0357; e-mail: iris@oikos.com;
www.oikos.com/
Provides information on energy efficiency and sustainable building construction. Includes the REDI 96 database of 1,700 companies for green building products. Search by topic.

The Passive Solar Industries Council (PSIC)
1511 K St. NW, Ste. 600
Washington, DC 20005
(202) 628-7400; fax (202) 393-5043; www.psic.org
The council promotes the affordable, environmentally sound design of residential, institutional, and commercial buildings. PSIC offers professional training, consumer education, and analysis tools nationwide for passive solar design and product information.
Publications: *Building Inside and Out*

Photovoltaic Systems Assistance Center (PVSAC)
Sandia National Laboratories
P.O. Box 5800, Mail Stop 0753
Albuquerque, NM 87185-0753
(505) 844-1548
The center offers information and assistance to the photovoltaic industry, public utilities, and system designers, and maintains a

database on the performance of
photovoltaic systems.

**Physicians for Social
Responsibility**
1101 Fourteenth St. NW, Ste. 700
Washington, DC 20005
(202) 898-0150; fax (202) 898-
0172; www.psr.org
Committed to eliminating weapons
of mass destruction, preserving a
sustainable environment, and
reducing violence and its causes.
Uses its members' expertise and
professional leadership influence
within the medical community
and strong links to policymakers
to address threats to human
welfare and survival. PSR is the
U.S. affiliate of International
Physicians for the Prevention of
Nuclear War, a network of
200,000 physicians in 80
countries. They work to protect
people from environmental health
hazards; to shift government
spending priorities away from
wasteful military expenditures; to
educate the medical community,
public, policymakers, and the
media about the human costs of
unnecessary military spending
and the environmental crisis; to
research the health effects of
environmental degradation; and to
promote international cooperation
and local community action.
Publications: *Medicine and Global
Survival* (quarterly international
journal), *PSR Monitor* (bulletin),
PSR Reports (members-only
newsletter)

**Plants for Clean Air Council
(PCAC)**

3458 Godspeed Road
Davidsonville, MD 21035
(410) 956-9036; fax (410) 956-
9039; www.plants4cleanair.org
Provides information regarding the
use of plants in removing certain
toxins from indoor air.

Pollution Prevention Yellow Pages
www2.southwind.net/~ebase/Lib/
Guides/Pollution/PollPreYell.txt
This is a directory of state and local
pollution prevention programs.

Population Action International
1120 19th St. NW, #550
Washington, DC 20036
(202) 659-1833; fax (202) 293-
1795; www.populationaction.org
Promotes public awareness,
population growth reduction
programs, and voluntary access to
family planning services.
Emphasis is on the relationship
between population and
environmental degradation.
Publications: several

**President's Council on
Sustainable Development**
730 Jackson Place, NW
Washington, DC 20503
(202) 408-5296; fax (202) 408-
6839; www.whitehouse.gov/pcsd/
The leading multiparty organization
in the United States on
sustainable development. Site
provides information on
sustainable development and
governmental policy in the
United States.
Publications: several

Rails-to-Trails Conservancy
1100 17th St. NW, 10th floor

Washington, DC 20036
(202) 331-9696; fax (202) 331-9680; RTCMail@Transact.org; www.railtrails.org
The conservancy seeks to convert thousands of miles of abandoned railroad corridors to public trails for walking, bicycling, horseback riding, cross-country skiing, wildlife habitat, and nature appreciation. Emphasis is on linking major metropolitan areas via rail-trails.
Publications: several

Rainforest Action Network (RAN)
221 Pine St., Ste 500
San Francisco, CA 94104
(415) 398-4404; fax (415) 398-2732; rainforest@ran.org; www.ran.org
The network works internationally in cooperation with other environmental and human rights organizations to protect rain forests. Emphasis is on Hawaii, Amazonia, and Southeast Asia.
Publications: *The World Rainforest Report*

Rainforest Alliance
65 Bleecker St.
New York, NY 10012
(212) 677-1900; fax (212) 677-2187; canopy@ra.org; www.rainforest-alliance.org
Promotes the conservation of the world's tropical forests by developing sound alternatives to the activities that cause tropical deforestation. Also provides public education for conservation. Emphasis is on "Smart Wood" certification, medicinal plant

projects, and nontimber forest products.
Publications: *Eco-Exchange*

Reef Relief
P.O. Box 430
Key West, FL 33041
(305) 294-3100; fax (305) 293-9515; reef@bellsouth.net; www.reefrelief.org
Protects the living coral reef of the Florida Keys. Emphasis is on regional public education and outreach programs to protect the coral reefs.
Publications: *ReefLine* (quarterly newsletter)

Renew America
1200 18th St. NW, Ste. 1100
Washington, DC 20036
(202) 721-1545; fax (202) 467-5780; renewamerica@counterpart.org; solstice.crest.org/environment/renew_america
Seeks to renew America's community spirit through environmental success. Emphasis is on identification, verification, and promotion of successful environmental programs in 20 categories, ranging from air pollution reduction to wildlife conservation.
Publications: *Environmental Success Index* (annual publication)

Resources for Global Sustainability
P.O. Box 3665
Cary, NC 27519-3665
(800) 724-1857; fax (919) 319-927; rgs@environmentalgrants.com; www.environmentalgrants.com

Focuses on disseminating information on funding to the environmental community. Maintains a large database on environmental grants.

Publications: *Environmental Grantmaking Foundations*

Rocky Mountain Institute (RMI)

1739 Snowmass Creek Rd.
Snowmass, CO 81654-9199
(970) 927-3851; fax (927) 927-3420; http://www.rmi.org

RMI's Green Development Services program researches environmentally and economically feasible opportunities for the building industry.

Publications: several

Save the Dunes Council, Inc.

444 Barker Rd.
Michigan City, IN 46360
(219) 879-3937; fax (219) 872-4875; std@savedunes.org; savedunes.org

Protects the Indiana dunes for public use and enjoyment by promoting the control of air, water, and waste pollution. Emphasis is on erosion and policy issues affecting the Indiana Lake Michigan shoreline, wetlands preservation, and groundwater protection.

Scenic America

801 Pennsylvania Avenue, SE
Washington, DC 20003
(202) 543-6200; fax (202) 543-9130; scenic@scenic.org; www.scenic.org

Preserves the scenic quality of America's communities and countryside. Provides information and technical assistance on scenic byways, tree preservation, economics of aesthetic regulation, and billboard and sign control.

Publications: *Viewpoints; The Grassroots Advocate*

Scientific Certification Systems, Inc, (SCS)

Park Plaza Building
1939 Harrison Street, Suite 400
Oakland, CA 94612
(510) 832-1415; fax (510) 832-0359; www.scs1.com

SCS is a for-profit, third-party certification organization that evaluates and certifies environmental claims made by manufacturers. Manufacturers may include the SCS label on their products. SCS will not release proprietary information, but will share the standards and processes used for evaluation. For example, the Forest Stewardship Council principles are used for the SCS Forestry Program.

Publications: Environmental Claims Program List of Certified Products & Claims; Forestry Management Program information

Sierra Club

85 Second St., 2nd floor
San Francisco, CA 94105-3441
(415) 977-5500; fax (415) 977-5799; www.sierraclub.org

Protects the wild places of the Earth and promotes the responsible use of the Earth's ecosystems and resources by educating the public. Emphasis is on old-growth forest protection, global warming,

wilderness/national parks
protection, toxic waste
regulations, and international
development lending.
Publications: *Sierra Magazine*

**Soil and Water Conservation
Society**
7515 NE Ankeny Rd.
Ankeny, IA 50021-9764
(515) 289-2331; fax (515) 289-
1227; swcs@swcs.org;
www.swcs.org
Promotes the conservation of soil,
water and related natural
resources.
Publications: *The Journal of Soil
and Water Conservation,
Conservation Voices Listening to
the Land*

**Southwest Network for
Environmental and Economic
Justice**
P.O. Box 7399
Albuquerque, NM 87194
(505) 242-0416; fax (505) 242-5609
The network supports the direct link
between economic and
environmental issues. It brings
together activists and grass-roots
organizations to address social,
racial, and economic injustices.
Emphasis is on EPA.

Steel Recycling Institute
680 Andersen Dr.
Pittsburgh, PA 15220-2700
(800) 876-7274, (800) 937-1226
(database); fax (412) 922-3213;
sri@recycle-steel.org;
www.recycle-steel.org
SRI maintains a database for
consumers seeking the nearest
location to recycle steel cans.

Publications: *The Recycling Magnet*
(quarterly newsletter)

**The Student Conservation
Association, Inc. (SCA)**
P.O. Box 550
Charlestown, NH 03603-0550
(603) 543-1700; fax (603) 543-
1828; www.sca-inc.org
Provides educational opportunities
for volunteers to assist with the
stewardship of public lands and
natural resources. Emphasis is on
encouraging youth (particularly
minorities and women) to pursue
careers in conservation and
resource management.
Publications: *Earth Work* (monthly
magazine)

TreePeople
12601 Mulholland Dr.
Beverly Hills, CA 90210
(818) 753-4600; fax (818) 753-4625
Urban forestry organization that
focuses on tree planting and
environmental education.
Emphasis is on training
volunteers as urban foresters.
Publications: *Seedling News*
(quarterly newsletter)

**Triangle J Council of
Governments**
4222 Emperor Blvd., Suite 200
P.O. Box 12276
Research Triangle Park, NC 27709
(919) 549-0551; fax (919) 549-
9390; www.tjcog.dst.nc.us
The council is an organization of
regional agencies involved in
economic and environmental
concerns.
Publications: several

Tropical Forest Foundation (TFF)
225 Reinekers Lane, Ste 770
Alexandria, VA 22314
(703) 518-8834; fax (703) 518-8974; tss@igc.apc.org
TFF is a coalition of industry, association, and environmental groups that focuses on preservation of tropical forests through sustainable forestry.

The Trust for Public Land (TPL)
116 New Montgomery St., 4th fl.
San Francisco, CA 94105
(415) 495-4014; fax (415) 495-4103; mailbox@tpl.org; www.tpl.org
TPL assists public agencies and communities in acquiring and protecting land of recreational, ecological, and cultural value for the public. Specializing in urban open space, TPL provides education and assistance for nonprofit land acquisition processes.
Publications: *Land and People*

Union of Concerned Scientists (UCS)
2 Brattle Square
Cambridge, MA 02238
(617) 547-5552; fax (617) 864-9405; ucs@ucsusa.org; www.ucsusa.org
UCS investigates the impact of advanced technology on society, focusing on energy policy, global environmental problems and arms control.
Publications: *Nucleus* (quarterly magazine)

United Nations Development Programme

www.un.org/undp/ppp/
Information on public/private partnerships for the urban environment and sustainable energy.

United Nations Environment Programme (UNEP)
Room DC2-0803, United Nations
New York, NY 10017
(212) 963-8138; fax (212) 963-7341; jfp@un.org
UNEP is the environmental agency of the United Nations. It helps to develop and coordinate environmental policies at the municipal, national, regional, and international levels by working with scientific agencies, the private and public sectors, nongovernmental organizations, legal institutions and others.
Publications: *Our Planet* (magazine), *Annual Report of the Executive Director,* and various regional and specialized newsletters

United Nations Population Fund (UNFPA)
220 E. 42nd St.
New York, NY 10017
(212) 297-5000; fax (212) 557-6416; www.unfpa.org
UNFPA assists developing countries with their population problems, and plays a leading role in the UN system in promoting population programs.
Publications: *Populi* (monthly), *The State of World Population* (annual report)

United Nations Commission on Sustainable Development

2 UN Plaza, Room DC2-2220,
New York, NY 10017
(212) 963-3170; fax (212) 963-
4260; www.un.org/esa/sustdev/
csd.htm
Provides information on initiatives
such as Agenda 21, Rio
Declaration, Conservation and
Sustainable Development of
Forests.

**U.S. Department of Commerce
(DOC), National Technical
Information Service**
Technology Administration
Springfield, VA 22161
(703) 605-6000, (703) 487-4650;
www.ntis.gov
Federal Government's central source
for the sale of scientific,
technical, engineering, and
related business information
produced by or for the U.S.
Government.

**U.S. Department of Energy
(DOE), Center of Excellence for
Sustainable Development**
Office of Energy Efficiency &
Renewable Energy,
Denver Regional Support Office,
1617 Cole Blvd.
Golden, CO 80401
(800) 363-3732; fax (303) 275-
4830; e-mail: sustainable.
development@hq.doe.gov;
www.sustainable.doe.gov
Provides energy efficiency and
renewable energy information.

**U.S. Department of Energy
(DOE), Energy Efficiency and
Renewable Energy
Clearinghouse (EREC)**
P.O. Box 3048

Herrifield, VA 22116
(800) 363-3732; fax (703) 893-
0400; doe.erec@nciinc.com;
www.eren.doe.gov/consumerinfo/
erec.html
The EREC provides information on
energy efficiency and energy
technology.
Publications: several

**U.S. Department of Energy
(DOE), National Energy
Information Center**
IF-048 Forrestal Building
1000 Independence Avenue, SW
Washington, DC 20585
(202) 586-8800;
infoctr@eia.doe.gov
Provides information on Department
of Energy (DOE) programs, and
distributes fact sheets and
publications on energy resources,
consumption, imports, exports,
and related economic and
statistical information.

**U.S. Department of Energy
(DOE), National Renewable
Energy Laboratory (NREL)**
1617 Cole Blvd.
Golden, CO 80401
(303) 275-3000; fax (303) 275-
4053; www.nrel.gov
NREL is a leading laboratory for
research and development of
renewable energy technologies.
Projects include energy-efficient
design and engineering of passive
and active solar buildings.

**U.S. Environmental Protection
Agency (EPA)**
401 M Street S.W.
Washington, DC 20460
www.epa.gov

Information for citizens, educators, researchers, government, and business. Provides information on EPA programs, initiatives, and publications.

U.S. Environmental Protection Agency (EPA), Asbestos Abatement/Management Ombudsman
Same as above—Mail Code 123QC
(800) 368-5888; fax (703) 305-6462; www.epa.gov
Provides the public sector informaiton on handling, abating, and managing asbestos.

U.S. Environmental Protection Agency (EPA), Indoor Air Quality Information Clearinghouse
P.O. Box 37133
Washington, DC 20013-7133
(800) 438-4318; fax (202) 484-1510; www.epa.gov/iedweb00/iaginfo.html
Information specialists provide information, referrals, publications, and database searches on indoor air quality. Information includes pollutants and sources, health effects, control methods, commercial building operations and maintenance, standards and guidelines, and federal and state legislation. The clearinghouse can also provide information on constructing and maintaining homes and buildings to minimize indoor air quality problems.

U.S. Environmental Protection Agency (EPA), Municipal Solid Waste Factbook

National Service Center for Environmental Publications
P.O. Box 42419
Cincinnati, OH 45242-2419;
www.epa.gov/epaoswer/non-hw/muncpl/factbook/index
(800) 490-9198; fax (513) 489-8695
Provides statistics on waste generation international material recycling rates, source reduction, and composting all available on disk. Also offers state-by-state stats on recycling rates, programs, contacts.

U.S. Environmental Protection Agency (EPA), Office of Ground Water and Drinking Water
(202) 260-5543; fax (202) 260-4383; www.epa.gov/OGWDW
This office works with states, tribes, and partners, to protect public health by ensuring safe drinking water and protecting groundwater.

U.S. Environmental Protection Agency (EPA), Office of Science and Technology
(202) 260-5400; www.epa.gov/ost
Develops sound, scientifically defensible standards, criteria, advisories, guidelines, limitations and standards guidelines.

U.S. Environmental Protection Agency (EPA), Office of Solid Waste and Emergency Response
(800) 424-9346; www.epa.gov/swerrims/index.htm
This office develops guidelines and standards for land disposal of hazardous wastes and underground storage tanks.

U.S. Environmental Protection Agency (EPA), Office of Wastewater Management
(202) 260-5850; www.epa.gov/owm

U.S. Environmental Protection Agency (EPA), Office of Wetlands, Oceans, and Watersheds
202-260-7166; www.epa.gov/
owowwtr1/tours/index.html
Seeks to create an industry-by-industry, consensus-building approach to environmental protection that is cleaner for the environment and cheaper for industries and taxpayers.

U.S. Environmental Protection Agency (EPA), Safe Drinking Water Hotline
(800) 426-4791; fax (703) 285-1101; www.epa.gov/watrhome/pubs/drinklink.html
Provides information about EPA's drinking water regulations and other related drinking water & ground water topics.

U.S. Environmental Protection Agency (EPA), $mart Growth Network
www.smartgrowth.org
For government, business, and civic sector leaders interested in creating metropolitan areas, cities, and towns that are environmentally, economically, and socially "smart."

U.S. Environmental Protection Agency, EPA Region 1
John F. Kennedy Federal Building
One Congress St.
Boston, MA 02203
(617) 565-3420
Region 1 includes: Connecticut, Maine, Massachusetts, New Hampshire, Rhode Island, and Vermont

U.S. Environmental Protection Agency, EPA Region 2
290 Broadway
New York, NY 10007-1866
(212) 637-4316
Region 2 includes: New Jersey, New York, Puerto Rico, and the Virgin Islands.

U.S. Environmental Protection Agency, EPA Region 3
841 Chestnut Building
Philadelphia, PA 19107
(215) 597-9800
Region 3 includes: Delaware, District of Columbia, Maryland, Pennsylvania, Virginia, and West Virginia.

U.S. Environmental Protection Agency, EPA Region 4
345 Courtland St., NE
Atlanta, GA 30365
(404) 347-4727
Region 4 includes: Alabama, Florida, Georgia, Kentucky, Mississippi, North Carolina, South Carolina, and Tennessee.

U.S. Environmental Protection Agency, EPA Region 5
77 West Jackson Boulevard
Chicago, IL 60604-3507
(312) 353-2000
Region 5 includes: Illinois, Indiana, Michigan, Minnesota, Ohio, and Wisconsin.

U.S. Environmental Protection Agency, EPA Region 6
First Interstate Bank Tower at Fountain Place
1445 Ross Avenue, 12th Floor, Ste. 1200
Dallas, TX 75202-2733
(214) 665-6444
Region 6 includes: Arkansas, Louisiana, New Mexico, Oklahoma, and Texas.

U.S. Environmental Protection Agency, EPA Region 7
726 Minnesota Avenue
Kansas City, KS 66101
(913) 551-7000
Region 7 includes: Iowa, Kansas, Missouri, and Nebraska.

U.S. Environmental Protection Agency, EPA Region 8
999 Eighteenth Street, Suite 500
Denver, CO 80202-2466
(303) 312-6312
Region 8 includes: Colorado, Montana, North Dakota, South Dakota, Utah, and Wyoming.

U.S. Environmental Protection Agency, EPA Region 9
75 Hawthorne St.
San Francisco, CA 94105
(415) 744-1305
Region 9 includes: Arizona, California, Hawaii, Nevada, American Samoa, and Guam.

U.S. Environmental Protection Agency, EPA Region 10
1200 Sixth Avenue
Seattle, WA 98101
(206) 553-1200

Region 10 includes: Alaska, Idaho, Oregon, and Washington.

U.S. Green Building Council
110 Sutter Street, Suite 906
San Francisco, CA 94104
(415) 445-9500; fax (415) 445-9911; www.usgbc.org
The council is a national, environmentally focused coalition of industry, professional, and environmental organizations that promotes green building policies, programs, and technologies. Emphasis is on the National Green Building Resource Center, National Green Building Rating System, and conferences.

U.S. House of Representatives, Law Library/Bill Status
(202) 225-1772; fax (202) 226-1399; law.house.gov/
Provides information regarding pending legislation, including environmental legislation. As there may be hundreds of bills pending, be specific in requests for information.

U.S. Office of Science and Technology Policy (White House)
Environmental Technology Strategy Staff Office of Science & Technology Policy
Room 443, Old Executive Office Bldg.
Washington, DC 20500
(202) 456-6202; www.whitehouse.gov/WH/EOP/OSTP
The Office's Environment Division provides research and

development on the environment and natural resource issues.

U.S. RCRA, Superfund & EPCRA Hotline

800-424-9346; www.epa.gov/ epaoswer/hotline/index.htm

The hotline is a publicly-accessible service that provides up-to-date information on several EPA programs.

Urban Ecology, Inc.

405 14th St., Ste 701
Oakland, CA 94612-2706
(510) 251-6330

Urban Ecology is an international organization dedicated to creating sustainable cities through use of ecology principles in urban planning and development. Emphasis is on land use planning, transportation, restoration, international education, and eco-city research.

Publications: *The Urban Ecologist* (quarterly newsletter)

Vanderbilt University Center for Environmental Management Studies

www.vanderbilt.edu/VCEMS/ VCEMShome.html

Provides centralized links to corporate environmental reports online.

Webdirectory

www.webdirectory.com/ General_Environment_ Interest_Groups/Offers links to environmental organizations.

The Wilderness Society

900 17th St. NW
Washington, DC 20006
(800) THE-WILD, (202) 833-2300; fax (202) 429-3959; www.tws.org; tws@tws.org

Protects wildlands and wildlife. Emphasis is on Arctic Wildlife Refuge, national forest policy, national parks, endangered species protection, and economics of public land use.

Publications: *Wilderness Year* (quarterly magazine)

The Wildlife Society

5410 Grosvenor Ln., Suite 200
Bethesda, MD 20814-2197
(301) 897-9770; fax (301) 530-2471; tws@wildlife.org; www.wildlife.org

The society is dedicated to conserving wildlife productivity and diversity through resource management. Emphasis is on education for wildlife managers.

Publications: *Journal of Wildlife Management*

World Resources Institute

10 G Street, NE, Ste. 800
Washington, DC 20002
(202) 729-7600; fax (202) 729-7610; www.wri.org

The institute helps governments, the private sector, nonprofit organizations, and others address human needs and economic growth while preserving natural resources. Emphasis is on forests, biodiversity, economics, technology, climate, energy, pollution, education, and governance.

Publications: several

World Society for the Protection of Animals (WSPA)
279 Perkins Street
P.O. Box 190
Boston, MA 02130
(617) 522-7000; fax (617) 522-7077; wspa@world.std.com; www.wspa.org.uk/home.html
The society is an international animal protection/wildlife conservation organization. Emphasis is on enacting animal protection legislation, disaster relief program to aid animal victims of disasters, animal spectacles, education, and less-developed countries.
Publications: *WSPA World*

Worldwatch Institute
1776 Massachusetts Ave. NW
Washington, DC 20036-1904
(202) 452-1999; fax (202) 296-7365; worldwatch@worldwatch.org
The institute is an environmental research institute. Emphasis is on interdependence of the world economy and its environmental support systems.

Publications: *State of the World, WorldWatch* (magazine), *The World Watch Papers, Vital Signs*

World Wildlife Fund
1250 24th St. NW, Ste. 500
Washington, DC 20037
(202) 293-4800; fax (202) 293-9211; wwf.us.org
The fund seeks to preserve endangered wildlife and wildlands by encouraging sustainable development. Emphasis is on conservation of tropical rain forests and preserving biological diversity.

Zero Population Growth (ZPG)
1400 16th St. NW, Ste. 320
Washington, DC 20036
(202) 332-2200; fax (202) 332-2302; info@zpg.org; www.zpg.org
ZPG seeks to achieve a sustainable balance between the Earth's population, its environment, and its resources. Emphasis is on education, urbanization and local growth issues, global warming, sustainability, transportation, and family planning.
Publications: *The ZPG Reporter* (bimonthly newspaper)

Summary of Environmental Issues in CSI MasterFormat™ Organization

To assist readers in asking appropriate questions regarding the greenness of a material, this appendix lists issues relative to resource management, toxicity/IEQ, and performance according to CSI MasterFormat sections.

This summary was developed by *theGreenTeam, Inc.,* and is the result of its ongoing work with building owners, building product manufacturers, green building trade/professional organizations, standards development organizations, and environmental organizations to develop sustainable building. This summary is intended to be a guide for researching environmental issues relative to building products. No warranty is made as to completeness or accuracy of information contained herein. References to manufacturers do not represent a guaranty, warranty, or endorsement thereof.

The summary of information is tabulated to correspond with the product summary in *The Green Home Product Guide,* co-authored by Dru Meadows and Charles E. Bell, founders of *theGreenTeam, Inc.* and lists issues relative to resource management, toxicity/IEQ, and performance according to CSI Masterformat™ sections.

theGreenTeam, Inc.
5822 S. New Haven
Tulsa, OK 74135
(918) 599-0011
fax: (918) 599-7567
email: dmeadows@busprod.com
http://home.earthlink.net/~arcvet/

DIVISION 1 **GENERAL REQUIREMENTS**

01100   SUMMARY: Identify owner's environmental goals and requirements, including energy efficiency, resource management, and specific project issues. Also, clearly indicate a team approach to addressing environmental issues.

01200   PRICE AND PAYMENT PROCEDURES: If submittal of updated Summary of Solid Waste Management and Environmental Protection Plan is required with Application for Payment, coordinate with Section 01351.

01231   ENVIRONMENTAL ALTERNATES: Identify options for green products. Use of this section will allow the owner to compare financial and practical viability of green product options for a particular project.

01300   ADMINISTRATIVE REQUIREMENTS: Require contractor to designate an on-site party responsible for instructing workers and overseeing the environmental goals for the project.

01310   PROJECT MANAGEMENT AND COORDINATION: Coordinate with Section 01351 for project quality control, coordination, and construction meetings. Review environmental procedures and status of Solid Waste Management and Environmental Protection Plan at each construction meeting.

01320   CONSTRUCTION PROGRESS DOCUMENTATION: Coordinate with Section 01351 and Section 01200 for periodic submittal of updated Summary of Solid Waste Management and Environmental Protection Plan. Where violation of environmental procedures requirements will irreversibly damage the site, identify requirements for documentation of progress at specific intervals. Documentation may also be useful for educational purposes.

01330   SUBMITTAL PROCEDURES: Clarify need for submission of material safety data sheets (MSDSs). Often owners and architects will incorporate a blanket request for MSDSs in response to environmental issues. While this may be appropriate, remember that interpreting chemical profile and test results requires understanding the health effects of exposure to the emitted chemicals, which is beyond the professional expertise of most architects; furthermore, adequate information is not available for most chemicals.

01351   ENVIRONMENTAL PROCEDURES: Identify environmental goals for construction waste management, indoor air quality, and environmental impact on the site. Specify a team approach to achieve these goals. The team— including contractor, designer, and owner—should agree upon an acceptable Solid Waste Management and Environmental Protection Plan, which outlines the project-specific methods to achieve the environmental goals specified. Specific methods will vary from project to project. For example, in a particular project area, there may be metal recycling facilities available but no wood recycling facilities. Because this section specifies recycling and reuse of construction waste, other Division 1 and Division 2 sections that include demolition and waste disposal requirements must be modified. Refer to sample section in Appendix C.

01400   QUALITY REQUIREMENTS: Include information required for conformance to regulatory requirements such as energy codes and National Pollutant Discharge Elimination System (NPDES). Coordinate with Section 01351.

01500   TEMPORARY FACILITIES AND CONTROLS: Coordinate with Section 01351 for temporary heating, cooling, and ventilating and progress cleaning and waste removal.

01600   PRODUCT REQUIREMENTS: This section addresses requirements for delivery, storage, and handling. Sometimes, it also specifies general requirements for materials and equipment identified as new. If you are specifying new materials made from recycled materials, that is acceptable. However, if you wish to allow reused materials, such as brick or millwork, edit your specifications accordingly.

01630   PRODUCT SUBSTITUTION PROCEDURES: Specify that substitutions may be considered when the contractor becomes aware of a product or procedure that is more environmentally sensitive.

01740   CLEANING: Require nontoxic cleaning materials and procedures. Coordinate with the Section 01351. Alternatives to more toxic commercial cleaning agents include: vinegar, citrus, borax, cornstarch, and baking soda.
- Abrasive cleaners: Substitute half lemon dipped in borax.
- Ammonia: Substitute vinegar, salt, and water mixture; or baking soda and water.
- Disinfectants: Substitute half cup borax in a gallon of water.
- Drain cleaners: Substitute one-fourth cup baking soda and one-fourth cup vinegar in boiling water.
- Upholstery cleaners: Substitute dry cornstarch.

01780   CLOSE-OUT SUBMITTALS: Require submittal of Final Summary of Solid Waste Management, as specified in Section 01351. Also, for government projects, require submittal of Resource Conservation and Recovery Act Project Summary, as specified in Section 01351. Require submittal of certifications and test data where appropriate. Several manufacturers have obtained independent certifications from Green Seal or Scientific Certification Systems. Sustainably harvested wood products may be labeled under the FSC principles. Refer to Section 06100, Rough Carpentry. Emissions testing has not been conducted for most products. Industries that have begun testing include paint manufacturers, carpet manufacturers, office furnishing manufacturers, floor covering adhesive manufacturers, and composite wood manufacturers. Verify that manufacturers have obtained the services of qualified health scientists to determine that their products are suitable for the intended use.

01810   COMMISSIONING: Indicate requirements for commissioning of facilities and facility systems to verify compliance with design, including optimum energy-efficient operations.

01820   DEMONSTRATION AND TRAINING: Require education for owner's personnel regarding both facility systems and the green materials in the building. Because the green items may be different from the systems and materials with which the owner's personnel are familiar, education about the environmental qualities as well as the operation and maintenance requirements may be necessary.

01830   OPERATION AND MAINTENANCE: Require maintenance instructions for specified products with attention to indoor air quality impacts of the recommended maintenance procedures and materials. Coordinate with Section 01820. Also identify maintenance contracts and green leases. Green leasing is a new and dramatic shift in the traditional perspective of leased equipment. Under a green lease, the product manufacturer is responsible for the disposition of the product at all times. Thus, when the customer no longer requires the use of the particular product or requires an updated model, the manufacturer would be obligated to reclaim it and refurbish it or disassemble it for recycling as appropriate. Coordinate with the appropriate technical section(s).

DIVISION 2   **SITE CONSTRUCTION**
02055   SOILS

Resource Management: Implement mulching and composting programs where appropriate to the project's scale and duration. Coordinate with Section 01351, Environmental Procedures, and Section 02230, Site Clearing. Soil amendment can be made from recycled scrap gypsum; coordinate with Section 09250, Gypsum Board.

Toxicity/IEQ: Coordinate with Section 01351, Environmental Procedures, to stockpile topsoil and to protect existing soils. Where soil tests indicate existing contamination, consider in situ treatment via phytoremediation instead of bioremediation and landfilling. Phytoremediation is an innovative technology that utilizes plants and trees to clean up contaminated soil and water. It is an aesthetically pleasing, solar-energy-driven, passive technique that can be used to clean up metals, pesticides, solvents, crude oil, polyaromatic hydrocarbons, and landfill leachates. Plants can break down (degrade) organic pollutants (those that contain carbon and hydrogen). Plants can also extract (phytoaccumulate) certain metal contaminants (nickel, zinc, and copper are the best candidates for removal by phytoextraction because they are the favorites of the approximately 400 known plants); the plants are harvested as necessary and either incinerated or composted to recycle the metals. Trees have longer tap roots and can act as organic pumps/filters. Poplar trees, for example, pull out of the ground 30 gallons of water per day. The pulling action of the roots decreases the tendency of surface pollutants to move downward toward groundwater/aquifers.

Performance: Traditional consideration focuses on bearing capacity and the amendments required for the selected landscaping elements. Environmental issues for performance should examine the potential to renew the soil, avoid erosion, and minimize stormwater runoff. Compost, for example can improve the quality of both sandy soil and clay soil by improving the ability of the soil to percolate and to hold water. By breaking up clay soil and by congealing sandy soil, compost aids the healthy root growth of plants as well as contributing to their nutritional needs. Similarly, the appropriate selection of plants can help rebuild the local ecosystem, including the soil.

02060

AGGREGATE

Resource Management: Aggregate fabricated from 100 percent recycled rubble or concrete is available. Due to the mass of the material and the corresponding energy/cost to transport, specify locally available sources. Fill material fabricated from 100 percent recycled tires is available.

Toxicity/IEQ: Toxicity is often a concern when utilizing recycled materials for aggregate, especially old tires. Tests are being performed by the University of Maine on the effect of tire chips on drinking water for chips placed both above and below the water table. To date, the accumulation of metals appears to be below secondary drinking water standards; some volatile and semi-volatile organic compounds have been detected for tire chips located below the water table.

Performance: Recycled porcelain, concrete, or stone may be expected to perform comparably to standard gravel/stone aggregate. Tire chips, 1″ to 2″ chips of waste steel and glass belted tires, have a low unit weight of 40 to 60 pcf versus the typical 125 pcf unit weight of gravel. Therefore, tire chips perform well where compressible, lightweight, stable fill is required, such as for retaining walls or for embankment construction where there is slope stability or excessive settlement caused by weak foundation soils and/or the weight of the embankment. Tire chips also insulate about eight times better than gravel in reducing frost penetration. The permeability of tire chips is greater than most gravel aggregate.

02220

SITE DEMOLITION

Resource Management: Collect, recycle, reuse, and dispose of demolished materials, as specified in Section 01351, Environmental Procedures, and as approved by the owner in the Solid Waste Management and Environmental Protection Plan.

Toxicity/IEQ: Coordinate with applicable regulations regarding detection and abatement of hazardous materials.

Performance: Thoughtful and considered disassembly, as opposed to wholesale demolition, will produce more usable "reusables" and will help prevent damage to items scheduled to remain.

02230

SITE CLEARING

Resource Management: Protect natural resources; collect, recycle, reuse, and dispose of demolished materials, as specified in Section 01351, Environmental Procedures, and as approved by the owner in the Solid Waste Management and Environmental Protection Plan. Identify organic debris that is free of disease, pest infestation, and chemical contamination and that is suitable for recycling on-site. Chip and compost suitable organic debris for use on-site. Stockpile where indicated on drawings or directed by the owner. Coordinate with mulch/compost requirements of Section 02900, Planting, and Section 02055, Soils.

Toxicity/IEQ: Coordinate with Section 02055, Soils, for phytoremediation of existing contaminated soils. Avoid composting diseased vegetation and animal waste (from carnivorous animals) in situ. Because the operations of commercial composting facilities are monitored and controlled to maintain the high temperatures required in the thermophyllic phase of composting (the thermophyllic phase of the average residential composting pile is only four to seven days and relies on thermophyllic bacteria that function at 104° to 170° F and that are extremely efficient at processing compostables) commercial composting can accept diseased vegetation and, in many cases, all types of animal waste. However, composting in situ is not generally so well controlled. If temperatures in the pile do not get hot enough to kill the undesirable organisms, those organisms can reinfest new vegetation when the compost is applied.

Performance: This section typically specifies removal of vegetation from the site, including stripping of sod and soil, in preparation for construction and landscaping. Where vegetation must be removed, coordinate with Section 01351, Environmental Procedures, to avoid loss of topsoil and contamination of waterways. Minimize site-clearing activities and identify indigenous vegetation to be protected in situ or relocated. Plants that are native and indigenous to the site will not only help to preserve biodiversity, but will perform better than most imported plants.

02340   SOIL STABILIZATION

Resource Management: Specify natural clay binders. Also, consider using fly ash to partially replace cement.

Toxicity/IEQ: Soil stabilization involves the addition and integration of foreign material in and on soil in order to "strengthen" the soil material for the intended construction. Consider the possible impact of such foreign materials on the ground water. Avoid asphalt soil stabilization methods and synthetic geotextile stabilization methods.

Performance: Performance is comparable for green methods and standard methods.

02360

SOIL TREATMENT

Resource Management: For soil treatment options, resource management issues closely parallel toxicity issues. The more environmentally friendly alternative to canvassing the construction site with poison is to investigate, evaluate, and adjust the local ecosystem such that the undesirable creatures are not attracted to materials and areas in which they are unwanted. For example, tree limbs or vegetation that touch the exterior walls or roof provide excellent transportation for unwanted, wood-boring insects. Rather than spraying the yard, consider relocating and/or trimming plants. For alternative termite control, consider designing a sand barrier around perimeter of the foundation. Because termites live in moist underground colonies and travel upward into buildings only to feed on the wood, they build shelter tubes above ground where they would be exposed to the outside air, which would dry them out and kill them. Termites are very capable of digging through soil. But, they are unable to dig through soil of certain grain size. Grains of size 1.6 to 2.5 mm particle size range (mesh 12 to 8) are too large for them to move, and the interstitial space is too small for them to move between the grains.

Toxicity/IEQ: This section typically specifies pesticides and herbicides to control unwanted vegetation, rodents, and insects. Avoid poisonous soil treatment. Utilize the least toxic treatment possible. Borates, for example, are less environmentally damaging than dioxins. Utilize alternative control methods where possible. For example, consider spot applications of gin/soap/vinegar (refer to organic gardening sources for additional recipes). For more pervasive unwanted vegetation, consider importing goats. Goats will eat just about anything and can leave a site bare and ready for tilling and replanting.

Performance: Alternative designs such as the termite sand barrier require certain preventative maintenance on the part of the building owner, such as keeping vegetation and dead leaves away from the building. Verify that the owner understands the maintenance involved and is willing to perform such maintenance. When used in combination with a termite flashing shield, a metal flashing between the sill plate and the foundation wall, the sand barrier can be extremely effective. If the termites do find an alternate route up the foundation to the wood sill plate, their shelter tube must extend around the angled drip of the flashing, easily exposing their location for spot chemical treatment. The sand barrier system has been approved by the City of Honolulu building code, but other municipalities may require a variance.

02370

 EROSION AND SEDIMENTATION CONTROL

Resource Management: Specify recycled content and natural fiber erosion control blankets. Avoid solid surfacing for erosion control.

Toxicity/IEQ: Consider the impact of foreign substances such as synthetic chemicals in geotextiles on the ecosystems and groundwater. Refer to Section 02340, Soil Stabilization.

Performance: By specifying plant materials in lieu of slope paving, erosion problems can be addressed without contributing to problems associated with stormwater runoff and flash flooding. Plants utilized for erosion control along drainage channels can form wildlife corridors that help preserve the biodiversity of the area. Coordinate with Section 02900, Planting. Coordinate with Section 02055, Soils, for improving performance of existing soils as a significant component of the local ecosystem.

02500

UTILITY SERVICES

Resource Management: Utility services include water, gas, sewerage, electrical power, and communication services brought to the building. Obviously, the preference is for the appropriate use of renewable resources such as wind or solar energy collected in situ, rainwater collection systems, and constructed wetlands for wastewater treatment. However, buildings that efficiently utilize common infrastructure may also be considered to be green. Many large complexes and even some urban areas are designed to take advantage of economies of scale via a central utilities plants. For example, buildings may tap into a central supply of hot water and chilled water to provide heating and cooling.

The routing of services across a site may impact local resources. Consider options for connecting to the infrastructure that preserve existing trees and minimize impact on the local ecosystem, even if it means adding a couple of feet to the service line.

In lieu of storm sewerage, consider minimizing the footprint of the structure and utilizing permeable paving. For permeable paving, refer to Section 02795, Pervious Pavement.

Toxicity/IEQ: Water quality is a growing concern in the United States. Most water treatment facilities are attempting to cope with industrial pollutants for which they were not originally designed. Also, many areas have grown so quickly that they have surpassed the capacity of the treatment facilities that serve them. Some municipalities have had to issue moratoriums on new construction based on water treatment capacity. All sources of drinking water contain some contaminants. Because water is the universal solvent, many materials are easily dissolved upon contact. The EPA has issued drinking water standards, or *maximum contaminant levels* (MCLs) for more than 80 contaminants, including: benzene (paint, plastic), 1,2-dichloroethane (paints), trichloroethylene (textiles, adhesives), vinyl chloride (PVC pipe), antimony (fire retardants, solder), barium (pigments, epoxy sealants), cadmium (galvanized pipe, paints), chromium (pigments), cyanide (steel, plastics), pentachlorophenol (wood preservatives), phthalate (PVC and other plastics), xylenes (paints), and lead (plumbing, solder, faucets). The EPA generally sets MCLs at levels that will limit an individual's risk of cancer from that contaminant to between 1 in 10,000 and 1 in 1,000,000 over a lifetime. In 1996, 4,151 systems of the nations approximately 55,000 community water systems, or 7 percent, reported one or more MCL violations, and 681 systems (less than 2 percent) reported violations of treatment technique standards.

Electromagnetic radiation is a growing concern relative to electric utility supply and electrically operated products. There is some evidence linking EM fields surrounding power lines to certain cancers. Refer to Section 16050—Basic Electrical Materials And Methods.

Performance: Design choices for material selection, systems selection, and general layout of building will greatly impact efficiencies and are addressed under other Sections. The performance of renewable energy systems is improving daily; refer to Section 13600—Solar And Wind Energy Equipment. Because of the state of flux in energy distribution systems, communication technologies, and urban approaches to water and waste management, perhaps the greatest performance issue for utility services is flexibility. Ideally, the building owner should be able to easily access, monitor, and, potentially, convert utility services as more efficient and environmentally friendly options are made available. The axiom of design for disassembly and reuse is particularly relevant to the work of this section.

02660   PONDS AND RESERVOIRS

Resource Management: This section includes not only
decorative ponds and retention basins, but also leaching pits
(simple biofiltration and graywater filtration systems).

Toxicity/IEQ: It is imperative to understand the local
ecosystem, the local climate, and the local drainage patterns
before installing a pond. Water in decorative ponds and
detention basins may become stagnant, and breed mosqui-
toes. Conversely, when appropriately designed and managed, it may contribute to the health of the local habitat as
well as perform the decorative and practical functions for
which it was intended.

Pond liners are typically fabricated from synthetic
chemicals and petroleum-based products. Consider using
natural, expanding clay soils where possible.

Graywater filtration systems rely primarily on mechanical processes to treat water. Water is filtered through carbon, sand, rock, and so on. Water can be treated to
advanced secondary standards.

Performance: Performance is comparable for green
methods and standard methods.

02670   CONSTRUCTED WETLANDS

Resource Management: Constructed wetlands address
the management of the Earth's fresh water resources. They
attempt to address water quality issues with a broad view
of the hydrologic cycle that involves less embodied energy
in the facility and less chemicals in the water. Because they
utilize natural systems to process wastewater, they also contribute to carbon sinking and may contribute to local habitats and wildlife corridors.

The amount of land required for constructed wetlands
will vary depending on the desired level of treatment and
the complexity of the system. Simple exterior wetland systems require 10 to 20 times more square footage than
greenhouse systems.

Toxicity/IEQ: Constructed wetlands treat water both
mechanically and biologically—not chemically. Water can
be treated to advanced tertiary standards and can process
metals, fats, greases, oils, gasoline, and some industrial toxins. The Federal Clean Water Act regulates water quality. Regional, state, and local governing agencies adopt
their own standards to regulate water treatment. Minimum
general standards for wastewater treatment are: secondary
wastewater, BOD_5 < 30 mg/l and TSS < 30 mg/l; advanced secondary wastewater, BOD_5 < 15 mg/l and TSS

< 30 mg/l; advanced tertiary wastewater, BOD_5 < 10 mg /l and TSS < 15 mg/l; pathogen removal required for beneficial public use, fecal coliform < 200/100 ml.

Performance: A constructed wetland is a system engineered and constructed for treatment of graywater, blackwater, and/or stormwater to levels that meet federal, state and local discharge requirements. They can be interior (greenhouse wetlands) or exterior. Constructed wetlands may serve individual facilities or whole municipalities. They can process metals, fats, greases, oils, gasoline, and some industrial toxins. They also produce usable byproducts such as nursery and water garden plants, compost, and methane gas.

Constructed wetlands may also produce potable water; however, local regulatory requirements for monitoring and acceptance of water treated by constructed wetlands may be challenging. Nevertheless, hundreds of constructed wetlands, 25 to 30 of which are sophisticated designs, currently are operational in the United States.

Maintenance requirements will vary with size— approximately a half-hour per day for 5,000 g.p.d. system to monitor computers and to trim and harvest plants and organisms. Blackwater treatment systems generally require a licensed wastewater operator.

02700   BASES, BALLASTS, PAVEMENTS, AND APPURTENANCES

Resource Management: Unless otherwise required in applicable state highway specifications, specify base course aggregate fabricated from minimum 30 percent recycled rubble or concrete and asphalt cement fabricated from minimum 15 percent recycled content asphalt. Refer to 02060—Aggregate for information on aggregate containing recycled tires.

Wheel stops made from 100 percent recycled plastic are available; refer to Section 06500—Structural Plastics.

Toxicity/IEQ: Refer to 02060—Aggregate for information on aggregate containing recycled tires. Refer to Section 06500—Structural Plastics for information on plastic lumber.

Performance: Due to stormwater runoff and albedo, pervious paving is preferable to solid surfacing. Refer to Section 02795—Pervious Paving. Where impervious paving is used, concrete paving is preferable to asphalt paving because of better albedo and maintenance requirements.

The US Green Building Council's green building rating system (LEEDS) recommends an albedo of less than 0.4 for paved surfaces.

Refer to 02060—Aggregate for information on aggregate containing recycled tires.

Refer to Section 06500—Structural Plastics for information on plastic lumber.

02795   PERVIOUS PAVEMENT

Resource Management: Pervious pavement includes interlocking pavers that allow water to percolate through the joints between the pavers and paving forms specifically designed to support soil and grass. Most of the paving forms that are designed to support soil and grass are fabricated from recycled plastic.

Toxicity/IEQ: It has been theorized that pervious pavement, especially pervious pavers that are designed to grow grass, provide biofiltration similar to graywater systems.

Performance: Specify pervious concrete paving or pervious pavers to minimize stormwater runoff from solid surfacing. Both are subject to failure under heavy loads. Contact product manufacturers for maximum load on pervious paving, and contact the Florida Concrete Paving Association for information regarding pervious concrete paving.

Pervious pavement can be up to 90 percent permeable; that is, under certain conditions, 90 percent of the moisture that hits the paved surface will percolate through the paved surface or evaporate and 10 percent will run off.

02800   SITE IMPROVEMENTS AND AMENITIES

Resource Management: Specify site amenities (planters, benches, waste receptacles, bicycle racks, play field equipment, fencing, etc.) manufactured from sustainably harvested wood, 100 percent postconsumer recycled plastic lumber, and recycled metals.

Toxicity/IEQ: Where possible, specify untreated, naturally rot-resistant, heartwood such as redwood, western cedar, cypress, elm, black locust, chestnut, in order to avoid chemicals in treated wood. Many South American species, such as Cuchi and Pau Lope, are also naturally rot-resistant. Untreated Cuchi wood has been used for more than 100 years as railroad ties in the tropical climate of South America. Refer to Section 06500—Structural Plastics for information on plastic lumber.

Performance: Performance is comparable for green methods and standard methods; however, maintenance requirements for plastic lumber will generally be significantly less than painted amenities. Refer to Section 06500—Structural Plastics for information on plastic lumber.

02900 PLANTING

Resource Management: Specify plants based on a xeriscaping approach, preferably one that utilizes indigenous plants appropriate to the local ecosystems. Where possible, specify appropriate companion planting, seasonal mixes, and habitat vegetation. Companion planting is an art practiced by most gardeners that takes advantage of complementary relationships between some plants, such as carrots and tomatoes or parsley and roses. Seasonal mixes utilize plants that thrive at various times of the year. Seasonal mixes are closely related to providing habitat vegetation. Many birds, animals, and insects—especially migratory creatures—depend upon certain plants flowering or seeding at specific times of the year and in certain regions.

Wood fiber mulch manufactured from 100 percent postconsumer paper content and yard trimming composts are available in most areas. Mulch can be made from recycled site debris. Coordinate with Section 01351—Environmental Procedures and Section 02230—Site Clearing. Soil amendment can be made from recycled scrap gypsum; coordinate with Section 09250—Gypsum Board. Waste gypsum board should be pulverized and spread evenly over the entire site area. Do not deposit it in areas that lack adequate drainage. Verify appropriate application rates with a landscaping consultant. Studies conducted through the Gypsum Association indicate that application rates may be as high as 22 tons per acre. However, in some areas, there may be regulatory restrictions on the disposal of construction waste on-site and a variance may be required.

Toxicity/IEQ: Specify an integrated pest management approach to plant establishment. Integrated pest management, according to the U.S. Department of Agriculture, Agricultural Research Service, is the judicious use and integration of various pest control tactics of the associated environment of the pest in ways that complement and facilitate the biological and other natural controls of pests to meet economic, public health, and environmental goals. Specify use of native beneficial insects. Specify use of appropriate companion plants, such as those with natural py-rethrums. Minimize chemical pesticides and fertilizers; where chemicals are required, specify the least toxic. Specify organic matter to support establishment of indigenous plants. Specify organic mulch products. Use inorganic materials such as sand or gypsum to improve workability and drainage of soil as appropriate to indigenous plants.

Performance: Xeriscaping utilizes indigenous plants, low-maintenance plants, that are tolerant of the site's existing soils and climate without supplemental irrigation or fertilization once established. Native plants will perform better than imported species and will require less maintenance. Where plants are imported to a region, it is advisable to monitor sufficiently to determine the relative invasiveness of the imported species. "Exotic" plants, plants not indigenous to a region, can blend into the local ecosystem, but they can also overrun it, suffocating indigenous plants and crippling habitats.

DIVISION 3
03100

CONCRETE
CONCRETE FORMS AND ACCESSORIES

Resource Management: This section includes both permanent and temporary forms for structural and architectural cast-in-place concrete. Resource-efficient options for permanent formwork include earth forms and insulated, stackable forms made of minimum 10 percent recycled polystyrene pellets and cement. Temporary forms (metal pan forms, wood forms, and corrugated paper forms) are generally reusable and easily recyclable. Most typically contain recycled contents. Specify reclaimed wood or sustainably harvested wood for wood forms. Refer to Section 06100—Rough Carpentry for information on sustainably harvested wood.

Toxicity/IEQ: There are 100 percent biodegradable, zero VOC form release agents available.

Performance: Permanent insulating formwork will conserve energy. Reuse temporary forms to the greatest extent possible. Coordinate with Section 01351 for reuse and recycling of spent formwork.

03200

CONCRETE REINFORCEMENT

Resource Management: Chairs and bolsters fabricated from recycled plastic are available. Fibrous reinforcement fabricated from recycled plastic is available. Steel reinforcement typically contains recycled steel. Refer to Section 05100—Structural Metal Framing for information regarding the impact of mining and smelting on the Earth's resources and for discussion of recycled content in the steel industry. Steel reinforcing containing 100 percent remelt steel is available.

Toxicity/IEQ: Refer to Section 06500—Structural Plastics for information on plastic products. Refer to Section 05100—Structural Metal Framing for information on steel products.

Performance: Performance is comparable for green methods and standard methods. Steel reinforcing may be easily separated with magnets from concrete aggregate during recycling operations. Separation of plastic from concrete aggregate may require water to float plastic shards.

03300 CAST-IN-PLACE CONCRETE:

Resource Management: Mining raw materials (aggregate and components of Portland cement: lime, oxides of calcium silicon, aluminum, and iron) produces soil erosion, pollutant runoff, and habitat loss. Materials for concrete manufacture are found throughout the United States, yet localized depletion of these resources may occur. Where pozzolanic cement is specified, natural pozzolans such as diatomaceous earths, volcanic ash, and pumicites may be used. Fly ash, a pozzolan created as a byproduct of coal combustion, may be used as a substitute for a maximum of 20 percent of Portland cement. Specify 20 percent fly ash or 30 percent ground granulated blast furnace slag content in cement and concrete as per ASTM standards (for cement: ASTM C 595, ASTM C 150, AASHTO M 240; for concrete: ASTM C 618, ASTM C 311, ASTM C 989, AASHTO M 302, ACI 266.R1). The production of concrete is extremely energy-intensive. Equipment required for mining, processing, mixing, and pouring at the site burn fossil fuel and generate pollution.

Toxicity/IEQ: The production of Portland cement generates large volumes of CO_2, a significant greenhouse gas, and dust. Some facilities have reduced their CO_2 production through energy efficiency improvements and through increased use of waste lime (instead of converting limestone to lime). Approximately 50 percent of the kilns in North America use hazardous waste as fuel. There is significant controversy over the burning of waste materials (tires, MSW, and hazardous materials) in cement kilns. The EPA and the Cement Kiln Recycling Coalition are addressing citizen concerns.

Concrete is relatively inert once cured. Admixtures, curing compounds, and sealers may emit VOCs, especially during the curing process. Specify water-based, zero or low VOC additives, sealers, and coatings. Verify that the curing compound is compatible with the specified floor sealer or finish. Specify temporary ventilation during placing and curing for interior work. Comply with applicable regulations and with South Coast Air Quality Management District regulations.

Hazardous materials may be "encapsulated" by being mixed with or imbedded in nonporous, durable concrete. However, consider future disassembly and possible options for recycling concrete that has encapsulated hazardous materials.

Performance: Coordinate with Section 01351 for reuse and pollution prevention. Return excess concrete to supplier and minimize water used to wash equipment. Concrete admixtures are now available that retard the setting of concrete so effectively that a partial load can be brought back to the ready mix plant for one or two days then reactivated for use. Cured waste concrete may be crushed and reused as fill or as a base course for pavement. It can also be used as aggregate in concrete manufacturing. Cured waste concrete still possesses an active cement ingredient that reduces the required virgin cement in recovered content mixes by 3 to 10 percent. Despite the recycling potential for concrete, most concrete waste in the United States (approximately 67 percent by weight, 53 percent by volume) is landfilled.

Performance in place is comparable for green methods and standard methods. Concrete construction provides thermal mass and durable construction.

03400   PRECAST CONCRETE

Resource Management: Plant fabrication handles raw materials and byproducts at a single location that allows greater efficiency and better pollution prevention than jobsite fabrication. Architectural items (planters, birdbaths, bollards) fabricated from lightweight and recycled content aggregates are available. The quantity and type of recycled materials vary from manufacturer to manufacturer, and include: cellulose, fiberglass, polystyrene, and rubber.

Autoclaved aerated concrete (AAC) is a type of lightweight precast concrete prevalent in Europe, Asia, and the Middle East, and recently became available through manufacturing facilities in the United States. It is made with Portland cement, silica sand or fly ash, lime, water, and aluminum powder or paste. The aluminum reacts with the products of hydration to release millions of tiny hydrogen gas bubbles that expand the mix to approximately five times the normal volume. When set, the AAC is cut into blocks or slabs and steam-cured in an autoclave. There is also a growing array of precast panel/CMU substitute products; refer to Section 04700—Simulated Masonry.

Toxicity/IEQ: Refer to Section 03300—Cast-In-Place Concrete. AAC uses less Portland cement by volume than cast-in-place concrete and traditional precast concrete. When fully cured, AAC forms microscopic crystals of the mineral tobormorite, a form of calcium silicate hydrate.

Performance: AAC is significantly lighter (about one-fifth the weight of traditional concrete) than normal concrete and can be formed into blocks or panels. AAC has the structural, fire-resistive, and acoustic properties of concrete, yet it is lightweight and can be cut with a saw much like a wood product. Coordinate with structural requirements of project. AAC is thermally efficient and considered to be more dimensionally stable than standard concrete.

DIVISION 4
04050

MASONRY

BASIC MASONRY MATERIALS AND METHODS

Resource Management: Refer to Section 03300—Cast-In-Place Concrete for information regarding Portland cement.

Toxicity/IEQ: Refer to Section 03300—Cast-In-Place Concrete for information regarding Portland cement.

VOCs may be emitted due to additives, sealers and coatings. Water-based, low VOC additives, sealers, and coatings are available. Specify temporary ventilation for interior work.

Performance: Performance is comparable for green methods and standard methods.

04210

CLAY MASONRY UNITS

Resource Management: Mining of clay, shale, soil, sand, limestone, and metal ores produces soil erosion, pollutant runoff, and habitat loss. Manufacturing waste is typically recycled in new units. Salvaged units are available in many communities. Brick firing produces fluorine and chlorine emissions. Select locally produced masonry units when available to minimize the environmental impact due to transportation of heavy material.

Toxicity/IEQ: Clay masonry is considered to be relatively inert. Because oil is commonly added (and burned away) during the production of brick, the manufacturer can use oil-contaminated soil that is free from hazardous contaminates. Although radon has been associated with certain soils, bricks do not produce abnormal exposure to radon gas, except in rare situations.

Performance: Performance is comparable for green methods and standard methods. Traditional masonry construction provides thermal mass and durable construction. Masonry is reusable and easily recyclable.

04220

CONCRETE MASONRY UNITS

Resource Management: Mining of clay, shale, soil, sand, limestone, and metal ores produces soil erosion, pollutant runoff, and habitat loss. Manufacturing waste is typically recycled in new units. Salvaged units are available in many communities. Industrial waste byproducts (air-cooled slag, cinders or bottom ash, ground waste glass and concrete, granulated slag and expanded slag) can be used for aggregate in concrete blocks although documenting this is often difficult. Refer to Section 03300—Concrete for information regarding use of fly ash and slag in concrete materials. Combustion emissions from mineral process, limestone calcining, and cement kiln operation include carbon dioxide and dust, and may include hazardous materials depending on waste burned in cement kilns. Select locally produced masonry units when available to minimize the environmental impact due to transportation of heavy material.

Toxicity/IEQ: Concrete masonry is considered to be relatively inert. The EPA has reported various aromatic and halogenated hydrocarbon emissions from concrete masonry units, ranging from 0.06 to 0.39 $\mu g/m^2$ per hour. Polystyrene foam insulation emissions include aromatic hydrocarbon emissions of 20 $\mu g/m^2$ per hour. Refer to Section 03300—Cast-In-Place Concrete for information regarding Portland cement.

Performance: Performance is comparable for green methods and standard methods. Traditional masonry construction provides thermal mass and durable construction. Masonry construction, when roughly textured, ribbed, or fluted, can help reduce noise by dispersing sound waves. Consider interlocking concrete masonry units for landscape retaining walls; interlocking concrete masonry units do not require mortar and are easy to disassemble and reuse. Masonry is reusable and easily recyclable. Autoclaved aerated (cellular) concrete is available; refer to Section 03400—Precast Concrete.

04290 ADOBE MASONRY UNITS

Resource Management: Adobe blocks are made from local clays/soils and dried in the sun, avoiding associated pollution of standard masonry manufacture. Primary ingredients include adobe soil and water. Adobe soils are principally from alluvial deposits and are acquired primarily as a byproduct of sand and gravel mining. Straw is sometimes added to prevent cracking. Moisture will disintegrate adobe; therefore, adobe is protected with cement plaster and overhangs. Also, adobe may be stabilized with asphalt emulsion. Asphalt emulsion is made by combining asphalt, a byproduct of crude oil distillation, with water and proprietary surfactants.

Toxicity/IEQ: Only limited VOC outgassing is associated with asphalt emulsion.

Performance: Adobe construction provides thermal mass. Sizes and shapes of adobe blocks vary, and include: structural bricks, face brick, and tiles. Adobe construction is suitable for a wide range of climates (not just American Southwest), including extremely cold and extremely wet. Performance may vary in accordance with the type of soil materials available locally. An unstabilized adobe wall without protection from rain will erode at rate of approximately 1 inch per 20 years in the American Southwest. Demolished adobe can disintegrate and return to the soil. Adobe is an indigenous construction technique; refer to Section 06700—Alternative Agricultural Products. Adobe construction dates back to the walls of Jericho (now located in Israel), around 8300 B.C.

Cob wall construction uses material similar to adobe (earth mixed with sand and straw) but requires no forming. The word cob comes from the early English building technique of using earth (mixed with sand and straw) to form organic shapes or "cobs" of the material, which is then placed to form walls. The cobs require no cement or mortar. The thick walls are sculpted, many times in curves with arches for doors and windows.

04295 RAMMED EARTH (*not a standard CSI Section*)

Resource Management: Rammed earth is a compacted mixture of earth, other soil materials, and Portland cement.

Toxicity/IEQ: Rammed earth construction is natural and nontoxic. It is frequently left unfinished on the interior. Refer to Section 03300—Cast-In-Place Concrete for information regarding Portland cement.

Performance: Lifts of the soil material are "rammed" within formwork, which is constructed on-site and removed after walls have undergone adequate curing. Tampers compact approximately 8 inches depth of mix into 4 inches of depth in each layer. The walls are characterized by "strata" of mixture indicating the construction technique. Walls (both interior and exterior) may be left exposed or plastered. Like adobe, rammed earth structures perform best in sunny climates, although they can withstand water. Rammed earth is an indigenous construction technique; refer to Section 06700—Alternative Agricultural Products. The Great Wall of China, constructed around 200 B.C., is made of rammed earth. Currently, approximately 15 percent of France's population reside in rammed earth structures. Rammed earth construction provides thermal mass, and is water- and fire-resistant.

Traditional rammed earth construction is not appropriate where subject to seismic loads. To comply with building codes in California, rammed earth construction has been used as infill for a post and beam structure, and has been pneumatically sprayed (similar to gunite) over reinforcing anchored to a concrete foundation.

04440   STONE

Resource Management: Quarrying stone produces soil erosion, pollution runoff, and loss of habitat. In some instances, quarry sites have been restored to approximate previous condition. From 15 percent to 90 percent of the stone can be wasted during the quarrying process due to chipping, trimming, and inferior materials. Most such waste is disposed of as fill at the quarry site or used for base aggregate in local road construction. Stone is available in this country and abroad. Use of local stone reduces transportation impacts.

Toxicity/IEQ: Toxicity/IEQ is comparable for green methods and standard methods. Radon may be a consideration in extremely rare circumstances.

Performance: Stone construction is very durable and can provide thermal mass. Stone is reusable and easily recyclable. However, excess and demolished stone is usually crushed and landfilled.

04700

SIMULATED MASONRY

Resource Management: Various alternative masonry products are available in block, plank and panel form. Depending on the particular manufacturer, components may include: cement, wood fibers, straw, recycled plastic, and expanded polystyrene foam beads.

Toxicity/IEQ: Like concrete masonry, simulated masonry is considered to be relatively inert. However, plastic and EPS components may outgas. Refer to Section 06500—Structural Plastics.

Performance: Methods of erection are similar to standard concrete masonry units although some products feature laying without mortar joints (dry stacking). Methods of insulating are also similar to concrete masonry units. Alternative masonry products tend to be lighter than standard CMU and more thermally efficient. Efficient recycling of mixed composition materials (e.g., synthetic plastic and cellulose) is problematic at this time as the technology to separate different materials is still evolving.

DIVISION 5
05050

METALS
BASIC METAL MATERIALS AND METHODS

Resource Management: Specify factory finishing rather than field-coating where possible. Plant fabrication/finishing handles raw materials and byproducts at a single location, which allows greater efficiency and better pollution prevention than job-site fabrication/finishing. Specify compliance with applicable VOC regulations and, where possible, with South Coast Air Quality Management District regulations (SCAQMD) for shop-applied coatings.

Powder coating is preferable to solvent-based coating application systems. Powder coating uses an electrostatic charge to adhere colored powder to metal. The powder remaining in the electrostatic chamber is "vacuumed" out and reused. Consider factory finishing that utilizes mechanical process rather than chemical. Mechanical processes such as abrasive blasting, grinding, buffing, and polishing do not generate as much hazardous waste as chemical and electrical processes.

Avoid electroplated coatings wherever possible. When electroplating is necessary, select one of the available replacement technologies listed by the U.S. EPA. The EPA has identified as toxic and/or polluting: cadmium plating materials, chromium plating materials, cyanide-based electroplating, and copper/formaldehyde-based electroless copper solutions. Available replacement technologies include the following: noncyanide copper plating, metal stripping, and zinc-plating; ion vapor deposition (IVD); physical vapor deposition (PVD); chromium-free substitutes for selected immersion processes; metal spray coating; and trivalent chromium plating for decorative applications. Zinc smelting for galvanizing generates toxic metals waste.

Green Seal recommends that anti-corrosive paint contain less than 250 g/l VOCs, less than 1.0 percent aromatic compounds by weight, and be free of the following compounds: halomethanes, methyl chloride; chlorinated ethanes, 1,1,1-trichloroethane; aromatic solvents, benzene, toluene (methyl benzene), ethylbenzene; chlorinated ethylenes-vinyl chloride; polynuclear aromatics—naphthalene; chlorobenzenes—1,2-dichlorobenzene; Phthalate esters -di (2-ethylhexyl) phthalate; butyl benzyl phthalate; di-n-butyl phthalate; di-n-octyl phthalate; diethyl phthalate; dimethyl phthalate; miscellaneous semi-volatile organics—isophorone; metals and their compounds—antimony; cadmium; haxavalent chromium; lead; mercury; preservatives—formaldehyde; ketones—methyl ethyl ketone; methyl isobutyl ketone; and miscellaneous VOCs— acrolein; acrylonitrile.

Toxicity/IEQ: Factory-applied finishes emit considerably fewer VOCs in situ than field-applied coatings because the primary outgassing occurs at the plant under controlled conditions.

Performance: Performance is comparable for green methods and standard methods. Powder coating is susceptible to damage due to field welding.

05100 STRUCTURAL METAL FRAMING

Resource Management: Mining raw materials (iron, limestone, coal) produces soil erosion, pollutant runoff, and habitat loss. Ore refinement produces heat, combustion emissions and requires significant amounts of water. Primary environmental concerns in the galvanizing process are related to the rinsing of the fabricated item, which contaminates the wastewater with metals and toxic chemicals. Supply of some of the raw materials (nickel, chromium, and manganese) is very limited. Production of new steel from recycled steel requires 39 percent of the energy required to process steel from virgin material. Traditional manufacturing procedures for processing steel include refining molten iron in either a basic oxygen furnace, an open-hearth furnace, or an electric-arc furnace. A new procedure, not readily available in the United States, is direct steelmaking that eliminates the iron ore agglomeration, cokemaking, ironmaking, and basic oxygen furnace and open hearth furnace; it also eliminates much of the associated pollution and energy inefficiencies.

Toxicity/IEQ: Steel does not outgas; however, the protective coat of oil found on some steel framing may irritate sensitive individuals if not removed prior to installation.

Performance: Where feasible, use bolted connections to allow for disassembly and reuse. Steel is easily recyclable because it can be magnetically separated from the waste stream. The overall recycling rate for the steel industry is approximately 66 percent. Recycled contents of particular products can vary greatly. Companies that manufacture their own steel for various steel fabrications can better document exact percentages in their products. Zinc can be recovered from both new and old galvanized steel products.

05500   METAL FABRICATIONS
Refer to Section 05100—Structural Metal Framing for information regarding steel. Refer to Section 05700—Ornamental Metal for information regarding other metals.

05700   ORNAMENTAL METAL
Resource Management: Mining raw materials produce soil erosion, pollutant runoff, and habitat loss. Ore refinement produces heat, combustion emissions, and requires significant amounts of water. Metal ores are a nonrenewable resource.

Copper has been used for roofing since ancient Greece (the Parthenon in Athens had copper shingles). Approximately 50 percent of the copper used in the United States comes from scrap, which is as usable as the primary copper refined from ore. Declining ore grades has led to increasingly large mines. Ore is crushed and mixed with water and surfactants to make the minerals float to the surface. After smelting, which separates the copper form the iron, sulfur, and other minerals, the copper is refined by fire or electrolytic processes. Sulfur dioxide is produced in copper smelting.

Aluminum is subject to corrosion and must have a protective coating (anodized or duranodic finish). Although aluminum beverage containers are readily recyclable in most communities, most are recycled into new beverage containers. Most aluminum building products contain virgin material. Aluminum is fabricated from bauxite, a mineral found primarily in tropical areas. A significant factor in the clearcutting of tropical rain forests is the desire to gain access to bauxite mines. Aluminum manufacture is water-intensive; wastewater contaminants include: aluminum, fluoride, nickel, cyanide, and antimony.

Wrought iron (iron that is fashioned or formed into intricate patterns) uses iron with a carbon content of 0.03 to 0.05 percent (ASTM A186); carbon is the ingredient that gives iron a fibrous nature and allows it to be malleable when heated. The lower the carbon content, however, the more resistant to corrosion.

Stainless steel is a family of iron-base alloys containing about 10.5 percent chromium or more and other elements such as nickel, manganese, molybdenum, sulfur, selenium, and titanium. Sixty commercial stainless steel types were originally recognized by the American Iron and Steel Institute (AISI) in three primary categories: austenitic stainless steels are chromium-nickel-manganese compositions (AISI Series 200 and 300); ferritic stainless steels are straight chromium steels (AISI Series 400) that are not hardenable by heat treatment; and martensitic stainless steels are straight-chromium (AISI Series 400) that are hardenable by heat treatment.

Toxicity/IEQ: Metal is inert and has virtually no impact on IAQ.

Performance: Performance is comparable for green methods and standard methods.

DIVISION 6   **WOOD AND PLASTICS**
06050   BASIC WOOD AND PLASTIC MATERIALS AND METHODS

Resource Management: Fasteners fabricated from up to 100 percent recycled steel are available. Refer to Section 05100—Structural Metal Framing, for information regarding steel. Wood products fabricated from reclaimed and remilled structural and nonstructural lumber is available.

Toxicity/IEQ: VOCs may be emitted during the curing process for adhesives and finishes.

Performance: Performance is comparable for green methods and standard methods. Structural lumber fabricated from reclaimed structural lumber generally performs better than comparable lumber available today, because most reclaimed lumber is from turn-of-the-century construction that utilized old-growth, tight-grained hardwood. Despite the demonstrated excellent structural performance, most building codes will require that such lumber/timber be regraded according to current methods.

06070   WOOD TREATMENT

Resource Management: There are hundreds of species of trees growing in the world's forests, but we tend to use only a few of them. The ones we do not use are often treated like weeds, left to rot or burned as waste. Using only a handful of tree species puts unbalanced pressure on our forest resources. Where possible, specify lesser known species. Some species of wood are naturally resistant to decay caused by the elements or termite attack. These include: black locust, black walnut, cedar, and redwood. Many South American species, such as Cuchi and Pau Lope, are also naturally rot-resistant. Untreated Cuchi wood has been used for over 100 years as railroad ties in the tropical climate of South America.

Toxicity/IEQ: There are three broad classes of wood preservatives: (1) creosote, which is generally used in railroad ties, utility poles, and pilings; (2) oilborne preservatives, such as pentachlorophenol and copper naphthenate, generally used for utility poles, assembly area roof supports, and glu-lam construction; and (3) waterborne preservatives, which are the most common preservatives used in residential, commercial, and industrial construction. Waterborne preservatives include: chromated copper arsenate (CCA), ammoniacal copper zinc arsenate (ACZA), ammoniacal copper arsenate (ACA), and ammoniacal copper quat (ACQ). Of these, ACQ is generally regarded as the least toxic. However, there are alternative products available that utilize borates, generally a mixture of borax and boric acid. Chlorothalonil, a mildewcide in paints and EPA-registered agricultural fungicide, may prove to be a viable alternative treatment. Copper napthenate, a water-insoluble copper soap of naphthenic acid—a byproduct of the petroleum refining industry—is being "rediscovered" and may find increased use in general construction. Borates, chlorothalonil, and copper napthenate are considered less toxic than the standard waterborne preservatives.

CCA is the most common waterborne preservative treatment. The EPA has listed the inorganic arsenical and chromium wastes (residuals, wastewater, treated wood drippage, and spent preservative) as hazardous. Wood treated with CCA may be burned only in approved incinerators, but it may be landfilled.

In use, wood preservatives are usually of fairly low volatility, but outgas for a very long time. While their emissions rates are not large and they do not generally result in high indoor air concentrations, many of the preservatives present health hazards, including chromium and arsenic.

Performance: Wood preservatives are used to make wood resistant to fungus growth and termite attack. Most building codes require that structural wood elements in direct contact with earth, embedded in concrete/masonry that is in direct contact with earth, or exposed to moisture be treated wood. Many allow alternative, decay-resistant species.

Borate-treated wood performs well relative to protection against decay due to fungus and insects. However, at their present state of development, they do not fix well in the lumber. Consequently, they should not be used in exposed applications where the borates can leach out. Where borate treatment is used, a variance from the building department may be required. The American Wood Preservers Association (AWPA) standards are commonly cited as approved treatment methods in building codes. AWPA is in the process of revising standards to address alternate preservative treatment, such as borate. Refer to Section 02360—Soil Treatment for information regarding sand barriers to termites.

06100   ROUGH CARPENTRY

Resource Management: Wood is a renewable resource. Harvesting of wood can produce soil erosion, pollutant runoff, increased levels of atmospheric carbon dioxide, global warming, and habitat loss. Approximately 80 percent of the world's ancient forests are gone. Less than 4 percent of the U.S. ancient forests remain. Forests provide many environmental benefits, including: habitats, potential sources for medicines, and climatic control. Many certified sources of sustainably harvested wood are available. Note that terminology tends to vary in accordance with the program emphasis (economic interest in timber versus environmental interest in forests). For example, "sustained yield" generally refers to the production of a given quality and quantity of timber on an annual basis, but "sustainable" refers to the preservation of the ecosystem. The American Forest and Paper Association (AF&PA), a national trade association of the forest, pulp, paper, and wood products industry, has developed a program called the Sustainable Forestry Initiative that promotes environmentally responsible forest management through self-certification.

Specify lumber bearing the Forest Stewardship Council (FSC) label. The FSC is the only independent, nonprofit, nongovernmental organization that trains, accredits, and monitors independent, third-party certifiers around the world. The FSC also promotes excellence in forestry management by helping to establish regional and international forest management standards.

For additional information regarding forests, tree farms, sustainably harvested wood, and nontimber products, contact the FSC or the Certified Forest Products Council. Refer to Appendix A for contact information.

Toxicity/IEQ: Toxicity/IEQ for rough carpentry framing is comparable for green methods and standard methods. Refer to Section 06050—Basic Wood And Plastic Materials And Methods for information regarding adhesives and finishes.

Performance: The quality of framing materials has decreased as the number of remaining old-growth, tight-grained trees has decreased. Old-growth trees are typically tall, with high canopies and few branches to produce knots along the thick portion of their trunks. The lumber produced from these trees produces high-grade (Architect Clear, Architect Custom Clear, Clear Heart, A Clear, and B Clear) and tight-grained pieces. Avoid these grades where possible. Also, avoid virgin lumber with grain more than 15 lines per inch, as it is likely to have come from temperate ancient forest trees. Specify least grade and grain to suit purpose. Maximize reclaimed and prefabricated lumber. Refer to Section 06170—Prefabricated Structural Wood.

06160

SHEATHING

Resource Management: Sheathing includes Oriented Strand Board (OSB), particleboard, chipboard, Medium Density Fiberboard (MDF) and hardboard. Refer to Section 06170—Prefabricated Structural Wood for information regarding resource management of composite wood products. Alternative products such as cellulose fiberboard (recycled newsprint), honeycomb cardboard (recycled paper or alternative agricultural fibers), and straw fiberboard (agricultural waste) are available and can serve many of the same purposes as MDF and particleboard; refer to Section 06700—Alternative Agricultural Products. Specify the sheathing product with the smallest component wood pieces (the most resource-efficient) that will meet performance requirements. Plywood is fabricated from layers of wood veneer and generally uses the largest component wood pieces. OSB is made from approximately six-inch long wood shavings oriented in different directions and bonded together with a synthetic resin. MDF uses smaller waste wood particles than OSB. Particleboard uses the smallest wood particles.

Toxicity/IEQ: Processed wood and wood waste products such as particleboard, chipboard, and hardboard often utilize formaldehyde-based resins as a binder or adhesive. Formaldehyde is considered a "probable" carcinogen even at low exposure levels. Interior grade particleboard is fabricated with urea-formaldehyde; exterior grade particleboard is fabricated with phenol resin, which is at least 10 times less toxic than urea formaldehyde. Particleboards that are formaldehyde-free are also available. Alternative binders include: paraffin wax (such as some cellulosic fiberboard) and methyl diisocyanate (such as straw fiberboard or some MDF).

ANSI A208.1 limits formaldehyde emissions in particleboard and ANSI A208.2 limits formaldehyde emissions in MDS. Current particleboard products have 80 percent to 90 percent lower emissions than those produced roughly one decade ago.

Performance: Performance is comparable for green methods and standard methods. MDF, particleboard, and alternative agricultural sheathing products function well in nonstructural applications, such as door cores and millwork.

06170

PREFABRICATED STRUCTURAL WOOD

Resource Management: Examples of prefabricated structural wood include: wood I-joists, prefabricated wood trusses, finger-jointed lumber, and composite panels. Prefabricated wood assemblies and composite wood panels are more resource-efficient than standard lumber. Prefabricated assemblies utilize sawdust, fibers, chips, and small pieces of lumber. Prefabricated wood generally contains preconsumer waste wood, although some trees are grown specifically for chipping.

Toxicity/IEQ: Adhesive binders used in prefabricated structural wood are any of several synthetic resins that pose varying degrees of human health risks.

Performance: By reducing lumber to component products and reassembling the component products in a manner that maximizes and standardizes the performance of each of the components, prefabricated structural wood can perform better with less material than conventional lumber/timber construction. Prefabricated wood is more difficult to recycle than standard lumber due to the binders.

06200

FINISH CARPENTRY (PREFABRICATED)

Resource Management: Refer to Section 06100—Rough Carpentry for information on wood as a renewable resource and on sustainable forestry. Sheathing materials manufactured from alternative agricultural products are available. Refer to Section 06700, Alternative Agricultural Products.

Plastic laminates are composed of thin layers of paper and thermosetting resins. Two types of resins, melamine and phenol, are used. Production of melamine and phenol resins is energy-intensive and generates air and water pollutants. Melamine resin contains melamine (produced from urea) and formaldehyde (produced from methanol); phenol resin contains phenol (produced from benzene and propylene, which in turn are obtained from crude oil and natural gas) and formaldehyde.

Two types of paper, kraft (brown, unbleached) and alpha-cellulose (white, bleached), are used. Paper manufacture is energy-intensive and generates air and water pollutants, including oxygen-depleting organics and toxic chlorinated compounds such as dioxins. Paper manufacture is considered to be one of the most polluting processes in manufacturing because of the bleach (chlorine) utilized in "whitening" the paper. Both types of paper are typically manufactured from virgin materials.

Pigments and inks color the decorative top layer of paper (the alpha-cellulose paper). The inks may also contain toxins such as titanium dioxide and phthalocyanine blue.

Alternatives to plastic laminate countertops include ceramic tile, linoleum, and alternative agricultural products.

Toxicity/IEQ: VOCs may be emitted during the curing process for adhesives and finishes. Low and zero VOC adhesives are available. Low VOC finishes for wood are available. Refer to Section 09900—Paints and coatings. Plastic laminates are relatively inert after manufacture.

Performance: Plastic laminates are easy to clean and disinfect, but can scratch easily. Plastic laminates are difficult to recycle because they are a composite material with thermosetting resins.

06500   STRUCTURAL PLASTICS

Resource Management: Plastic lumber is generally fabricated from 100 percent recycled pre- and postconsumer plastics (PET or HDPE, depending on the manufacturer). It may also contain recycled cellulose.

Toxicity/IEQ: As a substitute for treated lumber, it reduces potential leaching of chemicals used in wood treatment. Refer to Section 06070—Wood Treatment. Plastics are traditionally considered to be inert. Recent academic investigation, however, has indicated that plastics may not be as inert as previously believed. There is some evidence that plastic coatings commonly used to line food cans leach into the food. Once ingested, they may act as endocrine disrupters. To date, there have been no comparable studies researching the health impact of plastic building materials.

Performance: Structural plastic is perhaps a misnomer. CSI MasterFormat 1995 Edition includes "plastic lumber and other structural plastics" in this category. However, plastic lumber is not a substitute for structural wood members. It is formed in boards and posts and may be used for nonstructural applications such as fencing and benches. Plastic lumber is a durable, weather-resistant, and low-maintenance material. Plastic lumber is integrally colored and homogenous, and so does not require painting. It is recyclable.

One hundred percent recycled content plastic lumber may not perform well in lengths greater than 6 feet or where shear is a significant consideration (e.g., fencing, decking, and bollards). For such uses, specify plastic lumber with cellulose fiber. The cellulose fiber improves stability and resistance to screw pullout.

In 1997, the American Society for Testing and Materials, with significant assistance from the Plastic Lumber Trade Association, approved some of the first standards for plastic lumber: D 6108, Standard Test Method for Compressive Properties of Plastic Lumber and Shapes; D 6109, Standard Test Method for Flexural Properties of Unreinforced and reinforced Plastic Lumber; D 6111, Standard Test Method for Bulk Density and Specific Gravity of Plastic Lumber and Shapes by Displacement; D 6112, Standard Test Method for Compressive and Flexural Creep and Creep Rupture of Plastic Lumber and Shapes; and D 6118, Standard Test Method for Mechanical Fasteners in Plastic Lumber and Shapes.

06600   PLASTIC FABRICATIONS

Resource Management: Plastic fabrications include cultured marble, glass-fiber-reinforced plastic, and plastic formed to various profiles such as trim and planters. Many plastic formed profiles contain recycled plastic. A few manufacturers are experimenting with recycled fiberglass/plastic possibilities for consumer and building products.

Toxicity/IEQ: Refer to Section 06500—Structural Plastics.

Performance: Refer to Section 06500—Structural Plastics.

06700   ALTERNATIVE AGRICULTURAL PRODUCTS (*not a standard CSI Section*)

Resource Management: The number of species of plants and animals upon which society depends is exceptionally small relative to the number of species that are available and adequate to the purpose. By promoting the use of alternative agricultural products, the building industry not only can promote less toxic, renewable-resource, carbon-sinking products, but revitalize the market interest in a variety of flora and help to preserve the Earth's biodiversity. "Alternative agricultural products" refers to a growing market segment for the building industry (and other industries) that is capitalizing on little known and underutilized species. The most obvious substitutions are alternative lumber species. Specify alternate, nonendangered/nonthreatened species. The Convention on International Trade and Endangered Species (CITES) lists wood species that are endangered or threatened. Contact the Certified Forest Products Council for information regarding alternative lumber species, their characteristics and availability. Refer to Appendix A for contact information.

Perhaps an even greater potential for developing alternative agricultural building products exists in nontimber plants. Products fabricated from wheat straw, kenaf fibers, soy resins, and bamboo are currently available. There are several sources of fiberboard fabricated from straw and recycled cellulose. There is a decorative hardboard product fabricated from recycled cellulose and soy resins. There are form-release agents for concrete, and adhesives for laminated wood products fabricated from soy resins. Several universities, including Iowa State, the University of Arkansas, and the University of Nebraska, are involved in the research and development of soy adhesives for wood. There is flooring manufactured from bamboo, a fast-growing grass that may be harvested in four years. Starch-based plastics have penetrated the consumer market and are gaining ground in packaging. There are starch-based plastics and cellulose aggregate additives in development that might drastically alter construction procedures.

The Alternative Agricultural Research and Commercialization (AARC) Corporation, a wholly owned government corporation of the U.S. Department of Agriculture, makes equity investments in private companies to commercialize alternative agricultural products. Because the federal government has an equity position in these companies, Section 729 of the 1996 Federal Agricultural Improvement and Reform Act permits other federal agencies to establish set-asides and preferences for AARC-funded products, thus helping to improve the infrastructure and grow new, green industries. Some of the products developed with AARC assistance include: Environ by Phenix Biocomposites Inc., PrimeBoard by PrimeBoard Inc., Bio-Form by Leahy-Wolf Company, and Agriboard by Agriboard Industries.

Alternative fuels and the systems that utilize them (e.g., heaters that use corn for fuel) are available. Custom systems utilizing biofuels are available across the United States.

Toxicity/IEQ: Most of the alternative agricultural products are designed to replace petroleum- and synthetic chemical-based products, and have been specifically developed to be environmentally friendly.

Performance: Typically, only a limited number of wood species (relative to the tremendous diversity available) have approval by governing agencies based upon their documented structural characteristics (bending strength, compression strength, etc.), and by millwork fabricators based upon their physical characteristics (grain, luster, heartwood color, sapwood color, texture, odor, ease of drying, weathering, etc.) and woodworking characteristics (blunting effects, boring, carving, cutting resistance, gluing, mortising, molding, nailing, painting, planing, polishing, sanding, screwing, varnishing, veneering, etc.). Introducing alternative species for structural purposes may require a variance from the building department.

Alternative agricultural products are often based on indigenous materials. Indigenous materials include: straw, wool, coconut fibers, cactus juice, leaves, ice, and sod. Most governing agencies classify "indigenous" construction as "alternative" construction. Use of alternative or indigenous building materials and methods will probably require a variance from the building department. Fortunately, obtaining such a variance is easier than it was previously, due to the groundbreaking work of the Development Center for Appropriate Technology (refer to Appendix A for contact information) to develop sustainable model building codes, and the grassroots efforts in Arizona, California, and New Mexico to incorporate straw bale construction in building codes; refer to Section 06750—Straw Bale Construction.

Most alternative agricultural products perform adequately to the purpose for which they were designed. In some instances, however, the manufacturer does not have all the testing data typically used to describe performance requirements (i.e., compression, screw pull-out, etc.). Furthermore, such tests have often been specifically drafted and redrafted over the years to accommodate the petroleum- and/or synthetic chemical-based product that the alternative agricultural product is replacing. The standard test methods may not be appropriate to the new type of material. ASTM, ISO, and other standards organizations are only beginning to address this need.

06750   STRAW BALE CONSTRUCTION (not a standard CSI Section)

Resource Management: Straw is a renewable resource and an agricultural waste product that is typically burned, thus contributing to air pollution. Straw is often confused with hay, which is a food product; straw is the dry stems of cereal grains after the seed heads have been removed.

Toxicity/IEQ: Straw is natural and nontoxic, although some people may be allergic to it. While straw bales do not represent a food sources, they may provide a home for microbes, insects, and small animals, so it is important to encapsulate the bales inside and outside with Portland cement plaster.

Performance: Straw bale walls can be either load-bearing or nonload-bearing. Typically, straw bale walls are stacked bales pinned together using reinforcing bar (rebar) dowels, which are drilled or driven into the successive courses of bales.

Transverse loading testing in accordance with ASTM E-330, Test Method for Structural Performance of Exterior Windows, Curtain Walls, and Doors by Uniform Static Air Pressure Difference, resulted in a maximum deflection of 1.87″ at 20 psf for unstuccoed straw bale walls, and a maximum deflection of 0.13″ at 20 psf and a maximum deflection of 0.22″ at 50 psf for stuccoed straw bale walls.

Fire testing in accordance with ASTM E-119, Method for Fire Tests of Building Construction and Materials, resulted in a survived flame penetration for unstuccoed straw bale wall of 34 minutes, and for stuccoed straw bale walls of 120 minutes (the test discontinued at 120 minutes). The stuccoed straw bale walls survived the fire hose test with no indication of distress or failure.

The R-value for straw bale walls, as tested by Sandia Laboratories, is 2.67 per inch of thickness; thermal values for walls range from R-44 to R-52.

There are many jurisdictions that allow straw bale building under the alternative materials and methods provisions of the existing codes, but there are also some that have specific provisions for straw bale construction, including parts of Arizona (the City of Tucson, Pima County, Pinal County, the Town of Guadalupe); California (State Guidelines and several counties and municipalities); Boulder, Colorado; the state of New Mexico; and Austin, Texas.

DIVISION 7   **THERMAL AND MOISTURE PROTECTION**
07100   DAMPPROOFING AND WATERPROOFING
Resource Management: Natural materials such as bentonite clay are available (and have long been used) for waterproofing below grade. Many sheet membrane waterproofing materials contain a small percentage of recycled asphalt or rubber.

Zero-VOC, clear, penetrating water repellents for masonry, concrete, and stucco are available.

Toxicity/IEQ: VOCs may be emitted during the curing process. Comply with applicable regulations regarding toxic and hazardous materials, South Coast Air Quality Management District regulations, and as specified.

Performance: Performance is comparable for green methods and standard methods.

07200   THERMAL PROTECTION

Resource Management: Mining raw materials produces soil erosion, pollutant runoff, and habitat loss. Manufacture of plastic foams may emit benzene and other known carcinogens.

Insulation made from renewable resources such as cellulose are available. Straw, wool, coconut fibers, leaves, and sod are traditional and indigenous insulation materials; refer to Section 06700—Alternative Agricultural Products.

Insulation made from recycled materials such as cellulose and textiles and glass are available. Thermal batt insulation includes: glass fiber (can contain 5 percent to 30 percent recycled glass), cotton insulation (can contain 95 percent postindustrial recycled fiber), mineral wool (made from slag wool, an industrial byproduct from iron ore blast furnace, and rock wool, natural material such as basalt and diabase). Sprayed insulation includes: cellulose (which contains up to 75 percent postconsumer recovered paper). Loose fill insulation includes: perlite, vermiculite, polystyrene beads (which may contain recycled-content polystyrene, and cellulose (which contains up to 75 percent postconsumer recovered paper). Foamed in-place insulation includes: silicate foam (made from inorganic cementitious stabilizer, magnesium oxide, a catalyst, and compressed air) and polyicynene (petrochemical-based product, with foaming agent of carbon dioxide and water). Rigid board insulation includes: cellular glass foam, expanded polystyrene, extruded polystyrene, and polyurethane. Polyurethane typically uses an HCFC or an HFC blowing agent. Polyisocyanurate typically uses HCFC blowing agents.

The EPA's "Guideline for Procurement of Building Insulation Products Containing Recovered Materials" (40 CFR 248) recommends minimum recycled content for construction projects receiving federal funding. The EPA recommendations for insulation materials include: rock wool: slag 75 percent; fiberglass: glass cullet 20 percent to 25 percent; cellulose (loose-fill and spray-on): postconsumer paper 75 percent; perlite composite board: postconsumer paper 23 percent; plastic rigid foam: (polyisocyanurate/polyurethane): recovered material 5 percent; glass fiber-reinforced: recovered material 6 percent; phenolic rigid foam: recovered material 5 percent.

Avoid insulation materials manufactured with chemical compounds that have ozone-depleting potential, such as extruded polystyrene and polyisocyanurate board. Chlorofluorocarbons (CFCs) and hydrochlorofluorocarbons (HCFCs) have been widely used as blowing agents in the manufacture of insulation foams; they are known to contribute to depletion of the stratospheric ozone. CFCs have already been eliminated in the United States by Clean Air Act amendments, and HCFCs used in many plastic foams will be eliminated by 2020 or sooner. Carbon dioxide is an available replacement blowing agent, and is already being used by a few manufacturers.

Toxicity/IEQ: Adsorptive materials such as batt insulation may act as sinks for VOCs. Thermal and fireproof insulation materials do not necessarily need a soft, adsorptive surface; consider coating with a smooth and impermeable membrane to reduce the adsorption of VOCs. Design such that an impermeable layer is not located to create a moisture problem in the exterior envelope.

Synthetic insulations manufactured via polymerization or foaming and expansion emit VOCs that are known irritants, such as formaldehyde, xylene, and toluene. Most plastic foams release noxious and toxic chemicals when subject to intense heat or fire. The International Agency for Research on Cancer (IARC) identifies slag wool, rock wool, and fiberglass as "possible" carcinogens. OSHA requires warning labels and MSDSs for fiberglass material, identifying it as a "possible" carcinogen. The long, thin fibers of fibrous minerals are suspected of increasing the risk of cancer. Avoid the use of fiberglass and mineral fiber insulations in conditions that are exposed to the airstream. Fibrous glass insulation materials may contain formaldehyde-based resin binder materials. EPA classifies fiberglass as a "probable" carcinogen.

It is generally believed that airborne cellulose is nontoxic. However, cellulose insulation can contain chemical additives such as ammonium sulfate, boric acid, and sodium borate, for fire retardancy. The chemicals are considered to be stable under normal conditions (including typical attic conditions). Borates are considered to have low acute toxicity for mammals.

Performance: Insulation conserves energy. Avoid thermal bridging, especially with highly conductive metal framing systems. Loose-fill insulation materials can settle over time, thereby reducing their insulation value; however, loose-fill spray insulation can have an added binder to eliminate settling. Foil facing provides some resistance to air infiltration and adds radiant barrier if air space is provided in front of the foil.

07310   SHINGLES

Resource Management: Mining raw materials for the manufacture of fiberglass mat, stabilizers, and surfacing granules produces soil erosion, pollutant runoff, and habitat loss. Asphalt, modifiers, and fiberglass mat binders are derived from petrochemicals. Extraction of petroleum and natural gas can generate air and water pollution. Organic felt with a recycled fiber content is available in some asphalt shingles. Shingles manufactured from 100 percent recycled plastic and cellulose are available.

Toxicity/IEQ: Asphalt base shingles contain petroleum products, and will outgas, especially in warm, sunny climates. Since the material is on the exterior of the structure, there is generally little direct contamination of indoor air quality.

Performance: Provide light-colored roof surfaces to improve albedo. Asphalt shingles are recyclable, especially for paving, but the infrastructure necessary to effectively recycle them is not yet developed.

Recycled plastic shingles can have a class A fire rating, pass wind tests up to 110 mph, and be sawed and nailed like wood.

Photovoltaic shingles are available; refer to Section 13600—Solar And Wind Energy Equipment.

07320   ROOF TILES

Resource Management: Roof tiles may be fabricated from clay, fiber cement, concrete, or metal. Refer to Section 03300—Concrete for information regarding Portland cement. Fiber-cement roofing can include recycled-content fiber. Felt underlayment can include recycled content. Metal roofing tiles and panels can contain up to 100 percent recycled metal.

Toxicity/IEQ: Clay, concrete, fiber cement, and metal are considered inert. And because the material is on the exterior of the structure, there is generally little direct contamination of indoor air quality.

Performance: Provide light-colored roof surfaces to improve albedo. Clay, concrete, fiber cement, and metal are durable, fire- and insect-resistant, and easily disassembled. Clay, concrete, and fiber cement may be crushed and used for subbase material or fill.

07330   ROOF COVERINGS (SOD, GARDEN)

Resource Management: Obviously, sod and garden roofs offer an excellent opportunity to incorporate renewable resources into the built environment. Modern systems have evolved from traditional building techniques and include membranes and drainage layers appropriate to modern building needs. Some systems are available with drainage layers manufactured from recycled plastic.

Toxicity/IEQ: Garden and sod roofing systems are not only nontoxic, they have the capacity to improve environmental quality. Plants process carbon dioxide (carbon sinking). They can process certain types of toxins through their leaves and roots. Refer to Section 02055—Soils, for information on phytoremediation.

Performance: Garden and sod roof systems, when properly detailed and installed, can provide excellent thermal and acoustic insulation. Warranted garden roof systems have been used in Europe for decades. The plants will contribute to carbon sinking and can provide wildlife corridors, urban agriculture, and recreational areas. By using water in situ, they will also help minimize stormwater runoff and improve local hydrologic cycle functions. Care must be taken to design for anticipated live and dead loads.

07400   ROOFING AND SIDING PANELS

Resource Management: Can contain recycled content materials for steel, aluminum, and copper. Refer to Section 05050—Basic Metals Materials and Methods for information on metal finishing.

Toxicity/IEQ: Metal is considered inert. Composite panels generally utilize polystyrene insulation. Refer to Section 07200—Thermal Protection for information on polystyrene. Fibercement siding is also considered to be inert.

Performance: Provide light-colored roof surfaces to improve albedo. Composite panels that adhesively combine polystyrene and different metals are difficult to recycle. Fibercement siding is recyclable. Mechanical fastening aids in deconstruction for future recycling.

07500   MEMBRANE ROOFING

Resource Management: Membrane manufacturers are developing products fabricated from postconsumer materials.

Toxicity/IEQ: The cold adhesives used in adhesive application of roofing membranes are volatile chemicals that pose health and safety risks. They are combustible, harmful, or fatal if swallowed, and dangerous to inhale. Roofing adhesive that is water-based and/or low- VOC is available. Where a solvent-based adhesive is necessary, coordinate with temporary ventilation requirements in Section 01351—Environmental Procedures to close all air intakes near the work area to prevent solvent fumes from entering the building. Avoid polyvinyl chloride (PVC) membrane roofing, the most common thermoplastic membrane. Refer to Section 09651—Vinyl Flooring for information regarding PVC.

Performance: Provide light-colored roof surfaces to improve albedo (at ballasted membranes, provide light-colored ballast). ASTM has developed standards to quantify albedo. New product labels with the EPA and DOE, under the Energy Star program, indicate the solar reflective index. Use roof insulation systems as required by building location and energy calculations for building type and project requirements.

Membrane roofing is relatively durable. The average life expectancy of a coal tar built-up roof is 20 years; the average life expectancy of an asphalt built-up roof is 15 years. The average life expectancy of modified bitumen roofing is 15 years. The life expectancy of EPDM roofing is 20 years. Membrane roofing is difficult to recycle because of the variety of materials involved and because those materials are generally adhered to each other. While reuse and recycling of membrane roofing is not typical, it is possible. Mechanically fastened membranes will be easier to disassemble in the future, facilitating recycling of membrane and of substrate. Installation of a layer of sheathing between roofing insulation and roofing membrane may allow for membrane removal without damage to insulation.

07600   FLASHING AND SHEET METAL
             Refer to Section 05050—Basic Metals Materials and Meth-
             ods for information on metals and metal finishing.

07800   FIRE AND SMOKE PROTECTION
             Resource Management: Mineral wool has a high resis-
             tance to fire and is often used as a firesafing insulation.
             Mineral wool includes rock wool (from expanded perlite or
             other mineral) and slag wool (from steel, copper, or lead
             mill slag). Rock wool is no longer produced in the United
             States. The EPA recommends that mineral wool insulation
             contain at least 75 percent recovered slag.
             Toxicity/IEQ: Spray-on fireproofing fibers or other
             components may be released into indoor air. Dust problems
             can occur when fireproofing is drilled or otherwise pene-
             trated. Adsorptive materials may act as sinks for VOCs.
                 The International Agency for Research on Cancer
             (IARC) identifies slag wool and rock wool as "possible"
             carcinogens. The long, thin fibers of fibrous minerals are
             suspected of increasing the risk of cancer. Avoid the use of
             fiberglass and mineral fiber insulation in conditions that are
             exposed to the airstream.
             Performance: Performance is comparable for green
             methods and standard methods.

07900   JOINT SEALERS
             Resource Management: Avoid   polyvinyl   chloride
             (PVC) based products. Refer to Section 09651—Vinyl
             Flooring for information regarding PVC.
             Toxicity/IEQ: VOCs may be emitted during the curing
             process. Coordinate with temporary ventilation require-
             ments in Section 01351—Environmental Procedures. Seal-
             ants continue to outgas throughout their life. Specify
             sealants, particularly for interior applications, that are
             water-based and low VOC. Specify that curing-type interior
             sealants do not contain butyl rubber, neoprene, SBR (sty-
             rene butadiene rubber), or nitride. Avoid sealants containing
             aromatic solvents, fibrous talc, formaldehyde, halogenated
             solvents, mercury, lead, cadmium, chromium, and their
             compounds. The following sealants are generally consid-
             ered acceptable for indoor use: oleoresinous (small amounts
             of aliphatic hydrocarbons), acrylic emulsion latex, polysul-
             fide (small amounts of toluene vapors), polyurethane (small
             amounts of xylene and other solvents), and silicone (small
             amounts of xylene and other solvents). The following seal-
             ants should be avoided indoors: butyl rubber (aliphatic hy-

drocarbons), solvent-based acrylic (xylene), neoprene (xylene), styrene butadiene rubber (various VOCs—hexane, toluene, and xylene, depending on type), and nitrile (various VOCs—hexane, toluene, and xylene, depending on type).

Closed-cell backer rods outgas when ruptured. Opencell polyurethane backer rods are spongelike and may absorb moisture. Consider composite backer rods.

Performance: Reduces air infiltration and moisture penetration. Performance is comparable for green methods and standard methods. Verify that the proper sealant is specified for the given application. Improper selection can result in reapplication, air infiltration, and water damage

DIVISION 8
08050

DOORS AND WINDOWS
BASIC DOOR AND WINDOW MATERIALS AND METHODS

Resource Management: Refer to Division 6 for information related to wood and plastic. Refer to Division 5 for information related to metal.

Toxicity/IEQ: Plastics and factory coatings may outgas.

Performance: Specify window systems that are compatible with the calculated thermal loads of the building. This will reduce condensation not only on the glazing and sash, but also on the adjacent wall and other interior surfaces. For wood doors and windows, see comments in Division 6. Provide thermal break for exterior framing systems, and weather-stripping for doors in exterior frame to reduce thermal conductivity and improve energy efficiency

08100

METAL DOORS AND FRAMES

Resource Management: Core materials for metal doors vary widely, including fiberglass and plastic foams (polystyrene and polyurethane) for insulating doors, steel ribs, honeycomb paperboard (which often has recovered content), or a fire-resistive core (such as mineral fiber) for fire-rated doors. HFC-free, HCFC-free expanded polystyrene is the preferable insulating core; refer to Section 07200—Thermal Protection for information on blowing agents.

Where possible, specify factory finishing; refer to Section 05050—Basic Metal Materials And Methods. Where field finishing is required, specify a high solids, low VOC-durable coating such as a high-performance water-based acrylic paint. Avoid alkyd enamel paint, a solvent-based paint that emits large quantities of VOCs.

Toxicity/IEQ: Metal is inert and has virtually no impact on IAQ.

Performance: Specify an insulation core for exterior metal doors.

08200   WOOD AND PLASTIC DOORS

Resource Management: Doors fabricated from sustainably harvested wood are available. Specify doors that are certified under FSC principles. Some wood fiber composite doors have insulating cores; refer to Section 08100—Metal Doors and Frames.

Toxicity/IEQ: Refer to Section 06500—Structural Plastics. Refer to Section 09651—Vinyl Flooring for information regarding PVC.

Performance: Performance is comparable for green methods and standard methods. Refer to Section 08500—Windows for information regarding The National Fenestration Rating Council (NFRC) rating program.

08500   WINDOWS

Resource Management: Windows fabricated from sustainably harvested wood are available. Specify wood windows that are certified under FSC principles and/or are finger-jointed construction.

Toxicity/IEQ: Refer to Section 09651—Vinyl Flooring for information regarding PVC.

Performance: Specify low-conductivity frame, sash, and spacer materials. Wood has a high R-value. Metal conducts heat; metal frames should have a thermal break.

According to the EPA Energy Star standards for residential construction, in southern states, windows, doors, and skylights must have a U-factor of 0.75 or lower and a solar heat gain coefficient (SHGC) of 0.40 or lower; in the middle states, widows and doors must have a U-factor of 0.40 or lower and an SHGC of 0.55 or lower, and skylights must have a U-factor of 0.50 or lower and an SHGC of 0.55 or lower; and in northern states, windows and doors must have a U-factor of 0.35 or lower, and skylights must have a U-factor of 0.45 or lower.

Green Seal has developed standards for windows (GS-13) and window films (GS-14) that specify minimum requirements for energy efficiency, packaging, and labeling. The National Fenestration Rating Council (NFRC) has a rating program for a fixed set of environmental conditions and specific product sizes. While the ratings may not be directly applicable for determining seasonal energy performance, they nevertheless indicate general energy efficiency parameters. An NFRC label should include residential and nonresidential values for the U-factor, solar heat gain coefficient, and visible light transmittance. It should also indicate the specific product descriptions such as "Model xxx Casement, low-e, argon-filled."

08600   SKYLIGHTS

Resource Management: Resource management impacts are comparable for green methods and standard methods.

Toxicity/IEQ: Toxicity/IEQ is comparable for green methods and standard methods.

Performance: Daylight tubes that "pipe" or "duct" natural light into a space are available. Active tracking devices are available that follow the sun's path and maximize the amount of natural light directed through the skylight opening. Refer to Section 08500µWindows for information regarding The National Fenestration Rating Council (NFRC) rating program.

08700   HARDWARE

Refer to Section 05050—Basic Metals Materials and Methods for information on metals and metal finishing.

08800   GLAZING

Resource Management: Mining raw materials (sand, limestone, and soda ash) produces soil erosion, pollutant runoff, and habitat loss. Manufacturing is energy-intensive and can generate heat, air, and water pollution.

Recycled glass products are available for decorative architectural glass (stained glass and glass block).

Toxicity/IEQ: Glass is inert and has virtually no impact on IAQ. VOCs may be emitted from glazing compounds during the curing process.

Performance: Glazing technologies are improving rapidly. Control of light and heat transmittance, and the corresponding energy efficiency, is becoming much more sophisticated. At one end of the spectrum is the traditional insulated glazing. Typical, off-the-shelf energy efficiency specifications may call for double-glazed, low-E units with coating on the second surface (inner side of outer panel) in climates below 3,000 heating degree days, and on the third surface (outer side of inner panel) for climates at or over 3,000 heating degree days. At the other end of the spectrum, however, are photovoltaic spandrel panels and films that turn increasingly translucent/opaque when exposed to heat. Refer to Section 08900, Glazed CurtainWall.

08900 GLAZED CURTAIN WALL

Resource Management: Refer to Section 08800—Glazing for information regarding glass and refer to Section 05050—Basic Metal Materials and Methods for information regarding metals.

Toxicity/IEQ: Glass and metal are considered inert.

Performance: Photovoltaic curtainwall panel systems are available; refer to Section 13600—Solar And Wind Energy Equipment.

DIVISION 9 **FINISHES**

09050 BASIC FINISH MATERIALS AND METHODS

Resource Management: Many low-VOC, recycled-content products and alternative agricultural-content products are available for interior finishes. Refer to the individual sections for additional information.

Toxicity/IEQ: VOCs may be emitted from products, especially factory-packaged (e.g., shrink-wrapped) products, adhesives, and finishes during the curing process. Ventilate products prior to installation. Remove from packaging and ventilate in a secure, dry, well-ventilated space free from strong contaminant sources and residues. Ventilate away from other materials that may adsorb. Provide a temperature range of 60 degrees F minimum to 90 degree F maximum continuously for minimum 72 hours. Do not ventilate within limits of work unless otherwise approved by the owner. Coordinate with temporary ventilation in Section 01351—Environmental Procedures.

For most applications, low or zero-VOC adhesives are available.

Performance: Performance is comparable for green methods and standard methods for a broad range of finish materials. That is, there are many green products at low, middle, and high end of the performance and cost spectrum—just like standard materials and methods. Performance of a particular green product to a particular standard product may vary.

09100 METAL SUPPORT ASSEMBLIES

Resource Management: Refer to Section 05100—Structural Metal Framing, for information regarding steel.

Toxicity/IEQ: Thermal bridging at steel framing in exterior walls can create cold spots in the wall that promote the growth of mold.

Refer to Section 05100—Structural Metal Framing for information regarding steel.

Performance: Thermal bridging at exterior walls can negatively impact energy efficiency. Dimpled framing is being tested to determine if a dimpled leg, with less surface area in direct contact with sheathing materials, will improve performance. Proper design with sufficient insulation can address this problem as well.

Refer to Section 05100—Structural Metal Framing for information regarding steel.

09215   **PLASTER**

Resource Management: Mining raw materials (cement rock, limestone, clay, and/or shale) produces soil erosion, pollutant runoff, and habitat loss. Plaster includes Portland cement plaster and gypsum plaster and metal lath. Refer to Section 03300—Cast-In-Place Concrete, for information regarding Portland cement. Refer to Section 09250—Gypsum for information regarding gypsum and paper. Refer to Section 05100—Structural Metal Framing, for information regarding steel.

Toxicity/IEQ: Plaster is considered inert when cured. VOCs may be emitted from plaster additives during the curing process.

Performance: Performance is comparable for green methods and standard methods.

09250   **GYPSUM BOARD**

Resource Management: Mining raw materials (gypsum, limestone, clay, talc, mica, and perlite) produces soil erosion, pollutant runoff, and habitat loss. Gypsum is a non-renewable, although relatively abundant, resource. Calcining (heating at 325 to 340 degrees F to become the hemihydrate of calcium sulfate, stucco) produces significant air emissions; particulate emissions include: calcium sulfate dihydrate, calcium sulfate hemihydrate, anhydrous calcium sulfate, and gangue. Paper (cellulose) is a renewable resource. Paper manufacture is water- and energy-intensive. It generates significant air and water pollutants, including oxygen-depleting organics and toxic chlorinated compounds such as dioxins. Refer to Section 09651—Vinyl Flooring for information on dioxins as carcinogens and endocrine disrupters. According to the EPA's Toxic Release Inventory (TRI) data for 1988, the pulp and paper industry ranked fourth in U.S. industries for total discharges to land, water, and air of TRI pollutants. Most gypsum board products are manufactured with paper backing from primarily recycled paper and gypsum core containing minimum 10 percent recycled gypsum. Percentages vary depending on the manufacturing facility, and are generally increasing throughout the industry as manufacturing facilities upgrade.

Toxicity/IEQ: Additives used to produce waterproof gypsum board ("greenboard") and fire-resistant gypsum board may include VOCs. The paper backing may contain chemicals from previous uses (most paper backing contains recycled materials) and additives or chemicals used in the production of the paper itself. VOCs may be emitted from taping compounds and finishes during the curing process. VOC emissions from gypsum board can be minimized in the final building when gypsum installation is properly sequenced (i.e., installed prior to installation of potential sinks) and encapsulated (painted or coated). Coordinate with temporary ventilation in Section 01351—Environmental Procedures. Joint cement and texture compounds formulated with inert fillers and natural binders are available.

Performance: Performance is comparable for green methods and standard methods. Scrap gypsum can be recycled on-site as soil amendment; coordinate with Section 02900—Planting to identify requirements for gypsum soil amendment. Also, placing small scraps in interior wall cavities can add thermal mass and sound insulation.

09300   TILE

Resource Management: Mining raw materials (clay, silica, talc, feldspar, and limestone) for tile produces soil erosion, pollutant runoff, and habitat loss. Clay and sand are nonrenewable, although relatively abundant, resources. Adhesives for setting tile and for latex mortar and grout are typically derived from petrochemicals. Standard Portland cement mortar is composed of Portland cement, sand, and water; refer to Section 03300—Cast-In-Place Concrete for information regarding Portland cement. Pigments include a variety of crystalline materials obtained from the calcining of oxides of metals such as cobalt, nickel, aluminum, and chromium.

Manufacturing of ceramic tile is energy-intensive; however, there have been some energy efficiency improvements in firing techniques in recent years. Manufacture generates significant particulate emissions. Most manufacturers reclaim their fired scrap materials.

Tile containing recycled glass is available; generally, the recycled glass is preconsumer, industry waste such as windshield glass and waste from lightbulb manufacture. Tile containing feldspar tailings, a byproduct of the feldspar refining process, is available.

Toxicity/IEQ: Tile (ceramic and quarry) is inert, and cementitious mortar and grout is considered inert when cured. VOCs may be emitted from self-leveling cements and adhesives during the curing process. Avoid mortars, grout, and adhesives containing petroleum or plastic additives. Additives in latex formulations may include styrene butadiene rubber, acrylic resin, polyvinyl acetate, and ethylene vinyl acetate.

Performance: Tile is extremely durable and requires little maintenance. Performance is comparable for green methods and standard methods.

09400   TERRAZZO

Resource Management: Terrazzo flooring was originally developed as a byproduct of Italian mosaic artwork. As mosaic artists chipped marble tessera for their mosaic pieces, the marble and lime mortar tailings that fell to the floor were swept out on the terrace where there were trampled into the surface. Soon, such flooring was common on Italian terraces; hence, "terrazza." Today, the chips are generally not byproducts, but are specifically mined. Mining raw materials (marble, granite, quartzite, quartz, silica pebbles, sand, and components of Portland cement) produces soil erosion, pollutant runoff, and habitat loss. Underground mining of crushed stone is becoming more common due to increased environmental and economic benefits. In underground (room-and-pillar) mining, there is less overburden to be removed, and operations can continue all year long. Components of resins, primers and sealers are typically derived from petrochemicals. Refer to Section 03300—Cast-In-Place Concrete for information regarding Portland cement.

Terrazzo aggregate can contain recycled glass stone and glass aggregate.

Toxicity/IEQ: When cured, terrazzo is fairly inert. VOCs may be emitted from plastic matrix during the curing process and from sealers during curing and periodic maintenance. Coordinate with temporary ventilation in Section 01351—Environmental Procedures, especially where epoxy terrazzo systems are used. Waterborne acrylic sealers are available for most applications. Avoid epoxy sealers except where chemical or stain resistance is required. Avoid polyvinyl divider strips; refer to Section 09651—Vinyl Flooring for information on PVC.

Performance: Performance is comparable for green methods and standard methods. Terrazzo with glass aggregate has an apparent depth and luminescence that can be very beautiful. An alternative to sealing Portland cement terrazzo is to clean with a neutral cleaner/water solution. After several cleanings, the residue of cleaner on the floor will make it buffable. After approximately two months, the floor finish will have a patina that requires less maintenance.

09510   ACOUSTICAL CEILINGS

Resource Management: The major constituents of acoustical ceiling tiles are mineral wool (fabricated from slag and rock wool), cellulose, starch (primarily from corn), clay (for fire-rated products), fiberglass, and paint. Mining raw materials produces soil erosion, pollutant runoff, and habitat loss. Manufacture of acoustic ceiling tiles does not generate much waste because scrap material is recycled back into the process. Acoustic ceiling tile manufactured from recycled cellulose is available; generally, the recycled cellulose is preconsumer industry waste. Steel framing containing recycled steel is available. Refer to Section 05100—Structural Metal Framing for information regarding steel.

Toxicity/IEQ: Paints used in ceiling tiles and panels are low-VOC, water-based paints. Refer to Section 07200—Thermal Protection for information regarding slag wool, rock wool, and fiberglass as "possible" carcinogens. Avoid vinyl-faced ceiling tiles. PVC is used in the vinyl facing on some ceiling tiles. Refer to Section 09651—Vinyl Flooring for information regarding PVC.

Adsorptive materials may act as sinks for VOCs emitted from other sources. When the concealed spaces above suspended ceilings are used as return air plenums, both the upper and lower surfaces of the ceilings are exposed to the circulating air stream. And the temperatures at the ceiling surfaces are generally among the warmest in the interior space due to the thermal stratification that normally occurs. The increased temperature results in increased emissions of VOC from the ceiling materials.

Cornstarch used as a binder can, in the presence of moisture, fuel growth of bacteria and mold.

Performance: Performance of green materials for noise reduction coefficient (NRC) standards and light reluctance is comparable to standard materials. Cellulose ceiling tiles are suitable for dry areas and moderate acoustical requirements. Where acoustical demands are higher, specify mineral fiber tiles or cellulose tiles coated with low-VOC, water-based paint. Cellulose, mineral fiber, and glass fiber can absorb moisture in high humidity areas and promote microbial growth. In those areas, specify tiles with nonabsorptive cores such as glass fiber reinforced polyester.

WOOD FLOORING

09640

Resource Management: Wood flooring manufactured from reclaimed lumber and from alternative species is available. Bamboo, for example, is a fast-growing grass that can be finished into beautiful hardwood flooring. Refer to Section 06700—Alternative Agricultural Products for information on alternative species. Refer to Section 06100—Rough Carpentry for information on wood as a renewable resource and on sustainable forestry. Most stains and varnishes are derived from petrochemicals.

Toxicity/IEQ: Avoid wood floor finishes that are solvent-based polyurethanes. Water-based polyurethanes contain mostly aliphatic hydrocarbons instead of the mostly carcinogenic aromatic hydrocarbons found in solvent-based finishes. Other alternatives include waxes and citrus-based finishes.

Performance: Performance is comparable for green methods and standard methods. Bamboo has twice the stability of red oak and up to 90 percent of the hardness. Installation and maintenance is similar to a hardwood floor. Water-based polyurethanes may not perform as well as solvent-based in high-traffic areas.

VINYL FLOORING

09651

Resource Management: Many of the components of vinyl flooring are derived from petrochemicals. Resilient flooring manufactured from 100 percent recycled PVC is available in sheet, tile, and plank.

Vinyl flooring and vinyl composite tiles (VCTs) are manufactured from a variety of hazardous chemicals and nonrenewable petroleum-based resources, including ethylene dichloride and polyvinyl chloride (PVC). Manufacture of PVC produces many highly toxic byproducts, including:

dioxins, polychlorinated biphenyls (PCBs), and organo-
chlorines. Hundreds of substances known or suspected of
causing cancer and/or of disrupting our immune and reproductive systems are produced. There are two main
groups of hormone-disrupting chemicals associated with
PVC: dioxins (formed as a byproduct in the oxychlorina-
tion process) and phthalates (plasticisers). Phthalates are
"possible" carcinogens. Dioxins are known carcinogens
and are considered by many to be the most toxic man-made
chemical ever. In addition, other chemicals suspected as
hormone disrupters are used as additives in PVC, including:
organotins, cadmium, lead, and small quantities of alkyl-
phenols. Dioxins are released during the manufacture of
PVC and when PVC is burned or is recycled. Phthalates
are released during processing of plastics, during the product's life, and even after it is disposed. Internationally, use
of PVC is becoming more and more restricted. Communities in Germany, Austria, Japan, the Netherlands, Norway,
Sweden, and Denmark have PVC restrictions in place. Restrictions are also in various stages of development and implementation at the national level in Spain, Switzerland,
Denmark, and Sweden. The U.S. Environmental Protection
Agency is currently reassessing dioxin.

Titanium dioxide (TiO2) is a common white pigment
in resilient flooring. Manufacture of titanium dioxide can
produce sulfuric acid, metal sulfate, and metal chloride byproducts. According to NIOSH, titanium dioxide may cause
lung fibrosis, and is considered to be an occupational carcinogen.

Toxicity/IEQ: Vinyl flooring will outgas and, when
burned, will release hydrogen chloride, metal chlorides, and
dioxins. When vinyl flooring is incinerated, heavy metals
remaining in the ash must be treated as hazardous waste.

Most leveling compounds contain latex or polyvinyl acetate resins, and can emit VOCs, including 4-PC. Adhesives
may also be a source of VOCs. Factory-backed adhesive
tiles have fewer emissions than standard "wet" adhesive
installation. Low- and zero-VOC adhesives are available.
Some styles of plastic flooring are available in loose-laid
design (puzzle pieces that are tapped together with a rubber
mallet) that can be installed without adhesive.

Performance: Solid vinyl flooring has a static load resistance of up to 700 psi; vinyl composition tile (VCT) has
a static load resistance of up to 80 psi. Vinyl becomes brit-

tle as it ages, and the plasticizers migrate out of the material; vinyl-resilient flooring typically has a life span of 8 to 15 years. Consider solid vinyl products only where chemical resistance is required. Factory-backed adhesive tiles may not perform as well as "wet" adhesive installation in high-traffic areas.

09652   RUBBER FLOORING

Resource Management: Rubber floors may contain industrial and natural rubber. Industrial rubber is obtained through the polymerization of petroleum products. By varying the polymerization process, rubber with varying characteristics is produced. Natural rubber is a renewable raw material that is extracted from the sap of the tropical rubber plant (without harming the plant). Rubber flooring with 75 percent to 100 percent postconsumer recycled content is available.

Toxicity/IEQ: Rubber does not contain any PVCs, halogens (chlorine, bromine, iodine, fluorine), plasticizers, formaldehyde, or cadmium.

Performance: Rubber flooring is extremely hard-wearing and flame-retardant, and is permanently resilient. Antistatic and chemically resistant rubber flooring is available. No waxes are required to maintain rubber floors. Fewer color and pattern options are available for rubber than are available for linoleum or vinyl. Rubber is recyclable.

09653   LINOLEUM FLOORING

Resource Management: Linoleum is manufactured from cork, linseed oil, wood flour, and pine resin. Ground-up stone and wood are added for color. Backing is typically jute or polyglass. As agricultural products, cultivation of jute, flax (linseed oil), and pine can contribute to carbon sinking; they can also result in runoff of pesticides and chemical fertilizers. Wood flour and cork flour are typically obtained from preconsumer industrial wastes. Polyglass is a combination of fiberglass and polyester fibers. The finish coat is typically a waterborne acrylic. Titanium dioxide (TiO_2) is a common white pigment in resilient flooring. Refer to Section 09651—Vinyl Flooring for information on titanium dioxide.

Manufacture generates very little waste because nearly all manufacturing waste is recycled back into product.

Toxicity/IEQ: Linoleum is made predominantly from renewable resources, and while it has a distinctive odor, it emits no dangerous VOCs. Offgassing from linoleum may cause problems for persons with chemical sensitivity, especially during the first few days after installation. After a few days or weeks, the oxidation of the linseed oil decreases significantly.

Linoleum is naturally antibacterial because of the continuous oxidation of the linseed oil.

Performance: Linoleum is biodegradable and may be shredded and composted. It is very durable; linoleum flooring typically has a life span of 40 years (or more). Linoleum tile has a static load resistance of 700 psi; linoleum sheet has a static load resistance of 150 psi. Linoleum is water-resistant, but must be protected from moisture from the substrate both during and after installation.

Linoleum is available in sheet or tiles.

Linoleum can be maintained with a dry maintenance system and periodic buffing; it does not require (and may be damaged by) the periodic wet maintenance and refinishing that is typical on vinyl flooring.

09654   CORK FLOORING

Resource Management: Cork is a renewable resource harvested on a nine-year cycle. Some cork flooring is fabricated from bottle-cork industry waste. Manufacture involves few toxins and generates very little waste because nearly all manufacturing waste is recycled back into product.

Toxicity/IEQ: Cork is naturally antibacterial.

Performance: Cork provides good soundproofing and insulation. It may be used as an underlayment for ceramic or wood floors. It may also be finished flooring itself. Cork is biodegradable and recyclable. It is very durable; cork flooring typically has a life span of 40 years (or more).

09680   CARPET

Resource Management: Wool, cotton, jute, hemp, seagrass, and sisal rugs and carpets are available. Carpet manufactured from recycled PET (soda pop bottles) or from BASF nylon (sometimes called "6 again" nylon) is available. The BASF nylon is recyclable, and a close-the-loop infrastructure is developing within the carpeting industry, whereby manufacturers can reclaim and recycle carpeting manufactured from the BASF fiber. Previously, carpet manufacturers argued that old carpeting could not be recycled into new carpeting and that reclaimed synthetic carpet was recycled into roadbase aggregate and fill. Carpet pads manufactured from recycled textiles and waste carpets is available.

Toxicity/IEQ: Synthetic carpet fiber, backing, pad, adhesive, seam sealants, carpet treatment (mothproofing, antimicrobial, etc.) and floor-preparation chemicals are all potential sources of VOCs in indoor air. Carpet can contain more than 100 chemicals, including possible carcinogens. VOCs may be emitted from adhesives and from interaction of adhesive and carpet backing during the curing process. Install with tack strips (stretch-in method) over pads to avoid adhesive interaction with carpet backing. Hook-and-loop (Velcro) installation has been developed by 3M (called the TacFast system) and is available for carpeting from several mills. The carpet has a special loop backing that easily fastens and refastens to the companion hook strips adhered to the substrate. TacFast installation significantly reduces the VOCs due to adhesive carpet installation, making replacement of carpeting easier.

The Carpet and Rug Institute (CRI) addresses issues of IAQ and carpeting, and sponsors a green label program. CRI has established emission-level standards for: total volatile organic compounds (TVOCs), styrene; 4-PC (4 phenylcyclohexene), and formaldehyde. Green Seal recommends that carpets bear the CRI Indoor Air Quality Carpet Testing Program label or satisfy the State of Washington guidelines.

Carpeting also provides a sink for absorbing VOCs emitted from other sources and a home for a variety of bacteria, microbes, dust mites, and so on. Area rugs are a good alternative because they can be removed and cleaned outdoors by beating and letting the sun "bake" them.

Performance: Carpeting provides improved thermal and acoustic performance. Natural carpets are typically more expensive and require more care than most synthetic rugs, but they can age more beautifully.

In addition to the close-the-loop recycling programs developing in the carpet industry, a few manufacturers also have green lease programs.

09720   WALL COVERINGS

Resource Management: Cellulose (in wallpaper) is a renewable resource. Refer to Section 09250—Gypsum for information regarding paper. Polyvinyl chloride (in vinyl wall covering) is a significant environmental hazard. Refer to Section 09651—Vinyl Flooring, for information on PVC.

Wall coverings manufactured from recycled cotton, sustainably harvested wood, and natural materials such as sisal, jute, straw, and wool are available.

Toxicity/IEQ: Fabrics, plastics, and paper wall coverings all have unique potential chemical content and emission characteristics. Avoid vinyl wall covering due to the PVC content.

VOCs may be emitted from adhesives and backings during the curing process.

Performance: Performance is comparable for green methods and standard methods.

09900   PAINTS AND COATINGS

Resource Management: Most standard paints contain some materials that are derived from petroleum products. Titanium dioxide (TiO2) is a common white pigment in standard paint; refer to Section 09651—Vinyl Flooring for information regarding titanium dioxide. Paints manufactured from natural plant- and mineral-based finishes are available. They contain extracts from plant sources and minimally processed earth minerals, such as chalk or iron oxides. Solvents for natural paints include citrus oils and small amounts of low-odor petroleum solvents (dearomaticized isoparrafinics.) Milk-based paint contains lime, milk protein, clay, and earth pigments.

Recycled content paints are available.

Toxicity/IEQ: Paint products contain a variety of VOCs incorporated as drying agents, flattening agents, mildewcides, fungicides, preservatives, and others. Harmful chemicals found in paint include: methylene chloride, 1,1,1-trichloroethane, benzene, toluene, ethylbenzene, vinyl chloride, naphthalene, 1,2-di-chlorobenzene, di(2-ethylhexyl) phthalate, butyl benzyl phthalate, di-n-butyl phthalate, di-n-octyl phthalate, diethyl phthalate, dimethyl phthalate, isoprene, antimony, cadmium, hexavalent chromium, lead, mercury, formaldehyde, methyl ethyl ketone, methyl isobutyl ketone, acrolein, acrylonitrile. These VOCs have been measured in indoor air many months after application of the paints. South Coast Air Quality Management District (SCAQMD) has adopted VOC regulations; jurisdictions outside of California, including the federal government, have begun adopting similar regulations. Low-biocide paint is available. Low- and zero-VOC paint is available for both interior and exterior paint. Even "zero-VOC"-labeled paint may contain a maximum 1 gram/liter (white paint). There may be a slight increase in VOC for colored paint. Pigments can add as much as 5 percent to a paint's VOC content. Even natural paints may emit VOCs (natural VOCs), which may pose a problem for some chemically sensitive individuals.

Coordinate with temporary ventilation in Section 01351, Environmental Procedures.

Performance: Milk-based paint, the most common paint prior to this century, is not appropriate for exterior use or damp conditions.

Recycled-content paints, depending on the source of reclaimed paint products, may not meet VOC regulations. Some locals are developing regulatory language that exempts recycled-content paint from VOC restrictions. Recycled-content paint may also be limited in color depending on the source of reclaimed paint products. Sources of recycled content include community hazardous waste collection programs and contractor "left-overs."

The performance of low-VOC paint has improved considerably over the last several years. Specify compliance with applicable VOC regulations and SCAQMD VOC regulations, which continue to be some of the strongest VOC requirements in the country, and have contributed to the development of viable low-VOC paints. However, be careful when specifying particular VOC maximum contents relative to the type of paint and type of application. VOC regulations have been volatile themselves, and limits change frequently. Rule 1113, the SCAQMD rule covering paints and coatings, has the distinction of being one of the most amended pieces of regulations in U.S. history. As a guide, for general interior and exterior applications, use water-based latex primers and paints with no aromatic hydrocarbons and VOC content of fewer than 10 grams/liter; for applications subject to impact such as door frames, use water-based, 100 percent solids, high-performance acrylic instead of solvent-based paints; if solvent-based paint is required, use a product with a VOC content of fewer than 380 grams/liter and an aromatic hydrocarbon content less than 1 percent by weight; if epoxy paint is required, use a solvent-free, high-solids, zero-VOC epoxy.

Green Seal has developed standards for anticorrosive paints (GS-03) and for paints (GS-11); they specify minimum requirements for performance, utilizing applicable ASTM standards, VOC limitations, chemical component limitations, packaging, and labeling.

Ceramic coatings for field application over typical exterior cladding materials (masonry, stucco, wood) are also available. Ceramic coatings are low-emissivity paints that reflect radiant energy. Such coatings can generate energy savings of up to 30 percent during the cool season, and are extremely durable.

DIVISION 10	**SPECIALTIES**
10100	VISUAL DISPLAY BOARDS: Refer to Section 09654—Cork Flooring for information regarding cork.
10170	PLASTIC TOILET COMPARTMENTS

Resource Management: Toilet compartments with cores manufactured from minimum 50 percent recycled plastic are available.

Toxicity/IEQ: Refer to Section 06500—Structural Plastics.

Performance: Plastic partitions perform as well or better than most toilet partitions. They are water-resistant, graffiti-resistant, and nonabsorbent, with plastic face sheets permanently fused to plastic core. The pilaster shoes are one-piece-molded HDPE. Wall-mounting brackets are continuous, full-height, heavy-duty plastic.

10260	WALL AND CORNER GUARDS: Recycled plastic wall guards are available. Refer to Section 06500—Structural Plastics. Sustainably harvested wood wall guards are available. Refer to Section 06100—Rough Carpentry.
10270	ACCESS FLOORING:

Resource Management: Access flooring is fabricated with aluminum, steel, and medium-density fiberboard parts. At least one manufacturer, Camino Modular Systems, in Ontario, Canada, is reclaiming used access flooring and refurbishing it for reuse.

Toxicity/IEQ: Medium-density fiberboard generally contains formaldehyde. The concealed space between the raised floor and the structural floor can be a source of contaminants, either gaseous or particulate. However, it can also be used for locating sophisticated personal air control systems.

Performance: Performance is comparable for green methods and standard methods.

10290	PEST CONTROL

Resource Management: Integrated pest management is an environmentally sound system of controlling landscape pests. It includes well-timed nontoxic treatments and an understanding of the pest's life cycle and natural enemies.

Gardeners have been using this approach for centuries. For example, carnivorous insects such as ladybugs are often used to combat aphids; and certain plant combinations promote mutual health and growth (roses and parsley or carrots and tomatoes). Some plants, such as chrysanthemums, have natural pyrethrums. Integrated pest management works with the natural cycles of the ecosystem to take advantage of nature's pest controls. This not only minimizes introduction of toxic, synthetic chemicals, but can also help renew functioning ecosystems.

Proper design can also minimize the need for application of toxic chemicals. Refer to Section 02360—Soil Treatment

Toxicity/IEQ: Selection of materials, proper application, and proper scheduling of pesticide applications can reduce exposures of building occupants. Alternatives to more toxic commercial pest control agents include:
- Exterior plant insecticide: Substitute vinegar, soap, gin, and water mixture.
- Indoor plant insecticide: Substitute dishwater or bar soap and water.
- Mothballs: Substitute cedar chips and lavender flowers.

Performance: Because it addresses the problem, not just the symptom, alternative pest control can be more effective than standard chemical treatment methods. It does, however, tend to require certain preventative maintenance on the part of the building owner, such as preventing pest access to food sources. Verify that the owner understands the maintenance involved and is willing to perform such maintenance.

10300

FIREPLACES AND STOVES

Resource Management: Steel utilized on stoves is recycled material. Steel stoves used for heating that are manufactured from up to 100 percent postconsumer steel are available. Although local conditions vary, combustion appliances rely on a relatively inefficient use of natural resources that generates air emissions and contributes to global warming.

Toxicity/IEQ: Combustion appliances including fireplaces and wood stoves can be sources of organic and inorganic gases and of particulate matter. Smoke particles are possible carcinogens.

Performance: Cast-iron wood stoves, gas stoves, and fireplaces may be used for space heating. Efficiencies have improved in recent years, and range from 50 percent to 90 percent.

10800   TOILET, BATH, AND LAUNDRY ACCESSORIES

Resource Management: Automatic, sensor-operated hand dryers are available.

Toxicity/IEQ: Automatic hand dryers replace paper towels and eliminate their disposal and associated bacteria.

Performance: Performance is comparable for green methods and standard methods.

DIVISION 11   **EQUIPMENT**

11110   COMMERCIAL LAUNDRY AND DRY CLEANING EQUIPMENT

Resource Management: Ozonation is an alternative method for laundry (and dishwashing) that conserves water and minimizes chemical usage. With ozone laundering, washing time can be reduced by nearly half because the rinse cycle can be eliminated.

Toxicity/IEQ: Ozone oxidizes bacteria, viruses, and other contaminants without undesirable odors or byproducts. Ozone is ph neutral, and reduces chemical usage up to 95 percent. Ozone oxidizes contaminants up to 3,000 times faster than chlorine.

Performance: With the addition of ozone as an oxidant, laundry and dishwashing machines can run at lower wash temperatures for shorter cycles. In most situations (including hotels) laundry is cleaned as effectively with ozonation as with chemical laundry methods. Ozonation reduces chemical costs, chemical storage requirements, and labor expenses. It requires weekly, rather than daily, chemical check. And it prolongs life of equipment by reducing calcium and scale buildup.

11140   VEHICLE SERVICE EQUIPMENT

Resource Management: Electric charging stations and compressed natural gas (CNG) fueling stations are necessary for changing our transportation infrastructure. By utilizing alternative fuels, we can all help to reduce greenhouse gas emissions, especially one of the most significant—carbon dioxide. Carbon dioxide is a major greenhouse gas. In the upper levels of the atmosphere, carbon dioxide acts similarly to the windshield on a car, trapping heat. Atmospheric carbon dioxide concentrations are significantly greater than preindustrial levels. Much of the carbon dioxide buildup is due to automobiles, which have increased in number steadily since World War II.

Vehicle washing equipment routinely recycles water. Depending on the applicable regulatory requirements, auto service centers may reclaim tires and recycle oil.

Toxicity/IEQ: Equipment that promotes alternative fuel and recycling is always environmentally preferable and less polluting.

Performance: Specific performance evaluations are difficult since they tend to be apples-and-oranges comparisons.

11150   PARKING CONTROL EQUIPMENT

Resource Management: Traffic control speed bumps manufactured from recycled rubber are available. Parking stops manufactured from recycled plastic are available. Refer to Section 06500—Structural Plastics.

Toxicity/IEQ: Toxicity/IEQ is comparable for green products and standard products.

Performance: Performance is comparable for green methods and standard methods. Recycled rubber speed bumps often have longer life cycles than asphalt speed bumps. Recycled plastic parking stops often have longer life cycles than concrete parking stops; and, where colored stops are required, plastic outperforms concrete, as it is homogenous (including color) and does not require painting.

11160   LOADING DOCK EQUIPMENT

Resource Management: Bumpers manufactured from recycled tires are available.

Toxicity/IEQ: Toxicity/IEQ is comparable for green products and standard products.

Performance: Performance is comparable for green methods and standard methods.

11170   SOLID WASTE HANDLING EQUIPMENT

Resource Management: Reclamation and recycling options exist for almost every region for almost every material.

Toxicity/IEQ: Toxicity/IEQ is comparable for green methods and standard methods.

Performance: Composting and recycling equipment is available for commercial and residential use. Refer to Section 11450—Residential Equipment. Chute systems that allow for separate collection of solid waste are available for multistory construction.

11200   WATER SUPPLY AND TREATMENT EQUIPMENT

resource management: Rainwater harvesting systems are available for irrigation and potable water. The system can be as simple as a barrel under a downspout or as complex as a system with filters, settling tanks, pumps, UV radiation, and water purification treatment. Rainwater harvesting keeps rainwater on-site. It lessens the burden on municipal water facilities, and decreases erosion and flooding caused by runoff from impervious surfaces. Refer to Section 02670—Constructed Wetlands, for information regarding natural treatment of water. Refer to Section 11110—Commercial Laundry And Dry Cleaning Equipment for information regarding ozonation.

Toxicity/IEQ: Chlorine is routinely added to municipal water supplies and is likely to be a required additive for water collected/treated in situ and destined for potable use. Where such additives are necessary, iodine is a less toxic alternative.

Rainwater is generally of better quality than well and municipal tap water. The exception is near industrial sites where rainwater may be extremely acid. If you plan to use rainwater for drinking water, have it tested by a laboratory certified by the State Department of Health or the Environmental Protection Agency.

Performance: Performance is comparable for green methods and standard methods. In many instances, rainwater and water treated via constructed wetlands have tested better than the available municipal water. Rainwater is soft (hardness of zero) and can significantly reduce the quantity of detergents and soaps needed for cleaning.

11450   RESIDENTIAL EQUIPMENT

Resource Management: Several green manufacturers produce super-efficient appliances, and most standard, mainstream manufacturers now produce energy-efficient models. Current refrigerator models do not use CFC refrigerants; however, as of this writing, some still use insulation manufactured with HCFCs as blowing agents.

Some manufacturers have developed residential washers on the horizontal axis that require much less water. When used in combination with ionizing washer disks, they can significantly reduce water usage and pollution.

Toxicity/IEQ: Toxicity IEQ impact is comparable for green appliances and standard appliances. However, by virtue of their improved energy efficiency, green appliances contribute far fewer contaminants to the environment during their lifetime than do standard appliances.

Performance: Obviously, energy-efficient appliances require less energy to operate. Most perform the task for which they were designed comparably to the standard designs that they replace. Federal regulations require appliances to be labeled. indicating their energy performance (a bright yellow EER—energy efficiency rating—label). This is a developing field, and models are constantly being improved. Green Seal has developed standards for refrigerators (GS-20), clothes washers (GS-22), clothes dryers (GS-23), dishwashers (GS-24), and cooktops/ovens/ranges (GS-25), which specify minimum requirements for energy efficiency, water use, packaging, and labeling. And the EPA has developed minimum energy efficiency standards for Energy Star-labeled products. EPA Energy Star categories include: clothes washers, dishwashers, refrigerators, room air conditioners, televisions, VCRs, and computers.

Typically, horizontal axis washers are more efficient than top-loading; and side-by-side refrigerators are less efficient than top-bottom refrigerator/freezers.

Recycling systems are available and include under-the-counter containers to separate recyclables. They also include interior composting systems, which are generally a variation of standard garbage disposal. In some designs, the composting chute empties to an externally accessible composting bin.

11680   OFFICE EQUIPMENT

Resource Management: Office equipment historically has been available on a lease basis. Green leasing is a new, but dramatic shift in the traditional perspective of leased equipment. Under a green lease, the product manufacturer would be responsible for the disposition of the product at all times, meaning that when the customer no longer requires the use of the product or requires an updated model, the manufacturer would be obligated to reclaim it and refurbish it or disassemble it for recycling, as appropriate. This approach necessitates a revision of administrative services. It also requires a basic redesign of products to allow for future disassembly and upgrade. This has the potential to be cost-effective for manufacturers and customers alike. It is also extremely resource-efficient. Some major corporations, including Apple and Xerox, are exploring the possibilities of a green lease approach.

Toxicity/IEQ: Toxicity/IEQ is comparable for green products and standard products.

Performance: The EPA has developed minimum energy efficiency standards for Energy Star-labeled products. EPA Energy Star categories include: computers, copiers, facsimile machines, monitors, printers, and scanners.

DIVISION 12   **FURNISHINGS**

12050   FABRICS

Resource Management: Typical fabrics used in building products include: wool, worsted wool, wool and polyester blend, polyester, vinyl, modacrylic, silk and flax, nylon, and chlorofiber.

Wool, a natural fiber obtained from domesticated sheep, is valued for its absorbency, resiliency, insulation, and ability to take dye well. Wool has some environmental concerns relative to animal husbandry, including soil erosion due to over-foraging and pesticide runoff due to the immersion treatment (for parasites on sheep).

Polyester is produced from petroleum and natural gas. Manufacture of polyester fiber generates air emissions including polymer dust, volatized residual monomer, and fiber lubricants.

A variety of dyes are used, depending on the fabric and color desired. Many fabric dyes contain petrochemicals. Dyeing fabric is water-intensive and can generate toxic pollutants.

Draperies, upholstery, and wall coverings manufactured from organically grown natural fibers with nontoxic dyes are available. Organically grown cotton grown in certain colors is available. Some fabrics are also available that have recycled plastic (generally PET—soda pop bottles) content. Unfortunately, this combines petroleum-based plastics and organics in a way that is difficult to separate for future recycling.

Toxicity/IEQ: Dyes and fabric treatments, such as wrinkle-free or fire-resistant, can be toxic. Chemicals used for finishes and other purposes on fabrics can be sources of VOCs. Cornstarch and tapioca are used as sizing. Copper compounds, chromium compounds, and chlorinated phenol are used to inhibit mold and mildew. Silico-fluorides and chromium-fluorides, camphor, naphthalene, and paradichlorobenzene are used for mothproofing. Organic halogenphosphorous compounds, aryl bromophosphate, triethanolamine, and trimethylol melamine are used as flame retardants.

Performance: Fabric produced from natural fibers, especially when dyed with natural, nontoxic dyes, is biodegradable.

12100   ART

Resource Management: Many artists have embraced environmental ethics. Options range from lead-free, recycled-content stained glass to reclaimed, found-object sculpture to green statements beautifully expressed in traditional mediums.

Toxicity/IEQ: While many media can be very toxic during production, most are considered inert when cured/complete.

Performance: Performance is comparable for green methods and standard methods.

12400   FURNISHINGS AND ACCESSORIES

Resource Management: A variety of green furniture products are available, including products manufactured from sustainably harvested wood, recycled metal, recycled plastic, alternative agricultural materials, and organically grown fibers.

Toxicity/IEQ: Fabric coverings may act as sinks for VOCs. Refer to Section 12050—Fabrics.

Performance: Performance is comparable for green methods and standard methods.

12700   SYSTEMS FURNITURE

Resource Management: Several modular office furniture manufacturers have environmental lines that include reclaimed, refurbished furniture, furniture with recycled materials, and furniture with organic fibers/fabric.

Toxicity/IEQ: Fabric coverings may act as sinks for VOCs. They are constructed from various materials often including composite wood products, insulations, and adhesives that are all potential sources of VOC emissions. Freestanding, partial height partitions (or panels) can interfere with the proper distribution of ventilation air. Install panels according to plans prepared in harmony with the design of the HVAC system. Raising partition bottoms above the floor may improve air flow at workstations contained within partial height panel systems.

Performance: Performance is comparable for green methods and standard methods.

12800   INTERIOR PLANTS AND PLANTERS

Resource Management: Many recycled content planters are available. Refer to Section 06600—Plastic Fabrications, and Section 06500—Structural Plastics.

Toxicity/IEQ: There are potentially positive and negative impacts of plants on indoor air quality. Claims have been made that plants can remove contaminants from indoor air. The potential damage of plant materials and the associated growing media relate to elevated moisture levels and potential amplification of microbial contaminants. Where plants are used, planters should be well drained and the drainwater removed to the exterior.

Performance: Performance is comparable for green methods and standard methods.

DIVISION 13	**SPECIAL CONSTRUCTION**
13020	BUILDING MODULES

Resource Management: Prefabricated assemblies are more resource-efficient than field-constructed assemblies. Standardized shapes and processes mean less waste. Shop fabrication allows for environmental controls unavailable at the site, such as paint booths that can reclaim overspray.

Toxicity/IEQ: Prefabricated module units have been severely criticized for their poor IAQ. The same considerations and investigations conducted on field-constructed components should be exercised when reviewing prefabricated components.

Preengineered structures that are assembled on-site can provide the best of both worlds: minimal waste and good IAQ.

Performance: Performance is comparable for green methods and standard methods.

13080   SOUND, VIBRATION, AND SEISMIC CONTROL

Resource Management: Resource management is comparable for green methods and standard methods.

Toxicity/IEQ: Vibration transmitted through the building structure can cause occupant complaints similar to sick building syndrome complaints. Isolate mechanical equipment and other building equipment. Vibration sources can also include adjacent roadways or parking garages.

Performance: Performance is comparable for green methods and standard methods. In some cases, equipment life can be prolonged by appropriately dampening vibration.

13170   TUBS AND POOLS

Resource Management: Refer to Section 11110—Commercial Laundry And Dry Cleaning Equipment for information on ozonation.

Toxicity/IEQ: Ozonation is an alternative to chlorination. Chemical-free tub systems that utilize ozonation are available. Refer to Section 11110—Commercial Laundry And Dry Cleaning Equipment for information on ozonation.

Performance: Ozonation reduces total dissolved solids (TDS) so pools need to be drained less. Refer to Section 11110—Commercial Laundry And Dry Cleaning Equipment for information on ozonation.

13185 KENNELS AND ANIMAL SHELTERS

Resource Management: Concentrated animal feeding operations (CAFO) issues have focused public attention on the potential environmental damage from animal operations. Such damage includes destruction of native habitat, erosion, and contamination of waterways. Proper design and operations can mitigate the environmental impact. For example, by placing composting bins under cages of vegetarian animals such as birds and rabbits, the droppings can be easily composted.

Toxicity/IEQ: Improper management of kennels, animal shelters, and CAFO can produce some extremely unhealthy conditions. Select products that are easily maintained with nontoxic methods to help promote proper management. Depending on the scale of the CAFO operations, an NPDES permit may be required.

Performance: From a human perspective, performance is comparable for green methods and standard methods. From an animal perspective, green methods are likely to perform much better. Animals respond instinctively to healthy and environmentally appropriate conditions.

13400 MEASUREMENT AND CONTROL INSTRUMENTATION

Resource Management: The systems specified for energy and water use in a building can dramatically impact both the quantity and the quality of such resources. Monitors and controls that regulate use of electricity, gas, and water can help improve efficiencies.

Toxicity/IEQ: Various monitor and control equipment that maintains indoor air quality is available.

Performance: Monitoring and control systems can help prolong the life of energy and water equipment by preventing "spikes" in demand and by warning of potential problems.

13600   SOLAR AND WIND ENERGY EQUIPMENT
               Resource Management: Renewable, clean energy is, ul-
               timately, the only environmentally responsible option.
               Toxicity/IEQ: In many systems, battery storage is re-
               quired. While there are well-known concerns regarding the
               toxic components of batteries, overall the systems that util-
               ize renewable energy sources are significantly less hazard-
               ous than our continued dependence on non-renewable
               energy is to human health and environmental health.
               Performance: Many configurations of solar systems are
               available. In each, photovoltaic cells convert sunlight into
               electrical energy. Collected energy is usually stored in bat-
               teries and converted into AC electric for building use. Solar
               equipment is becoming more common for stand-alone
               items such as exterior lighting. Photovoltaic arrays can be
               designed to power the entire building. These may be
               mounted on the roof or ground. They may also be building-
               integrated. Thin-film photovoltaic systems that laminate
               thin-film photovoltaic film to one-fourth-inch glass are
               available. Wires collecting the energy are concealed in the
               standard glass-framing system. Also, photovoltaic roof
               shingles, developed primarily in response to Japan's Solar
               Roof initiative, are available. Systems using the sun's ra-
               diant energy to heat water are available. Panels are mounted
               either on the roof or ground, and water is piped to storage.
                  Wind-powered generators are available for residential
               and commercial applications. This is a rapidly changing
               field. Many of these systems, priced as luxury items only
               a few years ago, are today affordable.
13800   BUILDING AUTOMATION AND CONTROL
               Refer to Section 16500—Lighting, for information on oc-
               cupancy sensors.
13850   DETECTION AND ALARM
               Carbon monoxide detectors are available. These are similar
               in appearance and function to smoke detectors. Refer to
               Section 13400—Measurement And Control Instrumenta-
               tion.

DIVISION 14   **CONVEYING SYSTEMS**
14200   ELEVATORS
               Resource Management: Refer to Division 5 for infor-
               mation regarding metal products. Refer to the applicable
               Division 9 section for information regarding interior finish
               products.

Toxicity/IEQ: Hydraulic fluids and lubricants used in elevators can cause indoor air quality problems. Isolate lubricated equipment from the circulating air or air in the shaft, and pressurize elevator lobbies relative to the shaft to minimize escaping air from the shaft. Ventilate the shaft with negative pressure.

Performance: Performance is comparable for green methods and standard methods.

14900   TRANSPORTATION

Resource Management: This section typically specifies cars and motorized vehicles and equipment utilized in railroads, subways, and tramways. Public transportation that helps to minimize the use of individual vehicles is always environmentally preferable.

Toxicity/IEQ: Indoor environmental quality is not directly applicable for transportation equipment.

Performance: Performance is comparable for green methods and standard methods.

DIVISION 15   **MECHANICAL**

15050   BASIC MECHANICAL MATERIALS AND METHODS

Resource Management: The systems specified for energy and water use in a building can dramatically impact both the quantity and the quality of such resources. Energy-efficient and low-flow fixtures are readily available and required by code. Systems that promote more responsible use of energy and water by building occupants are also available. They range from reuse of waste heat via transfer piping to "preuse" of water via handwashing basin piped into the supply side of the toilet bowl.

Toxicity/IEQ: The primary IEQ consideration for domestic water supply is water quality, which, for most buildings, is largely determined by the municipal water treatment facility. Most water treatment facilities rely upon chemicals, including chlorine, to combat pathogens. Chlorine is highly reactive and readily forms chlorinated compounds, many of which are dangerous. Chlorinated hydrocarbons, such as DDT, have been and are used as pesticides. Water filter systems for chorine are available.

Performance: The primary environmental concern for mechanical systems is performance. Even when passive design is maximized for natural lighting, solar control of heat gain, natural ventilation, and water management, active systems are still commonly used. Mechanical systems may be stand-alone such as rainwater harvesting systems, constructed wetlands for wastewater management, solar power/water systems, or wind-power systems. More typically, one or more utility will be connected to "the grid" and may utilize high-efficiency systems. Generally, such systems are more expensive to install, but will pay for themselves over time. Refer to Section 11200—Water Supply and Treatment Equipment, Section 02670—Constructed Wetlands, and Section 13600—Solar and Wind Energy Equipment for information on these alternative technologies.

15080   MECHANICAL INSULATION

Resource Management: Refer to Section 07200—Thermal Protection.

Toxicity/IEQ: Refer to Section 07200—Thermal Protection.

Insulation may produce airborne fiberglass and microbial contamination. When soft, adsorptive duct linings become contaminated by particles, they can absorb up to 10 times more moisture; and moisture can contribute to microbial contaminants such us molds. Insulation for application to the outside of ductwork is preferable.

Performance: Specify minimum thickness in accordance with ASHRAE 90.1. Provide additional thickness to ensure that surface temperatures are below 100 degrees and to prevent condensation on cold surfaces.

15100   BUILDING SERVICES PIPING

Resource Management: Traditional metal piping has been largely replaced by PVC piping. Refer to Section 09651—Vinyl Flooring for information regarding manufacture of PVC.

Toxicity/IEQ: Specify traditional metal piping. Do not specify PVC piping. Refer to Section 09651—Vinyl Flooring for information regarding PVC. Several ionization options are available for preventing mineral buildup. These range from "drop-in" type toilet bowl cleaners to equipment spliced into piping runs.

Grease traps that utilize bacteria to decompose the grease are available. When the food source is exhausted, the bacteria turn on each other; therefore, the bacteria supply must be replenished each day. Natural strains of bacteria are generally used; these have an exceptionally high capacity for digesting specific organic compounds found in grease traps.

J-drains (traps) with removable panels for easy cleaning are available. These allow cleaning without use of polluting chemicals at sinks and lavatories.

Performance: Avoiding chemical pollution during operation typically means that the building owner must understand the operating system better and be willing to expend a pound of prevention instead of ten pounds of cure. Verify that owner's operating manuals include information regarding J-drains, grease traps, and so on.

15400
PLUMBING FIXTURES AND EQUIPMENT

Resource Management: Specify low-flow fixtures and automatic, sensor-operated faucets and flush valves. Most standard, mainstream companies have developed low-flow lines in response to building code requirements that require water-conserving fixtures. For faucets and aerators, specify a maximum 2.5 gallons/minute when measured at a flowing water pressure of 80 pounds per square inch. For water closets, specify maximum 1.6 gallons. Avoid gravity tank type water closets. For urinals, specify maximum 1.0 gallons/flush. For showerheads, specify maximum 2.5 gallons/minute when measured at a flowing water pressure of 80 pounds per square inch.

Composting toilets are available. Composting reduces water usage and creates soil amendment. Vacuum toilet systems, traditionally associated with water conservation in marine, air, and railroad transports are also available for application in commercial/residential buildings.

Toxicity/IEQ: Composting is the biological reduction of organic wastes to humus. It is a natural process that is critical for support of all terrestrial life. Although composting manure is a traditional and extremely valuable process, manure (especially from carnivorous animals) can promote unwanted bacteria and diseases if handled improperly. Refer to Section 02055—Soils.

Performance: When low-flow fixtures were first developed, many were deemed unsatisfactory because they could not deliver the pressure Americans were used to. More recent models do not have this problem, except for extremely high-pressure demands in some high-use areas.

Green Seal has developed standards for water efficient fixtures (GS-06), which specify minimum requirements for showerheads, faucets, toilets, packaging, and labeling.

Adjust automatic sensor-operated faucets and valves in accordance with manufacturer's instructions. Comply with ASHRAE 90.1 for minimum energy efficiency.

Vacuum toilets not only reduce water consumption, they reduce piping and can eliminate need for toilet vent pipes, allowing for flexibility in design layout.

15480   DOMESTIC WATER HEATERS

Resource Management: Refer to Section 15050—Basic Mechanical Materials and Methods.

Toxicity/IEQ: The primary IEQ consideration for domestic water supply is water quality, which, for most buildings, is largely determined by the municipal water treatment facility. Refer to Section 15050—Basic Mechanical Materials and Methods.

Performance: Energy efficiency is improved over older heaters because of new heating technologies and better tank insulation. Obviously, energy-efficient appliances require less energy to operate. Most perform the task for which they were designed comparably to the standard designs they replace. Federal regulations require appliances to be labeled indicating their energy performance (a bright yellow EER—energy efficiency rating—label). This is a developing field, and models are constantly being improved.

Instantaneous point-of-use (tankless, on-demand) electric water heaters are available for commercial and residential use. These are particularly effective when demand is located far away from domestic hot water mains.

15500   HEAT-GENERATION EQUIPMENT

Resource Management: Refer to Section 15050—Basic Mechanical Materials and Methods.

According to the EPA, space heating and cooling in residential buildings generate 420 million tons of carbon dioxide, a significant greenhouse gas, annually. According to the Department of Energy, Natural gas, used in about 55 percent of homes in the United States, is the most common heating fuel. Though it is perhaps the cleanest combustion fuel (compared with wood, oil, and coal) production and transmission of natural gas still results in emissions of methane, a greenhouse gas. Equipment that promotes conservation through high-efficiency and passive controls is a good solution to resource management concerns. Equipment that utilizes alternative, renewable, nonpolluting energy is also ideal.

Geothermal projects can result in overuse of the "commons" when the ground temperature in a microclimate is raised. This can affect both the local ecosystem and the performance of the geothermal equipment that has been designed around lower expected ground temperatures.

Toxicity/IEQ: Specify sealed combustion equipment to help maintain good IAQ.

Performance:: Reduce the heating demand through passive solar design. Specify high-efficiency equipment. The EPA has developed minimum energy efficiency standards for Energy Star-labeled products. EPA Energy Star categories include: furnaces, boilers, air-source heat pumps, gas-fired heat pumps, geothermal heat pumps, and programmable thermostats.

Gas-fired furnaces and boilers with efficiencies of 90 percent are available. Radiant electric heating equipment is available and can be efficient and cost-effective when heating loads are small. For larger loads, consider a heat pump. Specify air-source heat pumps in moderate climates and ground-source heat pumps in cold climates.

15600 REFRIGERATION EQUIPMENT

Resource Management: Refer to Section 15050—Basic Mechanical Materials and Methods.

Most refrigerants are greenhouse gases. Furthermore, they are used in HVAC and refrigeration equipment, huge consumers of electricity—the generation of which releases greenhouse gases. Alternative refrigerants include: hydrofluorocarbons (HFCs), hydrochlorofluorocarbons (HCFCs), ammonia, and hydrocarbons. HCFCs still impact the ozone layer and are scheduled to be phased out early in the twenty-first century. HFCs, while not damaging to the ozone layer (and so not slated for phase-out), are significant greenhouse gases. HFCs break down into trifluoroacetic acid and other compounds that accumulate in the hydrologic cycle and are toxic to wildlife.

Toxicity/IEQ: The primary IEQ concern is leaking of refrigerants from the system. Proper installation and maintenance can help prevent the release of refrigerants into the indoor environment and the atmosphere.

Performance: As of January 1, 1996, the production of CFCs and most other Class I ozone-depleting substances was banned in the United States and in other industrialized countries. HVAC and refrigeration equipment must rely on existing stockpiles of CFCs, black market CFCs, or be converted to use one of the alternative refrigerants.

Ammonia and hydrocarbons such as propane and isobutane perform very well as refrigerants and have been used in the past. They are, however, quite flammable. The Clean Air Act and many building codes prohibit hydrocarbon refrigerants; nevertheless, several European countries are reinvestigating this technology.

15700 HEATING, VENTILATING, AND AIR CONDITIONING EQUIPMENT

Resource Management: Maximize passive opportunities to reduce HVAC load. Refer to Section 15050—Basic Mechanical Materials and Methods and Section 15600—Refrigeration Equipment.

Toxicity/IEQ: HVAC systems can contribute to poor IAQ by failing to provide enough ventilation to dilute indoor contaminates to acceptable levels, by spreading contaminants introduced from outside sources and by generating contaminants within the HVAC system itself. The primary contaminants from HVAC systems are microbial and particulate. Design the system to prevent water collection. Specify nonwoven cotton fabric filters, not fiberglass filters.

Performance: Comply with ASHRAE 62 for ventilation; comply with ASHRAE 52 for filtration; comply with ASHRAE 55 for thermal comfort. Maintain positive pressure within the building. Comply with ASHRAE 90.1 for minimum energy efficiency. Provide economizer for systems with fan capacity of 5,000 cfm and higher and where required by codes.

Obviously, energy-efficient systems require less energy to operate. Most perform the task for which they were designed comparably to the standard designs that they replace. Federal regulations require appliances to be labeled, indicating their energy performance (a bright yellow EER—energy efficiency rating—label). This is a developing field, and models are constantly being improved.

The EPA has developed minimum energy efficiency standards for Energy Star-labeled products. EPA Energy Star categories include: furnaces, boilers, air-source heat pumps, gas-fired heat pumps, geothermal heat pumps, and programmable thermostats.

15800   **AIR DISTRIBUTION**
Resource Management: Refer to Section 15050—Basic Mechanical Materials and Methods.
Toxicity/IEQ: Locate outside air intakes away from potential sources of contamination (e.g., sources of motor vehicle emissions, building HVAC system exhausts). The air in rooms where contaminants are generated should be exhausted directly outdoors (e.g., labs, copying areas). ASHRAE Standard 62-1989 calls for delivery of ventilation air to occupant breathing zone. Amount is contingent upon carbon dioxide levels; other contaminants must be considered separately.
Performance: Properly sizing and sealing ductwork can improve energy efficiency.

15890   **DUCTWORK**
Resource Management: Refer to Section 15050—Basic Mechanical Materials and Methods and Division 5.

Toxicity/IEQ: Fiberboard ductwork has been implicated in microbial contamination. Metal surfaces can be cleaned more easily without fear of damaging the surface material. VOCs may be emitted from duct sealant during the curing process. They are very exposed to the air stream, so their emissions are very important. Fibrous glass insulation materials may contain formaldehyde-based resin binder materials. Install insulation so that unfaced fiberglass and mineral fiber insulation are not in contact with the airstream.

Performance: Properly sizing and sealing ductwork can improve energy efficiency.

15900   HVAC INSTRUMENTATION AND CONTROLS

Resource Management: Refer to Section 13400—Measurement And Control Instrumentation.

Toxicity/IEQ: Refer to Section 13400—Measurement And Control Instrumentation.

Performance: Sensors may be used to detect airflow, contaminant concentrations, thermal properties, or moisture content of air. Humidity control can help prevent microbial growth. Steam is preferable to liquid water as source.

15950   TESTING, ADJUSTING, AND BALANCING

Resource Management: Refer to Section 13400—Measurement And Control Instrumentation.

Toxicity/IEQ: Testing does not usually address IEQ issues. To better address IEQ issues relative to the HVAC system, coordinate with Section 01351 and Section 01810.

Performance: Provide preoccupancy ventilation as specified in Section 01351, Environmental Procedures; provide prior to final testing, adjusting, and balancing of HVAC system. Coordinate with commissioning; refer to Section 01810—Commissioning.

DIVISION 16   **ELECTRICAL**
16050   BASIC ELECTRICAL MATERIALS AND METHODS

Resource Management: Refer to Section 15050—Basic Mechanical Materials and Methods.

Toxicity/IEQ: Many studies have indicated an apparent link between exposure to electromagnetic fields (for example, under overhead power lines) and an increased risk of cancer. A link between electrical wiring configurations in the home and the incidence of childhood cancer has also been indicated. Most studies have concentrated on the magnetic, not the electric, component of electromagnetic fields. This is primarily because the human body is a good conductor, so the penetration of electric fields into the body itself is minimal. Magnetic fields, on the other hand, readily penetrate the body. However, recent studies have demonstrated that electromagnetic fields can attract and concentrate aerosols of all types, including known carcinogenic aerosols, natural aerosols containing the radioactive radon decay atoms of radon gas, and bacteria. The effect is primarily due to the electric, rather than the magnetic, field component.

Performance: Coordinate with Division 8 and Division 15 to minimize load requirements and improve energy efficiency.

16100
WIRING METHODS
Resource Management: Refer to Section 15050—Basic Mechanical Materials and Methods.

Toxicity/IEQ: Some experimentation with twisting of wires has been done to control the generation of electromagnetic fields. Theoretically, twisting is effective not so much because it brings wires closer together, but because the actual geometry of the twisted wires makes their fields cancel. A certain number of twists per foot will be optimum for a certain frequency (presumably 60 Hz for North American power wiring). Twisting is used to reduce electromagnetic interference from inverter wires. Inverters are devices that typically take low-voltage DC electricity and convert it to high-voltage AC electricity. The low-voltage side of inverters can carry very large currents, and are, therefore, large generators of EMF. Twisting of wires is also commonly used inside audio electronics and computers to prevent internal interference.

Performance: Performance is comparable for green methods and standard methods.

16500
LIGHTING
Resource Management: Refer to Section 15050—Basic Mechanical Materials and Methods. Maximize the use of natural lighting.

Toxicity/IEQ: Currently, products are not legally permitted to be manufactured with PCBs. Lead is commonly used in solder for ballasts on HID lamps; however, many manufacturers now crimp ballasts rather than solder. Mercury is commonly used in fluorescent lamps; however, some manufacturers have developed low-mercury fluorescent lamp products containing maximum 20 ppm of mercury.

Light quality is also a consideration for IEQ. Full-spectrum lighting is preferred in all normal applications because it approximates natural daylight. Full-spectrum lamps and filters are available.

Performance: Comply with National Energy Policy Act requirements for lighting products. Energy-efficient HID, sodium, halogen, and fluorescent lamps are available. Green Seal has developed standards for compact fluorescent lamps (GS-05), which specify minimum requirements for performance, energy efficiency, mercury content, packaging, and labeling.

Occupancy sensors are available to turn lights on when a room or covered area is occupied and off when unoccupied. Passive infrared and ultrasonic operation are common. Specify with adjustable time delay for turning lights off.

Photoelectric control is available for exterior lighting. Specify that photoelectric control be completely self-contained and, adjustable, in NEMA 1 weatherproof enclosure with adjustable 0 to 15 minute minimum time delay to provide a dead band zone for temporary changes in daylighting. Specify automatic operation as follows:

• Daylight-only lighting level, 50 footcandles or more: No fixtures on.
• Daylight-only lighting level less than 25 footcandles: All fixture lamps activated.

Footcandle lighting level readings should be measured at grade.

Full-spectrum lamps provide better light quality than conventional standard artificial lighting; full-spectrum lamps are neither more nor less energy-efficient. They generally cost more than the fluorescent and incandescent lamps they replace; however, the full-spectrum filters can be a very cost-effective compromise since they are reusable.

16530

EMERGENCY LIGHTING

Resource Management: Refer to Section 15050—Basic Mechanical Materials and Methods.

Toxicity/IEQ: Toxicity/IEQ is comparable for green methods and standard methods.

Performance: Light emitting diode (LED) lighting is available, and is much more efficient than compact fluorescent lighting. LEDs last from 80 to 500 years. Specify LED type with maintenance-free battery back-up for 120 minutes; UL listed.

Sample Sections and Forms

To assist readers in the process of selecting and specifying green building materials, this appendix provides sample forms, intended to be used only as guides. Language is presented for example only and no warranty or guaranty is made as to completeness or accuracy of information contained herein.

The following samples forms and specification sections were developed by *theGreenTeam, Inc.,* and are the result of its ongoing work with building owners, building product manufacturers, green building trade/professional organizations, standards development organizations, and environmental organizations to develop sustainable building. The sample forms and specification sections are intended to be a guide for researching and implementing green building products. No warranty is made as to completeness or accuracy of information contained herein. References to manufacturers do not represent a guaranty, warranty, or endorsement thereof.

- Environmental Impact Questionnaire
- Indoor Air Quality Emission Test Report
- Section Format
- Sample Section 01231
- Sample Section 01351
- Sample Technical Section—Section 10170

theGreenTeam, Inc.
5822 S. New Haven
Tulsa, OK 74135
(918) 599-0011
fax: (918) 599-7567
email: dmeadows@busprod.com

http://home.earthlink.net/~arcvet/

The following sample specification section was developed by Ross Spiegel and is the result of his ongoing work to develop sustainable buildings. The sample specification section is intended to be a guide for researching and implementing green building products. No warranty is made as to completeness or accuracy of information contained herein. References to manufacturers do not represent a guaranty, warranty, or endorsement thereof.

• Sample Section 01630

Ross Spiegel
Michael A. Shiff & Associates, Inc.
1103 E. Las Olas Blvd., Suite 200
Ft Lauderdale, FL 33301-2315
(954) 463-8900, Extension 24
fax: (954) 463-8552
email: Ross_Spiegel_MAS@compuserve.com

> SPECIFIER NOTE: THIS DOCUMENT IS INTENDED TO BE A GUIDE FOR RESEARCHING ENVIRONMENTAL ISSUES RELATIVE TO BUILDING PRODUCTS. ISSUES ARE ORGANIZED UNDER THREE PRIMARY CATEGORIES: RESOURCE MANAGEMENT, TOXICITY, AND PERFORMANCE.

ENVIRONMENTAL IMPACT QUESTIONNAIRE (EIQ)

I. DIRECTIONS
   A. Complete the following questionnaire and submit for review to:

   _____

   _____

   _____

   _____

   B. Relate information concerning only one product per questionnaire.

   C. All questions may not apply to every product or manufacturer. It is not expected that the manufacturer will have addressed all of the environmental concerns expressed in the EIQ.
      1. Respond to every question even if response is "not available," "not applicable," or "no."
      2. Attach additional sheets as required. Reference additional sheets to correspond with the question number.

II. IDENTIFICATION
   A. Material/Product: _____

   Brand Name: _____

   Manufacturer: _____

   What is the primary use or application for this product? _____

   _____

   _____

   _____

B. Contact for EIQ:

Name: _____ Title: _____

Address: _____ Zip Code: _____

Telephone: _____ Fax: _____ Date: _____

III. RESOURCE MANAGEMENT

A. Renewable Resources:
   1. List renewable resources used as product raw materials. Provide percentage amounts in relation to complete (100 percent) product.

   Renewable Resource   *Percentage*

   _____   _____

   _____   _____

   _____   _____

   _____   _____

   2. Does manufacturer obtain product raw materials or fabricate this product outside of the United States: ____Y ____N?
      a. If yes, are United States environmental standards or more strict standards followed in these countries: ____Y ____N?
      b. List countries involved.

      _____

      _____

B. Managed Resources:
   1. Does extraction of product raw materials or fabrication of this product affect endangered specie(s): ____Y ____N?
      a. If yes, list species and describe effect, including mitigation methods for negative effects.
      Endangered Species   *Effect*

      _____   _____

      _____   _____

   2. Products Containing Wood: Are wood materials obtained from certified sustainable forestry operations: ____Y ____N?
      a. If yes, provide name of certification organization for each wood species being used in this project.
      Species   *Certification Organization*

      _____   _____

      _____   _____

b. If no, state where the product resources are produced and describe forestry operations.

Product Resources   *Forestry Operations*

_____   _____

_____   _____

C. Recycled Content:
  1. List recycled materials used as product raw materials; distinguish preconsumer and postconsumer materials. Provide percentage amounts in relation to complete (100 percent) product.

    Recycled Material   *Percent Preconsumer*   *Percent Postconsumer*

_____   _____   _____

_____   _____   _____

D. Embodied Energy:
  1. Product Transport:
    a. Where are raw materials acquired? Identify state and country.

      Raw Material   *Source (State and Country)*

_____   _____

_____   _____

_____   _____

    b. Describe means of transporting raw materials to the manufacturing plant.

      Raw Material   *Transportation*

_____   _____

_____   _____

    c. Where is product manufactured/fabricated? Identify state and country.

_____

    d. Is the product warehoused locally, regionally, or nationally?

_____

    e. Describe means of transporting product to distribution facilities.

_____

  2. Production Energy: List energy sources used in production process; indicate which are renewable energy sources (e.g., wind, solar). Provide percentage amounts in relation to complete (100 percent) product.

Energy Sources	*Renewable*	*Percentage*
_____	___Y ___N	_____
_____	___Y ___N	_____
_____	___Y ___N	_____

3. Provide an embodied energy study of the product from extraction of raw materials through production and assembly. Include an estimate for the total number of BTUs required per pound of finished products. Identify parameters for study.

_____

4. Describe measures the manufacturer has taken to minimize energy usage in the production process.

_____

_____

_____

_____

E. Reuse/Recyclability/Disposal:
  1. Reuse:
      a. Can product be reused directly (in same or similar use): ____Y ____N?
      b. If yes, discuss possibility of direct reuse of the product after project demolition.

_____

_____

  2. Recycling:
      a. Can product be recycled: ___Y ____N?
      b. If yes, list the parts of the product that can be postconsumer recycled into raw materials for the product and the parts that can be postconsumer recycled into other types of items. Provide percentage amounts in relation to complete (100 percent) product.

Postconsumer—Raw	*Postconsumer— Other*	*Percentage*
_____	_____	_____
_____	_____	_____
_____	_____	_____

      c. If yes, describe the process of separation of the parts for postconsumer recycling from the product.

_____

_____

d. If yes, list current markets using recycled materials from the product.

_____

_____

e. If yes, estimate the practical number of times this item can be recycled. _____

3. Describe the manufacturer's policy and program to facilitate the recycling or reuse of its product by accepting product returns at the end of their "useful life."

_____

_____

IV. TOXICITY/HAZARDOUS MATERIALS

A. Toxic/Hazardous Byproducts:

1. List the production wastes involved with the manufacture of this item. Distinguish the production wastes between toxic and nontoxic. Provide percentage amounts in relation to complete (100 percent) product.

Toxic	_Nontoxic_	_Percentage_
_____	_____	_____
_____	_____	_____
_____	_____	_____
_____	_____	_____

2. Estimate the quantity of waste produced per unit of finished product.

_____

3. Is reclamation of production waste done on site: ____Y ____N? with outside services: ____Y ____N?

a. If outside services are used, list companies involved.

_____

_____

4. Is waste water reclaimed by manufacturer: ____Y ____N?

a. If yes, describe process of recycling/reuse of waste water.

_____

_____

_____

_____

_____

5. Describe the manufacturer's active steps to minimize or eliminate production wastes; include process of liquid and solid waste material treatment or reclamation if performed at manufacturing site.

_____

_____

_____

_____

6. Describe the manufacturing procedures and chemicals involved that would be considered better than industry standard.

_____

_____

_____

B. Toxic/Hazardous Contents (carcinogens and other hazards inherent in product/material):
1. Provide a complete chemical profile of the item; include all chemical components and provide percentage amounts in relation to complete (100 percent) product; identify biocides (mildewcides or in-can preservatives) and carcinogens listed by any of the following:
   a. United States Environmental Protection Agency (EPA) Carcinogen Assessment Group (CAG) list of carcinogens.
   b. Clean Air Act Sections 109, 111, and 112.
   c. The National Toxicology Program's latest published "Annual Report on Carcinogens."
   d. IARC Human Carcinogens (Groups 1, 2A, and 2B).
   e. California Proposition 65

Chemical	Carcinogen		Percentage
_____	__Y	__N	_____
_____	__Y	__N	_____
_____	__Y	__N	_____
_____	__Y	__N	_____
_____	__Y	__N	_____

C. Material Safety Data Sheet (MSDS):
   1. Provide Material Safety Data Sheet.
      a. Articles: Finished products that are manufactured off-site and shipped to the project for installation while conforming to Title 29 of the Code of Federal Regulations; OSHA Hazard Communication Regulation 29CRF 1910.1200, Section (b)5 and Section (c) are defined as articles. If by being defined as an article an MSDS has not been developed for a particular product, provide MSDS on raw materials, goods, and items used in the fabrication of that article.

D. Outgassing/Reactivity:
   1. Chlorofluorocarbon (CFC):
      a. Are CFCs or HCFCs used in the manufacture and/or content of the item specified: _____Y _____N?
      b. If CFCs or HCFCs were previously used in the product and/or its manufacture, describe measures taken by manufacturer to eliminate their use.

      _____

      _____

      _____

   2. Indoor Air Quality (IAQ):
      a. Does the product outgas (emit) carcinogens or other hazardous substances into the air after installation, including final curing/drying: _____Y _____N?
      b. If yes, submit IAQ test report.

E. Electromagnetic Radiation:
   1. Does the product emit electromagnetic radiation: _____Y _____N?
   2. If yes, at what rate per hour? _____
   3. If yes, describe methods for installation, use, and maintenance of product to minimize generation of and occupant exposure to electromagnetic radiation.

      _____

      _____

F. Compliance with Regulations (Environmental Statutory Compliance):
   1. Does the manufacturer meet all federal, state, and local environmental laws, including laws governing air emissions, waste water treatment, and solid waste disposal/treatment: _____Y _____N?
   2. Has the manufacturer met the above criteria for the previous five years: _____Y _____N?

3. List these applicable standards.

_____

_____

_____

4. Does the product meet applicable industry standards, such as ASTM, Green Seal, manufacturing standards, LA or NY research report numbers, and UL approvals:
   _____Y_____N? List these standards. _____

_____

_____

V. PERFORMANCE: INSTALLATION
A. Environmental Procedures/Precautions:
   1. Describe special procedures and precautions to be used while handling and installing the product:

_____

_____

_____

_____

   2. Identify accessories, such as fasteners, sealers, and adhesives that are nontoxic (or less toxic than industry standard), energy-efficient, or recycled or recyclable products.

_____

_____

_____

_____

B. Installation Energy:
   1. Product Transport: List the means to transport the finished product to the construction site.

_____

_____

   2. Installation: List energy means and describe energy requirements for installation of the product.

_____

_____

C. Construction Waste:
    1. List the recommended method(s) for proper products disposal; stipulate preferred method and restrictions that may apply.

_____

_____

_____

    2. Comment on the environmental impact of the product as a waste material.

_____

_____

_____

    3. Packaging:
      a. Describe packaging for the product.

_____

_____

_____

      b. Does manufacturer accept return of used packaging for reuse: ____Y ____N?
      c. If yes, state limitations and procedures for packaging return.

_____

_____

_____

VI. PERFORMANCE: OPERATIONS
    A. Maintenance
      1. Describe the recommended cleaning and maintenance procedures for the product, using products that have minimal VOC emission.

_____

_____

_____

      2. Estimate the "useful life" expectancy for this product.

_____

      3. Are replacement parts available: ____Y ____N?
        a. If yes, can replacement parts be installed in the field: ____Y ____N?
      4. Provide a copy of the life cycle analysis for this product.

5. Provide a copy of the manufacturer's warranty for this product.

B. Energy Efficiency (energy required to operate/maintain):
   1. Estimate BTUs required to operate the product when new: _____;
      after five years: _____; after ten years: _____.

C. Compliance with Regulations (Environmental Statutory Compliance):
   1. Does the product meet all federal, state, and local environmental laws, including laws governing energy efficiency and air emissions: ____Y ____N?
   2. Has the product met the above criteria for the previous five years: ____Y ____N?
   3. List these applicable standards.

   _____

   _____

   _____

   _____

   _____

   _____

   _____

VII. CORPORATE COMMITMENT
   A. Corporate Environmental Policy:
      1. Provide copy of manufacturer's stated environmental policies.

END OF ENVIRONMENTAL IMPACT QUESTIONNAIRE

SPECIFIER NOTE: THIS DOCUMENT IS INTENDED TO BE A GUIDE FOR EVALUATING INDOOR AIR QUALITY ISSUES RELATIVE TO BUILDING PRODUCTS.

INDOOR AIR QUALITY EMISSION TEST REPORT

I. DIRECTIONS
A. Complete the following and submit for review to:

_____

_____

_____

_____

B. Relate information concerning only one product, material, or accessory item per test report.

C. It is not expected that the manufacturer will have addressed all of the environmental concerns expressed in the Indoor Air Quality Emission Test Report.
  1. Respond to every question even if response is "not available," "not applicable," or "no."
  2. Attach additional sheets as required. Reference additional sheets to correspond with the question number.

II. IDENTIFICATION
A. Material/Product: _____

Brand Name: _____

Manufacturer: _____

What is the primary use or application for this product? _____

_____

_____

B. Testing Laboratory:

Name: _____

Phone number: _____

Address: _____

Contact Person: _____

III. TEST PARAMETERS AND PROCEDURES

A. Test Objectives: Describe the purpose of the testing and the intended use of the results:

_____

_____

_____

B. Facilities and Equipment:
  1. Describe the facilities and equipment; indicate sensitivity of the analytical system.

_____

_____

_____

_____

C. Experimental Design:
  1. Describe test conditions, including temperature, humidity, air exchange rate, and test materials loading.

  Temperature: _____

  Humidity: _____

  Air exchange rate: _____

  Test materials loading: _____

  General test conditions: _____

_____

_____

D. Sample Description:
  1. Describe the sample(s) tested, including the type of material(s) or product(s), brand name or other identification as appropriate, size or quantity tested, and sample selection process (e.g., random).

  Material/product: _____

  Brand name: _____

  Manufacturer: _____

  Size/quantity: _____

  Sample selection process: _____

_____

2. For wet samples or samples applied to a substrate, describe the sub-strate and methods to attach the sample to the substrate and to seal the sample edges.

Substrate: _____

Attachment methods: _____

Sealing methods: _____

_____

E. Experimental Procedures: Describe the experimental procedures used during testing, including details of the sampling and analysis techniques.
1. Identify date(s) of testing: _____
2. Identify duration of exposure: _____
3. Were standardized test procedures, such as ASTM D5116, *Guide for Small-Scale Environmental Chamber Determination of Organic Emissions from Indoor Materials/Products*, used: ____Y ____N?
a. If yes, cite standards: _____

_____

_____

_____

_____

b. If no, describe the experimental procedures used during testing and analysis:

_____

_____

_____

_____

IV. TEST RESULTS
A. Data Analysis: Describe the accuracy of the test results.

_____

_____

_____

_____

_____

B. Discussion and Conclusions:

1. Discuss the relevance of the findings and provide conclusions. For example, describe the effect of temperature and/or air exchange rate on emission factors. Note any anomalies and describe data treatment to address such data.

   _____

   _____

   _____

   _____

   _____

   _____

   _____

2. List all substances identified in a sample of the air emitted from product; indicate amounts detected in parts per million (ppm); identify carcinogens that appear on any of the following lists:
   a. United State Environmental Protection Agency (EPA) Carcinogen Assessment Group (CAG) list of carcinogens.
   b. Clean Air Act Sections 109, 111, and 112.
   c. The National Toxicology Program's latest published "Annual Report on Carcinogens."
   d. IARC Human Carcinogens (Groups 1, 2A, and 2B).
   e. California Proposition 65.

Substance	_Carcinogen_	_ppm_
_____	___Y ___N	_____
_____	___Y ___N	_____
_____	___Y ___N	_____
_____	___Y ___N	_____
_____	___Y ___N	_____
_____	___Y ___N	_____
_____	___Y ___N	_____

3. Provide instructions, requirements, or recommendations on minimizing the impact of emissions from the products on workers installing the items and on indoor air quality in the completed building. Include information on original installation of the item, maintenance, and eventual removal from the facility.

   Installation: _____

   _____

_____

_____

Maintenance: _____

_____

_____

_____

Removal/disposal: _____

_____

_____

_____

C. Other reports: If other reports and evaluations have been performed for
the product, submit copies.

END OF INDOOR AIR QUALITY EMISSION TEST REPORT

SPECIFIER NOTE: THIS DOCUMENT IS INTENDED TO BE A FORMAT GUIDE FOR INCORPORATING ENVIRONMENTAL ISSUES INTO STANDARD CONSTRUCTION SPECIFICATIONS. TOPICS OTHER THAN ENVIRONMENTAL TOPICS ARE NOT ADDRESSED.

ENVIRONMENTAL SPECIFICATIONS FORMAT

SECTION 00000

TITLE

PART 1 GENERAL

1.01 SUMMARY
    A. Section includes:
        1.
        x. Environmental requirements for work of this section.

1.02 REFERENCES

SPECIFIER NOTE: STANDARDS ARE BEING DEVELOPED RAPIDLY BY MANY SEGMENTS OF THE BUILDING INDUSTRY TO SUPPORT MARKET DEMANDS FOR PRODUCTS AND SERVICES THAT ADDRESS ENVIRONMENTAL ISSUES. VERIFY CURRENT STANDARDS APPROPRIATE TO [TITLE OF SECTION]. THE FOLLOWING ARE EXAMPLES.

    A. American Society of Heating Refrigerating and Air Conditioning Engineers (ASHRAE):
        1. ASHRAE/IES 90.1: Energy-Efficient Design of New Buildings Except Low-Rise Residential Buildings.

    B. American Society for Testing and Materials (ASTM):
        1. ASTM C618: Specification for Fly Ash and Raw or Calcined Natural Pozzolan for Use as a Mineral Admixture in Portland Cement Concrete.
        2. ASTM D5116: Guide for Small-Scale Environmental Chamber Determination of Organic Emissions from Indoor Materials/Products.

  C. Green Seal:
     1. GS5: Environmental Standard for Compact Fluorescent Lamps.
     2. GS6: Environmental Standard for Water-Efficient Fixtures.

  D. Forest Stewardship Council:
     1. Smart Woods Program.

  E. Scientific Certification Systems (SCS):
     1. Forest Conservation Program.

1.03 SUBMITTALS

SPECIFIER NOTE: VERIFY GREEN SUBMITTAL REQUIREMENTS. FOR PROPRIETARY SPECIFICATIONS, SUBMITTAL OF MANUFAC-TURER'S PRODUCT DATA MAY NOT BE REQUIRED. VERIFY THAT REVIEWER HAS THE EXPERTISE REQUIRED TO ASSESS THE SUBMITTALS.

  A. Submit manufacturer's product data, including:
     1. Emission data: Conduct materials testing according to the general guidelines of ASTM D5116.
     2. Material Safety Data Sheets.
     3. Recycled-content data: Indicate percentage of preconsumer and postconsumer recycled contents.
     4. Energy performance data.
     5. Corporate environmental statement of manufacturer.
     6. Maintenance data.

  B. Submit certification evidencing compliance with requirements for:
     1. Sustainably harvested wood.
     2. Low-flow water fixtures.

1.0X ENVIRONMENTAL REQUIREMENTS

SPECIFIER NOTE: THIS ARTICLE SPECIFIES ENVIRONMENTAL PERFORMANCE REQUIREMENTS. LOCATE PARAGRAPH 1.0X AT END OF PART 1.

COORDINATE REQUIREMENTS WITH MATERIALS SPECIFICA-TIONS UNDER PART 2; WHERE PRESCRIPTIVE SPECIFICATIONS ARE USED AND SUBSTITUTIONS ARE NOT ALLOWED, QUALITY CONTROL REQUIREMENTS UNDER THIS PARAGRAPH MAY BE REDUNDANT. NEVERTHELESS, USE OF THIS PARAGRAPH WILL HELP CLARIFY GREEN ISSUES FOR THE CONTRACTOR.

   A. Resource Management:

SPECIFIER NOTE: INCLUDE REQUIREMENTS REGARDING THE USE OF AND THE ENVIRONMENTAL IMPACT TO THE EARTH'S RENEWABLE PERPETUAL RESOURCES (FORESTS, GRASSLANDS, WATER, SOLAR ENERGY, WIND ENERGY, ETC.) AND TO THE EARTH'S MANAGED RESOURCES (ENDANGERED SPECIES, BOTH FLORA AND FAUNA).

INCLUDE REQUIREMENTS REGARDING THE USE OF RECYCLED CONTENT MATERIAL. INDICATE MINIMUM PERCENTAGES OF PRECONSUMER AS APPROPRIATE.

INCLUDE REQUIREMENTS FOR MANUFACTURER RECLAIM PROGRAMS AND/OR LEASING OPTIONS. LEASING OPTIONS WITH A MANUFACTURER WHO COMMITS TO RECLAIM, REUSE, AND RECYCLE PRODUCTS FURNISHED UNDER [TITLE OF SEC-TION] MAY BE NEGOTIABLE AS A SEPARATE CONTRACT BETWEEN OWNER AND MANUFACTURER. COORDINATE SEPA-RATE CONTRACT INFORMATION WITH SUMMARY OF WORK.

FOLLOWING ARE EXAMPLES.

   1. Renewable Resources:
      a. Wood: Provide products from sustainably harvested wood/sus-tainably managed forest as certified under the Forest Stewardship Council Smart Woods Program or the SCS Forest Conservation Program.
      b. Water: Provide equipment that minimizes water usage.

1) Water closets, lavatory faucets, and faucet aerators: Certified under GS 6.
2. Managed Resources:
   a. Aluminum: Products containing aluminum manufactured from raw materials obtained in areas currently or historically supporting tropical rain forests are not permitted.
3. Recycled Content: Provide [TITLE OF SECTION] manufactured from recycled materials.
   a. Preconsumer recycled content: Minimum __ percent of complete product.
   b. Concrete: Type F or Type C fly ash in accordance with ASTM C618 may be used as a substitute for a maximum of 20 percent of Portland cement.
4. Reuse/Recyclability/Disposal: Provide [TITLE OF SECTION] for which secondary markets or leasing programs exist.
   a. Carpet: Furnished and installed by manufacturer under separate contract. Coordinate installation with carpet manufacturer.

B. Toxicity/Hazardous Materials:

SPECIFIER NOTE: MANY ENVIRONMENTAL ISSUES, ESPECIALLY THOSE RELATED TO HAZARDOUS MATERIALS, ARE BEING ADDRESSED THROUGH LESISLATION/REGULATION AS WELL AS THROUGH INDUSTRY STANDARDS. VERIFY APPLICABILITY OF LOCAL, STATE, AND FEDERAL REGULATIONS TO PRODUCTS FURNISHED UNDER [TITLE OF SECTION].

FOLLOWING ARE EXAMPLES.

---

1. Toxic/Hazardous Contents: Products containing carcinogens listed by any of the following will not be permitted.
   a. EPA-CAG list of carcinogens.
   b. Clean Air Act, Sections 109, 111, and 112.
   c. The National Toxicology Program's latest published "Annual Report on Carcinogens."
   d. IARC, Human Carcinogens (Groups 1, 2A, and 2B).
2. Outgassing/Reactivity:
   a. Formaldehyde: Products containing urea-formaldehyde will not be permitted.
   b. Chlorofluorocarbons (CFCs): Products and equipment requiring or using CFCs during the manufacturing process will not be

permitted. Products and equipment requiring or using CFCs during normal operation will not be permitted.

    c. Volatile Organic Compounds (VOCs):

        1) Paints, Coatings, Sealers: Comply with South Coast Air Quality Management District (SCAQMD) rules and regulations.

C. Performance:

SPECIFIER NOTE: INCLUDE REQUIREMENTS FOR ENERGY EFFACING, ENVIRONMENTAL IMPACT OF ACCESSORIES, AND MAINTENANCE DURING OPERATIONS.

INCLUDE REQUIREMENTS FOR EFFICIENCY OF INSTALLATION, MINIMIZATION OF CONSTRUCTION WASTE, AND/OR RECLAMATION OF CONSTRUCTION WASTE. COORDINATE WITH ENVIRONMENTAL PROCEDURES IN PART 3.

FOLLOWING ARE EXAMPLES.

---

    1. Energy Efficiency: Provide equipment that is energy-efficient as demonstrated by comparative industry standards.

        a. Lamps and Ballasts.

        b. Compact Fluorescent Lamps: Certified under GS5.

        c. HVAC System: Minimum __ EER (energy efficiency rating) as referenced in ASHRAE 90.1.

        d. Motors.

        e. Appliances.

    2. Environmental Impact of Accessories:

        a. Adhesives: Nontoxic, water-based.

        b. Concrete placement accessories:

            1) Formwork: Reuse forms to greatest extent possible without damaging structural integrity of concrete and without damaging aesthetics of exposed concrete.

            2) Mixing equipment: Return excess concrete to supplier; minimize water used to wash equipment.

            3) Moisture curing: Prevent water runoff.

    3. Maintenance:

        a. Products that require toxic or hazardous materials for maintenance will not be permitted.

    4. Construction waste:

        a. Provide products from manufacturers with reclamation program for packaging.

---

    b. Provide products from manufacturers with reclamation program for construction scrap and waste materials.

PART 2 PRODUCTS

> SPECIFIER NOTE: IDENTIFY SPECIFIC MANUFACTURERS, MATERIALS, FINISHES, AND FABRICATION REQUIREMENTS IN APPROPRIATE PART 2 PARAGRAPHS; BECAUSE NEW TECHNOLOGIES AND PRODUCTS MAY BE DIFFICULT TO LOCATE, CONSIDER IDENTIFYING CONTACT PERSON AND PHONE NUMBER FOR GREEN PRODUCTS.

PART 3 EXECUTION

3.0X ENVIRONMENTAL PROCEDURES

> SPECIFIER NOTE: SPECIFY GREEN INSTALLATION REQUIREMENTS UNDER THIS PARAGRAPH. LOCATE PARAGRAPH 3.0X AT END OF PART 3.
>
> FOLLOWING ARE EXAMPLES.

A. Indoor Air Quality:
   1. Temporary ventilation: During and immediately after installation of products/materials that may negatively impact indoor air quality of completed Work, provide temporary ventilation as specified in Section 1350—Environmental Procedures.
   2. Cleaning: Use nontoxic materials and procedures.

B. Construction Waste Management: As specified in Section 1350—Environmental Procedures, and as follows:
   1. Reuse of packaging by manufacturer: Coordinate reclamation of packaging with [TITLE OF SECTION] manufacturer.
   2. Reuse of scrap and waste materials by manufacturer: Sort as required by manufacturer and coordinate reclamation of scrap and waste materials with [TITLE OF SECTION] manufacturer.

END OF SECTION

> SPECIFIER NOTE: THIS SECTION IS SIMILAR TO THE STANDARD SECTION 01230—ALTERNATES, BUT EMPHASIZES ENVIRONMENTAL CONSIDERATIONS FOR MATERIALS AND PRODUCTS. EDIT TO SUIT LOCATION AND PROJECT.

SECTION 01231

ENVIRONMENTAL ALTERNATES

PART 1 GENERAL

1.1 SUMMARY

    A. Section includes: Alternates to be submitted to Owner with Bid.

       1. Submission procedures.

       2. Documentation of changes to Contract Sum/Price and Contract Time.

> SPECIFIER NOTE: EDIT BELOW TO SUIT PROJECT. COORDINATE WITH BID FORM.

    B. Related Documents:

       1. Agreement: Incorporating monetary value of accepted Alternates.

       2. [Instructions to Bidders,] Bid Form, [Supplements to Bid Forms]: Requirements for Alternates.

1.2 DEFINITIONS

    A. Alternate: The net amount to be added to or deducted from the Base Bid Price for work identified in Schedule of Alternates.

1.3 SUBMISSION REQUIREMENTS

    A. Extent of Alternates:

       1. Determine the full extent of Work affected by proposed Alternates.

       2. Coordinate related work and modify surrounding work to integrate the Work of each Alternate.

          a. Include as part of each Alternate, miscellaneous devices, accessory objects, and similar items incidental to or required for a complete installation whether or not mentioned as part of the Alternate.

    B. Submission Form: Complete Schedule of Alternates below and attach to Bid.

---

1. Substitutions are permitted. Submit a request for substitution for any manufacturer not named in accordance with Section 01600—Product Requirements.

C. Schedule: A Schedule of Alternates is included at the end of this section. Specification sections referenced in the schedule contain requirements for materials and methods necessary to achieve the Work described under each alternate.
   1. Alternates describe environmental requirements.
   2. Conform to Contract Documents for requirements for performance, appearance, workmanship, and materials not modified under the alternate bids.

1.4 SELECTION AND AWARD OF ALTERNATES

A. Acceptance or Rejection: Alternates quoted on Schedule of Alternates and attached to Bid will be reviewed and accepted or rejected at the Owner's option. None, any, or all alternates may be accepted or rejected by the Owner.

B. Bids will be evaluated on the Base Bid. After selection of a Contractor, consideration will be given to alternates and Base Bid Price adjustments.

C. Accepted alternates will be identified in the Owner-Contractor Agreement.

PART 2 PRODUCTS—Not Used

PART 3 EXECUTION

SPECIFIER NOTE: SCHEDULE OF ALTERNATES INCLUDES POSSIBLE OPTIONS. PRODUCTS AND MANUFACTURERS ARE EXAMPLES ONLY AND NO WARRANTY OF SUITABILITY IS GIVEN BY THEIR INCLUSION HEREIN. EDIT TO SUIT PROJECT.

EDIT ALTERNATES BELOW BY ADDING AND/OR DELETING ALTERNATES FOR THE SPECIFIC CONDITIONS AND REQUIREMENTS OF THE PROJECT SITE.

3.1 SCHEDULE OF ALTERNATES

A. Alternate Number 1: State the amount to be added to or deducted from the Base Bid Price if degradable, natural-fiber erosion control blankets are provided for the erosion control blankets and erosion control geo-

textiles as specified in Section 02370—Slope Protection and Erosion Control.
  1. WS072, WS072B, WS052, or CFS072B by GreenFix America (800-929-2184).
  2. Or equal.
  Add: _____ dollars or Deduct: _____ dollars.

B. Alternate Number 2: State the amount to be added to or deducted from the Base Bid Price if reinforcing steel fabricated from minimum 90 percent postconsumer recycled steel is provided for reinforcing bars and wire as specified in Section 03200—Concrete Reinforcement.
  1. SMI-Texas (210-372-8200).
  2. Or equal.
  Add: _____ dollars or Deduct: _____ dollars.

C. Alternate Number 3: State the amount to be added to or deducted from the Base Bid Price if expansion joint fillers fabricated from 100 percent postconsumer recycled newsprint is provided in lieu of expansion joint fillers as specified in Section 03300—Cast-In-Place Concrete.
  1. Homex 300 by Homosote (800-257-9491).
  2. Or equal.
  Add: _____ dollars or Deduct: _____ dollars.

D. Alternate Number 4: State the amount to be added to or deducted from the Base Bid Price if mortar mix furnished in reusable bulk bags is provided for the mortar specified in Section 04100—Masonry Mortar and Grout. Submit documentation from mortar mix manufacturer stating that mortar packaging from installed materials is reused or recycled.
  1. SpecMix (612-490-1665).
  2. Or equal.
  Add: _____ dollars or Deduct: _____ dollars.

E. Alternate Number 5: State the amount to be added to or deducted from the Base Bid Price if sustainably harvested wood as certified in accordance with Forest Stewardship Council (FSC) Principles and Criteria is provided in lieu of lumber as specified in Section 06100—Rough Carpentry. Submit documentation of FSC-accredited certification for installed materials.
  1. Certified Forest Products Council (503-590-6600).
  2. Or equal.
  Add: _____ dollars or Deduct: _____ dollars.

F. Alternate Number 6: State the amount to be added to or deducted from the Base Bid Price if 100 percent remelt steel fasteners are provided in lieu of fasteners as specified in Section 06100—Rough Carpentry.
  1. Maze Nails (815-223-8290).

2. Or equal.
    Add: _____ dollars or Deduct: _____ dollars.

G. Alternate Number 7: State the amount to be added to or deducted from the Base Bid Price if sustainably harvested wood as certified in accordance with Forest Stewardship Council (FSC) Principles and Criteria is provided in lieu of lumber as specified in Section 06175—Wood Trusses. Submit documentation of FSC-accredited certification for installed materials.
    1. Certified Forest Products Council (503-590-6600).
    2. Or equal.
        Add: _____ dollars or Deduct: _____ dollars.

H. Alternate Number 8: State the amount to be added to or deducted from the Base Bid Price if sustainably harvested wood as certified in accordance with Forest Stewardship Council (FSC) Principles and Criteria is provided in lieu of lumber as specified in Section 06200—Finish Carpentry. Submit documentation of FSC-accredited certification for installed materials.
    1. Certified Forest Products Council (503-590-6600).
    2. Or equal.
        Add: _____ dollars or Deduct: _____ dollars.

I. Alternate Number 9: State the amount to be added to or deducted from the Base Bid Price if 100 percent remelt steel fasteners are provided in lieu of fasteners as specified in Section 06200—Finish Carpentry.
    1. Maze Nails (815-223-8290).
    2. Or equal.
        Add: _____ dollars or Deduct: _____ dollars.

J. Alternate Number 10: State the amount to be added to or deducted from the Base Bid Price if organic asphalt shingles with membrane fabricated from minimum 50 percent recycled cellulose in shingle mat substrate are provided in lieu of fiberglass shingles as specified in Section 07310—Shingles. Color as approved by Owner from manufacturer's standard palette. Submit samples for initial selection purposes in form of manufacturer's color charts or chips showing full range of colors, textures, and patterns available.
    1. Atlas (770-933-4461).
    2. Certainteed (800-274-8530).
    3. Tamko (800-641-4691).
    4. Or equal.
        Add: _____ dollars or Deduct: _____ dollars.

K. Alternate Number 11: State the amount to be added to or deducted from the Base Bid Price if walkway pads fabricated from minimum 90

percent postconsumer recycled rubber tires are provided in lieu of walk-way pads as specified in Section 07510—Built-Up Bituminous Roofing.
1. Roof-Gard Pads by Humane Manufacturing (800-369-6263).
2. Or equal.
   Add: _____ dollars or Deduct: _____ dollars.

L. Alternate Number 12: State the amount to be added to or deducted from the Base Bid Price if walkway pads fabricated from minimum 90 per-cent postconsumer recycled rubber tires are provided in lieu of walkway pads as specified in Section 07550—Modified Bituminous Membrane Roofing.
1. Roof-Gard Pads by Humane Manufacturing (800-369-6263).
2. Or equal.
   Add: _____ dollars or Deduct: _____ dollars.

M. Alternate Number 13: State the amount to be added to or deducted from the Base Bid Price if tile manufactured from recycled glass is provided in lieu of ceramic tile as specified in Section 09310—Ceramic Tile. Color as approved by Owner from manufacturer's standard pal-ette. Submit samples for initial selection purposes in form of manufac-turer's color charts or chips showing full range of colors, textures, and patterns available.
1. Prominence by GTE (717-724-8323).
2. Traffic Tile by Terra Green Ceramics (317-935-4760).
3. Or equal.
   Add: _____ dollars or Deduct: _____ dollars.

N. Alternate Number 14: State the amount to be added to or deducted from the Base Bid Price if 1/8-inch thick linoleum sheet with natural jute backing is provided in lieu of vinyl tile and vinyl sheet flooring as specified in Section 09650—Resilient Flooring. Color as approved by Owner from manufacturer's standard palette. Submit samples for initial selection purposes in form of manufacturer's color charts or chips show-ing full range of colors, textures, and patterns available.
1. Marmoleum by Forbo Industries (800-842-7839)
2. DLW Linoleum by Gerbert (717-299-5035)
3. Or equal.
   Add: _____ dollars or Deduct: _____ dollars.

O. Alternate Number 15: State the amount to be added to or deducted from the Base Bid Price if carpet manufactured from postconsumer recycled plastic or postconsumer recycled carpet is provided in lieu of carpet as specified in Section 09680—Carpet. Color as approved by Owner from manufacturer's standard palette. Submit samples for initial selection purposes in form of manufacturer's color charts or chips show-ing full range of colors, textures, and patterns available.

1. Image Carpets (800-722-2504).
2. Interface (800-336-0225).
3. Or equal.
   Add: _____ dollars or Deduct: _____ dollars.

END OF SECTION

SECTION 01351

ENVIRONMENTAL PROCEDURES

SPECIFIER NOTE: THIS SECTION INCLUDES REQUIREMENTS FOR WASTE MANAGEMENT AND THE PROTECTION OF NATURAL RESOURCES. THIS SECTION EMPHASIZES A TEAM APPROACH, INCLUDING OWNER, DESIGN PROFESSIONAL, AND CONTRACTOR, TO ADDRESS ENVIRONMENTAL ISSUES. THIS SECTION DOES NOT ADDRESS REQUIREMENTS FOR ENVIRONMENTAL IMPACT STATEMENTS OR ENVIRONMENTAL IMPACT REPORTS. REFERENCES TO ORGANIZATIONS, PROGRAMS, AND MANUFACTURERS IN THIS SECTION DO NOT REPRESENT A GUARANTY, WARRANTY, OR ENDORSEMENT THEREOF. COORDINATE WITH REQUIREMENTS OF OTHER SECTIONS; VERIFY THAT PRODUCTS AND INSTALLATION METHODS SPECIFIED IN OTHER SECTIONS ARE ENVIRONMENTALLY APPROPRIATE. EDIT TO SUIT LOCATION AND PROJECT.

PART 1 GENERAL

1.01 SUMMARY

A. Section includes: Procedures for achieving the most environmentally conscious Work feasible within the limits of the Construction Schedule, Contract Sum, and available materials, equipment, and products.
   1. Participate in promoting efforts of Owner and Architect to create an energy-efficient and environmentally sensitive structure.
   2. Use recycled-content, toxic-free, and environmentally sensitive materials, equipment, and products.
   3. Use environmentally sensitive procedures.
      a. Protect the environment, both on-site and off-site, during demolition and construction operations.
      b. Prevent environmental pollution and damage.
      c. Effect optimum control of solid wastes.

SPECIFIER NOTE: COORDINATE REQUIREMENTS FOR WASTE COLLECTION AND DISPOSAL AND FOR ENVIRONMENTAL PROTECTION SPECIFIED UNDER THIS SECTION WITH WORK SPECIFIED UNDER RELATED SECTIONS. EDIT BELOW TO SUIT PROJECT.

B. Related Sections:
   1. Section 01025—Measurement and Payment: Applications for payment.
   2. Section 01200—Project Meetings: Preconstruction conference.
   3. Section 01500—Construction Facilities and Temporary Controls: Temporary ventilation, environmental protection, waste collection, and disposal operations.
   4. Section 01630—Product Substitution Procedures.
   5. Section 01700—Contract Close-out: Cleaning and final submittals.
   6. Section 02070—Selective Demolition: Salvage and waste disposal operations.
   7. Section 02100—Site Preparation: Tree and plant protection.
   8. Section 02230—Site Clearing: Removal and storage of existing vegetation and topsoil.

1.02 DEFINITIONS

SPECIFIER NOTE: VERIFY VENTILATION REQUIREMENTS FOR INDOOR AIR QUALITY. "ADEQUATE" REQUIREMENTS FOR ONE MATERIAL MAY NOT BE "ADEQUATE" FOR ANOTHER; FOR EXAMPLE, CARPET CAN CONTAIN OVER 100 CHEMICALS, INCLUDING POSSIBLE CARCINOGENS, AND MAY REQUIRE MORE COMPLEX VENTILATION TO ACCELERATE OFFGASSING PRIOR TO INSTALLATION. MATERIALS/PRODUCTS THAT GENERALLY REQUIRE TEMPORARY VENTILATION FOR OFFGASSING INCLUDE: ADHESIVES, WOOD PRESERVATIVES, COMPOSITE WOOD PRODUCTS, PLASTICS, WATERPROOFING, INSULATION, FIREPROOFING, SEALANTS/CAULKING, ACOUSTICAL CEILINGS, RESILIENT FLOORING, CARPET, PAINTING, SEALERS/COATINGS, WALL COVERINGS, MANUFACTURED CASEWORK, AND FURNITURE. FOR MORE INFORMATION AND INFORMATION ON CURRENT FEDERAL ACTIVITIES FOR IAQ, CONTACT EPA INDOOR AIR QUALITY INFORMATION CLEARING HOUSE (800) 438-4318/(202) 484-1307; NATIONAL PESTICIDES TELECOMMUNICATION NETWORK (800) 858-7378; NATIONAL INSTITUTE FOR OCCUPATIONAL SAFETY AND HEALTH (800) 35-NIOSH; AND THE DEPARTMENT OF ENERGY (DOE) OFFICE OF CONSERVATION AND RENEWABLE ENERGY (800) DOE-3732.

A. Adequate ventilation: Ventilation, including air circulation and air changes, required to cure materials, dissipate humidity, and prevent accumulation of dust fumes, vapors, or gases.

B. Construction and demolition waste: Includes solid wastes, such as building materials, packaging, rubbish, debris, and rubble resulting from construction, remodeling, repair, and demolition operations.
   1. Rubbish: Includes both combustible and noncombustible wastes, such as paper, boxes, glass, crockery, metal and lumber scrap, metal cans, and bones.
   2. Debris: Includes both combustible and noncombustible wastes, such as leaves and tree trimmings that result from construction or maintenance and repair work.

C. Chemical waste: Includes petroleum products, bituminous materials, salts, acids, alkalis, herbicides, pesticides, organic chemicals, and inorganic wastes.

D. Environmental pollution and damage: The presence of chemical, physical, or biological elements or agents that adversely affect human health or welfare; unfavorably alter ecological balances; or degrade the utility of the environment for aesthetic, cultural, or historical purposes.

E. Hazardous materials: Includes pesticides, biocides, and carcinogens, as listed by recognized authorities, such as the Environmental Protection Agency (EPA) and the International Agency for Research on Cancer (IARC).

F. Interior final finishes: Materials and products that will be exposed at interior, occupied spaces, including flooring, wall covering, finish carpentry, and ceilings.

SPECIFIER NOTE: VERIFY CLASSIFICATION OF LANDFILL(S) AS APPROPRIATE TO LOCATION OF PROJECT. FOR EXAMPLE, IN CALIFORNIA, UNDER THE CALIFORNIA CODE OF REGULATIONS, TITLE 23, SPECIFY CLASS III LANDFILL. FOR INFORMATION ON SOLID WASTE LANDFILLS AND DISPOSAL REGULATIONS, CONTACT APPLICABLE SOLID WASTE AGENCY. THE RCRA (RESOURCE CONSERVATION RECOVERY ACT) HOTLINE MAINTAINS CURRENT LISTS OF STATE SOLID AND HAZARDOUS WASTE MANAGEMENT OFFICIALS. CONTACT RCRA AT (800) 424-9346. EDIT BELOW TO SUIT PROJECT.

G. Municipal Solid Waste Landfill: A permitted facility that accepts solid, nonhazardous waste such as household, commercial, and industrial waste, including construction and demolition waste.

H. Packaged dry products: Materials and products that are installed in dry form and are delivered to the site in manufacturer's packaging, including carpets, resilient flooring, ceiling tiles, and insulation.

I. Sediment: Soil and other debris that has been eroded and transported by storm or well production runoff water.

J. Sanitary wastes:
   1. Garbage: Refuse and scraps resulting from preparation, cooking, distribution, or consumption of food.
   2. Sewage: Domestic sanitary sewage.

K. Wet products: Materials and products installed in wet form, including paints, sealants, adhesives, and special coatings.

SPECIFIER NOTE: COORDINATE BELOW WITH SECTION 01600, MATERIALS AND EQUIPMENT, FOR SUBSTITUTION REQUIREMENTS. INDICATE UNIQUE PROCEDURES APPLICABLE FOR PROPOSAL OF ENVIRONMENTAL SUBSTITUTIONS.

1.03 SUBSTITUTIONS

A. Notify Owner when Contractor is aware of materials, equipment, or products that meet the aesthetic and programmatic intent of Contract Documents but are more environmentally sensitive than materials, equipment, or products specified or indicated in the Contract Documents.

B. Requirements of Section 01630—Product Substitution Procedures, apply except as follows:
1. Prior to submitting detailed information required under Section 01630, submit the following for initial review by Owner and Architect:
   a. Product data including manufacturer's name, address, and phone number.
   b. Description of the differences of the proposed substitution from specified product. Include description of environmental advantages of proposed substitution over specified product.
2. Submit additional information as directed by Architect.

SPECIFIER NOTE: COORDINATE BELOW WITH SECTION 01200, PROJECT MEETINGS, FOR PRECONSTRUCTION MEETING REQUIREMENTS.

1.04 PRECONSTRUCTION MEETING

A. After award of Contract and prior to the commencement of the Work, schedule and conduct meeting with Owner and Architect to discuss the proposed Solid Waste Management and Environmental Protection Plan and to develop a mutual understanding relative to details of environmental protection, recycling, and rebate programs.

1.05 SUBMITTALS

A. Solid Waste Management and Environmental Protection Plan: Not more than 10 days after the preconstruction meeting, prepare and submit a Solid Waste Management and Environmental Protection Plan including, but not limited to, the following:

1. List of federal, state, and local laws, regulations, and permits concerning environmental protection, environmental pollution and damage, hazardous materials, construction and demolition waste, chemical waste, sanitary waste, sediment, water, air, and noise pollution that are applicable to the Contractor's proposed operations.
2. List species of fish and wildlife that require specific attention, along with measures for their protection.

SPECIFIER NOTE: CONTRACTOR IS REQUIRED TO PRESERVE THE NATURAL RESOURCES ON THE SITE AND TO RESTORE RESOURCES DAMAGED DURING CONSTRUCTION OPERATIONS; REFER TO ENVIRONMENTAL CONTROLS AS SPECIFIED HEREIN. THEREFORE, IT IS NECESSARY TO ESTABLISH EXISTING CONDITION OF NATURAL RESOURCES ON THE SITE. IF OWNER HAS NOT ADEQUATELY DOCUMENTED EXISTING CONDITIONS, CONTRACTOR MAY BE REQUIRED TO DO SO. EDIT BELOW AS APPRORPAITE.

3. Procedures to be implemented to provide the required environmental protection and to comply with the applicable laws and regulations.
   a. Document existing conditions.
4. List of the recycling facilities, reuse facilities, municipal solid waste landfills, and other disposal area(s) to be used. Include:
   a. Name, location, and phone number.
   b. Copy of permit or license for each facility.
5. Procedures for Recycling/Reuse Program.

SPECIFIER NOTE: DELETE BELOW IF PROJECT DOES NOT QUALIFY FOR REBATE PROGRAMS.

6. Procedures for Rebate Program(s).
7. Schedule for application of interior finishes.
8. Revise and resubmit Solid Waste Management and Environmental Protection Plan as required by Owner.
   a. Approval of the Contractor's Solid Waste Management and Environmental Protection Plan will not relieve the Contractor of

responsibility for adequate and continuing control of pollutants and other environmental protection measures.

SPECIFIER NOTE: COORDINATE BELOW WITH SECTION 01025, MEASUREMENT AND PAYMENT, FOR APPLICATION FOR PAYMENT REQUIREMENTS.

B. With each Application for Payment as specified in Section 01025, submit the following:
   1. Updated Summary of Solid Waste Disposal and Diversion. Submit on form in Appendix A of this Section. Include manifests, weight tickets, receipts, and invoices specifically identifying the Project and waste material for:
      a. Municipal Solid Waste Landfills.
      b. Recycling Centers.
      c. Nonprofit Organizations.
   2. Records of noise level. Indicate procedures for measurement and for dealing with any problems and the alternatives implemented for mitigating actions.
C. With Record Submittals as specified in Section 01700, submit the following:
   1. Final Summary of Solid Waste Disposal and Diversion. Submit on form in Appendix A of this Section.

SPECIFIER NOTE: RESOURCE CONSERVATION AND RECOVERY ACT PROJECT SUMMARY IS USEFUL ON FEDERAL PROJECTS AND ON OTHER PROJECTS REQUIRING DOCUMENTATION OF MATERIALS WITH RECYCLED CONTENT UTILIZED IN CONSTRUCTION. DELETE BELOW IF PROJECT DOES NOT REQUIRE DOCUMENTATION OF MATERIALS WITH RECYCLED CONTENT.

   2. Resource Conservation and Recovery Act Project Summary. Submit on form in Appendix B of this Section.

SPECIFIER NOTE: DELETE BELOW IF PROJECT DOES NOT QUALIFY FOR REBATE PROGRAMS. IF REBATE PROGRAMS ARE APPLICABLE, COORDINATE WITH SECTION 01700, CONTRACT CLOSE-OUT FOR CLOSE-OUT SUBMITTAL REQUIREMENTS.

3. Three-ring binder with rebate information and product documentation as required, or Owner to qualify for Rebate Programs.

PART 2 PRODUCTS

Not Used

PART 3 EXECUTION

3.01 RECYCLING AND REUSE

SPECIFIER NOTE: IDENTIFY TYPES OF MATERIALS TO BE RECYCLED OR REUSED. VERIFY AVAILABILITY OF LOCAL FACILITIES CAPABLE OF PROCESSING THE MATERIALS AND NOTE ANY SPECIAL LIMITATIONS IMPOSED BY LOCAL FACILITIES ON THE CONDITION OF MATERIALS ACCEPTED.

CONSIDER HIGHEST AND BEST OF EACH MATERIAL (REUSE IS MORE EFFICIENT THAN RECYCLING); FOR EXAMPLE, MANY BUSINESSES COLLECT ITEMS SUCH AS USED PAINT, BRICK, OR METAL FABRICATIONS FOR REUSE. ALSO, SOME MANUFACTURERS ACCEPT USED PACKAGING FROM THEIR PRODUCTS FOR REUSE. CONSIDER RECYCLING OR REUSING MATERIAL ON SITE; FOR EXAMPLE, CRUSHED GYPSUM MAY BE USED AS SOIL AMENDMENT IN SOME AREAS.

COORDINATE WITH SPECIFIC PROJECT MATERIALS AND REQUIREMENTS. THE FOLLOWING IS AN EXAMPLE.

A. Collection: Implement a recycling/reuse program that includes separate collection of waste materials of the following types:
   1. Asphalt.
   2. Concrete.
   3. Porcelain plumbing fixtures.
   4. Metal.
      a. Ferrous.
      b. Nonferrous.
   5. Wood, nails, and staples allowed.
   6. Debris.
   7. Glass, colored glass allowed.
   8. Red clay brick.
   9. Paper.
      a. Bond.

      b. Newsprint.

      c. Cardboard and paper packaging materials.

    10. Plastic.

SPECIFIER NOTE: MANY TYPES OF PLASTICS MAY BE MIXED TOGETHER TO MAKE PLASTIC LUMBER. HOWEVER, SOME FA-CILITIES OPERATE PREDOMINANTLY FOR THE CONSUMER SEC-TOR AND REQUIRE SEPARATION OF PLASTIC BY "CONSUMER" TYPES. MILK JUGS ARE GENERALLY FABRICATED FROM HDPE; PLASTIC WRAP AND PLASTIC BAGS ARE GENERALLY FABRI-CATED FROM LDPE; PLASTIC SODA BOTTLES ARE GENERALLY FABRICATED FROM PET.

---

      a. High-density polyethylene (HDPE).

      b. Low-density polyethylene (LDPE).

      c. Polyethylene terephthalate (PET).

      d. Polystyrene.

      e. Other.

    11. Gypsum.

    12. Paint and paint cans.

    13. Others as appropriate.

SPECIFIER NOTE: IDENTIFY LOCAL RECYCLING CENTERS AND WASTE HAULERS. SOURCES FOR THIS INFORMATION INCLUDE STATE SOLID WASTE OFFICES AND ENVIRONMENTAL PROTEC-TION AGENCY (EPA) REGIONAL OFFICES, WASTE MANAGE-MENT DIVISION. LIST CENTERS THAT ACCEPT MATERIAL IDENTIFIED ABOVE FOR RECYCLING/REUSE. THE FOLLOWING IS AN EXAMPLE.

    B. Recycling/Reuse Centers: The following is a partial list for contrac-tor's information only. For more information, contact the Integrated Solid Waste Management Office, City Hall.

SPECIFIER NOTE: FOR INFORMATION ON RECYCLING/REUSE OF ASPHALT, CONTACT THE ASPHALT RECYCLING AND RE-CLAIMING ASSOCIATION (410) 267-0023.

---

1. Asphalt.
2. Concrete.
3. Porcelain plumbing fixtures.
4. Metal.

SPECIFIER NOTE: OPTIONS FOR COMPANIES THAT ACCEPT WOOD WASTE INCLUDE WOOD RECYCLING INC. (800) 982-8732.

---

5. Wood, clean, and mixed (nails and staples allowed).
6. Debris.
7. Glass.
8. Red clay brick.
9. Paper.

SPECIFIER NOTE: FOR INFORMATION ON RECYCLING/REUSE OF PLASTIC, CONTACT THE VINYL ENVIRONMENTAL RE-SOURCE CENTER OF THE VINYL INSTITUTE AT (800) 969-8469, THE ASSOCIATION OF FOAM PACKAGING RECYCLERS (202) 974-5351, AND THE AMERICAN PLASTICS COUNCIL AT (800) 2-HELP-90.

---

10. Plastic.
11. Gypsum.

SPECIFIER NOTE: OPTIONS FOR COMPANIES THAT ACCEPT USED PAINT AND USED PAINT CANS FOR REUSE INCLUDE THE GREEN PAINT COMPANY (800) 527-8866 AND MAJOR PAINT CO. (310) 542-7701. GREEN PAINT HAS PROGRAMS TO ACCEPT USED PAINT FROM CONTRACTORS. MAJOR PAINT HAS PROGRAMS TO ACCEPT USED PAINT FROM PUBLIC AND PRIVATE AGENCIES (NOT CONTRACTORS). FOR MORE INFORMATION ON FACILITIES THAT ACCEPT USED STEEL CANS, CONTACT THE STEEL CAN RECYCLING INSTITUTE (SCRI) AT (800) YES-1-CAN/(800) 937-1226.

---

12. Paint and paint cans.

C. Handling:
   1. Clean contaminated materials prior to placing in collection containers. Deliver materials free of dirt, adhesives, solvents, petroleum contamination, and other substances deleterious to recycling process.
   2. Arrange for collection by or delivery to the appropriate recycling or reuse facility.

SPECIFIER NOTE: IDENTIFY LOCAL AND REGIONAL REUSE PROGRAMS. ALSO, IDENTIFY NONPROFIT ORGANIZATIONS SUCH AS SCHOOLS, LOCAL HOUSING AGENCIES, AND PUBLIC ARTS PROGRAMS THAT ACCEPT USED MATERIALS. IDENTIFY SPONSOR AGENCY AND CONTACT FOR EACH PROGRAM. THE FOLLOWING ARE EXAMPLES.

D. Participate in Re-Use Programs:

SPECIFIER NOTE: FOR INFORMATION ON THE NATIONAL MATERIALS EXCHANGE NETWORK CONTACT THE PACIFIC MATERIALS EXCHANGE (509) 466-1532; MODEM ACCESS THROUGH (509) 466-1019/(800) 858-6625. THE FOLLOWING IS AN EXAMPLE.

   1. California Materials Exchange (CAL-MAX) Program sponsored by the California Integrated Waste Management Board.
      a. CAL-MAX is a free service provided by the California Integrated Waste Management Board, division of the California Environmental Protection Agency, designed to help businesses find markets for materials that traditionally would be discarded. The premise of the CAL-MAX Program is that material discarded by one business may be a resource for another business.
      b. To obtain a current Materials Listings Catalog, call CAL-MAX/California Integrated Waste Management Board. Contact CAL-MAX at (916) 255-2369.
   2. Materials For The Arts (MFA) sponsored by the Department of Cultural Affairs.
      a. MFA is a materials exchange that accepts waste and excess materials from private donors and distributes them to various nonprofit art organizations throughout the city. Contact _____.

SPECIFIER NOTE: FOR INFORMATION ON LOCAL ACTIVITIES OF HABITAT FOR HUMANITY, CONTACT THE NATIONAL HOTLINE (800) HABITAT.

3. Habitat for Humanity, a nonprofit housing organization that rehabilitates and builds housing for low-income families.
   a. Sites requiring donated materials vary. Contact _____.

SPECIFIER NOTE: IDENTIFY RECIPIENT OF MONIES RECOVERED FROM REUSE AND REBATE PROGRAMS. IF MONIES WILL NOT ACCRUE TO CONTRACTOR, EDIT BELOW.

E. Rebates, tax credits, and other savings obtained for recycled or reused materials accrue to Contractor.

3.2 REBATE PROGRAMS

A. Execute final implementation of Rebate Programs. Obtain information packets from each sponsoring agency prior to starting Work. Document installation of products eligible for rebates under the following programs:

SPECIFIER NOTE: IDENTIFY PROGRAMS FROM UTILITIES AND GOVERNMENTAL AGENCIES UNDER WHICH PROJECT QUALIFIES FOR A REBATE. IDENTIFY CONTACT FOR EACH PROGRAM. THE FOLLOWING ARE EXAMPLES.

1. Energy Efficiency Incentive Program for Small and Medium-Size Commercial and Industrial Customers: Sponsored by the Department of Water and Power (DWP). Contact _____.
2. Commercial New Construction, Design Advantage: Sponsored by the Department of Water and Power (DWP). Contact _____.
3. Commercial Energy Efficiency Program: Sponsored by _____. Contact _____.

> SPECIFIER NOTE: COORDINATE ENVIRONMENTAL CONTROLS
> WITH SECTIONS 01500—CONSTRUCTION FACILITIES AND TEM-
> PORARY CONTROLS; 01700-CONTRACT CLOSEOUT; 02070-
> SELECTIVE DEMOLITION; AND 02100-SITE PREPARATION FOR
> REQUIREMENTS FOR ENVIRONMENTAL PROTECTION, CLEAN-
> ING, AND WASTE DISPOSAL. EDIT BELOW TO SUIT PROJECT.

3.03 ENVIRONMENTAL CONTROLS

A. Protection of natural resources: Preserve the natural resources within the project boundaries and outside the limits of permanent work performed under this Contract in their existing condition or restore to an equivalent or improved condition as approved by Owner, upon completion of the Work.

1. Confine demolition and construction activities to work area limits indicated on the Drawings.

   a. Temporary construction: As specified in Section 01500—Construction Facilities and Temporary Controls.

   b. Salvage operations: As specified in Section 02070—Selective Demolition.

   c. Disposal operations for demolished and waste materials that are not identified to be salvaged, recycled, or reused:

      1) Remove debris, rubbish, and other waste materials resulting from demolition and construction operations from site.

      2) No burning permitted.

      3) Transport materials with appropriate vehicles, and dispose off-site to areas that are approved for disposal by governing authorities having jurisdiction.

      4) Avoid spillage by covering and securing loads when hauling on or adjacent to public streets or highways. Remove spillage, and sweep, wash, or otherwise clean project site, streets, or highways.

      5) Comply with applicable regulations.

2. Water resources: As specified in Section 02230—Site Clearing and as follows:

   a. Comply with requirements of the National Pollutant Discharge Elimination System (NPDES) and the State Pollutant Discharge Elimination System (SPDES).

   b. Oily substances: Prevent oily or other hazardous substances from entering the ground, drainage areas, or local bodies of water.

      1) Store and service construction equipment at areas designated for collection of oil wastes.

   c. Mosquito abatement: Prevent ponding of stagnant water conducive to mosquito breeding habitat.

  d. Prevent runoff from site during demolition and construction op-
     erations.

SPECIFIER NOTE: COORDINATE BELOW WITH WORK SPECIFIED
IN DIVISION 2-SITE CONSTRUCTION.

---

3. Land resources: Prior to construction, identify land resources to be
   preserved within the Work area. Do not remove, cut, deface, injure,
   or destroy land resources, including trees, shrubs, vines, grasses,
   topsoil, and land forms without permission from Owner.
   a. Earthwork: As specified in Section 02300—Earthwork and as
      follows:
      1) Erodible soils: Plan and conduct earthwork to minimize the
         duration of exposure of unprotected soils, except where the
         constructed feature obscures borrow areas, quarries, and
         waste material areas. Clear areas in reasonably sized incre-
         ments only as needed to use the areas developed. Form earth-
         work to final grade as shown. Immediately protect side slopes
         and back slopes upon completion of rough grading.
      2) Erosion and sedimentation control devices: Construct or in-
         stall temporary and permanent erosion and sedimentation
         control features as required.

SPECIFIER NOTE: FOR OLD-GROWTH AND OTHER SIGNIFICANT
TREES AND PLANTS, IT MAY BE USEFUL TO HAVE A MORE AG-
GRESSIVE APPROACH TO PROTECTION THAN THE STANDARD
PROHIBITIONS. THE FOLLOWING IS AN EXAMPLE.

---

   b. Tree and plant protection: As specified in Section 02100—Site
      Preparation, and as follows:
      1) Prior to start of construction, tag each tree and plant sched-
         uled to remain with value as identified by Owner. In the event
         of damage to tree or plant, Owner may, at Owner's discre-
         tion, deduct the indicated value of the damaged tree or plant
         from the Contract Sum.
4. Air Resources: Prevent creation of dust, air pollution, and odors.
   a. Use water sprinkling, temporary enclosures, and other appropri-
      ate methods to limit to lowest practical level dust and dirt rising
      and scattering in air.

---

       1) Do not use water when it may create hazardous or other adverse conditions such as flooding and pollution.

   b. Store volatile liquids, including fuels and solvents, in closed containers.

   c. Properly maintain equipment to reduce gaseous pollutant emissions.

   d. Interior final finishes: Schedule construction operations involving wet products prior to packaged dry products to the greatest extent possible, in accordance with approved Solid Waste Management and Environmental Protection Plan.

SPECIFIER NOTE: COORDINATE BELOW WITH SECTION 01500—CONSTRUCTION FACILITIES AND TEMPORARY CONTROLS. EDIT BELOW TO SUIT PROJECT.

---

   e. Temporary Ventilation: As specified in Section 01500—Construction Facilities and Temporary Controls, and as follows:

SPECIFIER NOTE: MOST OF THE EMISSIONS FROM WET PRODUCTS WILL OCCUR DURING THE FIRST FEW HOURS OR DAYS AFTER INSTALLATION; HOWEVER, MANY MATERIALS/PRODUCTS CONTINUE TO EMIT FOR WEEKS, MONTHS, AND YEARS. EMISSION RATES GENERALLY DECREASE OVER TIME.

---

       1) Provide adequate ventilation during and after installation of interior wet products and interior final finishes.

SPECIFIER NOTE: PACKAGED DRY PRODUCTS FREQUENTLY PRODUCE A BURST OF EMISSIONS WHEN THEY ARE INITIALLY REMOVED FROM PACKAGING. THE INITIAL BURST IS SIGNIFICANTLY HIGHER THAN THE EMISSIONS A WEEK OR A MONTH LATER; FOR EXAMPLE, CARPET BACKED BY STYRENE BUTADIENE RUBBER LATEX (SBR) TENDS TO EMIT SIGNIFICANTLY HIGHER QUANTITIES OF 4-PHENYLCYCLOHEXENE (4-PC) DURING THE FIRST DAY THAN AT THE END OF A WEEK, BUT WILL CONTINUE TO EMIT AT LOW LEVELS FOR SEVERAL MONTHS. FOR MORE INFORMATION ON CARPET VENTILATION, CONTACT THE CONSUMER PRODUCT SAFETY COMMISSION AT (800) 638-2772, PRESS 1, PAUSE, PRESS 000, PAUSE, PRESS 129.

---

2) Provide adequate ventilation of packaged dry products prior to installation. Remove from packaging and ventilate in a secure, dry, well-ventilated space free from strong contaminant sources and residues. Provide a temperature range of 60 degrees F minimum to 90 degree F maximum continuously during the ventilation period. Do not ventilate within limits of Work unless otherwise approved by Architect.

SPECIFIER NOTE: COORDINATE BELOW WITH OWNER'S OCCUPANCY REQUIREMENTS AND WITH INDOOR AIR QUALITY IMPLICATIONS OF MATERIALS SPECIFIED FOR PROJECT. IN GENERAL, THE HIGHER THE VENTILATION RATE AND THE LONGER THE VENTILATION PERIOD AFTER INSTALLATION, THE LOWER THE RESIDUES WHEN THE SPACE IS OCCUPIED. HOWEVER, HIGH PERCENTAGES OF OUTSIDE AIR MAY NOT BE APPROPRIATE IN HUMID CLIMATES OR INDUSTRIAL AREAS.

WHERE OWNER REQUIRES AIR QUALITY MONITORING, CONFORM TO STANDARD TESTS AND PROCEDURES. THE EPA HAS PUBLISHED METHODS FOR AIR QUALITY MONITORING COVERING THE NAAQS CRITERIA POLLUTANTS AND A COMPENDIUM OF INDOOR AIR QUALITY SAMPLING AND ANALYTICAL METHODS. ADDITIONAL METHODS INCLUDE THE STANDARDS THAT HAVE BEEN ADOPTED BY ASTM OR NIOSH, ACCORDING TO THEIR AVAILABILITY AND APPLICABILITY.

WHERE CHAMBER TESTING IS REQUIRED, SPECIFY TESTING UNDER ASTM D5116 GUIDE FOR SMALL-SCALE ENVIRONMENTAL CHAMBER DETERMINATION OF ORGANIC EMISSIONS FROM INDOOR MATERIALS/PRODUCTS.

---

3) Preoccupancy ventilation: After final completion and prior to initial occupancy, provide adequate ventilation for minimum five days. Preoccupancy ventilation procedures:
   a) Use supply air fans and ducts only.
   b) Temporarily seal exhaust ducts.
   c) Temporarily disable exhaust fans.
   d) Provide exhaust through operable windows or temporary openings.
   e) Provide temporary exhaust fans as required to pull exhaust air from deep interior locations. Stair towers may be used for exhausting air from the building during the temporary ventilation.

  f) After preoccupancy ventilation and prior to final testing and balancing of HVAC system, replace air filters and make HVAC system fully operational.

5. Fish and Wildlife Resources: Manage and control construction activities to minimize interference with, disturbance of, and damage to fish and wildlife.

6. Noise Control: Perform demolition and construction operations to minimize noise. Perform noise-causing work in less sensitive hours of the day or week as directed by owner.

  a. Repetitive, high-level impact noise will be permitted only between the hours of 8:00 A.M. and 6:00 P.M. Do not exceed the following dB limitations:

Sound Level in dB	*Time Duration of Impact Noise*
70	More than 12 minutes in any hour
80	More than 3 minutes in any hour

  b. Provide equipment, sound-deadening devices, and take noise abatement measures that are necessary for compliance.

  c. Maximum permissible construction equipment noise levels at 50 feet (dB):

EARTHMOVING	*dB*	*MATERIALS HANDLING*	*dB*
FRONT LOADERS	75	CONCRETE MIXERS	75
BACKHOES	75	CONCRETE PUMPS	75
DOZERS	75	CRANES	75
TRACTORS	75	DERRICKS IMPACT	75
SCRAPERS	80	PILE DRIVERS	95
GRADERS	75	JACK HAMMERS	75
TRUCKS	75	ROCK DRILLS	80
PAVERS, STATIONARY	80	PNEUMATIC TOOLS	80
PUMPS	75	SAWS	75
GENERATORS	75	VIBRATORS	75
COMPRESSORS	75		

  d. At least once every five successive working days while work is being performed above 55 dB noise level, measure sound level for noise exposure due to the construction.

END OF SECTION

Appendix A

SUMMARY OF SOLID WASTE DISPOSAL AND DIVERSION

Project Name: _____ Project Number: _____

Contractor Name: _____ License Number: _____

Contractor Address: _____

Solid Waste Material	Date Material Disposed/ Diverted	Amount Disposed/ Diverted (ton or cu. yd)	Municipal Solid Waste Facility (name, address, & phone number)	Recycling/Reuse Facility (name, address, & phone number)	Comments (if disposed, state why not diverted)
Asphalt					
Concrete					
Metal					
Wood					
Debris					
Glass					
Clay brick					
Paper/ Cardboard					
Plastic					
Gypsum					
Paint					
Carpet					
Other:					

Signature: _____ Date: _____

Appendix B

RESOURCE CONSERVATION AND RECOVERY ACT— PROJECT SUMMARY

Project Name: _____ Project Number: _____

Contractor Name: _____ License Number: _____

Contractor Address: _____

1.0 EPA GUIDELINE ITEMS

A. Fly Ash:
  1. Total dollar amount of concrete and cement provided for this project. $_____.
  2. Total dollar amount of concrete and cement containing fly ash provided for this project. $_____.
  3. Were there any technical impediments to increasing the amount of concrete and cement containing fly ash provided for this project? _____.

     a. If yes, please explain. _____

        _____

        _____

        _____.

B. Building Insulation Products:
  1. Total dollar amount of building insulation products provided for this project. $_____.
  2. Total dollar amount of building insulation products containing recycled materials provided for this project. $_____.
  3. Were there any technical impediments to increasing the amount of building insulation products containing recycled materials provided for this project? _____.
     a. If yes, please explain. _____

        _____

        _____

        _____.

C. Carpet:
  1. Total dollar amount of carpet provided for this project.
                                                              $_____.

---

2. Total dollar amount of carpet containing recycled materials provided for this project. $_____.

3. Were there any technical impediments to increasing the amount of carpet containing recycled materials provided for this project?

_____.

  a. If yes, please explain. _____

_____

_____

_____.

D. Floor Tiles (resilient):

1. Total dollar amount of floor tile (resilient) provided for this project. $_____.

2. Total dollar amount of floor tile (resilient) containing recycled materials provided for this project. $_____.

3. Were there any technical impediments to increasing the amount of floor tile (resilient) containing recycled materials provided for this project? _____.

  a. If yes, please explain. _____

_____

_____

_____.

E. Floor Tiles (ceramic):

1. Total dollar amount of floor tile (ceramic) provided for this project. $_____.

2. Total dollar amount of floor tile (ceramic) containing recycled materials provided for this project. $_____.

3. Were there any technical impediments to increasing the amount of floor tile (ceramic) containing recycled materials provided for this project? _____.

  a. If yes, please explain. _____

_____

_____

_____.

F. Hydraulic Mulch:

1. Total dollar amount of hydraulic mulch provided for this project. $_____.

2. Total dollar amount of hydraulic mulch containing recycled materials provided for this project. $_____.

3. Were there any technical impediments to increasing the amount of hydraulic mulch containing recycled materials provided for this project? _____.
a. If yes, please explain. _____

_____

_____

_____.

G. Compost:
1. Total dollar amount of compost provided for this project.
$_____.
2. Total dollar amount of compost containing recycled materials provided for this project. $_____.
3. Were there any technical impediments to increasing the amount of hydraulic mulch containing recycled materials provided for this project? _____.
a. If yes, please explain. _____

_____

_____

_____.

2.0 SPECIFICATIONS

NOT USED

3.0 SOLID WASTE PREVENTION

A. Total dollar amount of solid waste disposed (landfill) for this project.
$_____.

B. Total weight of solid waste disposed (landfill) for this project.
$_____.

4.0 RECYCLING

A. Total dollar value of solid waste diverted from landfill and recycled or reused for this project. (Express as total dollar amount for solid waste disposal in landfill for equivalent type and amount of diverted waste.)
$_____.

B. Total weight of solid waste diverted from landfill and recycled or reused for this project. (Express as total weight for solid waste disposal in landfill for equivalent type and amount of diverted waste.)

$_____$.

5.0 COMMENTS

A. Comments and suggestions for increasing amount of recycled materials used in construction materials.

_____

_____

_____.

B. Comments and suggestions for improving solid waste prevention and recycling efforts during construction.

_____

_____

_____

_____

_____

_____.

Signature: _____ Date: _____

SPECIFIER NOTE: THIS SECTION IS A SAMPLE SECTION WHICH MAY BE USED FOR CONTROLLING THE SUBMITTAL OF SUBSTITUTION REQUESTS DURING BIDDING AND CONSTRUCTION. IT SHOULD BE EDITED TO SUIT A SPECIFIC PROJECT AND LOCATION.

SECTION 01630

PRODUCT SUBSTITUTION PROCEDURES

PART 1 GENERAL

1.01 SECTION INCLUDES

A. Contractor's options in selection of products.

B. Requests for substitution of products.

1.02 RELATED REQUIREMENTS

A. Document 00200—Instructions to Bidders: Times for submittal of requests for substitutions during the Bidding period.

B. Document 00700—General Conditions: Times for submittal of requests for substitutions during the Bidding period.

C. Section 01310—Project Management and Coordination: Coordination of construction.

D. Section 01334—Shop Drawings, Product Data, and Samples: Product data submittals.

E. Section 01770—Closeout Procedures: Record documents; operation and maintenance data.

1.03 OPTIONS

A. Products Specified by Reference Standards or by Description Only: Any product meeting those standards.

Project Name/Project No.   01630-1   Product Substitution Procedures

B. Products Specified by Naming One or More Manufacturers with a Provision for Substitutions: Submit a request for substitution for any manufacturer not specifically named.

C. Products Specified by Naming Several Manufacturers: Products of named manufacturers meeting specifications; no options, no substitutions.

D. Products Specified by Standard of Comparison: Products of named manufacturer; submit a request for substitution for any manufacturers not specifically named as meeting specifications.

1.04 LIMITATIONS ON SUBSTITUTIONS

A. Requests for substitutions of products will be considered only during bidding up to 14 days prior to the date of bid opening. Requests received after receipt of bids will be considered only in case of product unavailability or other conditions beyond control of Contractor, his or her subcontractors, or suppliers. Contractor shall order products sufficiently in advance of date they will be needed on project to avoid necessity for submission of a substitution request.

B. Substitutions will not be considered when indicated on shop drawings or product data submittals without separate formal request, when requested directly by subcontractor or supplier, or when acceptance will require substantial revision of Contract Documents.

C. Substitute products shall not be ordered or installed without written acceptance.

D. Only one (1) request for substitution for each product will be considered. When substitution is not accepted, provide specified product.

E. Architect/Engineer will determine acceptability of substitutions.

1.05 REQUESTS FOR SUBSTITUTIONS

A. Submit separate request for each substitution. Document each request with complete data substantiating compliance of proposed substitution with requirements of Contract Documents.

B. Identify product by Specifications section and Article numbers. Provide manufacturer's name and address, trade name of product, and model or catalog number. List fabricators and suppliers as appropriate.

C. Attach product data as specified in Section 01334.

D. List similar projects using product, dates of installation, and names of Architect/Engineer and Owner.

E. Give itemized comparison of proposed substitution with specified product, listing variations, and reference to Specifications section and Article numbers.

F. Give quality and performance comparison between proposed substitution and the specified product.

G. Give cost data comparing proposed substitution with specified product and amount of net change to Contract Sum.

H. List availability of maintenance services and replacement materials.

I.   State effect of substitution on construction schedule and changes required in other work or products.

1.06 CONTRACTOR REPRESENTATION

A. Request for substitution constitutes a representation that Contractor has investigated proposed product and has determined that it is equal to or superior in all respects to specified product.

B. Contractor will provide the same warranty for substitution as for specified product.

C. Contractor will coordinate installation of accepted substitute, making such changes as may be required for Work to be complete in all respects.

D. Contractor certifies that cost data presented is complete and includes all related costs under this Contract.

E. Contractor waives claims for additional costs related to substitution, which may later become apparent.

1.07 SUBMITTAL PROCEDURES

A. Submit three (3) copies of request for substitution.

B. Architect/Engineer will review Contractor's requests for substitutions with reasonable promptness.

C. Acceptance by the Architect/Engineer, if given, will be made by addendum issued no later than seven (7) days prior to receipt of bids.

D. No substitutions are allowed under the Lump Sum Base Bid unless approved by addendum.

E. For accepted products, submit shop drawings, product data, and samples under provisions of Section 01334.

PART 2 PRODUCTS

Not Used

PART 3 EXECUTION

Not Used

END OF SECTION

BIDDER'S/GENERAL CONTRACTOR'S SUBSTITUTION
REQUEST FORM

To: <u>Name of Architect/Engineer</u>

Project: <u>Name of Project</u>

We hereby submit for your consideration the following product instead of the specified item for the above project:

Drawing No.: _____ Drawing Title: _____

Section: _____ Paragraph: _____ Specified Item: _____

Proposed Substitution: _____

Attach complete technical data, including laboratory tests, if applicable. Include complete information on changes to Drawings and/or Specifications which proposed substitution will require for its proper installation.

Fill in Blanks Below:
A. Does the substitution affect dimensions shown on Drawings?
   Yes _____ No _____ If yes, clearly indicate changes below.

   _____

   _____

   _____

B. Will the undersigned pay for changes to the building design, including engineering and detailing costs caused by the requested substitution?
   Yes _____ No _____ If no, fully explain below.

   _____

   _____

C. What effect does substitution have on other Contracts or trades?

   _____

D. Manufacturer's guarantees of the proposed and specified items are:
   _____ Same _____ Different (explain on attachment)

E. Itemized comparison of specified item(s) with the proposed substitution; list significant variations:

   _____

   (Use separate sheet if necessary)

F. Accurate cost data comparing proposed substitution with product specified:

   _____

(Use separate sheet if necessary)

(FORM CONTINUED ON NEXT PAGE)

G. Reasons for substitution:

_____

_____

_____

H. What effect does substitution have on construction schedule?

_____

I. Designation of maintenance services and sources:

_____

(Attach additional sheets if required)

CERTIFICATION OF EQUAL PERFORMANCE AND ASSUMPTION OF LIABILITY FOR EQUAL PERFORMANCE, EQUAL DESIGN, AND COMPATIBILITY WITH ADJACENT MATERIALS.

The undersigned states that the function, appearance, and quality are equal or superior to the specified item.

Signature shall be by person having authority to legally bind their firm to the above terms. Failure to provide legally binding signature will result in retraction of approval.

Submitted by:

_____
Firm (Contractor)

_____

_____
Address

_____
Signature & Title

Date: _____

Telephone: _____

For Use by Architect/Engineer:

[_] Accepted [_] Accepted As Noted

[_] Not Accepted [_] Received Too Late

By: _____

Date: _____

Remarks: _____

_____

_____

_____

END OF FORM

SAMPLE TECHNICAL SECTION*

SECTION 10170

PLASTIC TOILET COMPARTMENTS

*The format for this sample technical specification section follows SectionFormat™, CSI Publication No. MP-2-2, "A Recommended Format for Construction Specification Sections," published by the Construction Specifications Institute, 601 Madison Street, Alexandria, VA 22314-1791.

SectionFormat provides a format for organizing specification text within an established structure. It provides consistency from section to section within a project manual.

The format for the pages within this sample technical specification section follows PageFormat™, CSI Publication No. MP-2-3, published by the Construction Specifications Institute, 601 Madison Street, Alexandria, VA 22314-1791.

PageFormat provides a means of organizing specification section pages in an orderly and uniform manner.

PART 1 GENERAL

1.01 SUMMARY
  A. Work Includes:
    1. Solid plastic toilet compartments, floor-mounted, head rail-braced.
    2. Solid plastic urinal screens, wall-mounted with floor-mounted pilaster brace.
    3. Attachment hardware.

  B. Related Documents: The Contract Documents, as defined in Section 01110—Summary of Work, apply to the Work of this Section. Additional requirements and information necessary to complete the Work of this Section may be found in other Documents.

  C. Related Sections:
    1. Section 06100—Rough Carpentry: Framing and plates within walls for partition attachment.
    2. Section 10810—Toilet Accessories: Coordinate compartment installation with subsequent accessory installation.

1.02 REFERENCES
  A. American National Standards Institute (ANSI):
    1. ANSI A117.1—Specifications for Making Buildings and Facilities Accessible to and Usable by Physically Handicapped People.

1.03 SUBMITTALS
  A. Section 01330—Submittal Procedures: Procedures for submittals.

1. Product Data: Panel construction, hardware, and accessories.
2. Shop Drawings: Partition plan, elevation views, dimensions, door swings, details of wall and floor supports and connections.
3. Samples: Two 2-inch by 3-inch samples of partition indicating finish and color.

1.04 QUALITY ASSURANCE

A. Regulatory Requirements: Conform to ANSI A117.1 code for access for the handicapped operation of toilet compartment door and hardware.

1.05 DELIVERY, STORAGE, AND HANDLING

A. Section 01600—Product Requirements: Transport, handle, store, and protect products.

1.06 ENVIRONMENTAL REQUIREMENTS

A. Resource Management:
   1. Recycled Content: Provide solid plastic compartments and screens with core manufactured from minimum 50 percent recycled plastic.

PART 2 PRODUCTS

2.01 MANUFACTURERS

A. Subject to compliance with project requirements, manufacturer's offering specified items which may be incorporated in the Work include the following:
   1. Comtec (717) 348-0997.
   2. Santana (800) 368-5002 or (717) 343-7921.

2.02 MATERIALS

A. Solid plastic compartments and screens: water-resistant, graffiti-resistant, nonabsorbent, with plastic face sheets permanently fused to plastic core.
   1. Panels: 1-inch thickness.
   2. Doors: 1-inch thickness.
   3. Pilasters: 1-inch thickness.

B. Pilaster Shoes: 3 inches high; one piece-molded HDPE.

C. Attachments:
   1. Screws and Bolts: Stainless steel; tamper-proof type.
   2. Wall-Mounting Brackets: Continuous, full-height, heavy-duty plastic in accordance with toilet compartment manufacturer's instructions.

D. Hardware: Chrome-plated nonferrous cast pivot hinges, gravity type, adjustable for door close positioning; nylon bearings; black anodized aluminum door latch; door strike and keeper with rubber bumper; cast alloy chrome-plated coat hook and bumper.

2.03 FABRICATION

A. Solid Plastic: 1/4-inch radius beveled edges.

B. Hardware and Attachments: Predrilled by manufacturer; provide for protection of dissimilar metals.
   1. Floor-Mounted Anchorage: Corrosion-resistant anchoring assemblies with threaded rods, lock washers, and leveling adjustment nuts at pilasters for structural connection to floor. Provide shoes at pilasters to conceal anchorage.

2.04 FINISHES

A. Compartments and Screens: Color as selected by Architect/Owner from manufacturer's standard colors.

B. Pilaster Shoes: Color to match core of solid plastic compartments and screens.

PART 3 EXECUTION

3.01 EXAMINATION

A. Section 01700—Execution Requirements: Verification of existing conditions before starting work.

B. Verification of Conditions: Verify that field measurements, surfaces, substrates, and conditions are as required and ready to receive Work.
   1. Verify correct spacing of plumbing fixtures.
   2. Verify correct location of built-in framing, anchorage, and bracing.

C. Report in writing to Architect/Owner prevailing conditions that will adversely affect satisfactory execution of the Work of this section. Do not proceed with Work until unsatisfactory conditions have been corrected.

D. By beginning Work, Contractor accepts conditions, and assumes responsibility for correcting unsuitable conditions encountered at no additional cost to the Owner.

3.02 INSTALLATION

A. Install partitions secure, rigid, plumb, level, and square in accordance with manufacturer's published instructions.
   1. Provide for adjustment due to minor floor variations.

2. Install adjacent components for consistency of line and plane.

B. Maintain 1/2-inch space between wall and panels and between wall and pilasters. Attach panel brackets securely to walls using anchor devices.

C. Attach panels and pilasters to bracket with through-sleeve tamper-proof bolts and nuts. Locate head rail joints at pilaster center lines.

D. Anchor urinal screen panels to walls and to floor in accordance with manufacturer's instructions to suit supporting wall construction.

E. Conceal floor fastenings with pilaster shoes.

F. Equip each door with hinges, one door latch, and one coat hook and bumper. Align hardware to uniform clearance at vertical edges of doors, not exceeding 1/4 inch.
   1. Provide hardware at handicapped toilet with operating hardware complying with ANSI A117.1.

3.03 CONSTRUCTION
A. Interface with Other Work:
   1. Coordinate placement of support framing and anchors in walls.

B. Site Tolerances:
   1. Maximum Variation From True Position: 1/4 inch.
   2. Maximum Variation From Plumb: 1/8 inch.

3.04 ADJUSTING
A. Adjust and align hardware to uniform clearance at vertical edge of doors, not exceeding 3/16 inch.

B. In-Swinging Doors: Adjust hinges to locate doors in partial open position when unlatched.

C. Out-Swinging Doors: Adjust hinges to gently return doors to closed position.

D. Adjust adjacent components for consistency of line or plane.

3.05 ENVIRONMENTAL PROCEDURES
A. Indoor Air Quality:
   1. Clean Surfaces: Use nontoxic materials and procedures.
   2. Remove protective masking.

END OF SECTION

GLOSSARY

1,1,1-Trichloroethane Included in fabric and carpet manufacture and in a variety of cleaners, it is observed offgassing. 1,1,1-Trichloroethane is considered capable of causing fertility problems and developmental defects, and may also have health impacts on wildlife. Chlorinated solvents such as 1,1,1-Trichloroethane deplete stratospheric ozone.

Abatement Reduction of the degree or intensity of, or elimination of pollution. (As defined by the EPA.)

Acetone A moderately toxic, highly volatile, and flammable solvent used in nail polish removers, glues, paint strippers and other products. Considered less toxic than aromatic hydrocarbons such as toluene and xylene, it causes symptoms similar to, but slightly more severe than, those of ethyl alcohol.

Acid Leachates Water that has become acidic after seepage through landfills; potentially very damaging to fish habitats, drinking water supplies, and so on.

Acrylics A family of plastics used for fibers, rigid sheets, and paints and caulkings.

Action Levels (1) Regulatory levels recommended by EPA for enforcement by FDA and USDA when pesticide residues occur in food or feed commodities for reasons other than the direct application of the pesticide. As opposed to "tolerances," which are established for residues occurring as a result of proper usage, action levels are set for inadvertent residues resulting from previous legal use or accidental contamination. (2) In the Superfund program, the existence of a contaminant concentration in the environment high enough to warrant action or trigger a response under SARA and the National Oil and Hazardous Substances Contingency Plan. The term is also used in other regulatory programs. (As defined by the EPA.)

Activated Carbon A highly adsorbent form of carbon used to remove odors and toxic substances from liquid or gaseous emissions. In waste treatment, it is used to remove dissolved organic matter from waste drinking water. It is also used in motor vehicle evaporative control systems. (As defined by the EPA.)

Acute Exposure A single exposure to a toxic substance that may result in severe biological harm or death. Acute exposures are usually characterized as lasting no longer than a day, as compared to longer, continuing exposure over a period of time. (As defined by the EPA.)

Acute Toxicity The ability of a substance to cause severe biological harm or death soon after a single exposure or dose. Also, any poisonous effect resulting from a single short-term exposure to a toxic substance. (As defined by the EPA.)

Administrative Order A legal document signed by EPA directing an individual, business, or other entity to take corrective action or refrain from an activity. It describes the violations and actions to be taken, and can be enforced in court. Such orders may be issued, for example, as a result of an administrative complaint whereby the respondent is ordered to pay a penalty for violations of a statute. (As defined by the EPA.)

Adsorption Removal of a pollutant from air or water by collecting the pollutant on the surface of a solid material; for example, an advanced method of treating waste by which activated carbon removes organic matter from wastewater. (As defined by the EPA.)

Advanced Treatment A level of wastewater treatment more stringent than secondary treatment; requires an 85 percent reduction in conventional pollutant concentration or a significant reduction in nonconventional pollutants. Sometimes called tertiary treatment. (As defined by the EPA.)

Advanced Wastewater Treatment Any treatment of sewage that goes beyond the secondary or biological water treatment stage and includes the removal of nutrients such as phosphorus and nitrogen and a high percentage of suspended solids. (As defined by the EPA.)

Aeration A process that promotes biological degradation of organic matter in water. The process may be passive (as when waste is exposed to air) or active (as when a mixing or bubbling device introduces the air). (As defined by the EPA.)

Aerobic Life or processes that require, or are not destroyed by, the presence of oxygen.

Aerobic Treatment Process by which microbes decompose complex organic compounds in the presence of oxygen and use the liberated energy for reproduction and growth. (Such processes include extended aeration, trickling filtration, and rotating biological contactors.)

Agricultural Pollution Farming wastes, including runoff and leaching of pesticides and fertilizers; erosion and dust from plowing; improper disposal of animal manure and carcasses; crop residues and debris. (As defined by the EPA.)

Air Pollutant Any substance in air that could, in high enough concentration, harm humans, other animals, vegetation, or material. Pollutants may include almost any natural or artificial composition of airborne matter capable of being airborne. They may be in the form of solid particles, liquid droplets, gases, or in combination thereof. Generally, they fall into two main groups: (a) those emitted directly from identifiable sources and (b) those produced in the air by interaction between two or more primary pollutants, or by reaction with normal atmospheric constituents, with or without photoactivation. Exclusive of pollen, fog, and dust, which are of natural origin, about 100 contaminants have been identified. Air pollutants are often grouped in categories for ease in classification; some of he categories are: solids, sulfur compounds, volatile organic chemicals, particulate matter, nitrogen compounds, oxygen compounds, halogen compounds, radioactive compounds, and odors. (As defined by the EPA.)

Air Pollution The presence of contaminants or pollutant substances in the air that interfere with human health or welfare or produce other harmful environmental effects. (As defined by the EPA.)

Air Quality Standards The level of pollutants prescribed by regulations that are not be exceeded during a given time in a defined area. (As defined by the EPA.)

Airborne Particulates Total suspended particulate matter found in the atmosphere as solid particles or liquid droplets. Chemical composition of particulates varies widely, depending on location and time of year. Sources of airborne particulates include: dust, emissions from industrial processes, combustion products from the burning of wood and coal, combustion products associated with motor vehicle or nonroad engine exhausts, and reactions to gases in the atmosphere. (As defined by the EPA.)

Algae Simple rootless plants that grow in sunlit waters in proportion to the amount of available nutrients. They can affect water quality adversely by lowering the dissolved oxygen in the water. They are food for fish and small aquatic animals.

Alternative Compliance A policy that allows facilities to choose among methods for achieving emission reduction or risk reduction, instead of command-and-control regulations that specify standards and how to meet them. Use of a theoretical emissions bubble over a facility to cap the amount of pollution emitted while allowing the company to choose where and how (within the facility) it complies. (As defined by the EPA.)

Alternative Fuels Substitutes for traditional liquid, oil-derived motor vehicle fuels like gasoline and diesel. Includes mixtures of alcohol-based fuels with gasoline, methanol, ethanol, compressed natural gas, and others.

Ammonia Substance used extensively in large industrial refrigeration applications, highly poisonous to humans. Ammonia is a gas that is intensely irritating to the skin, eyes, and the respiratory tract, even in low concentrations. Household ammonia is a 5 percent to 10 percent solution of ammonia in water, and like other types of cleaning products with ammonia, it gives off ammonia gas vapors. Environmental impact from household use probably is minimal, although use of ammonia-based fertilizers can lead to groundwater pollution with nitrates. Ammonia reacts with chlorine bleach to produce toxic and irritating chloramines.

Anaerobic A life or process that occurs in, or is not destroyed by, the absence of oxygen.

Aquifer An underground geological formation or group of formations containing water. Aquifers are sources of groundwater for wells and springs.

Asbestos (1) From the Greek adjective meaning unquenchable; the name for a number of extremely hardy fibrous silicate minerals that occur in rock formations throughout the world. Includes chrysotile, amosite, crocidolite, tremolite, anthophylite, and actinolite. (2) A mineral fiber that can pollute air or water and cause cancer or asbestosis when inhaled. EPA has banned or severely restricted its use in manufacturing and construction.

Asbestos Abatement Procedures to control fiber release from asbestos-containing materials in a building or to remove them entirely, including removal, encapsulation, repair, enclosure, encasement, and operations and maintenance programs.

ASHRAE Standard 62 Ventilation for Acceptable Indoor Air Quality. Details two methods for compliance: the Ventilation Rate Procedure and the Indoor Air Quality Procedure. Rapidly becoming the standard of care for building ventilation and indoor air quality.

Assay A test for a specific chemical, microbe, or effect. (As defined by the EPA.)

Attainment Area An area considered to have air quality as good as or better than the national ambient air quality standards as defined in the Clean Air Act. An area may be an attainment area for one pollutant and a nonattainment area for others. (As defined by the EPA.)

Background Level (1) The concentration of a substance in an environmental media (air, water, or soil) that occurs naturally or is not the result of human activities. (2) In exposure assessment, the concentration of a substance in a defined control area, during a fixed period of time before, during, or after a data-gathering operation. (As defined by the EPA.)

Bacteria Microscopic living organisms that can aid in pollution control by metabolizing organic matter in sewage, oil spills, or other pollutants. Bacteria in soil, water, or air can also cause human, animal, and plant health problems.

Bacteria Sink Porous materials that allow the growth of biological contaminants within the material.

Bake-out A process used to remove VOCs from a building by elevating the temperature in the unoccupied, fully furnished, and ventilated building.

Banking A system for recording qualified emission reductions for later use in bubble, offset, or netting transactions. (As defined by the EPA.)

BEN EPA's computer model for analyzing a violator's economic gain from not complying with the law.

Bentonite A colloidal clay, expansible when moist, commonly used to provide a tight seal around a well casing.

Benzene A clear, colorless, flammable liquid (CH), derived from petroleum and used to manufacture DDT (a prohibited insecticide), detergents, other strains of insecticides, and motor fuels. Benzene is included in the formulation of paints, adhesives, and resins, and can offgas. Benzene is considered a carcinogen.

Beryllium A metal hazardous to human health when inhaled as an airborne pollutant. It is discharged by machine shops, ceramic and propellant plants, and foundries.

Best Management Practice (BMP) Methods that have been determined to be the most effective, practical means of preventing or reducing pollution from nonpoint sources. (As defined by the EPA.)

Bioaccumulants Substances that increase in concentration in living organisms as they take in contaminated air, water, or food, because the substances are very slowly metabolized or excreted. (As defined by the EPA.)

Bioaccumulation *See* to Biological Magnification.

Bioassay A test to determine the relative strength of a substance by comparing its effect on a test organism with that of a standard preparation. (As defined by the EPA.)

Biodegradable Capable of decomposing under natural conditions.

Biodiversity Refers to the variety and variability among living organisms and the ecological complexes in which they occur. Diversity can be defined as the number of different items and their relative frequencies. For biological diversity, these items are organized at many levels, ranging from complete ecosystems to the biochemical structures that are the molecular basis of heredity. Thus, the term encompasses different ecosystems, species, and genes. (As defined by the EPA.)

Biological Contaminants Contaminants that include bacteria, viruses, molds, pollen, animal and human dander, insect and arachnid excreta (dust mites).

Biological Control In pest control, the use of animals and organisms that eat or otherwise kill or out-compete pests. (As defined by the EPA.)

Biological Magnification Refers to the process whereby certain substances such as pesticides or heavy metals move up the food chain, work their way into rivers or lakes, and are eaten by aquatic organisms such as fish, which in turn are eaten by large birds, animals or humans. The substances become concentrated in tissues or internal organs as they move up the chain. (As defined by the EPA.)

Biological Oxygen Demand (BOD) An indirect measure of the concentration of biologically degradable material present in organic wastes. It usually reflects the amount of oxygen consumed in five days by biological processes breaking down organic waste. (As defined by the EPA.) The greater the BOD, the greater the degree of pollution.

Biomass All of the living material in a given area; often refers to vegetation. (As defined by the EPA.)

Biome Entire community of living organisms in a single major ecological area. (As defined by the EPA.)

Bioremediation Use of living organisms to clean up oil spills or remove other pollutants from soil, water, or wastewater; use of organisms such as non-harmful insects to remove agricultural pests or counteract diseases of trees, plants, and garden soil. (As defined by the EPA.)

Biosphere The portion of Earth and its atmosphere that can support life. (As defined by the EPA.)

Biota The animal and plant life of a given region. (As defined by the EPA.)

Blackwater Water that contains animal, human, or food waste. (As defined by the EPA.)

Bloom A proliferation of algae and/or higher aquatic plants in a body of water; often related to pollution, especially when pollutants accelerate growth. (As defined by the EPA.)

BOD5 The amount of dissolved oxygen consumed in five days by biological processes breaking down organic matter. (As defined by the EPA.) *See also* Biological Oxygen Demand.

Bog A type of wetland that accumulates appreciable peat deposits. Bogs depend primarily on precipitation for their water source, and are usually acidic and rich in plant residue with a conspicuous mat of living green moss. (As defined by the EPA.)

Borax A sodium salt of boron, used as a laundry whitener and general purpose cleaner. Slightly less toxic than boric acid.

Boric Acid A boron compound used as an insecticide, particularly against ants and fleas. Although it is considered moderately toxic, boric acid is not volatile and thus does not emit toxic vapors. Formerly used to clean and dress wounds, boric acid is absorbed through broken skin, and deaths have occurred from that use. The major hazard from household use is accidental ingestion or inhalation of dust.

Bottle Bill Proposed or enacted legislation that requires a returnable deposit on beer or soda containers and provides for retail store or other redemption. Such legislation is designed to discourage use of throwaway containers. (As defined by the EPA.)

Bottom Ash The nonairborne combustion residue from burning pulverized coal in a boiler; the material that falls to the bottom of the boiler and is removed mechanically; a concentration of noncombustible materials, which may include toxics. (As defined by the EPA.)

British Thermal Unit (BTU) Unit of heat energy equal to the amount of heat required to raise the temperature of 1 pound of water by 1 degree F at sea level.

Bromotrifluoromethane A fire suppression agent (Halon 1301) primarily designed for areas containing delicate, expensive, or irreplaceable equipment; used because of its ability to suppress fires without leaving undesirable residue.

Brownfields Abandoned, idled, or under-used industrial and commercial facilities/sites where expansion or redevelopment is complicated by real or perceived environmental contamination. They can be in urban, suburban, or rural areas. EPA's brownfields initiative helps communities mitigate potential health risks and restore the economic viability of such areas or properties. (As defined by the EPA.)

Building-Related Illness Diagnosable illness whose cause and symptoms can be directly attributed to a specific pollutant source within a building (e.g., Legionnaire's disease, hypersensitivity, pneumonitis.) (As defined by the EPA.) Building-related illnesses are generally considered more serious than sick building syndrome (SBS) conditions and are clinically verifiable diseases that can be attributed to a specific source or pollutant within a building. The symptoms of the disease persist after leaving the building, unlike SBS, where the occupant experiences relief shortly after leaving the building. *See also* Sick Building Syndrome.

Butyls Synthetic rubber resins used for flexible sheet products and durable, solvent-based caulkings.

Byproduct Material, other than the principal product, generated as a consequence of an industrial process or as a breakdown product in a living system. (As defined by the EPA.)

Cadmium (Cd) A heavy metal that accumulates in the environment.

Carbon Dioxide (CO$_2$) A colorless, odorless gaseous product of human respiration.

Carbon Monoxide (CO) A colorless, odorless, poisonous gas produced by incomplete fossil fuel combustion. Found in soldering, in gas appliances, and in other combustion sources. Carbon monoxide can slow down your brain and your reflexes and dim your vision. Most people don't realize how little carbon monoxide it takes to be poisonous to the human body. Only 50 parts of CO per million parts of air, by volume, is considered dangerous. Carbon monoxide doesn't suffocate you, it kills you by chemical action. It's an asphyxiant; it combines directly with your blood so the body can't carry oxygen to the tissues.

Carbon Tetrachloride (CCl4) Compound consisting of one carbon atom and four chlorine atoms. Once widely used as a industrial raw material, as a solvent, and in the production of CFCs. Use as a solvent ended when it was discovered to be carcinogenic.

Carboxyhemoglobin Hemoglobin in which the iron is bound to carbon monoxide (CO) instead of oxygen. (As defined by the EPA.)

Carcinogen Any substance that can cause or aggravate cancer. (As defined by the EPA.)

Carrying Capacity (1) In recreation management, the amount of use a recreation area can sustain without loss of quality. (2) In wildlife management, the maximum number of animals an area can support during a given period. (As defined by the EPA.) The term is commonly used by environmentalists to refer to the planetary capacity for human population growth and impact.

CAS Registration Number A number assigned by the Chemical Abstract Service to identify a chemical.

Categorical Exclusion A class of actions that either individually or cumulatively would not have a significant effect on the human environment and therefore would not require preparation of an environmental assessment or environmental impact statement under the National Environmental Policy Act (NEPA). (As defined by the EPA.)

Chemical Stressors Chemicals released to the environment through industrial waste, auto emissions, pesticides, and other human activity that can cause illnesses and even death in plants and animals. (As defined by the EPA.)

Chemical Treatment Any one of a variety of technologies that use chemicals or a variety of chemical processes to treat waste.

ChemNet Mutual aid network of chemical shippers and contractors that assigns a contracted emergency response company to provide technical support if a representative of the firm whose chemicals are involved in an incident is not readily available. (As defined by the EPA.)

Chlorinated Hydrocarbons (1) Chemicals containing only chlorine, carbon, and hydrogen. These include a class of persistent, broad-spectrum insecticides that linger in the environment and accumulate in the food chain. Among them are DDT, aldrin, dieldrin, heptachlor, chlordane, lindane, endrin, Mirex, hexachloride, and toxaphene. Other examples include TCE, used as an industrial solvent. (2) Any chlorinated organic compounds including chlorinated solvents such as dichloromethane, trichloromethylene, chloroform.

Chlorinated Solvent An organic solvent containing chlorine atoms (e.g., methylene chloride and 1,1,1-trichloromethane). Chlorinated solvents are found in aerosol spray containers, highway paint, and dry cleaning fluids.

Chlorination The application of chlorine to drinking water, sewage, or industrial waste to disinfect or to oxidize undesirable compounds.

Chlorine A chemical used to purify water and a bleaching agent. A movement begun in Europe to ban products containing chlorine has spread to the United States. Concerns focus on the discharge of organic compounds into oceans and waterways.

Chlorofluorocarbons (CFCs) A family of inert, nontoxic, and easily liquefied chemicals used in refrigeration, air conditioning, packaging, insulation, or as solvents and aerosol propellants. Because CFCs are not destroyed in the lower atmosphere, they drift into the upper atmosphere where their chlorine components destroy ozone.

Chlorophenoxy A class of herbicides that may be found in domestic water supplies and cause adverse health effects.

Chronic Effect An adverse effect on a human or animal whereby symptoms recur frequently or develop slowly over a long period of time. (As defined by the EPA.)

Chronic Exposure Multiple exposures occurring over an extended period of time or over a significant fraction of an animal's or human's lifetime—usually seven years to a lifetime. (As defined by the EPA.)

Chronic Toxicity The capacity of a substance to cause long-term poisonous health effects in humans, animals, fish, and other organisms. (As defined by the EPA.)

Cistern Small tank or storage facility used to store water for a home or farm; often used to store rainwater.

Class I Area Under the Clean Air Act, a Class I area is one in which visibility is protected more stringently than under the national ambient air quality standards; includes national parks, wilderness areas, monuments, and other areas of special national and cultural significance. (As defined by the EPA.)

Class I Substance One of several groups of chemicals with an ozone depletion potential of 0.2 or higher, including CFCS, halons, carbon tetrachloride, and methyl chloroform (listed in the Clean Air Act), and HBFCs and ethyl bromide (added by EPA regulations). (As defined by the EPA.)

Class II Substance A substance with an ozone depletion potential of less than 0.2. All HCFCs are currently included in this classification. (As defined by the EPA.)

Clearcut Harvesting all the trees in one area at one time, a practice that can encourage fast rainfall or snowmelt runoff, erosion, sedimentation of streams and lakes, and flooding, and destroys vital habitat. (As defined by the EPA.)

Climate Change Also referred to as "global climate change," the term is sometimes used to refer to all forms of climatic inconsistency, but because the Earth's climate is never static, the term is more properly used to imply a significant change from one climatic condition to another. In some cases, "climate change" has been used synonymously with the term "global warming"; scientists, however, tend to use the term in the wider sense to also include natural changes in climate. (As defined by the EPA.)

Closed-Loop Recycling Reclaiming or reusing wastewater for nonpotable purposes in an enclosed process. (As defined by the EPA.)

Code of Federal Regulations (CFR) Document that codifies all rules of the executive volumes, known as titles. Title 40 of the CFR (referenced as 40 CFR) lists all environmental regulations.

Cogeneration The consecutive generation of useful thermal and electric energy from the same fuel source.

Coliform Index A rating of the purity of water based on a count of fecal bacteria.

Commissioning The start-up phase for a new or remodeled building. This phase includes testing and fine-tuning the HVAC and other systems to assure proper functioning and adherence to design criteria. Commissioning also includes preparation of the system operation manuals and instruction of the building maintenance personnel.

Compost The relatively stable humus material that is produced from a composting process by which bacteria in soil mixed with garbage and degradable trash break down the mixture into organic fertilizer.

Composting The controlled biological decomposition of organic material in the presence of air to form a humuslike material. Controlled methods of composting include mechanical mixing and aerating, ventilating the materials by dropping them through a vertical series of aerated chambers, or placing the compost in piles out in the open air and mixing it or turning it periodically.

Compressed Natural Gas (CNG) An alternative fuel for motor vehicles; considered one of the cleanest because of low hydrocarbon emissions and because its vapors are relatively nonozone producing. However, vehicles fueled with CNG do emit a significant quantity of nitrogen oxides.

Conservation Preserving and renewing, when possible, human and natural resources. The use, protection, and improvement of natural resources according to principles that will ensure their highest economic or social benefits. (As defined by the EPA.)

Conservation Easement Easement that restricts a landowner to land uses that are compatible with long-term conservation and environmental values. (As defined by the EPA.)

Constructed Wetland Any of a variety of designed systems that approximate natural wetlands, using aquatic plants, and can be used to treat wastewater or runoff.

Contaminant Any physical, chemical, biological, or radiological substance or matter that has an adverse effect on air, water, or soil. (As defined by the EPA.)

Copper Naphthenate One of the copper compounds used as a wood preservative. Because of its relatively low acute toxicity to humans, it is considered a safer alternative to pentachlorophenol and creosote. Copper compounds, including copper naphthenate, are highly toxic to aquatic organisms. Copper accumulates in soils, and concentrates in marine and fresh water organisms.

Criteria Pollutants The 1970 amendments to the Clean Air Act required EPA to set National Ambient Air Quality Standards for certain pollutants known to be hazardous to human health. EPA has identified and set standards to protect human health and welfare for six pollutants: ozone, carbon monoxide, total suspended particulates, sulfur dioxide, lead, and nitrogen oxide. The term "criteria pollutants" derives from the requirement that the EPA must describe the characteristics and potential health and welfare effects of these pollutants. It is on the basis of these criteria that standards are set or revised. (As defined by the EPA.)

Cryptosporidium A protozoan microbe associated with the disease cryptosporidiosis in humans. The disease can be transmitted through ingestion of drinking water, person-to-person contact, or other pathways, and can cause acute diarrhea, abdominal pain, vomiting, fever, and can be fatal, as it was in the Milwaukee episode.

Cumulative Exposure The sum of exposures of an organism to a pollutant over a period of time. (As defined by the EPA.)

Degree-day A rough measure used to estimate the amount of heating required in a given area; is defined as the difference between the mean daily temperature and 65 degrees F. Degree-days are also calculated to estimate cooling requirements.

Department of Energy (DOE) The DOE originated with the race to develop the atomic bomb during World War II, and resulted in the Atomic Energy Commission. By the mid-1970s, the Atomic Energy Commission was abolished and two new agencies were created: the Nuclear Regulatory Agency, to regulate the nuclear power industry, and the Energy Research and Development Administration, to manage the nuclear weapon, naval reactor, and energy development programs. However, the extended energy crisis of the 1970s soon demonstrated the need for unified energy organization and planning. In 1977, the Department of Energy assumed the responsibilities of the Federal Energy Administration, the Energy Research and Development Administration, the Federal Power Commission, and parts and programs of several other agencies. Today, the DOE mission includes ensuring the energy security of the nation, maintaining the safety of our nuclear stockpile, and developing energy innovations and technology.

Diatomaceous Earth (Diatomite) A chalklike material (fossilized diatoms) used to filter out solid waste in wastewater treatment plants; also used as an active ingredient in some powdered pesticides. Both natural diatomaceous earth (DE) and swimming pool grade come from the same fossil sources but are processed differently. The pool grade is chemically treated and partially melted, and consequently contains crystalline silica, which can be a respiratory hazard.

Diazinon An insecticide. In 1986, the EPA banned its use on open areas such as sod farms and golf courses because it posed a danger to migratory birds. The ban did not apply to agricultural, home lawn, or commercial establishment uses.

Dibenzofurans A group of organic compounds, some of which are toxic.

Dichloro-Diphenyl-Trichloroethane (DDT) The first chlorinated hydrocarbon insecticide chemical name. It has a half-life of 15 years and can collect in fatty tissues of certain animals. The EPA banned registration and interstate sale of DDT for virtually all but emergency uses in the United States in 1972 because of its persistence in the environment and accumulation in the food chain.

Dinoseb A herbicide that is also used as a fungicide and insecticide. It was banned by the EPA in 1986 because it posed the risk of birth defects and sterility.

Dioxin Any of a family of compounds known chemically as dibenzo-p-dioxins. Concern about them arises from their potential toxicity as contaminants in commercial products. Tests on laboratory animals indicate that it is one of the more toxic anthropogenic (man-made) compounds.

Dissolved Oxygen (DO) The oxygen freely available in water, that is vital to fish and other aquatic life and for the prevention of odors. DO levels are considered a most important indicator of a water body's ability to support desirable aquatic life. Secondary and advanced waste treatment are generally designed to ensure adequate DO in waste-receiving waters.

Ecological Impact The effect that a human-caused or natural activity has on living organisms and their nonliving (abiotic) environment. (As defined by the EPA.)

Ecological Indicator A characteristic of an ecosystem that is related to or derived from a measure of biotic or abiotic variable that can provide quantitative information on ecological structure and function. An indicator can contribute to a measure of integrity and sustainability. (As defined by the EPA.)

Ecology The relationship of living things to one another and their environment, or the study of such relationships. (As defined by the EPA.)

Ecosphere The "biobubble" that contains life on earth, in surface waters, and in the air. (As defined by the EPA.)

Ecosystem The interacting system of a biological community and its nonliving environmental surroundings. (As defined by the EPA.)

Electric and Magnetic Fields (EMF) *See* Electromagnetic Spectrum.

Electromagnetic Spectrum A continuum of electric and magnetic radiation, encompassing all wavelengths from electricity, radio, and microwaves, at the low-frequency end to infrared, visible light, and ultraviolet light in the midrange, to X rays and gamma rays at the high-frequency end of the spectrum.

Embodied Energy The total energy that a product may be said to "contain," including all energy used in growing, extracting, and manufacturing it, and energy used to transport it to the point of use. The embodied energy of a structure or system includes the embodied energy of its components, plus the energy used in construction.

Emission Pollution discharged into the atmosphere from smokestacks, other vents, and surface areas of commercial or industrial facilities; from residential chimneys; and from motor vehicle, locomotive, or aircraft exhausts. (As defined by the EPA.)

Emissions Trading The creation of surplus emission reductions at certain stacks, vents, or similar emissions sources, and the use of this surplus to meet or redefine pollution requirements applicable to other emissions sources. This allows one source to increase emissions when another source reduces them, maintaining an overall constant emission level. Facilities that reduce emissions substantially may "bank" their "credits" or sell them to other facilities or industries. (As defined by the EPA.)

Encapsulation The treatment of asbestos-containing material with a liquid that covers the surface with a protective coating or embeds fibers in an adhesive matrix to prevent their release into the air. (As defined by the EPA.)

Endangered Species Animals, birds, fish, plants, or other living organisms threatened with extinction by anthropogenic (human-caused) or other natural changes in their environment. Requirements for declaring a species endangered are contained in the Endangered Species Act. (As defined by the EPA.)

Endangerment Assessment A study to determine the nature and extent of contamination at a site on the National Priorities List and the risks posed to public health or the environment. The EPA or the state conducts the study when a legal action is to be taken to direct potentially responsible parties to clean up a site or to pay for it. An endangerment assessment supplements a remedial investigation. (As defined by the EPA.)

End-of-the-pipe Technologies such as scrubbers on smokestacks and catalytic convertors on automobile tailpipes that reduce emissions of pollutants after they have formed. (As defined by the EPA.)

Endrin A pesticide toxic to freshwater and marine aquatic life that produces adverse health effects in domestic water supplies.

Energy Management System A control system capable of monitoring environmental and system loads and adjusting HVAC operations accordingly in order to conserve energy while maintaining comfort. (As defined by the EPA.)

Energy Recovery Obtaining energy from waste through a variety of processes (e.g., combustion).

Environmental Assessment An environmental analysis prepared pursuant to the National Environmental Policy Act (NEPA) which assesses the potential environmental and cumulative impacts of a project and possible ways to minimize effects of a project on the environment.

Environmental Audit An independent assessment of the current status of a party's compliance with applicable environmental requirements or of a party's environmental compliance policies, practices, and controls. (As defined by the EPA.)

Environmental Chamber A stainless steel, nonreactive testing device, with a known air volume and dynamically controlled air change rate, temperature and humidity. Emission rates are commonly determined by placing materials or furniture into a small or large stainless steel environmental chamber then measuring the release of volatile vapors from the products over a specified time period. Rates are measured in $\mu g/m^2 \cdot hr$ (micrograms per square meter per hour) or $mg/m^2 \cdot hr$ (milligrams per square meter per hour).

Environmental Equity/Justice Equal protection from environmental hazards for individuals, groups, or communities, regardless of race, ethnicity, or economic status. This applies to the development, implementation, and enforcement of environmental laws, regulations, and policies, and implies that no population of people should be forced to shoulder a disproportionate share of negative environmental impacts of pollution or environmental hazard due to a lack of political or economic strength levels.

Environmental Fate The destiny of a chemical or biological pollutant after release into the environment.

Environmental Fate Data Data that characterize a pesticide's fate in the ecosystem, considering factors that foster its degradation (light, water, microbes), pathways, and resultant products.

Environmental Impact Statement A document required of federal agencies by the National Environmental Policy Act for major projects or legislative proposals significantly affecting the environment. A tool for decision making, it describes the positive and negative effects of the undertaking and cites alternative actions.

Environmental Indicator A measurement, statistic, or value that provides a proximate gauge or evidence of the effects of environmental management programs or of the state or condition of the environment.

Environmental Protection Agency (EPA) Established in 1970 to consolidate the federal government's environmental regulatory activities under the jurisdiction of a single agency, the mission of the EPA is to protect human health and to safeguard the natural environment. The EPA ensures that federal environmental laws are enforced fairly and effectively.

Environmental Site Assessment The process of determining whether contamination is present on a parcel of real property. (As defined by the EPA.)

Environmental Tobacco Smoke Mixture of smoke from the burning end of a cigarette, pipe, or cigar, and smoke exhaled by the smoker. (As defined by the EPA.)

Erosion The wearing away of land surface by wind or water, intensified by land-clearing practices related to farming, residential or industrial development, road building, or logging. (As defined by the EPA.)

Ethylbenzene A part of paint formulations, and associated with some carpeting, it is observed offgassing in the home, in office furniture products, in office buildings, and in subject's breath. Ethylbenzene is a chronic toxin, capable of causing fertility problems and developmental defects. Ethylbenzene will also potentially have health impacts on wildlife.

Eutrophication The slow aging process during which a lake, estuary, or bay evolves into a bog or marsh and eventually disappears. During the later stages of eutrophication, the water body is choked by abundant plant life due to higher levels of nutritive compounds such as nitrogen and phosphorus. Human activities can accelerate the process. (As defined by the EPA.)

Evapotranspiration The loss of water from the soil both by evaporation and by transpiration from the plants growing in the soil.

Exotic Species A species that is not indigenous to a region.

Feedstocks The raw material used in manufacturing a product, such as the oil or gas used to make a plastic.

Fluorides Gaseous, solid, or dissolved compounds containing fluorine that result from industrial processes. Excessive amounts in food can lead to fluorosis.

Fluorocarbons (FCs) Any of a number of organic compounds analogous to hydrocarbons in which one or more hydrogen atoms are replaced by fluorine. Once used in the United States as a propellant for domestic aerosols, they are now found mainly in coolants and some industrial processes. FCs containing chlorine are called chlorofluorocarbons (CFCs). They are believed to be modifying the ozone layer in the stratosphere, thereby allowing more harmful solar radiation to reach the Earth's surface. (As defined by the EPA.)

Flush-out A process used to remove VOCs from a building by operating the building's HVAC system at 100 percent outside air for a specific period of time.

Fly ash Very fine ash waste collected from the flue gases of burning coal, smelting, or waste incineration.

Formaldehyde A colorless, gaseous compound used in an aqueous solution as a preservative, disinfectant, and curing agent. It is used widely in production of adhesives, plastics, preservatives, fabric treatments, and others, and commonly emitted by indoor materials that are made with its compounds. It is highly irritating if inhaled and is now listed as a probable human carcinogen. Urea formaldehyde and gaseous byproducts are detrimental to human health. Formaldehyde earned notoriety through its widespread use as a component in urea formaldehyde insulation. Formaldehyde exposure causes sensitization in a significant fraction of people exposed. Formaldehyde causes cancer in animal tests.

Friable Capable of being crumbled, pulverized, or reduced to powder by hand pressure.

Fungi Parasitic lower plants (including molds and mildew) lack chlorophyll, needing organic material and moisture to germinate and grow.

General Services Administration (GSA) One of the three central management agencies in the federal government (the Office of Personnel Management and the Office of Management and Budget are the others). GSA provides the buildings and supplies that enable federal employees to accomplish their work. It also provides workspace, security, furniture, equipment, supplies, tools, computers, and telephones. GSA negotiates contracts that account for $40 billion of goods and services bought annually from the private sector.

Geothermal/Ground Source Heat Pump Underground coils used to transfer heat from the ground to the inside of a building.

Global Warming An increase in the near-surface temperature of the Earth. Global warming has occurred in the distant past as the result of natural influences, but the term is most often used to refer to the warming predicted to occur as a result of increased emissions of greenhouse gases. Scientists generally agree that the Earth's surface has warmed by about 1 degree F in the past 140 years. The Intergovernmental Panel on Climate Change (IPCC) recently concluded that increased concentrations of greenhouse gases are causing an increase in the Earth's surface temperature and that increased concentrations of sulfate aerosols have led to relative cooling in some regions, generally over and downwind of heavily industrialized areas. (As defined by the EPA.)

Graywater Domestic wastewater composed of washwater from kitchen, bathroom, and laundry sinks, tubs, and washers. (As defined by the EPA.)

Greenhouse Effect The warming of the Earth's atmosphere attributed to a buildup of carbon dioxide or other gases; some scientists think that this buildup allows the sun's rays to heat the Earth, while making the infrared radiation atmosphere opaque to infrared radiation, thereby preventing a counterbalancing loss of heat. (As defined by the EPA.)

Greenhouse Gas A gas, such as carbon dioxide or methane, that contributes to potential climate change. (As defined by the EPA.)

Groundwater The supply of freshwater found beneath the Earth's surface, usually in aquifers, which supply wells and springs. Because groundwater is a major source of drinking water, there is growing concern over contamination from leaching agricultural or industrial pollutants or leaking underground storage tanks. (As defined by the EPA.)

Groundwater Disinfection Rule A 1996 amendment of the Safe Drinking Water Act requiring the EPA to promulgate national primary drinking water regulations requiring disinfection as for all public water systems, including surface waters and groundwater systems. (As defined by the EPA.)

Habitat The place where a population (e.g., human, animal, plant, microorganism) lives; includes its surroundings, both living and nonliving. (As defined by the EPA.)

Habitat Indicator A physical attribute of the environment measured to characterize conditions necessary to support an organism, population, or community in the absence of pollutants; for example, salinity of estuarine waters or substrate type in streams or lakes. (As defined by the EPA.)

Hazard (1) Potential for radiation, a chemical, or other pollutant to cause human illness or injury. (2) In the pesticide program, the inherent toxicity of a compound. Hazard identification of a given substances is an informed judgment based on verifiable toxicity data from animal models or human studies. (As defined by the EPA.)

Hazard Assessment Evaluation of the effects of a stressor or the determination of a margin of safety for an organism conducted by comparing the concentration that causes toxic effects with an estimate of exposure to the organism. (As defined by the EPA.)

Hazard Communication Standard An OSHA regulation that requires chemical manufacturers, suppliers, and importers to assess the hazards of the chemicals that they make, supply, or import; and to inform employers, customers, and workers of these hazards through MSDS information. (As defined by the EPA.)

Hazard Evaluation A component of risk evaluation that involves gathering and evaluating data on the types of health injuries or diseases that may be produced by a chemical and on the conditions of exposure under which such health effects are produced. (As defined by the EPA.)

Hazardous Air Pollutants Air pollutants that are not covered by ambient air quality standards but that, as defined in the Clean Air Act, may present a threat of adverse human health effects or adverse environmental effects. Such pollutants include asbestos, beryllium, mercury, benzene, coke oven emissions, radionuclides, and vinyl chloride. (As defined by the EPA.)

Hazardous Chemical An EPA designation for any hazardous material requiring an MSDS under OSHA's Hazard Communication Standard. Such substances are capable of producing fires and explosions or adverse health effects like cancer and dermatitis. Hazardous chemicals are distinct from hazardous waste. (As defined by the EPA.)

Hazardous Ranking System The principal screening tool used by the EPA to evaluate risks to public health and the environment associated with abandoned or uncontrolled hazardous waste sites. The HRS calculates a score based on the potential of hazardous substances spreading from the site through the air, surface water, or groundwater, and on other factors such as density and proximity of human population. This score is the primary factor for determining whether the site should be on the National Priorities List, and if so, the ranking it should have compared to other sites on the list. (As defined by the EPA.)

Hazardous Substance (1) Any material that poses a threat to human health and/or the environment. Typical hazardous substances are toxic, corrosive, ignitable, explosive, or chemically reactive. (2) Any substance designated by the EPA to be reported if a designated quantity of the substance is spilled in the waters of the United States or is otherwise released into the environment. (As defined by the EPA.)

Hazardous Waste Byproducts of society that can pose a substantial or potential hazard to human health or the environment when improperly managed. Possesses at least one of four characteristics (ignitability, corrosivity, reactivity, or toxicity), or appears on special EPA lists. (As defined by the EPA.)

Hazardous Waste Landfill An excavated or engineered site where hazardous waste is deposited and covered. (As defined by the EPA.)

Hazards Analysis Procedures used to (a) identify potential sources of release of hazardous materials from fixed facilities or transportation accidents; (b) determine the vulnerability of a geographical area to a release of hazardous materials; and (c) compare hazards to determine which present greater or lesser risks to a community. (As defined by the EPA.)

Hazards Identification Providing information on which facilities have extremely hazardous substances, what those chemicals are, how much there is at each facility, how the chemicals are stored, and whether they are used at high temperatures. (As defined by the EPA.)

Heat Island Effect A "dome" of elevated temperatures over an urban area caused by structural and pavement heat fluxes and pollutant emissions. (As defined by the EPA.)

Heat Pump An electric device with both heating and cooling capabilities. It extracts heat from one medium (the heat source) at a lower temperature and transfers it to another (the heat sink) at a higher temperature, thereby cooling the first and warming the second. (As defined by the EPA.)

Heavy Metals Metallic elements with high atomic weights (e.g., mercury, chromium, cadmium, arsenic, and lead) that can damage living things at low concentrations and tend to accumulate in the food chain. (As defined by the EPA.)

Heptachlor An insecticide that was banned from use on some food products in 1975 and from all of them 1978. It was allowed for use in seed treatment until 1983. More recently, it was found in milk and other dairy products in Arkansas and Missouri where dairy cattle were illegally fed treated seed.

High Efficiency Particulate Arrestance (HEPA) A designation for very fine air filters (usually exceeding 98 percent atmospheric efficiency), typically used only in surgeries, clean rooms, or other specialized applications.

Hydrogen Sulfide A very odorous, toxic, and explosive gas produced by some bacteria in the absence of oxygen. Produces acids on contact with water.

Indicator (1) In biology, any biological entity or processes or community whose characteristics show the presence of specific environmental conditions. (2) In chemistry, a substance that shows a visible change, usually of color, at a desired point in a chemical reaction. (3) A device that indicates the result of a measurement; for example, a pressure gauge or a moveable scale. (As defined by the EPA.)

Indoor Air Pollution Chemical, physical, or biological contaminants in indoor air. (As defined by the EPA.)

Indoor Air Quality (IAQ) According to the EPA (Environmental Protection Agency) and NIOSH (National Institute of Occupational Safety and Health) good indoor air quality includes: introduction and distribution of adequate ventilation air, control of airborne contaminants, and maintenance of acceptable temperature and relative humidity. According to ASHRAE Standard 62, good indoor air quality is defined as "air in which there are no known contaminants at harmful concentrations as determined by cognizant authorities and with which a substantial majority (80 percent or more) of the people exposed do not express dissatisfaction."

Integrated Pest Management (IPM) A mixture of chemical and other, non-pesticide, methods to control pests. (As defined by the EPA.) IPM commonly refers to an environmentally sound system of controlling landscape pests, which includes well-timed nontoxic treatments and an understanding of the pest's life cycle.

Invasive Commonly used to refer to an exotic plant adapted to very similar growing conditions as those found in the region to which it is imported. Because such a species usually has no natural enemies (pests, diseases, or grazers), it flourishes so strongly that it disrupts the native ecosystem and forces out native plant species, resulting in habitat loss, water-table modification, and other serious problems.

Joint and Several Liability Under CERCLA, this legal concept relates to the liability for Superfund site cleanup and other costs on the part of more than one potentially responsible party (i.e., if there were several owners or users of a site that became contaminated over the years, they could all be considered potentially liable for cleaning up the site). (As defined by the EPA.)

Lagoon (1) A shallow pond where sunlight, bacterial action, and oxygen work to purify wastewater; also used for storage of wastewater or spent nuclear fuel rods. (2) Shallow body of water, often separated from the sea by coral reefs or sandbars. (As defined by the EPA.)

Landfills (1) Sanitary landfills are disposal sites for nonhazardous solid wastes spread in layers, compacted to the smallest practical volume, and covered by material applied at the end of each operating day. (2) Secure chemical landfills are disposal sites for hazardous waste, selected and designed to minimize the chance of release of hazardous substances into the environment. (As defined by the EPA.)

LC 50/Lethal Concentration Median-level concentration, a standard measure of toxicity that tells how much of a substance is needed to kill half of a group of experimental organisms in a given time. (As defined by the EPA.)

LD 50/Lethal Dose The dose of a toxicant or microbe that will kill 50 percent of the test organisms within a designated period. The lower the LD 50, the more toxic the compound. (As defined by the EPA.)

Leachate Water that collects contaminants as it trickles through wastes, pesticides, or fertilizers. Leaching may occur in farming areas, feedlots, and landfills, and may result in hazardous substances entering surface water, groundwater, or soil. (As defined by the EPA.)

Leachate Collection System A system that gathers leachate and pumps it to the surface for treatment. (As defined by the EPA.)

Lead (Pb) A heavy metal that is hazardous to health if breathed or swallowed. It was once used in oil-based paints and printing inks, and still is used in some motor fuels, some pigments, and solders. Older homes may contain layers of lead-bearing paint, which pose a toxic hazard if disturbed. Many lead compounds cause cancer. Like other metals, lead is not biodegraded in the environment.

Legionella A genus of bacteria, some species of which have caused a type of pneumonia called Legionnaires Disease.

Lethal Dose Low (Ldlo) The lowest dose in an animal study at which lethality occurs. (As defined by the EPA.)

Level of Concern (LOC) The concentration in air of an extremely hazardous substance above which there may be serious immediate health effects to anyone exposed to it for short periods. (As defined by the EPA.)

Life Cycle Cost An accounting method that extends beyond capital cost into maintenance and replacement costs, environmental costs, and so on.

Life Cycle of a Product All stages of a product's development, from extraction of fuel for power to production, marketing, use, and disposal. (As defined by the EPA.)

Lifetime Average Daily Dose Figure for estimating excess lifetime cancer risk. (As defined by the EPA.)

Lifetime Exposure Total amount of exposure to a substance that a human would receive in a lifetime (usually assumed to be 70 years).

Limit of Detection (LOD) The minimum concentration of a substance being analyzed that has a 99 percent probability of being identified. (As defined by the EPA.)

Lindane A pesticide that causes adverse health effects in domestic water supplies and is toxic to freshwater fish and aquatic life.

Low Emissivity (low-E) Windows Window technology that reduces the amount of energy loss through windows by inhibiting the transmission of radiant heat while allowing sufficient light to pass through.

Material Safety Data Sheet (MSDS) A compilation of information required under the OSHA Communication Standard on the identity of hazardous chemicals, health, and physical hazards, exposure limits, and precautions. Section 311 of SARA requires facilities to submit MSDSs under certain circumstances.

Materials Recovery Facility (MRF) A facility that processes residentially collected, mixed recyclables into new products available for market.

Maximum Acceptable Toxic Concentration For a given ecological effects test, the range (or geometric mean) between the no observable adverse effect level and the lowest observable adverse effects level. (As defined by the EPA.)

Maximum Tolerated Dose The maximum dose that an animal species can tolerate for a major portion of its lifetime without significant impairment or toxic effect other than carcinogenicity. (As defined by the EPA.)

Mercury (Hg) Heavy metal that can accumulate in the environment, and is highly toxic if breathed or swallowed. *See also* Heavy Metals.

Methane A colorless, nonpoisonous, flammable gas created by anaerobic decomposition of organic compounds. A major component of natural gas used in the home.

Microclimate (1) Localized climate conditions within an urban area or neighborhood. (2) The climate around a tree or shrub or a stand of trees. (As defined by the EPA.)

Montreal Protocol Treaty, signed in 1987, that governs stratospheric ozone protection and research and the production and use of ozone-depleting substances. It provides for the end of production of ozone-depleting substances such as CFCS. Under the protocol, various research groups continue to assess the ozone layer. The Multilateral Fund provides resources to developing nations to promote the transition to ozone-safe technologies.

Moratorium During the negotiation process, a period of 60 to 90 days during which the EPA and potentially responsible parties may reach settlement but no site response activities can be conducted. (As defined by the EPA.)

Multiple Chemical Sensitivity (MCS) A diagnostic label for people who suffer multisystem illnesses as a result of contact with or proximity to a variety of airborne agents and other substances. (As defined by the EPA.)

Mutagen/Mutagenicity An agent that causes a permanent genetic change in a cell other than that which occurs during normal growth. Mutagenicity is the capacity of a chemical or physical agent to cause such permanent changes. (As defined by the EPA.)

National Ambient Air Quality Standards (NAAQS) Standards established by the EPA that apply for outdoor air throughout the country. *See also* Criteria Pollutants, State Implementation Plans, Emissions Trading.

National Emissions Standards for Hazardous Air Pollutants (NESHAPS) Emissions standards set by the EPA for an air pollutant not covered by NAAQS that may cause an increase in fatalities or in serious, irreversible, or incapacitating illnesses. Primary standards are designed to protect human health; secondary standards are designed to protect public welfare (e.g., building facades, visibility, crops, and domestic animals). (As defined by the EPA.)

National Estuary Program A program established under the Clean Water Act Amendments of 1987 to develop and implement conservation and management plans for protecting estuaries and restoring and maintaining their chemical, physical, and biological integrity, as well as controlling point and nonpoint pollution sources. (As defined by the EPA.)

National Institute of Occupational Safety and Health (NIOSH) An agency of the Centers for Disease Control of the Department of Health and Human Services. NIOSH is the research arm of OSHA, the Occupational Safety and Health Administration.

National Pollutant Discharge Elimination System (NPDES) A provision of the Clean Water Act that prohibits discharge of pollutants into waters of the United States unless a special permit is issued by the EPA, a state, or where delegated, a tribal government on a Native American reservation. (As defined by the EPA.)

National Priorities List (NPL) The EPA's list of the most serious uncontrolled or abandoned hazardous waste sites identified for possible long-term remedial action under Superfund. The list is based primarily on the score a site receives from the Hazard Ranking System. The EPA is required to update the NPL at least once a year. A site must be on the NPL to receive money from the Trust Fund for remedial action. (As defined by the EPA.)

National Response Center The federal operations center that receives notifications of all releases of oil and hazardous substances into the environment. Open 24 hours a day, it is operated by the U.S. Coast Guard, which evaluates all reports and notifies the appropriate agency. (As defined by the EPA.)

Native Used in reference to plants, a plant whose presence and survival in a specific region is not due to human intervention. Certain experts argue that plants imported to a region by prehistoric peoples should be considered native. The term for plants that are imported and then adapt to survive without human cultivation is "naturalized."

Nonaqueous Phase Liquid (NAIL) Contaminants that remain undiluted as the original bulk liquid in the subsurface—for example, spilled oil. (As defined by the EPA.)

Nonpoint Sources Diffuse pollution sources (i.e., without a single point of origin or not introduced into a receiving stream from a specific outlet). The pollutants are generally carried off the land by stormwater. Common nonpoint sources are agriculture, forestry, urban, mining, construction, dams, channels, land disposal, saltwater intrusion, and city streets. (As defined by the EPA.)

Occupational Safety and Health Administration (OSHA) OSHA resides under the U.S. Department of Labor. OSHA implements the provisions of the 1970 Occupational Safety and Health Act. It establishes and enforces protective standards for employees in the workplace.

OECD Guidelines Testing guidelines prepared by the Organization of Economic and Cooperative Development of the United Nations. They assist in preparation of protocols for studies of toxicology, environmental fate, and so on. (As defined by the EPA.)

Offgas/Outgas A process of evaporation or chemical decomposition through which vapors are released from materials.

Oxidizer Any agent or process that receives electrons during a chemical reaction.

Ozonation/Ozonator Application of ozone to water for disinfection or for taste and odor control. The ozonator is the device that does this.

Ozone (O3) Found in two layers of the atmosphere, the stratosphere and the troposphere. In the stratosphere (the atmospheric layer 7 to 10 miles or more above the Earth's surface) ozone is a natural form of oxygen that provides a protective layer shielding the Earth from ultraviolet radiation. In the troposphere (the layer extending up 7 to 10 miles from the Earth's surface), ozone is a chemical oxidant and major component of photochemical smog. It can seriously impair the respiratory system and is one of the most widespread of all the criteria pollutants for which the Clean Air Act required the EPA to set standards. Ozone in the troposphere is produced through complex chemical reactions of nitrogen oxides, which are among the primary pollutants emitted by combustion sources; hydrocarbons, released into the atmosphere through the combustion, handling, and processing of petroleum products; and sunlight. (As defined by the EPA.)

Ozone Depletion Destruction of the stratospheric ozone layer, which shields the Earth from ultraviolet radiation harmful to life. This destruction of ozone is caused by the breakdown of certain chlorine and/or bromine-containing compounds (chlorofluorocarbons or halons), which break down when they reach the stratosphere and then catalytically destroy ozone molecules. (As defined by the EPA.)

Ozone Hole A thinning break in the stratospheric ozone layer. Designation of amount of such depletion as an "ozone hole" is made when the detected amount of depletion exceeds 50 percent. Seasonal ozone holes have been observed over both the Antarctic and Arctic regions, part of Canada, and the extreme northeastern United States. (As defined by the EPA.)

Ozone Layer The protective layer in the atmosphere, about 15 miles above the ground, that absorbs some of the sun's ultraviolet rays, thereby reducing the amount of potentially harmful radiation that reaches the Earth's surface. (As defined by the EPA.)

Pathogens Microorganisms (e.g., bacteria, viruses, or parasites) that can cause disease in humans, animals and plants.

Pay-as-You-Throw Systems under which residents pay for municipal waste management and disposal services by weight or volume collected, not a fixed fee. (As defined by the EPA.)

Peak Electricity Demand The maximum electricity used to meet the cooling load of a building or buildings in a given area.

Peak Levels Levels of airborne pollutant contaminants much higher than average or occurring for short periods of time in response to sudden releases.

Phenols Organic compounds that are byproducts of petroleum refining, tanning, and textile, dye, and resin manufacturing. Low concentrations cause taste and odor problems in water; higher concentrations can kill aquatic life and humans.

Phosphates Certain chemical compounds containing phosphorus.

Photochemical Smog Air pollution caused by chemical reactions of various pollutants emitted from different sources.

Photosynthesis The manufacture by plants of carbohydrates and oxygen from carbon dioxide mediated by chlorophyll in the presence of sunlight.

Photovoltaic Having the capacity to generate electricity from the energy of sunlight, using photocells.

Phytoplankton That portion of the plankton community composed of tiny plants; for example, algae, diatoms.

Phytoremediation Low-cost remediation option for sites with widely dispersed contamination at low concentrations. (As defined by the EPA.)

Phytotoxic Harmful to plants.

Phytotreatment (Phytoremediation) The cultivation of specialized plants that absorb specific contaminants from the soil through their roots or foliage. This reduces the concentration of contaminants and incorporates them into biomasses that may be released back into the environment when the plant dies or is harvested. (As defined by the EPA.)

Plasticizers Chemicals added to soft plastics to preserve their flexibility. These agents offgas slowly, eventually rendering the plastic brittle.

Point Source A stationary location or fixed facility from which pollutants are discharged; any single identifiable source of pollution (e.g., a pipe, ditch, ship, ore pit, factory smokestack). (As defined by the EPA.)

Pollutant Generally, any substance introduced into the environment that adversely affects the usefulness of a resource or the health of humans, animals, or ecosystems. (As defined by the EPA.)

Pollution Generally, the presence of a substance in the environment that, because of its chemical composition or quantity, prevents the functioning of natural processes and produces undesirable environmental and health effects. Under the Clean Water Act, for example, the term has been defined as the man-made or man-induced alteration of the physical, biological, chemical, and radiological integrity of water and other media. (As defined by the EPA.)

Pollution Prevention (1) The Identification of areas, processes, and activities that generate excessive waste products or pollutants in order to reduce or prevent them through alteration or elimination of a process. Such activities, consistent with the Pollution Prevention Act of 1990, are conducted across all EPA programs and can involve cooperative efforts with such agencies as the Departments of Agriculture and Energy. (2) The EPA has initiated a number of voluntary programs in which industrial or commercial "partners" join with the agency in promoting activities that conserve energy, conserve and protect water supplies, reduce emissions or find ways of utilizing them as energy resources, and reduce the waste stream. Among these are: Agstar, to reduce methane emissions through manure management; Climate Wise, to lower industrial greenhouse-gas emissions and energy costs; Coalbed Methane Outreach, to boost methane recovery at coal mines; Design for the Environment, to foster the inclusion of environmental considerations in product design and processes; Energy Star programs, to promote energy efficiency in commercial and residential buildings, office equipment, transformers, computers, office equipment, and home appliances; Environmental Accounting, to help businesses identify environmental costs and factor them into management decision making; Green Chemistry, to promote and recognize cost-effective breakthroughs in chemistry that prevent pollution; Green Lights, to spread the use of energy-efficient lighting technologies; Indoor Environments, to reduce risks from indoor air pollution; Landfill Methane Outreach, to develop landfill gas-to-energy projects; Natural Gas Star, to reduce methane emissions from the natural gas industry; Ruminant Livestock Methane, to reduce methane emissions from ruminant livestock; Transportation Partners, to reduce carbon dioxide emissions from the transportation sector; Voluntary Aluminum Industrial Partnership, to reduce perfluorocarbon emissions from the primary aluminum industry; WAVE, to promote efficient water use in the lodging industry; Wastewi$e, to reduce business-generated solid waste through prevention, reuse, and recycling. (As defined by the EPA.)

Polychlorinated biphenyls (PCB) Organo-halogen compounds, or compounds containing chlorine, bromine, or fluorine with organic chemicals. In construction, polychlorinated biphenyls are commonly found in fluorescent light fixture ballasts and electrical power transformers.

Poly Ethylene Terephthalate (PET) A polyester plastic used widely in soft drink bottles.

Polymer A natural or synthetic chemical structure where two or more like molecules are joined to form a more complex molecular structure (e.g., polyethylene in plastic). (As defined by the EPA.)

Polyvinyl Chloride (PVC) (1) A polymer derived from oil or liquid natural gas and salt (sodium chloride). The liquid natural gas or petroleum is refined and reacted with chlorine from the salt to form vinyl chloride monomer. Vinyl chloride monomer, a known carcinogen, is polymerized to form PVC resin. (2) A tough, environmentally indestructible plastic that releases hydrochloric acid when burned. (As defined by the EPA.)

Postconsumer A reclaimed waste product that has already served a purpose to a consumer, such as used newspaper. Waste from industrial processes is not considered postconsumer.

Preconsumer Materials/Waste Materials generated in manufacturing and converting processes, such as manufacturing scrap and trimmings and cuttings. Includes print overruns, over-issue publications, and obsolete inventories. (As defined by the EPA.)

Project XL An EPA initiative to give states and the regulated community the flexibility to develop comprehensive strategies as alternatives to multiple current regulatory requirements in order to exceed compliance and increase overall environmental benefits. (As defined by the EPA.)

Pyrethrum and Pyrethrins Pyrethrum is made from powdered flowers of the chrysanthemum family. The active insecticidal ingredient is pyrethrin. Some people are acutely sensitive to pyrethrum. Adverse reactions range from contact dermatitis and asthmalike attacks to anaphylactic reactions with peripheral vascular collapse. As early as 1934, a cross-reaction between ragweed allergies and pyrethrum sensitivities was noted in the medical literature. Some pyrethrum formulations include petrochemicals as solvents and propellants, as well as synergists to make them more toxic. Pyrethrum and pyrethrins are used for pest control.

Radon A colorless naturally occurring, radioactive, inert gas formed by radio-active decay of radium atoms in soil or rocks. Trace radon emissions may be detected after excavating into subsoil for building foundations.

Rainwater Harvesting The practice of collecting, storing, and using precipitation from a catchment area such as a roof.

Recharge The process by which water is added to a zone of saturation, usually by percolation from the soil surface (e.g., the recharge of an aquifer). (As defined by the EPA.)

Recharge Rate The quantity of water per unit of time that replenishes or refills an aquifer. (As defined by the EPA.)

Reclamation In recycling, the restoration of materials found in the waste stream to a beneficial use, which may be for purposes other than the original use. (As defined by the EPA.)

Recombinant Bacteria A microorganism whose genetic makeup has been altered by deliberate introduction of new genetic elements. The offspring of these altered bacteria also contain these new genetic elements; that is, they "breed true." (As defined by the EPA.)

Recombinant DNA The new DNA that is formed by combining pieces of DNA from different organisms or cells.

Recycle/Reuse Minimizing waste generation by recovering and reprocessing usable products that might otherwise become waste (e.g., recycling aluminum cans, paper, and bottles, etc.). (As defined by the EPA.)

Red Tide A proliferation of a marine plankton that is toxic and often fatal to fish, perhaps stimulated by the addition of nutrients. A tide can be red, green, or brown, depending on the coloration of the plankton.

Remediation (1) Cleanup or other methods used to remove or contain a toxic spill or hazardous materials from a Superfund site. (2) For the Asbestos Hazard Emergency Response program, abatement methods including evaluation, repair, enclosure, encapsulation, or removal of greater than 3 linear feet or square feet of asbestos-containing materials from a building. (As defined by the EPA.)

Renewable A renewable product can be grown or naturally replenished or cleansed at a rate that exceeds human depletion of the resource.

Reuse Using a product or component of municipal solid waste in its original form more than once; for example, refilling a glass bottle that has been returned or using a coffee can to hold nuts and bolts. (As defined by the EPA.)

Riparian Habitat Areas adjacent to rivers and streams with a differing density, diversity, and productivity of plant and animal species relative to nearby uplands. (As defined by the EPA.)

Riparian Rights Entitlement of a land owner to certain uses of water on or bordering the property, including the right to prevent diversion or misuse of upstream waters. Generally a matter of state law. (As defined by the EPA.)

Risk A measure of the probability that damage to life, health, property, and/or the environment will occur as a result of a given hazard. (As defined by the EPA.)

Risk Assessment Qualitative and quantitative evaluation of the risk posed to human health and/or the environment by the actual or potential presence and/or use of specific pollutants. (As defined by the EPA.)

Risk Characterization The last phase of the risk assessment process that estimates the potential for adverse health or ecological effects to occur from exposure to a stressor and evaluates the uncertainty involved. (As defined by the EPA.)

Runoff That part of precipitation, snow melt, or irrigation water that runs off the land into streams or other surface water. It can carry pollutants from the air and land into receiving waters. (As defined by the EPA.)

Sand Filters Devices that remove some suspended solids from sewage. Air and bacteria decompose additional wastes that filter through the sand so that cleaner water drains from the bed. (As defined by the EPA.)

Secondary Effect Action of a stressor on supporting components of the ecosystem, which in turn impacts the ecological component of concern. (As defined by the EPA.)

Secondary Treatment The second step in most publicly owned waste treatment systems during which bacteria consume the organic parts of the waste. It is accomplished by bringing together waste, bacteria, and oxygen in trickling filters or in the activated sludge process. This treatment removes floating and settleable solids and about 90 percent of the oxygen-demanding substances and suspended solids. Disinfection is the final stage of secondary treatment. (As defined by the EPA.)

Semivolatile Organic Compounds Organic compounds that volatilize slowly at standard temperature (20 degrees C and 1 atm pressure). (As defined by the EPA.)

Septic System An on-site system designed to treat and dispose of domestic sewage. A typical septic system consists of tank that receives waste from a residence or business and a system of tile lines or a pit for disposal of the liquid effluent (sludge) that remains after decomposition of the solids by bacteria in the tank and must be pumped out periodically.

Septic Tank An underground storage tank for wastes from homes not connected to a sewer line. Waste goes directly from the home to the tank.

Shading Coefficient The amount of the sun's heat transmitted through a given window compared with that of a standard 1/8-inch-thick single pane of glass under the same conditions.

Sick Building Syndrome (SBS) Syndrome whereby occupants of a building experience acute health and/or comfort effects that appear to be linked to time spent therein, but where no specific illness or cause can be identified. Complaints may be localized in a particular room or zone, or may be spread throughout the building. (As defined by the EPA.)

Sink Place in the environment where a compound or material collects. (As defined by the EPA.) In buildings, sinks are surfaces that tend to capture volatile compounds from air and then release them later. Carpets, gypsum board, ceiling tile, and upholstery are all sinks.

Sinking In buildings, generally refers to the absorption of VOCs by sinks ('soft' building materials). See also adsorption and sinks.

Solvents Found in adhesives, coal tar pitch and coal tar roofing, metal cleaners, putty, impermeable paints and coatings, pipe cements (polyurethane resins), wire coverings, transformers. Aliphatic hydrocarbons, aromatic hydrocarbons, petroleum naphtha, tetrachloroethylene, toluene are found in solvents.

Source Reduction Reducing the amount of materials entering the waste stream from a specific source by redesigning products or patterns of production or consumption (e.g., using returnable beverage containers). Synonymous with waste reduction. (As defined by the EPA.)

Species (1) A reproductively isolated aggregate of interbreeding organisms having common attributes and usually designated by a common name. (2) An organism belonging to such a category. (As defined by the EPA.)

Superfund The program operated under the legislative authority of CERCLA and SARA that funds and carries out EPA solid waste emergency and long-term removal and remedial activities. These activities include establishing the National Priorities List, investigating sites for inclusion on the list, determining their priority, and conducting and/or supervising cleanup and other remedial actions. (As defined by the EPA.)

Surface Runoff Precipitation, snow melt, or irrigation water in excess of what can infiltrate the soil surface and be stored in small surface depressions; a major transporter of nonpoint source pollutants in rivers, streams, and lakes. (As defined by the EPA.)

Sustainable Sustainable practices and sustainable communities meet the needs of present generations without compromising those needs for future generations. To be truly sustainable, a human community must not decrease biodiversity, must not consume resources faster than these are renewed, must recycle and reuse virtually all materials, and must rely primarily on resources of its own region. Ecological/environmental sustainability is defined by the EPA as the maintenance of ecosystem components and functions for future generations.

Tertiary Treatment Advanced cleaning of wastewater that goes beyond the secondary or biological stage, removing nutrients such as phosphorus, nitrogen, and most BOD and suspended solids. (As defined by the EPA.)

Thermal Pollution Discharge of heated water from industrial processes that can kill or injure aquatic organisms. (As defined by the EPA.)

Thermal Stratification The formation of layers of different temperatures in a lake or reservoir. (As defined by the EPA.)

Threshold The dose or exposure level below which a significant adverse effect is not expected. (As defined by the EPA.)

Threshold Level Time-weighted average pollutant concentration values, exposure beyond which is likely to adversely affect human health. (As defined by the EPA.)

Threshold Limit Value (TLV) The concentration of an airborne substance to which an average person can be repeatedly exposed without adverse effects. TLVs may be expressed in three ways: (a) TLV-TWA, time-weighted average, based on an allowable exposure averaged over a normal 8-hour workday or 40-hour workweek; (b) TLV-STEL, short-term exposure limit or maximum concentration for a brief specified period of time, depending on a specific chemical (TWA must still be met); and (c) TLV-C, ceiling exposure limit or maximum exposure concentration not to be exceeded under any circumstances (TWA must still be met). (As defined by the EPA.)

Tight Buildings Buildings that are designed to let in minimal infiltration air in order to reduce heating and cooling energy costs. In actuality, buildings typically exhibit leakage that is on the same order as required ventilation; however, this leakage is not well distributed and cannot serve as a substitute for proper ventilation.

Total Dissolved Solids (TDS) All material that passes the standard glass river filter; now called total filtrable residue. Term is used to reflect salinity.

Total Petroleum Hydrocarbons (TPH) Measure of the concentration or mass of petroleum hydrocarbon constituents present in a given amount of soil or water. The word "total" is a misnomer; few, if any, of the procedures for quantifying hydrocarbons can measure all of them in a given sample. Volatile ones are usually lost in the process and not quantified, and nonpetroleum hydrocarbons sometimes appear in the analysis.

Total Suspended Particles (TSP) A method of monitoring airborne particulate matter by total weight.

Total Suspended Solids (TSS) A measure of the suspended solids in wastewater, effluent, or water bodies, determined by tests for total suspended nonfilterable solids.

Total Volatile Organic Compound (TVOC) Compound measured in $\mu g/m^3$ (micrograms per cubic meter).

Toxaphene Chemical that causes adverse health effects in domestic water supplies and is toxic to freshwater and marine aquatic life.

Toxicant A harmful substance or agent that may injure an exposed organism. (As defined by the EPA.)

Toxic Chemical Any chemical listed in the EPA rules as "toxic chemicals subject to Section 313 of the Emergency Planning and Community Right-to-Know Act of 1986." (As defined by the EPA.)

Toxic Chemical Release Form Information form required of facilities that manufacture, process, or use (in quantities above a specific amount) chemicals listed under SARA, Title III. (As defined by the EPA.)

Toxicity The degree to which a substance or mixture of substances can harm humans or animals. Acute toxicity involves harmful effects in an organism through a single or short-term exposure. Chronic toxicity is the ability of a substance or mixture of substances to cause harmful effects over an extended period, usually upon repeated or continuous exposure, sometimes lasting for the entire life of the exposed organism. Subchronic toxicity is the ability of the substance to cause effects for more than one year but less than the lifetime of the exposed organism. (As defined by the EPA.)

Toxicity Assessment Characterization of the toxicological properties and effects of a chemical, with special emphasis on establishment of dose-response characteristics. (As defined by the EPA.)

Toxicity Testing Biological testing (usually with an invertebrate, fish, or small mammal) to determine the adverse effects of a compound or effluent. (As defined by the EPA.)

Toxic Pollutants Materials that cause death, disease, or birth defects in organisms that ingest or absorb them. The quantities and exposures necessary to cause these effects can vary widely. (As defined by the EPA.)

Toxic Release Inventory Database of toxic releases in the United States compiled from SARA, Title III, Section 313 reports. (As defined by the EPA.)

Toxic Substance A chemical or mixture that may present an unreasonable risk of injury to health or the environment. (As defined by the EPA.)

Toxic Waste A waste that can produce injury if inhaled, swallowed, or absorbed through the skin. (As defined by the EPA.)

Trichloroethylene Found in solvents and used in the formulations of paints, varnishes, lacquers, and dyes, trichlorethylene is observed offgassing. It is considered a carcinogen and a chronic toxin, and has the capability of causing fertility problems and developmental defects.

Troposphere   The layer of the atmosphere closest to the Earth's surface.

United States Postal Service (USPS)   For the last decade, the United States Postal Service has been committed to sustainable principles. In 1993, the postmaster general issued the USPS *Environmental Policy and Guiding Principles,* which can be summarized as follows Meet or exceed all applicable environmental laws; incorporate environmental considerations into the business planning process; foster the sustainable use of natural resources by promoting pollution prevention reducing waste, recycling, and reusing material; expect every employee to take ownership and responsibility for the USPS's environmental objectives; work with customers to address mutual environmental concerns; measure progress on protecting the environment; encourage suppliers, vendors, and contractors to comply with similar environmental protection policies. The USPS has developed a Green Addendum to the USPS specifications that specifies low-VOC and recycled-content products. In 1998, the USPS opened the first green post office in Fort Worth, Texas.

Urban Runoff   Stormwater from city streets and adjacent domestic or commercial properties that carries pollutants of various kinds into the sewer systems and receiving waters. (As defined by the EPA.)

Urethanes   A family of plastics (polyurethanes) used for varnish coatings, foamed insulations, highly durable paints, and rubber goods.

Variable Air Volume (VAV)   A method of modulating the amount of heating or cooling effect that is delivered to a building by the HVAC system. The flow of air is modulated, rather than the temperature. VAV systems typically consist of VAV boxes that throttle supply airflow to individual zones, some mechanism to control supply fanflow to matchbox demand, and the interconnecting ductwork and components.

Vinyl Chloride   A chemical compound used in producing some plastics, that is believed to be oncogenic.

Volatile   Any substance that evaporates readily.

Volatile Organic Compound (VOC)   Any organic compound that participates in atmospheric photochemical reactions, except those designated by EPA as having negligible photochemical reactivity. Volatile organic compounds are chemical compounds based on carbon and hydrogen structures and are vaporized at room temperatures.

Waste Exchange   Arrangement by which companies exchange their wastes for the benefit of both parties.

Waste Stream   The total flow of solid waste from homes, businesses, institutions, and manufacturing plants that is recycled, burned, or disposed of in landfills or segments thereof, such as the "residential waste stream" or the "recyclable waste stream." (As defined by the EPA.)

Watershed The land area that drains into a stream; the watershed for a major river may encompass a number of smaller watersheds that ultimately combine at a common point. (As defined by the EPA.)

Watershed Approach A coordinated framework for environmental management that focuses public and private efforts on the highest-priority problems within hydrologically defined geographic areas, taking into consideration both ground- and surface water flow. (As defined by the EPA.)

Watershed Area A topographic area within a line drawn to connect the highest points uphill of a drinking water-intake into which overland flow drains. (As defined by the EPA.)

Wetlands An area that is saturated by surface or groundwater, with vegetation adapted for life under those soil conditions such as swamps, bogs, fens, marshes, and estuaries. (As defined by the EPA.)

Xenobiota Any biotum displaced from its normal habitat; a chemical foreign to a biological system.

Xeriscape™ A trademarked term referring to water-efficient choices in planting and irrigation design. It refers to seven basic principles to conserve water and protect the environment. These include: planning and design, use of well-adapted plants, soil analysis, practical turf areas, use of mulches, appropriate maintenance, and efficient irrigation.

Xylene Found in paints, varnishes, lacquers, solvents, xylenes are included in the formulations of paints, adhesives, and some furniture products, and are observed offgassing. Xylenes are considered to be a chronic toxin capable of potentially causing fertility problems and developmental defects. Xylenes will also have potential health impacts on wildlife.

INDEX